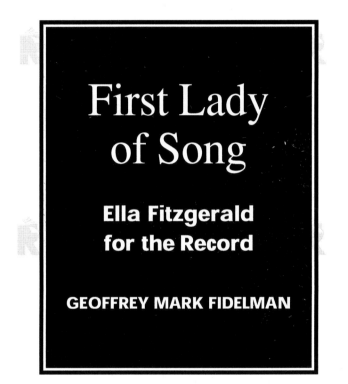

First Lady of Song

Ella Fitzgerald for the Record

GEOFFREY MARK FIDELMAN

REPLICA BOOKS

A DVISION OF BAKER & TAYLOR
BRIDGEWATER, NJ

Baker & Taylor Cataloging-in-Publication Data

Fidelman, Geoffrey Mark.
First lady of song : Ella Fitzgerald for the record /
Geoffrey Mark Fidelman. —1st Replica Books ed.
p.   cm.
ISBN 0735100969
Originally published: Secaucus, N.J. : Carol Pub. Group, c1994.
Includes discography and index.
1. Fitzgerald, Ella. 2. Jazz musicians - United States - Biography.
3. Singers - United States - Biography. I. Title.
ML420.F52 F5 1999
782.42165'092 [B]-dc 21

FIRST LADY OF SONG

Ella Fitzgerald

For the Record

Geoffrey Mark Fidelman

A CITADEL PRESS BOOK
Published by Carol Publishing Group

Carol Publishing Group Edition, 1996

A Citadel Press Book
Published by Carol Publishing Group
Citadel Press is a registered trademark of Carol Communications, Inc.

Editorial Offices: 600 Madison Avenue, New York, N.Y. 10022
Sales and Distribution Offices: 120 Enterprise Avenue, Secaucus,
    N.J. 07094
In Canada: Canadian Manda Group, One Atlantic Avenue, Suite 105,
    Toronto, Ontario M6K 3E7

Queries regarding rights and permissions should be addressed to:
Carol Publishing Group, 600 Madison Avenue, New York, N.Y. 10022

Manufactured in the United States of America
10 9 8 7 6 5 4 3 2 1

Library of Congress Cataloging-in-Publication Data

Fidelman, Geoffrey Mark.
    First lady of song : Ella Fitzgerald for the record /
    by Geoffrey Mark Fidelman.

First Lady of Song

This book is dedicated to Ella Fitzgerald, whose music has enriched my life beyond all measure . . .

To Norman Granz, whose vision and dedication to jazz enabled Ella to share her gift unhampered by mediocrity or indifference . . .

To all the fans, whose amazing demographics transcend all categories except love and good taste . . .

And to Michael, who gave me something to live for, body and soul.

Contents

Foreword

$\mathscr{I}$n gilding the lily of Miss Fitzgerald, I'll let Ella's contemporaries speak for themselves:

PEARL BAILEY: "Ella is simply the greatest singer of them all."

FRANK SINATRA: "The best way to start any musical evening is with this girl. It don't get better than this."

BING CROSBY: "Man, woman, or child, she's simply the greatest."

LUCILLE BALL: "Ella's amazing! My daughter says that every time she makes a mistake, it becomes a hit record."

VINCENTE MINNELLI: "If you want to learn how to sing, listen to Ella Fitzgerald."

ANDY WILLIAMS: "She brings out the best in everybody, making everyone work that much harder to keep up with her."

JO STAFFORD: "It is so much fun to sing with Ella. It is so nice to sing with someone who does more than make a pretty noise."

DORIS DAY: "The one radio voice that I listened to above others belonged to Ella Fitzgerald. There was a quality to her voice that fascinated me, and I'd sing along with her, trying to catch the subtle ways she shaded her voice, the casual yet clean way she sang the words."

DAVID CROSBY: "Oh, wow, Ella . . . she's real cool!"

MILDRED BAILEY: "Ella is one of my favorite singers, one whose interpretations I especially admire."

PERRY COMO: "She has been one of my all-time favorites for many years and still is—she's terrific!"

MEL TORMÉ: "Ella's fabulous . . . one of the greatest singers alive."

PAT BOONE: "Every other singer, male or female, if they're lucky, they listen to Ella."

RICHARD PERRY: "She is the most thorough professional I have worked with, every working moment was pure joy."

MARTY PAICH: "She is amazingly creative, bringing so much more to a song than just as a singer. She is a first-class musician and the most gracious person in the world."

JOE PASS: "She always encouraged me to create and take my turn in our duets, never playing the star."

BENNY CARTER: "I was there from the beginning and it was obvious from the start what she had that night at the Apollo. My goodness what she's done with it."

TOMMY FLANAGAN: "Ella had an almost musical mental telepathy with me so we could improvise wildly and she would never falter for even a moment."

JIMMY ROWLES: "Everything is music. Music comes out of her. When she walks down the street, she leaves notes."

LOUIE BELLSON: "There is no voice like that lady. She has it all. She's complete."

ED THIGPEN: "Ella's musicianship is just incredible. Playing with her is like playing with a full orchestra."

BILLY MAY: "Ella knows her stuff. You can't fool her. She's the best at what she does."

IRA GERSHWIN: "I never knew how good our songs were until I heard Ella Fitzgerald sing them."

KETER BETTS: "There are only geniuses in music, math, and chess. Ella is a genius."

BILLY STRAYHORN: "Ella is the boss lady. That's all!"

BOB BACH: "Ella Fitzgerald has been called the greatest and The First Lady of Song and almost every other superlative for so long now that it begins to become one of those accepted bromides like 'an apple a day keeps the doctor away,' etc."

Metronome MAGAZINE: "The greatest pop singer of them all."

Playboy MAGAZINE: "The greatest jazz singer in the world."

Ebony MAGAZINE: "The number one vocalist in the land."

LEONARD FEATHER: "If one all-around queen of jazz vocalists could be chosen, it would have to be Ella Fitzgerald."

BENNY GREEN: "How many songs has Ella guaranteed a kind of immortality merely by recording them?"

HENRY PLEASANTS: "She commands . . . an extraordinary range of two octaves and a sixth . . . this is a greater range, especially at the bottom, than is required or expected of most opera singers."

and

ELLA FITZGERALD: "I've had some wonderful love affairs and some that didn't work out. I don't want to dwell on that and I don't want to put people down, but I think all the fabulous places I've been, the wonderful things that have happened for me, the great people I've met—that ought to make a story."

.

Acknowledgments

$\mathcal{M}$y gratitude is offered to the following individuals, companies, corporations, and institutions for their invaluable help with support, research, and the granting of interviews, helping to make this book as accurate and interesting as possible:

Those who made music or show business memories with Ella and contributed greatly to the legend:

Van Alexander; Steve Allen; Louie Bellson; Keter Betts; Joshua Brand; Benny Carter; David Crosby; Tommy Flanagan; Rudy Hill, and especially Lee Hirschberg of Warner Brothers/Reprise Records; Steve Lang; Victor Lobl; John Masius; Billy May; Bob Merlis; Marty Paich; Patricia Laird Pinney; Joe Pass; Richard Perry; Paul Smith; Jo Stafford; Val Valentin; Paul Weston; Andy Williams; and Mike Wofford.

A special debt to all of those who allowed me to quote them but could only do so anonymously; I have respected your privacy and appreciate your trust.

Those who shared their research or assisted me in mine:

UCLA Television archivist Dan Einstein and Lou Kramer of the UCLA Film and Television Archives; Woody Wise; Stuart Shostak of Shokus Video; Ted Gonzales of KCET-TV Los Angeles; Linda Haven of WTTW Chicago; Susan Dangel and Bill Cosel of Mugar Productions; Matthew Hutchinson, Mark Stevenson, and Diana Valentine of MTM Enterprises; Susan Rubio and Jeff Sotzing of Carson Productions; Carol MacDonald; Loren Nizinsky; Jerry Kritzberg; Todd Bernstein; David Little; Martin Isaacson; Andy McKae of MCA Records;

Orrin Keepnews; Michael Lang of Verve Records; Peter Pullman; Phil Schaap; Andy Powell; Chris Nickens; Guy Vespointe; Terry Woodson; John Fell; Sherry DeBiaso of Capitol Records; James Gavin; Will Freedwald; Roseann Peppard; Kirk Roberts and Eric Miller of Fantasy, Inc.; Joe Gues and Angie Hill of Brown Kraft; Chip Lightman; Catherine De Meis of Sofa Entertainment; Coyne Steve Sanders; Dan Morganstern, Don Luck, Fran Cosgrove and especially Esther of the Institute of Jazz Studies at Rutgers University; Malcolm Leo and Kristie Hannum of Malcolm Leo Productions; Steven Adler and Jerome Seven of Bob Banner Productions; Diana Weisman of Meadowlane Productions; and William Egan and Lee Silverstein of Mark Goodson Productions.

A very special thanks to Paul Surratt and the Archives of Music Preservation for opening their vaults to me; their assistance was invaluable to making this book more accurate. Anyone desiring to write about good music should make this their first stop.

I am forever in the debt of my wonderful agent, Robert Simpson, of the Roslyn Targ Agency. His calm, reassuring demeanor was very helpful on those days when I was freaking out. His skill as an agent and negotiator was indispensable. His belief in this book will never be forgotten.

My thanks go to my editor at Carol Publishing, Allan J. Wilson. His insight and understanding of this book, his dry sense of humor, and his years as an editor were instrumental in making this a better book. May this be the first of many together.

Introduction

$\mathcal{E}$lla Fitzgerald. The name conjures up thoughts of the Savoy Ballroom; the Chick Webb, Duke Ellington, and Count Basie bands; hot jazz, sweet ballads, and recordings by the thousands. There is so much more to this career, touched by genius, the famous and the infamous. I had started out to write a book about a career in music, but I found I could not tell the whole story unless I included more. It was fascinating before I got started, and while the amount of material involved was voluminous, I was even more fascinated with the story *behind* the music when I finished.

This was not an easy book to write. Those who worked for her during the time this book was researched were tremendously protective of her. Almost to the point of paranoia. Therefore, this is an unauthorized biography.

The book started with an idea from Val Valentin, longtime recording engineer for Verve and Capitol Records. Valentin holds incredible esteem in the industry, having worked with Frank Sinatra, Ella, Connie Francis, Nat Cole, and many others. A mutual acquaintance (in fact an old flame from his boyhood days) introduced us, and a friendship resulted. Still handsome, Val carried a twinkle in his eye and a head full of memories in a body that was well over seventy. Everyone in the business knew him, and not an unkind word was said of him. He was very, very nice to me, a person who could do nothing for him in return except offer friendship.

Val was, at that time, working in the office of Norman Granz, Ella Fitzgerald's longtime manager and producer. Val's job, it seemed, was

Vice President in charge of looking after Ella's needs. When asked why this man, literally one of the founders of the modern recording industry, was doing this kind of work, his answer was simple: "I love her. We have been friends for over forty years. Norman would give me the shirt off his back if I asked for it. So now, Norman has asked me to do this. I do it with a full heart."

"It" included driving Ella to her doctor's appointments, dealing with her household workers, having leaks in her roof fixed, traveling with her whenever she was able to work, and fulfilling her every request. Val was a very spiritual person, and did not consider this a comedown. He'd had a big career, and now he was helping his friends.

At lunch with me one day in Beverly Hills, the topic of misinformation came up. So much of what had been previously written about Ella was, as he said, "so much horseshit." He worried that the truth of her career would never be set straight. "You know, young man, you ought to write a book. Ella and Norman are getting old and are not in good health. When I die, all the memories will die with me."

Once I told Val that I was indeed going to write such a book, and submitted to him a sample chapter, he was enthusiastic but cautious. "You must get Norman's approval," he said. "Write him a letter, and I will make sure he sees it. This is so well written [his words, not mine] that I'm certain he will want to meet you." I outlined my ideas for the book, and gave the letter to Maryjane Outwater, Granz's personal assistant for more than thirty years.

I never heard from Granz. Valentin got more and more hedgy. While he did indeed share reminiscences with me, he asked me not to directly quote him in the book. I have not. Later, I found that much of what he told me was already in the public record. Maryjane, although always polite (and always took my calls), was cool and unsupportive of the book idea. While I do thank her for giving me Tommy Flanagan's phone number, that same number was offered to me by at least three other people.

I promised Val that I would not do anything he would not be happy with, i.e., making claims that this book was authorized. I still hoped Granz would relent and cooperate, but that notion soon died. While Ella was nice enough to send me an autographed photo (something she rarely did any longer due to advancing arthritis in her hands), she would not be interviewed. She was very ill; this I understood. I wanted to interview anyone who had ever worked with her, mostly to talk about the music.

I tried to contact Frank Sinatra to talk about the television shows they had done together. To do this, I had to contact Susan Reynolds and his public relations people, and then forward a letter stating my intentions.

Even the phone number of Mr. Sinatra's P.R. people was not easy to find. I did not get it from Val. In my letter, I told Ms. Reynolds that, while Mr. Granz and Miss Fitzgerald were not cooperating with the book, they were well aware it was being written. I told them that in my letter to Mr. Granz I had offered him a first look at the book, with the proviso that I would change anything he felt was untrue or would hurt Ella. I offered the same promise to Mr. Sinatra, and mentioned that Val and Maryjane had been pleasant and helpful in getting me started.

I received a letter back, stating that Mr. Sinatra did not allow interviews about his friends, and did not want to cooperate with an unauthorized book. He was kind enough to send me an autographed picture and wish me good luck. I was a little disappointed, but I didn't think twice about it.

When next I called Val, he was furious. "Young man, we are very unhappy with you," he bellowed at me. "How dare you tell Frank Sinatra's people that this book was authorized and that we were helping you with it?" I tried to explain that I had told them it *was* unauthorized, that Mr. Sinatra would not cooperate *because* of that fact. I offered to show him a copy of the letter I had sent. I told him exactly what I had said, and what my intentions had been. Val said that Sinatra's people were furious, and that I had seriously injured his long-standing friendship with the Chairman of the Board by trying to use his name. Why, I inquired, would Mr. Sinatra send me a picture if he were angry with me? And why, if I were lying, would I be willing to produce the letter?

A little more banter was parlayed back and forth as Valentin started to calm down. Finally, I realized our friendship was on very shaky ground. I asked if I should stop calling him. He said, "Maybe you'd better let it rest for a while, until things blow over." He never took my calls again.

The only other person contacted for this book who refused an interview was (now the late) Dinah Shore. Her advancing cancer made it impossible for her to meet with me. While her people did not mention her illness, it was a well-known but well-kept industry secret. Happily, many of her television shows with Ella became available to me for viewing. Certainly, her comments would have been enlightening, but, like Ella herself, the lady was simply too ill to talk.

Literally hundreds of people were interviewed for this book, and thousands of hours of video, film, and recordings were perused. I had personally seen Miss Fitz more than twenty-five times in concert, so was able to write of her performances firsthand.

Many times in this book, I quote people who wished to remain anonymous. Most of the time, this was because people feared hurting Ella, or feared for their careers should their identities become known. Paranoia and fear are not new in show business. These requests for anonymity have been gladly filled.

Why was this book so important for me to write, despite the obstacles? Let me tell you about the first time I saw Ella perform in concert.

Norman Granz had booked Ella into Avery Fisher Hall in March of 1978, but the date had to be canceled due to (her musical director) Tommy Flanagan's heart attack. Ella would not appear without him. When Tommy felt better, the date was made up the following June 4. Roy Eldridge appeared as a guest artist, although he and Ella did not work together that night. Jimmie Smith filled in for regular Bobby Durham on drums, but Keter Betts was still helming the bass after almost fifteen years at that point.

Ella was in top spirits, top voice, and I was enthralled. Wearing a white and blue sequined gown and her trademark gold hoop earrings, Miss Fitz came on stage to a five-minute standing ovation. I had never seen anything like it before. Having viewed Liza Minnelli, Bette Midler, Richard Burton, Ethel Merman, Zero Mostel, Mary Martin, and many other stars received with incredible audience reaction, this was somehow different. Certainly any of those performers had the ability to whip an audience into a near frenzy of cheering.

With Ella, the greeting was less frenetic and more respectful. All kinds of people were standing and applauding. In many cases, a well-placed fan club or small group could institute a near riot in an audience. For many stars, their vociferous gay followings could keep an audience on its feet in adulation. For Ella, the ovation came from *everybody*. The audience was young, old, black, white, straight, gay, Asian, punk, jazz, heavy metal, big band, disco, and anything in between. This was not the furiousness of the fanatic, but the love, respect, and awe of the general public. The performer in front of them had lived, worked, hurt, loved, survived, delivered, and was the absolute best at what she did.

And still delivered. When we all settled down, Ella launched into "Goody-Goody," a song she seemed never to sing with the same arrangement twice.

I was lucky to be catching her at the height of the Pablo years. She was still able to do all of the wonderful things she had always been famous for, though surely with several rough edges. I had rushed to see her because friends said she was ill and wouldn't be singing much longer. She only sang for fourteen more years.

For a person to have such an impact on popular society, and to have absolutely nothing substantive written about her, floored me. This was a cultural gap that needed to be filled, for the sake of scholarship and musical history. For the sake of examining an enigma.

Ella had been ill for many years. Why didn't she want to retire? Why did she still want to work, even if she was not often physically able? By that time in her life, she defined herself by her career. Ella *was* that concert, or that album. Like the bunny in the commercials, she just kept going and going. Her only album of the '90s (actually recorded in 1989 and released in 1990) won her yet another Grammy Award as Best Female Jazz Artist. Only her health forced her to end any long-term career plans.

It wasn't the money; Mr. Granz had seen to it that Ella was financially independent. After more than fifty years before the public, she simply lived for that moment when she could receive the love of her audiences. For more than ten years, she risked her health and indeed her life to receive it. I believe the answer lies in a line from one of Ella's bop classics, "Mr. Paganini": "When the voice is boppin'/ T'ain't no need in stoppin'." T'ain't no need indeed.

This is the story of a woman who lived to perform, and most of her life's action occurred on stage. Never being truly comfortable with her relatives or friends without some tie to her music, the sacrifice made to be "First Lady" was genuine. This book is a labor of love and respect. Ella Fitzgerald deserves them both.

GEOFFREY MARK FIDELMAN
Oceanside, New York
July, 1994

The Decca Years

Chapter One

1917–1935

$\mathcal{B}$y the time 1935 rolled around, Ella Jane Fitzgerald was already on the road to musical immortality. The product of a broken home by common-law parents, she was born in Newport News, Virginia, reputedly on April 25, 1918. However, according to Ella's birth certificate and later school records, she was actually born a year earlier. This date would become a sticking point in her life, especially when her fortieth and seventy-fifth birthdays were celebrated to much fanfare.

Originally, Ella was made a year younger so it would add to her "little girl" image with the Chick Webb band; later it helped bridge the age gap between herself and younger husband Ray Brown. As Ella was never one to allow the truth to interfere with good public relations, she never bothered to correct her birthdate long after it made no difference to anyone.

Her father William and her mother Tempe (short for Temperance, a highly unlikely name) were never legally married. They lived at 2050 Madison Avenue, with William nine years older than the independent Tempe. After World War I, her parents separated, and Tempe moved the family to Yonkers, New York. Mother and daughter moved in with Tempe's Portuguese lover Joseph Da Silva, often referred to as Ella's stepfather. This again was press agentry in an effort to sanitize her childhood.

Joseph was undoubtedly a nurturing influence on her music and cultural awareness, and she spoke of this part of their relationship with great affection for the rest of her life. However, what she chose not to recall was the child abuse she was subjected to in her teens.

The ersatz Da Silva family lived in an ethnically mixed area of Italians, Spaniards, and African Americans at 27 Clinton Street. It was in this environment that Ella grew into young womanhood. In 1923, Ella's folks presented her with a sister, Frances. Two years later, they moved to 72 School Street.

"Growing up in a mixed neighborhood," she once recalled, "I had mostly Italian friends. First time I ran into a prejudice thing, a boy came in from another school and called me 'nigger.' Well, I pushed him, he fell down, and the other kids thought I had hit him—so I became a heroine at the school! They made him apologize, and after that everyone looked up to me, thought I was real bad. I was about eleven." Actually, this fight probably occurred with a girl named Josephine Attanasio. And while Ella did give her a bloody nose, the fight was about Ella's bullying of Josephine's younger sister, not about race issues.

While Tempe worked for a caterer and a laundry and extra income came from Joseph's ditchdigging and chauffeuring, Ella needed to add to the family coffers. To earn money for herself, Ella ran numbers (she was a messenger who picked up the bets and later made payoffs as necessary). She also was a lookout for (as she would refer to it) a "sporting house. Oh yes, I had a very interesting young life!"

Recalling her "stepfather," she would later chuckle, "If I would have had any idea that one day I would be recording songs in Portuguese, I would have paid a lot more attention when he tried to teach it to me!" With a characteristic lack of candor, Ella has never publicly discussed growing up in a mixed neighborhood in Yonkers and especially what that meant in the late 1920s and early '30s.

Most urban areas were divided by race, religion, income, or national background, much as they still are in today's supposed enlightened times. People rarely visited "other" neighborhoods unless they were just passing through. Some people lived their entire lives without ever traveling outside of their "section." The only equalizer was the depression: European or African or Christian or Jew, everyone was hurting.

Today, having parents of mixed heritage, if not totally acceptable to everyone, is certainly commonplace and not likely to receive a raised eyebrow. In the cloudy days of the early 1930s, having an African mother and a Portuguese "stepfather," a man her mother wasn't even married to, would put a sensitive young girl into the smallest of subcultures, always somehow less than.

One can try and laugh off a childhood where, to belong and to survive, it was necessary to consort with gamblers and prostitutes, but it is obvious that Ella never quite "fit in." Her lack of perceived acceptance led to her being painfully thin ("they had to give me milk in school to bring up my weight") and shy. Yet, shyness should not be confused with not being sharp. She always presented herself as an innocent, but she did not become the First Lady of Song without knowing exactly what was going on around her, and how to make the most of it.

Like many young people, of both European and African ancestry, Ella was caught up in the culture of the 1930s. Previous to this time, popular music came from Broadway, vaudeville, or that new invention, the wireless radio. People gathered around the piano to sing the popular sheet music of the day, or played the early phonograph records that were available. Adults controlled what was considered appropriate, and young people had to wait to come of age to be involved. Suddenly, a new music emerged that grabbed the ears of young people, and for the first time in history, teenagers had their own musical voice: the sound of big band jazz.

This "new" music was an outgrowth of ragtime, Dixieland, and the early jazz of the Charleston era. The mecca for this new type of entertainment was the Apollo Theater in Harlem. Pilgrimages to the Apollo brought glimpses of such legends as Chick Webb, Fletcher Henderson, Billie Holiday, Benny Carter, and many others. Ella and her friends traveled the train down to Harlem and spent many happy hours at the Apollo taking in the talent. Her idol was terpsichorist Snakehips Tucker, and she toyed with the idea of calling herself "Snakehips" Fitzgerald. Ella, very lithe as a teenager, fancied herself as a hep dancer, and thought seriously of pursuing a career kicking up her heels. "Everybody in Yonkers thought I was a good dancer," she once said. "I really wanted to be a dancer, not a singer."

This was not an unusual thought for young black people of that era, even those with solid families and religious backgrounds such as she. Opportunities were slim for all young people during the Great Depression, and much worse for black youth. Many African Americans found their living in show business. They played vaudeville on the "Chitlin' " circuit, danced in black honky-tonks and speakeasies and, if they were lucky, landed a small role in a Broadway show, review, radio program, or motion picture. As hard as this life was, it was often preferable to washing clothes, shining shoes, or scrubbing toilets. Ella was luckier than most, having a fairly stable home life until her teens. However, those performers really stirred up the talent inside her, and she often talked of dancing. To the teenager of the early 1930s, big band jazz *was* dancing.

In a 1991 interview, childhood friend Charles Gulliver recalled: "She didn't sing so much at all, really, but she loved to dance. She was some dancer, oh yeah! She was a terrific dancer! We used to go down to . . . the Savoy. We'd learn all the latest dances. We took the trolley car to the subway station, then subway to New York, and we'd come out at 125th Street." Ella and Gulliver teamed up and decided to try their luck as professional dancers. They began to get some gigs in Yonkers as a dance team. It is at this point that the details of Ella's early life get extremely blurry.

Most of what has been published through the years placed Ella in Yonkers until her big break. However, the truth of her life before her celebrity is neither that simple nor palatable. For one thing, it was reported that not long after Ella made her debut at the Apollo, Tempe died saving the life of a child. Yet more recent stories blamed her death on a heart attack. Here's how Ella remembered it in the early 1980s:

"There was a little Italian boy who just loved my mother so. If his mother couldn't get him to eat, she'd just say to my mother, 'Please come and make him eat!' He'd come and stay with us. He wanted to go with my mother anywhere she wanted to go. And they were in the car one day. She was holding him. My cousin, who was driving the car, stopped the car fast. To save the little boy from hitting the front, my mother grabbed him and hit her head. She got fifty-four stitches in her head. They didn't have all the medicines they have now, and it didn't heal."

Ella's aspirations for Yonkers success were ended with her mother's death. Joe Da Silva turned increasingly to alcohol, and turned increasingly to young Ella for "comfort." Whether he was simply taking out his anger on the youngster, or actually saw her as a sex object, in short time Ella was removed from the house by Tempe's sister Virginia. Frances joined them shortly thereafter at their home on 145th Street in Harlem, when Joe died of a heart attack.

While Ella became close to her cousin Georgiana (who in later years became her traveling companion and wardrobe mistress), she did not like life in her aunt's house. She visited Yonkers as often as possible to see her chums, but after a while they began to go their separate ways. Hating her new life, Ella became increasingly unhappy, and her behavior became increasingly irascible and hostile. She tried to drop out of school, but was sent to the Riverdale Children's Association, which was a setting not as loose as a high school but not as restrictive as a reform school. It should have been more restrictive, for soon Ella left the school and her aunt's house to live on the streets.

Ella's street life greatly hindered her ability to get anywhere or do anything to better her lot. She lived hand to mouth, often unwashed, ill fed, and with no permanent address. While some interviewed for this book rumored that Ella traded her body for a safe place to sleep, there is no substantiating evidence that she was ever a prostitute. As strange as it may seem, it is possible to cling to certain moral values while ignoring others. Tempe had, it seems, filled Ella with religion. There were some things Ella did because she had to; there were some things she did because she wanted to; there were some things she never did because she couldn't.

Now, the legend and the truth come together chronologically. The Apollo Theater in Harlem had a policy of having an amateur night, a performance of new talent after the "real" show was over to showcase newcomers in competition. The concept of having these showcases began at Harlem's Lafayette Theater on 132nd Street in 1933. The winner received a prize of a trophy, cash, or perhaps a professional booking. Contestants were encouraged to write their names, addresses, and phone numbers on a card and drop it in a box. Amateurs would be contacted by pulling the cards out of the box at random, and told when to come to perform. More than half of the 200,000 African Americans living in Harlem were on relief (the depression idiom for welfare), and these shows were great morale boosters.

Although she always claimed she was egged on by her friends ("one day two girlfriends and I made a bet—a dare"), Ella and some of her street companions put their names on those cards, and the powers in the universe that make things happen pulled out Ella's entry in January of 1934. Accompanied by her encouraging compatriots, she attended at the prescribed time, running through her dance routine in her head.

The Apollo show ended with the Edwards Sisters, a "flash" act featuring an amazing amount of energetic dancing. As Ella described them, "They were the dancingest sisters around!" She realized she couldn't possibly follow them with her amateur dancing. As luck would have it, she was the first one called to perform. "My legs turned to water and a million butterflies played tag in my stomach," she would later say. Her friends pushed her out on stage, "and when I looked where I thought the audience should be, all I saw was a big blur." Someone from the audience yelled, "What's *she* gonna do?" The Apollo Theater was known for its tough audiences, who made an art form out of heckling. They had seen the best, and when they saw real talent, their enthusiasm would be wild and unbridled. However, whenever they were faced with something less than spectacular, or when they "smelled fear," their rowdy disapproval could have turned the Rock of Gibraltar into Pebble Beach.

The master of ceremonies sensed Ella's panic, and inquired if she wanted to sing instead. With the audience's encouragement, she asked if the house band knew the Hoagy Carmichael song "Judy." She later asserted that she knew the lyrics because her mother used to play Connee Boswell's record of this song over and over. Strangely enough, music historian Will Friedwald claims there is no trace of such a recording to be found today.

Ella sang the number, resting on Boswell's style to get her through it. The audience response was so positive that it required an encore. The only other song Ella knew was what she referred to as the flip side to "Judy," "Believe It Beloved." Needless to say, Ella won first prize, $25. Had she not won the contest, Ella would never have pursued a career as a vocalist. She called that evening, "the turning point of my life. Once up there, I felt the acceptance and love from the audience—I knew I wanted to sing before people the rest of my life."

Also of great coincidence was the attendance that night of a young saxophonist and arranger, Benny Carter. Benny immediately saw the potential in young Ella's singing, and introduced himself to Ella after the show. "I'm not sure if I was the M.C. that night" (he wasn't), recalled Carter, "but immediately I could see not only her talent but her reaction to the audience. Although she was nervous, and still gets nervous before every performance, she loved them, and they loved her back. It was obvious from the start what she had that night at the Apollo, and my goodness what she's done with it." It was both wonderful and amazing that they were still close friends and recording companions more than fifty-five years later.

What made Ella so special that night was the incredible reaction she and the audience had to one another. It wasn't her voice, which was still thin and tentative, and her style was that of Connee Boswell's. She was a gawky teenager, not well dressed or well groomed, and she never claimed to be a great beauty. Yet, it was like two people who meet and become instant best friends. It was a chemical reaction, two individual elements that when combined caused a huge fizz.

Carter introduced Ella to Fletcher Henderson several days after her debut, but Fletcher was not particularly impressed (one wonders how many times he must have kicked himself over *that* one), saying, "I just don't see much in her."

Ella began a routine of playing and winning all the amateur contests in Harlem, adding "The Object of My Affection" to her repertoire. The only stumbling point was one night at the Lafayette when she attempted to sing "Lost in a Fog," dressed all in black to look sophisticated. "The pianist didn't know the chord changes and I really *did* get lost," Ella remembered many years later. She was booed off the stage. However, total failure quickly turned to total triumph as she continued on with her three songs, winning every talent show in which she was entered. Finally, the talented teen won a professional booking as her prize: a week at the Harlem Opera House with the Tiny Bradshaw band for $50. At this time, she also got her first mention in the press. *New York Age* referred to her then forthcoming

Harlem Opera House appearance in January 1935: ". . . and Ella Fitzgerald, the last name a prize winner at a recent audition contest at
the Harlem Opera House."

There is a story about Ella that has resurfaced time and again,
purportedly occurring around this time. It is simply apocryphal. Supposedly, the CBS radio network got wind of Ella's uptown triumphs,
and wanted to feature her on a show starring Arthur Tracy, "The
Street Singer," whose big hit was "Here Lies Love." The sad tale
continues that just as the contract was to be signed, Ella's mother
died, leaving no one to sign her contracts.

While it was impossible to track down the exact date of Ella's
mother's passing, an underaged girl would still have had a guardian
appointed by the courts. New York had a very strong family court
system, even then. Had such a contract been offered, CBS would
have requested such a guardian be appointed. William S. Paley, chairman of CBS, was not a man to be put off. Ella's aunt, Virginia Williams, could have provided the necessary signature. Finally, Mr. Tracy
himself recently was quoted as saying that he had no intention of
hiring Ella, and in fact had never heard of her until her days with the
Decca record label.

Much of Ella's early career was similarly wrapped in the gauze of
publicity agents.

It was at the end of that week at the Opera House that Ella first
crossed paths with Chick Webb, the drumming bandleader. As Ella
reminisced: "Tiny Bradshaw's band was on that show. They put me
on right at the end, when everybody had on their coats and was getting
ready to leave. Tiny said, 'Ladies and gentlemen, here is the young
girl that's been winning all the contests,' and they all came back and
took their coats off and sat down again."

Chick was due in with his band the following night, and, as they
used to say, he caught her act. While Chick was impressed, he had
no desire to add a female vocalist to his organization. Intervention
came in the person of Bardu Ali, front man for the Webb band.

Chick (born William Henry Webb, Jr., in 1909) was handicapped
as a baby with tuberculosis of the spine. A fall down a flight of stairs
as a toddler partially paralyzed his legs. His diminutive size (just over
four feet) earned him the nickname "Chick." Due to his physical
limitations, Ali conducted the band while Webb played the drums

(and played them extremely well, a dynamo who would be more of a legend today if not for his untimely death).

Ali took Ella backstage into Chick's dressing room (it has been rumored that she was "smuggled" in, but the small dressing rooms in these theaters preclude the drama of this version) and induced the bandleader to listen while she sang a few songs. Webb felt he had no need for a girl singer since he already had a young male singer, Charlie Linton, and didn't see the need to add to the payroll expenses.

Finally, he relented and allowed Ella a tryout when the band played at Yale University. "Well, we're playing Yale tomorrow," he remarked with a question mark in his voice. "Get on the band bus and if they like you there, you've got a job." If the hipsters at Yale accepted her, he felt she might actually work out for a while. Chick and Ella never had a reason to look back, and the singer banked a cool $12.50 a week in her first months with the band, upped to $15.00 when they started taking up regular residence at the Savoy Ballroom.

Chapter Two

1936–1937

$\mathcal{T}$he first time she came into my office," said Moe Gale, who was Webb's manager and eventually handled those same chores for Ella, "she looked terrible. Her hair disheveled, her clothes just terrible. I said to Chick, 'My God, what can you do with this girl?' Chick answered, 'Mr. Gale, you'd be surprised what a beauty parlor and some makeup and nice clothes can do.' " Gale's office was Consolidated Radio Artists at the RKO Building on West Forty-eighth Street in New York. Gale was also a stockholder in the Savoy Ballroom.

Much has been made of Ella's appearance at this time. Charlie Linton helped Ella find a room on 122nd Street and Seventh Avenue in the German-owned boardinghouse where he resided. This was Ella's first permanent address in quite a while. However, Ella had no inkling as to how to care for and groom herself. As impossible as it may sound, the only way to put it is that Ella was disgusting. She was not entirely to blame for this. With her mother's death (and precious little time spent with her Aunt Virginia), the normal lessons a young girl learns about hygiene and grooming went untaught. The companions she met during her time on the street certainly did not add to this education. She literally did not know to use soap and water on a regular basis. Webb trombonist Sandy Williams took her as one would take a child and taught her how to bathe. To her credit, she saw what was necessary to learn, and adapted quickly to it.

Just as it took time for Ella to develop her vocal style, so it was with her stage appearance. Saxophonist and onetime Webb arranger Edgar Sampson once recalled: "We all kidded her. It would always be 'Hey, Sis, where'd you get those clothes?' We all called her Sis. And 'Sis, what's with that hairdo?' But she always took it in good spirits."

At this point in the story, it has often been written that poor orphaned Ella was adopted by Chick Webb and his wife, Sallye. It's a great story, but simply not true. Chick was allowed legal guardianship so that Ella could travel and record with the band. The adoption pretense was necessary to deflect any rumors that Chick might be having sex with his new underaged vocalist.

While never publicized, many bandleaders had dalliances with their "canaries." Once while in a New York hotel, bandleader Russ Morgan was in flagrante delicto with his singer when the maid walked in. Embarrassed, they ended their fellatio session, but the story was all over town in hours, causing the girl to leave the city and be temporarily replaced while things cooled down. This was important stuff back then. Nowadays, they'd go on Geraldo and get applause.

Ella began to tour with the band using the time as an education, learning from Chick how to be a professional and learning from the band how to be an instrumentalist. She always strove to be one of the guys, and while she was most certainly exposed to the marijuana, drinking, pep pills, prostitution, and gambling that were part and parcel of big band business, her bandmates tried as they could to insulate her from the worst of it. "She was always the lady tomboy," recalled one former member. "She wanted to be a part of everything we did musically, but when things got down and dirty she remained a highly interested observer."

In May 1935, she got her first review, from George T. Simon of *Metronome* magazine. In assessing the Webb organization, he offered, "Miss Fitzgerald should go places."

Ella's musical schooling was from topflight jazz musicians at the peak of their form, so it is no wonder that as her singing style developed, she often sounded like another instrument in the band. One of her early musical mentors was a sideman in the Webb organization, the late Dizzy Gillespie. "I learned a lot from those musicians," Ella has said, "and I'm very grateful for it. When they used to have the after-hours jam sessions at Minton's and Monroe's Uptown House, I used to sneak in with them. And I feel that I learned what little bop I do have by following Dizzy around to these different places. I feel that was my education. He is a wonderful teacher, and I am very grateful to him." She needed to learn fast because she was about to enter a place that would become like a second home to her: the recording studio.

Ella finally went before the microphone to cut her first sides for Decca, the label to which the Webb band was under contract. She reminisced: "I'll never forget it; the record was 'Love and Kisses.' After we made it the band was in Philadelphia one night when they wouldn't let me in at some beer garden where I wanted to hear it on the jukebox. So I had some fellow who was over twenty-one go in and put a nickel in while I stood outside and listened to my own voice coming out." For the most part, Ella remained with the label for the next twenty years.

On June 12, 1935, Ella cut her first 78s, the aforementioned "Love and Kisses" and a second tune, "I'll Chase the Blues Away." Strangely, the latter was released on the subsidiary label Brunswick, rather than on Decca. Another review of Ella's singing (by *New York Age*) from this period was her first rave: "During the Webb band presentation, Charlie Linton sings rather well, but it takes Ella Fitzgerald to send the audience into a vociferous display of enthusiasm. Her voice is seemingly tinged with honey, and she sings with a rhythmic tempo that puts her over with a bang."

It was four more months before Ella returned to the studio, this time for "Rhythm and Romance" and "I'll Chase the Blues Away" (rerecorded from her first step up to the mike) on October 12. During this time, the youngster was sharpening her chops, traveling with the band in between gigs at the Savoy Ballroom, the spiritual home of the Webb group.

The Savoy Ballroom ("The World's Most Famous Ballroom" was one of its nicknames) was opened at the end of the Charleston age on March 6, 1926. Located in the heart of Harlem on Lenox Avenue near 140th Street, it took up a whole floor of a block-long building. Unusual for its time, the Ballroom admitted anyone who could afford to get in. The Savoy was one happening place, packed to the rafters with teenagers and young adults who wanted to "swing" to the music that exploded on the bandstand. Every sort of person congregated there, from middle-class teens looking to cut loose to professional criminals looking to score and the entire spectrum in between. Alcohol and drugs increased the momentum, with otherwise laid-back customers sweating and straining to keep up with the "shucking and jiving." Young people would rehearse for hours before going to the Savoy; they worked on new dance steps and tried to look sharp on the dance floor. Not until the disco days of the late 1970s would such a combination of music, energy, lighting, rhythm, sweat, alcohol, and drugs come together in one place on a regular basis.

The huge stage offered two bandstands, where orchestras could alternate in nonstop music. It was not easy to do well at the Savoy; if the dancers didn't dig the music and dance, the band was out. These double bandstands, which could also disappear from view for dramatic effect, easily led themselves to a staple of the Savoy: the battle of the bands.

The Webb band was the unofficial "house" band, the one most often booked and the most popular with the regulars. Certainly, having a stockholder in the Ballroom as their agent didn't hinder the frequent bookings of the Webb ensemble. As other bands came and went, Webb alternated sets with the "visitors." Each set got louder and progressively more energized. Sometimes, both bands played the same number, each trying to whip the young hepsters into an ever-growing frenzy.

Only once did Webb lose such a battle; it took the genius of Duke Ellington to hand the band a defeat. The Duke of Ellington had no desire to enter such a battle. He was secure with his music and his musicians. When Webb enthused to sideman Teddy McRea, "We're gonna make this cat work tonight!," Ellington wanted no part of it. He pulled Chick aside and whispered, "Look, man, we got the place full, we ain't gettin' no more money, why knock our brains out?" Usually Ellington was more colorful with his language, but he wanted to make his point clear. Unfortunately, Webb was stubborn.

The Duke and his men, with singer Ivie Anderson, played first, followed immediately by Webb and his group. The latter tried hard to "swing" Duke off the stand, and the audience saw something special brewing. They egged the Ellington Orchestra on to fight back musically. Duke realized he would have to go along, and blew several windows out before Chick admitted he had met his match.

Not only was Ella getting a musical education, she was getting invaluable life experience. Additionally, she was learning how to sing in front of anybody and everybody. The Webb sets at the Savoy were becoming something of a legend in the music business, much different than those of "sweeter" bands who performed in much more controlled environments. Ella saw the incredible opportunity presented to her to learn, and knew only she could take advantage of it. She taught herself to sight-read the music, so she could be fast in rehearsals. She wrote the lyrics down on homemade flash cards, shuffling them faster and faster until she had the lyrics down perfectly. There was never an instance where the band was ready to go and she wasn't.

The first popular standard Ella warbled on wax was "My Melancholy Baby," backed with "All My Life" on March 17, 1936. These cuts were recorded with Teddy Wilson and His Orchestra, rather than with Chick, again for the Brunswick label. Ella's vocals on these cuts appeared courtesy of Billie Holiday. Lady Day had temporarily left Wilson without a singer so she could tour with Jimmie Lunceford's band. As much as Ella gilded the lily of Billie's memory in later years, Billie was not a big fan of Ella's at that time. Teddy much preferred Ella's voice to Billie's, feeling Billie was overly influenced by Louis Armstrong. It has been reported that Billie would catch Ella at the Savoy, and then remark with disdain, "A great band like that with Ella. That bitch"—and then leave in a huff.

Ella rarely strayed from the Webb fold, but several gems appear with Wilson, Benny Goodman, and others. These early recordings featured the band, with Ella's vocal stuck in the middle after the first chorus as more of an afterthought than an attraction.

Her voice sounded young because she was young, although her youth was played up and she probably added a little more of it to her vocals than was natural. There was little vibrato and her instantly identifiable style was hardly in evidence, but there was something in the voice that was pleasing to the ear and the heart. Like other women-children vocalists popular at the time (Judy Garland, Rose Marie, Shirley Temple, and Deanna Durbin to name a few), there was the promise of maturity in the selection of songs dichotomized by the girlish interpretations of the lyrics.

At this point in her career, her recordings were pleasant attempts at vocalizing but nothing more. Ella and Chick returned to recording double harness on April 7 in New York (all of the preceding recordings were made in New York, as were all of her recordings during the next several years) and again on June 2 to do seven sides that were no more distinguished than their predecessors. When songs were chosen to record, the band was always considered first and foremost. After all, she was only the girl singer. It was not yet evident that people were beginning to come to the Savoy as much to hear the youthful vocalist as to dance to the band.

The first recording that became part of the legend of Ella was a song called "(If You Can't Sing It) You'll Have to Swing It." The song in itself was nothing more than a cute novelty tune taken at a fox-trot tempo. Martha Raye featured this song in her act for years, doing a comic turn with it in much the same tempo as this original recording with Ella. What does shine through even in this early cut are several of the vocal trademarks that would, in a few years, become part of the unmistakable Fitzgerald style.

Ella often played with time, speeding up or slowing down or bending it against the steady rhythm of her accompaniment. While it was done on a very simple level here, Ella's ease in using time was surely evident. Another "Ella-ism" was the breaking up of syllables on the vowel, singing words like hand as "ha-and" or Paganini as "Pa-ha-ha-ganini," harmonically inserting other notes before going to the one in the melody. These two vocal tricks appeared throughout Ella's entire career, not interfering with her singing but adding to it, as Ella had the genius to know when and how to use them.

The final Ella-ment, the one for which she was perhaps best known, was the art of scat singing. Although it was not developed anywhere near to the sophistication of her later work, Ella threw in several bits of scat throughout "You'll Have to Swing It." Here, then, was the first real hint of the style that was to become the backbone of the career of Ella Fitzgerald. As no surprise to many who have followed Ella's career, this song, renamed "Mr. Paganini," appeared time and again in both studio and live cuts, and was much requested at her concerts over fifty-five years later. Also recorded at this session were three more sides, the most popular of which was "Vote for Mr. Rhythm," which was reissued several times on both albums and CDs.

In October of 1936, Ella was approached by the King of Swing, Benny Goodman, to help on a recording date when his regular vocalist fell ill. With Chick Webb's blessing, Ella eagerly agreed and went to the RCA studios (Goodman's record label) in New York on October 5. Three cuts were waxed, including "Didja Mean It" and "Oh, Yes, Take Another Guess." The gem here, the next of the famous Fitzgerald recordings, was "Goodnight My Love." Introduced by Shirley Temple in movies, this cut was ensured a place in recording history not only by the magic of Ella and Benny together, but because it (like the other two cuts) had to be pulled from distribution less than two weeks after it was issued. Decca, long known for its possessive nature when it came to the artists recording for them, threatened to sue RCA for unauthorized use of Ella Fitzgerald. Never mind that such a release could only enhance Ella's stature (thereby enhancing her sales potential as well as that of the Webb organization); Decca owned Ella and that was that. The 78 became an instant collector's item, only put in general release later by RCA as a special 45 rpm record long after Ella left Decca. It is a shame that these were the only commercial recordings by Ella and Benny; their styles blended beautifully, even in these early days in both their careers. In fact, Ella made an early radio appearance on November 10, 1936, with Goodman on his "Camel Caravan" series.

It has been reported that during this time, Ella had an affair with Goodman tenor sax man Vido Musso. Supposedly, she became pregnant, and had to take a three-month leave of absence from the band after her botched abortion, which left her barren. If this is true, and I could not find the usual two sources to verify it, it might explain a lot about Ella's choices for the rest of her life. To some women, not being able to give birth might not matter. Perhaps to Ella, knowing she could never have a family of her own motivated her to seek her "pleasure" in life from two sources: her career (primarily) and men (secondarily).

The abortion, and her forced time off from touring, would also explain why Ella was singing with the Teddy Hill band at the Savoy during this time. Additionally, she appeared weekly on Moe Gale's "Goodtime Society" radio broadcasts without Webb.

It was around this time that Ella first crossed paths with someone who would loom large in her recording career, Billy May. May was then a sideman with the Charlie Barnet orchestra, when the Barnet organization played in a battle of the bands with the Webb group at the Savoy Ballroom. "We [the musicians] all hung out together, mostly at the hotel on 126th Street near Seventh Avenue where many of the Webb players lived including, I believe, Ella. We sat around pitching ideas and drinking champagne, but it was almost twenty-five years before I would orchestrate for Ella's *Harold Arlen Songbook* [see the Verve Years]," recalled May.

Ella returned to the Decca fold that same month to record with a subgroup of the Webb band called "Ella Fitzgerald and Her Savoy Eight." Clearly, Decca (who already had a reputation for promoting singing "personalities" as well as jazz bands) had its sights on Ella as a solo artist, looking to milk her growing popularity. Over the following twenty years, Decca promoted, recorded (and in some cases misrecorded) such well-known singers as Al Jolson; Sophie Tucker; Ethel Merman; Mary Martin; Danny Kaye; Sammy Davis, Jr.; Carmen McRae; Bing Crosby; and Carol Burnett. With the exceptions of Jolson, Tucker, and Burnett, all of them did excellent work for Decca, but did their best work after leaving the label to achieve more artistic freedom.

As Ella began to fashion her emerging style, she also began to hit her stride in popularity. Appearing with the band, she was a work in progress. Before the audience, she would hone her talent, watching and listening to the reaction of the crowd. Within a year, Ella was billed above the name of the band (and in larger letters) on all publicity; within two years she was called "the First Lady of Song." On November 18 and 19, Ella and the Savoy Eight did cover versions of four already popular songs: "My Last Affair" and "Organ Grinder's Swing" (which Ella would rerecord thirty and forty years later, respectively; see The Verve Years and The Pablo Years), and "Shine" and "Darktown Strutters' Ball." Ella was still resting on her little-girl sound, although she was taking more of a featured place within the arrangements.

Over the next year and a half, Ella would alternately record with the Webb big band and then with the smaller Savoy Eight. While there were many interesting cuts in the mix ("Dedicated to You" and "Big Boy Blue" were done with the Mills Brothers in early 1937; "Crying Mood," "Bei Mir Bist Du Schoen," and "Holiday in Harlem" were other early favorites), and several Ella would give more attention to later in her career ("Rock It for Me," "All or Nothing at All"), her work here is basically more of the same. Decca had found a formula that worked, and worked it for all it was worth.

Ella moved again during this period, this time to a larger hotel-style apartment on Seventh Avenue near 142nd Street. The reason for her move was drummer Jo Jones, the newest man in her life. While the affair didn't last long, the name of the hotel was immortalized in song: the Woodside Hotel was the inspiration for "Jumpin' at the Woodside."

Another battle of the bands took place on May 11, 1937, that would live in music infamy. This time, the opposing team was led by Benny Goodman, with drummer Gene Krupa bringing up the rear. Goodman had wisely done a little musical espionage, visiting the Savoy to watch the Webb assembly in action. Chick had gotten wind of Goodman's forthcoming visit, and cannily changed the tempos of all his arrangements to throw Benny off.

The night of the battle, more than four thousand people jammed the Ballroom, while over five thousand eager onlookers jammed the streets surrounding it. With five policemen keeping the peace inside, the city called in the riot squad and the fire department to defuse any potential trouble on the street. Inside, Webb gave his group a pep talk. He pulled Ella aside to say, "This is the turning point of this band. You know how much this means to me."

As usual, the visitors began first. Back and forth, the bands traded efforts. This time, Webb was not to be put down. By the time Ella was introduced, the bands were running neck and neck, with Webb having a slight edge. She began the first of several numbers, with the attendees stopping in their tracks. Rather than continuing to dance, they stood arm-in-arm, swaying to her vocalizing. Chick ended the set with a drum solo, leaving Goodman and Krupa shaking their heads with their mouths open. Both Webb and Ella became forces to be reckoned with.

In 1937, Ella won her first *Down Beat* poll, giving her top female vocal honors (the male was Bing Crosby). Jimmie Lunceford offered Ella $75 to leave Webb, but Ella stuck with her mentor. He applauded her loyalty (and growing fame) by eventually raising her salary to $125 per week. Only Chick's forthcoming illness would break the mold, changing forever the direction of Ella's career.

Chapter Three

1938–1939

*T*he last of the great band battles involving the Webb band took place on January 16, 1938. This time the challenger was the swing-ingest band of them all, the Count Basie Orchestra. That very night, Basie had appeared with Benny Goodman at Goodman's knockout Carnegie Hall concert. Basie went from one gig downtown right to his gig at the Savoy. Billie Holiday was his vocalist that night. Although the band magazines were divided over the winner (*Metronome* for Webb, *Down Beat* for Basie), Ella won out hands down over Billie, rocking the whole crowd with her infectious singing.

Another apocryphal story: Webb was hospitalized in the spring of 1938, while the band waited for him to recover in New York. Bored and concerned (for their futures as well as for Webb's failing health), Ella and the guys fooled around with some music to play for him in the hospital to cheer him up. Ella remembered an old nursery rhyme that had been a favorite of hers as a child, and with Ella reworking the words and the guys collaborating on the music, the Webb organization went to visit him in April of 1938 to cheer him up with their "new" song. Chick, delighted with the gesture but more delighted with the music, insisted that they all go into the studio to record it as soon as he was well. On May 2, 1938, the group went into Decca's studios in New York and cut "A-Tisket A-Tasket."

The above anecdote makes a great story, but once again the sharp pin of truth must burst the bubble of fiction. To prick that piece of imagination brings to the foreground a young arranger, Van Alexander. He had been one of the "hep-cats" who hung out at the Savoy ("the Home of Happy Feet") to dance and be cool. "I arranged music, and thought I was pretty good," chuckled Van in a recent interview. With the brazen confidence of youth, he went up to Chick Webb during one of the band breaks. "I told him I had written some great arrangements for the band, and he asked if I could bring them around the next day for him to hear. Chick was always open to musical input, and felt he had nothing to lose by listening to me," remembered Alexander [who was still called Al Feldman; Van came from his Dutch middle name and Alexander was his first name, changed when his solo career really got started], "so he agreed."

All he had to do now was go home and write those wonderful arrangements he had bragged about, because he had nothing on paper. Obviously, he was talented *and* fast, because he came back the next day and was hired to arrange for Webb, which by this point meant arranging for Ella.

The band went to Boston in April 1938 to play at Levaggi's nitery, where they were also broadcasting nightly on the radio. Ella approached Van about an idea she had concerning a favorite childhood nursery rhyme: could they swing it? "I turned her down flat, bemoaning the incredible amount of work Chick was giving me to come up with fresh arrangements every day for the radio show," recalled Van. No more was mentioned until a few days later, when Ella again approached him, persistent, red hot to do this song. Ella had already learned to push for what she wanted musically, willing to fight for what she felt was good for her. "She put it on the line, and told me that if I didn't do the arrangement, she'd bring in someone from the outside who would," recalled Alexander. "Naturally, I didn't want to alienate Ella *or* Chick."

At the risk of her going to another arranger, Van agreed to work on it that night, and stayed up until dawn working out a concept that would be right for both Ella and the band. She gave the arrangement the once-over, but felt the lyrics and bridge needed work. It was Ella who changed "walking on down the avenue" to "trucking on down the avenue," and added several other "hep" asides to make the song as we know it today. It was her idea, and her now-evident style, that made it so special; it was Van Alexander who put the structure together and arranged it. They both gladly shared equal credit for the song. Van also became well-known for his own band as well as for background music on such television classics as "Hazel," "Bewitched," "The Donna Reed Show," "I Dream of Jeannie," "Dennis the Menace," and the latter-day theme song of "The Dean Martin Show." Alexander entered Ella's life again in the early and mid-1950s, as he wrote several arrangements for her to use in supperclubs.

Also not told in the official stories of the making of "Tisket" was Ella's dalliance with President Roosevelt's son. He would bring his chauffeured limousine to the club and escort her home every night. He was heard to say, "I am the future of this country!" Not only was he not the future of the country, he was not in the future of Ella Fitzgerald. When Ella left Boston, the affair was over.

Chick put "Tisket" on the air almost immediately, and the band played it nightly for almost a month, making the song tight and well rehearsed before that day in the studio came on May 2, 1938. Despite the fact that she was already over twenty years old, Ella was able to inject into this song enough of that same little-girl quality to make it extremely appealing. The difference here was that vocally Ella had her tongue in her cheek, and her humor came through on the cut. Needless to say, this was an enormous song for Ella, forever recognized as her theme song all over the world. It appeared on the "Hit Parade" for nineteen weeks. "If they'd been giving out gold records in those days I imagine we'd have gotten one," said Ella. She rerecorded it for Verve (both in the studio and live; see The Verve Years) and Columbia (see The Pablo Years), and each time the single sold very well.

There was something incredibly appealing about Ella's way with this deceptively simple song. Not a concert or club date went by since that May day in 1938 where Ella didn't work at least four bars of the song into her performance to appease the audience. The icing on the cake was Ella's name appearing on the label as lyricist, beginning her ASCAP rating as a writer of lyrics with no small talent. While Chick

Webb's name appears on several of Ella's songs, along with such standards as "Don't Be That Way" and "Stompin' at the Savoy," he never actually wrote anything. It was his band, he gave these songs the exposure they needed to catch on, so his name appeared on the sheet music. This was a very common practice back then, and no one ever raised an eyebrow.

Eight more sides were made at this recording session and on the following day, with "I'm Just a Jitterbug" being the most interesting. The impact of "Tisket" hadn't been felt yet, so it was pretty much business as usual. When Ella and Chick returned to the studio on June 9, it was obvious that Ella was now the featured player, and her style was becoming more adult in its presentation.

"Pack Up Your Sins and Go to the Devil" and "Everybody Step" had been featured by Ethel Merman in Irving Berlin's movie musical *Alexander's Ragtime Band*. Both are earthy numbers, although Ella was able to inject quite a bit more innocence than the brassier Miss Merman. "MacPherson Is Rehearsin' (to Swing)" was a near-miss follow-up to "You'll Have to Swing It," and "Ella" not only features Miss Fitz's lyrics but capitalized on her growing fame.

Ella's fame was also growing as a woman who attracted men. Between May and August 1938, Ella had an affair with Louis Jordan, a sideman with Webb until he was fired because he was upstaging Ella. Jordan truly liked and respected Ella, and although he was a married man, he wasn't beyond trying to "influence" Ella to leave Webb and join his band. Ella allowed herself to enjoy what he had to offer, but would not leave Chick.

Another romance in January 1939 was a little more contrived. Ella began to see Heywood Henry, baritone sax man for the Erskine Hawkins band. It didn't take long for the fling to be over, as both parties (and clients of Moe Gale) parted company after all possible publicity had been milked.

It was just after this time that Ella made the first of her big mistakes concerning her love life. Her fellow bandmates often teased her about her "innocence," although in this case they were not necessarily referring to her virginity or lack thereof. In later years, Ella would say, "My one regret in life is that I loved a little too easily and a little too often."

What happened has been described in two ways by the lady in

question. "There was this guy who kind of hung around after the shows, and I guess he kind of liked me. Anyway, the guys in the band said he wanted to marry me, and bet me that I wouldn't. I had to win the bet, so I married him." In later years, her version changed to, "I went and got married on a bet. I was that stupid; the guy bet me I wouldn't marry him. The guys in the band were all crying when I told them."

As Val Valentin might say, that's just horseshit. Barney Kornegay was a penny-ante con man and sharpie who saw Ella as a meal ticket and a way to pay off his gambling debts. Miss Fitz simply would not believe that her Romeo had feet of clay. Moe Gale hired investigators to prove Kornegay's criminal past, and at this point Ella became a believer. Since she had no grounds for divorce (they were a lot harder to get in those days), the attorneys decided to sue for annulment, under the grounds that Kornegay had married Ella under false pretenses (not revealing his criminal past). The loathsome Lothario fought bitterly against losing his meal ticket, but in the end our Heroine prevailed. Ella was obviously trying to spread her wings as an adult, and perhaps felt she needed the umbrella of marriage to sanctify the fact that she was sexually active. "I got an annulment and the judge told me, 'You just keep singing "A-Tisket A-Tasket" and leave these men alone,' " she would later recall, but Ella would always have trouble with the opposite sex.

The August 17 session further showed how Ella was growing out of her little-girl mold. "Wacky Dust" was an obvious salute to cocaine with extremely sophisticated lyrics. Many years later, the Manhattan Transfer wisely revived the number, electronically copying the Webb arrangement almost note for note and pastiching Ella's vocals. "I Can't Stop Loving You" and "Woe Is Me" (from the session on the following day) were some of Ella's best ballad singing up to that point. Her last session of 1938 on October 6 featured two standouts. "FDR Jones" was fun and lively, successfully covered by Judy Garland on *her* early Decca sessions. "I Found My Yellow Basket" was a natural follow-up to "Tisket," but failed to make the same big splash.

Her twenty-first year, 1939, brought major upheaval as great success and great personal tragedy rocked Ella's life. She recorded thirty-two sides over the next twelve months, and before it was over was the nominal leader of her own big-time orchestra. As the year unfolded, so did her figure, metamorphosing from willowy to zaftig. Although some singers have problems with extra weight, Ella's voice just filled out and matured.

The first session of the year on February 17 produced two hit songs, Charlie Shavers's "Undecided" and " 'Tain't What You Do." The former featured extremely confident vocals by Ella as well as crisp and precise playing by the band (with an infectious saxophone solo by Hilton Jefferson and hot drumming by the very ill Webb). Although the transition from drum solo to vocal before the last chorus was very abrupt, it caught the ear nicely, giving the song a cute "hook." Ella's voice still sounded young, but there was a solid presentation in her style that belied her age and lack of experience. It was a superior effort by all concerned, rising it above the mist of half-forgotten big band trivia to definitive hit status.

The latter (a cover version of Jimmie Lunceford's recent record) harked back to what had been Ella's bread and butter with the band: a novelty song, rhythmic but insipid. After a full chorus by the orchestra (often Ella wasn't heard until the second chorus on many of the Webb recordings), the interesting aspects of this tune included a lively trombone solo by Sandy Williams, an unusual vocal chorus by the band, and above all an ending that would live in the annals of jazz! Ella can be given credit for naming an entire musical genre by her use of the soon-to-be-famous term "rebop" in her wordless vocal. She included it in her repertoire until the band broke up in 1941.

Also recorded at the same session was "My Heart Belongs to Daddy," Ella's first attempt at Cole Porter. While the band did swing to Porter's beguine, she was gagged by ersatz lyrics that sanitized all the original sophistication and meaning. It was a decade before Ella approached the song again for Decca (with Ellis Larkins), and thirty-three years before she would meet the original, spicy lyrics on her only album for Atlantic Records. It's not that Ella was more or less innocent than any other young woman of that era; in an interview several years ago Mary Martin told me she didn't get the illicit implications of the song she introduced on Broadway until salty Sophie Tucker explained them to her.

A typical evening's entertainment from the band at that time was preserved on Olympic records in a set recorded at the Savoy Ballroom. Opening with "Oh, Johnny," the band blasts through such numbers as "Blue Lou," "Diga Doo," "I Want the Waiter (With the Water)," "Limehouse Blues," " 'Tain't What You Do," "Traffic Jam," "I'm Confessin' That I Love You," "Breakin' Down," and "Swing Out." This is the earliest known recording of Ella singing live in front of an audience. Her voice was clear and sounds very much like her recordings of that time.

The band continued to prosper, with the group playing the Park Central Hotel as well as two dates at the Paramount Theater when they weren't holding court at the Savoy.

Ella and Chick continued to record while his health kept a steady decline. The March 2, 1939, session provided yet another popular novelty song, "Chew-Chew-Chew (Your Bubble Gum)." It is interesting to note the beginning of a dichotomy that characterized the rest of Ella's Decca recordings: beautiful ballads on one hand and girlish novelty numbers on the other. "Chew" gained great popularity during 1939 due to its swinging dance tempo, but it was in fact a misguided follow-up to the earlier "Chewing Gum." An amusing side note was the band's referring to Ella as "Sis" during this recording; musicians called her by that name for over six decades. Unfortunately for Ella, "Chew" was even better than "It's Slumbertime Along the Swanee" and "Sugar Pie" from the same date.

When Chick and Ella recorded together one last time, the eight sides made on April 21 again mingled standards such as "Little White Lies" with novelties like "Coochi-Coochi-Coo." This session also yielded a song that would stay with Ella through the years: "Don't Worry 'Bout Me." Certain songs seemed to follow her from era to era and record label to record label. She sang it, swung it, caressed it, and medleyed it, each time finding a way to bring something new to the number and make it sound fresh (see The Verve Years and The Pablo Years for other versions of this song). It was the first of the really sophisticated love songs Ella was allowed to warble, and when she was given a wider berth, her maturity emerged. Interestingly enough, her vocal line here was matched almost note for note on her 1979 recording of the number with the full Count Basie Orchestra, although the accompaniment here was primarily by rhythm section only.

The other songs from this session were not nearly as satisfying, as Ella and the band fought for musical supremacy. "If You Ever Change

Your Mind" had a fine piano solo but suffered from a mediocre arrangement. "Little White Lies" had a typical fox-trot instrumental introduction, but the tempo was too fast to be effective as a vocal. Ella did take liberties with the melody, but the band didn't offer the necessary support. "Coochi-Coochi-Coo" was simply too young for her at this point; even its range made the high notes seem forced.

The discussion here of these last few songs is significant: not only were they typical of Ella's recordings at the time, but they were the *best* of what she was offered. It wasn't that Decca had no taste or that Chick Webb didn't have more sophisticated ideas; the problem was to find the right niche for her. Ostensibly too young and innocent to be torching for her lost man, she was nevertheless too mature musically to be coochi-cooing, either. Additionally, the orchestra was primarily a dance band, specializing in the fox trot and pseudo-boogie-woogie of the era. Even Frank Sinatra was initially saddled with the same problem: virtually all big band vocalists were hired to be ornaments to the festive musical package of their particular band. On special occasions, particularly with Frank and Ella, the ornaments shone more brightly than the package.

Sadly, Chick's health precluded any more touring (except for one last "blast" on a riverboat outside of Washington, D.C.), and for all intents and purposes these recordings marked the end of his orchestra. Webb was taken from the riverboat to Johns Hopkins Hospital in his native Baltimore. Pneumonia had overtaken him, his condition too fragile to fight it off. On the day he died, June 16, 1939, he asked his mother to lift him up. He simply stated, "Sorry, I gotta go!," and died in his mother's arms. When Chick passed, Ella Fitzgerald became the undisputed star of the organization.

Chapter Four

1939–1941

𝒞hick Webb was buried in Baltimore (where the services were held). To attend, the band traveled north from Montgomery, Alabama, where it had been fulfilling a previously booked engagement. It was a broiling hot and humid day. Throngs of people surrounded the funeral chapel. Trolley cars and buses stopped, with people perched on top to catch a glimpse of "their" great musician's last hurrah and/or a look at Ella. The chapel was filled to capacity ("It was the biggest funeral I had ever seen," recalled Moe Gale) with Ella and the band sitting in the front pews. After several oratories for Chick, Ella came to the podium and sang "My Buddy," and then saxophonist Teddy McRea did a tenor-sax solo.

Gale decided the band should keep going, with Ella's name out front and one of the saxophone men in charge of the music. Bill Beason was the first of several drummers attempting to fill Webb's sticks. Giving a statement to the press, he said, "According with Mr. Webb's wishes, Miss Fitzgerald has succeeded to the leadership of the band." Ella later remembered, "I felt like quitting, but the fact that people like me and I like people kept me going." However, all was not smooth sailing.

"Clearly, Ella was not comfortable fronting the band," recollects a band member who wishes to remain anonymous. "She was good at singing her numbers and posing for photographs, but she wasn't savvy enough yet to lead a group. Also, she used to piss some of the guys off with her 'play pretty for the people' everytime someone took a solo. She would just talk through their playing." Obviously, it was Gale who was pulling the strings in the shadows, booking the band and deciding on songs and presentation. At first there wasn't any real change in the sound of the band or the types of songs recorded, however some of the spirit definitely seemed missing.

The first sides by "Ella Fitzgerald and Her Famous Orchestra" were on June 29. Three of the five selections proved popular and one became a classic. Both "Betcha Nickel" and "I Want the Waiter (With the Water)" achieved momentary popularity on the charts, assuring that the band could remain successful without its drummer at the helm (although both songs had been featured with the band before Webb's demise). "Waiter" even moved Ella along on the maturity meter, since its lyrics implied the singer to be a mother, i.e., an adult. The first gem, though, was the ballad "Stairway to the Stars." Although this number had first been made popular by Glenn Miller, the more enduring identification is with Ella, for she rerecorded it again live many years later and had a second huge hit with it (see The Verve Years).

As the months moved on, the band did seem to have more than a passing likeness to the sound of the Glenn Miller band, especially in the trumpet and piano solos. In many of its recordings during this period, the band would be reminiscent of Miller, Basie, or Lunceford. Without Webb, the group began to lose its edge and its identity; Van Alexander had left (and changed his name) to front his own group, and some of the "sound," the musical image that made one band sound different from another, traveled with him.

Remember, there were dozens of big bands at this time, and quite often more than a half-dozen would record the same song. While much has been made of the mythos of bands searching for their sound (it was the basic plot for the movie The Glenn Miller Story), there were similarities between many of the bands, and what distinguished them quite often was the personality of the leader and the singer(s) indigenous to each. Bandleader Artie Shaw has been quoted as saying, ". . . So much has been made about [Miller] searching for that sound. Lots of bands had [similar sounds], but quite honestly Miller should have lived and 'Chattanooga Choo-Choo' should have died."

On her return to the studio that August, it was obvious that the musical direction was changing, albeit in very small steps. "My Last Goodbye" sounded almost as if it were played by the Desi Arnaz Orchestra due to the long instrumental introduction featuring a flute, a trademark of the Arnaz band. Ella's contribution is distinguished by a slight nasality, attributable to a head cold. It is worth noting that she was now singing ballads whose lyrics imply the point of view not of a schoolgirl, but of a woman. This more mature attitude affected not only the choice of songs, but the manner in which they were interpreted. Only in the censored lyrics of "Billy (I Always Dream of Billy)," where the reference to getting a nocturnal thrill was changed to a reference to a dream, are we once again reminded of the problems Ella faced in trying to change her musical image.

Ella's last session of 1939 was not as satisfying as the previous one. While I will spare the reader a discussion of such tripe as "My Wubba Dolly," the only chance for Ella to show her musical chops came with the haunting "Moon Ray." Ella was featured right from the beginning, and it was treated much more like a ballad than a dance tune. The colorful arrangement featured a fine piano solo by Tommy Fulford, with Ella moving her voice all over the song in one of her loosest recorded vocal lines up to that time. While "You're Gonna Lose Your Gal" was strictly a dance arrangement, with another very long instrumental intro, Ella did get to inject quite a bit of "personality" into the piece, in much the same way as Patty Andrews and Martha Raye were doing at the time.

It is interesting that a young African-American performer like Ella would be influenced by such performers of European ancestry as Connee Boswell, Raye, or Andrews. While it was the smoothness and sweet delivery that attracted Fitzgerald to Boswell, it was the energy and delivery of Raye and Andrews that caught Ella's ear. Certainly, there were other people recording at that time who could have influenced her, but it wasn't until she began to record straight ballads that the deep creative influences of such wonderful people as Billie Holiday, Ethel Waters, and Louis Armstrong became evident.

It is during this time that one could hear the emergence of a recording artist becoming a mature interpreter of the popular song. It is an engrossing process, this blossoming of talent. It is much different than the blossoming of celebrity, for often talent has a much longer gestation period. For Ella, it had taken five years of celebrity status before her vocal maturity began to exhibit itself in her recordings of 1940.

Now a star in her own right, with the band carrying her name, Ella's fame rose considerably. She was named *Metronome*'s number-one female singer in both 1939 and 1940. The session on October 12, 1939, was noteworthy for the fact that it was done in Chicago while on tour (as opposed to New York) and contained the first song recorded with the new band that Ella did not sing, "Lindy Hopper's Delight." As this *was* still a band and not just a backup group for Ella, the band was still greatly featured in the arrangements, and the young jitterbugs of the day wanted instrumentals they could dance to without the distraction of a vocalist.

There were several more such recordings made between 1939 and 1941, although each carried Ella's name on the label. Also, as with other bands, the record label insisted on consistently timed releases to appease the growing demand for this kind of music, whether or not each cut would become a number-one hit.

The recording industry was much different then, ruled by the ever-changing juke boxes and top DJs in each major city. As there were no albums as we know them today, it was important to release the 78s often to keep the band's name before the buying public. Ella's band was vying for attention with such legends as Glenn Miller, Tommy Dorsey, Jimmy Dorsey, Jimmie Lunceford, Benny Goodman, Harry James, Count Basie, Duke Ellington, Artie Shaw, Bob Crosby, and others. Vocalists in competition included Frank Sinatra, Connie Haines, Helen O'Connell, the Modernaires, Rudy Vallee, Bing Crosby, Judy Garland, Frances Langford, Billie Holiday, Doris Day, Dinah Shore, Helen Humes, Dinah Washington, and Pearl Bailey. The economy began to swing up from the depths of the depression, and people bought radios, record players (or Victrolas, as the RCA product was called), and records. People had been dancing their way through the dark years, and ballrooms were everywhere.

The year 1940 brought several wonderful examples of a solid, well-organized band working in tandem with a seasoned vocalist. A five-year veteran of professional show business, Ella was growing in her art, reflected in her vocal stylings and choices of music. Certainly Decca controlled what was recorded, but Ella just as certainly had some input as well. This year also brought a considerable shake-up in the old Webb organization, with Bobby Stark, Tommy Fulford, Sandy Williams, Nat Story, and Wayman Carver leaving before the year was even two weeks old. Handling much of these details was, of course, manager Moe Gale.

Her first session of the year, on January 26, produced three excellent swing ballads, "Is There Somebody Else?," "Sugar Blues," and "The Starlit Hour." "Sugar Blues" featured a very fluid vocal line that demonstrated how her breath control was improving; she was learning not only how to breathe but *where.* In "Starlit Hour," her famous vibrato became much more evident. Previously, her voice had just trailed off at the end of an extended note; now that note was sustained until she was through with it. Another Fitzgerald trademark, the vocal "yodel" at the beginning of a word, made itself clearly heard here for the first time.

She followed those songs with a February session that included "Sing Song Swing" and "Baby Won't You Please Come Home." By today's standards, the former seems extremely dated and racist (dealing with Asians), and the latter got the attention from Ella it deserved in the early 1960s (see The Verve Years). "Baby" was once again a turn toward more mature material, with a lovely sax solo at the break by Eddie Barefield. "If It Weren't for You" was a typical song for the band at the time; the orchestration was topnotch and the band was playing more as a unit than they had since Chick's passing. It's too bad that "Imagination" had to be taken at that same old fox-trot tempo—Ella was still being given very little opportunity to sing a flat-out ballad.

An interesting sidelight occurred at this time while the band was on the West Coast playing a date in Los Angeles. Some of the band's sidemen were invited to work at occasional jam sessions for an extra $6. The coordinator of these sessions was a young Norman Granz. "Sure, he used my musicians, but he didn't want me; he just didn't dig me," said Ella. Granz later loomed large in Ella's life, but not for eight more years, and not with Decca.

Continually touring and then playing at the Savoy, the band took time out only for sessions in the recording studio. The sides on March 20 were all instrumentals for the band, so Ella did not sing in the studio again until May 9. Only producing three sides, the session did provide three winners in the quality category. "Deedle-De-Dum" appeared to be yet another novelty song, but it was one with a difference. It was not a *childish* novelty, and as a song was a great finger-snapper. While the lyrics are old-fashioned (how many of you know what a hurdy-gurdy is?), one perceives that Ella was having fun, and even got to rip out a scat coda before she was through. "Shake Down the Stars" was several steps in the direction toward giving Ella a chance to show a more sophisticated sentiment. With orchestra accompanying her (instead of the other way around), there was a specter of Lady Day in Ella's bending of notes and the stealing of time. Perhaps Ella was also harking back to Billie's main influence, Satchmo. "Gulf Coast Blues" was important in the Fitzgerald mythos in that it was her first real stab at the blues form; she took to it like a duck to water. She was obviously very comfortable in the easy tempo of this blues. It was also the first time Ella got a chance to add something new and important to her style—sensuality. Certainly a great part of any adult persona, Ella would add more and more of this quality into her art as time went by.

Ella's personal life was that of many performers who lived on the road: long, hard hours of performing, learning new songs, recording, and traveling, balanced against taking relaxation and pleasure where it could be found. None of the people interviewed for this book wanted to comment on her behavior during this time for the record, but there were several comments made with the promise of anonymity:

"She was getting a lot of attention and she liked it. There would always be guys hanging around after the shows and sometimes she'd go out and have a good time."

"Ella always wanted to be with the guys, to do what they did. Unfortunately, she followed their example in ways that ended up hurting her."

"She was not a wild woman, especially in comparison with some of her contemporaries, but by this time she was certainly no innocent babe in the woods."

The September 25 recording session produced nothing out of the ordinary. "Five O'Clock Whistle" is probably best remembered by fans of animation: it was used as background or mood music in a spate of cartoons produced in the 1940s and '50s. Again the band took on a sound that suggests Glenn Miller, and Ella once again was hampered by the dance tempo. Adult for its day, the tag of the lyric clearly implied an errant husband.

The date in November further exemplifies that dichotomous recording relationship that would last for the rest of her tenure at Decca: some great standards sprinkled in with Tin Pan Alley duds and novelties. "Cabin in the Sky" and "Taking a Chance on Love" had been featured by the extraordinary Ethel Waters on Broadway and in the movies. While Ella fell well short of the pathos and drama of the Waters versions, these were certainly noteworthy efforts.

She attacked both songs in a very straight-forward manner; for the first time the recording was totally hers, not a dance band recording with vocal. *Any* group of musicians could have been supporting her; there was no sense of the old Webb guard being present. "I'm the Lonesomest Gal in Town," her last recording of 1940, had a "down and dirty" feel to it, perhaps more suited to Mae West or Ethel Merman than Miss Fitz. While she may have moved too far into the area of the earthy lyric, it was very healthy for her growth as a performer. One of her last Decca recordings, "Hard Hearted Hanna," is a direct descendent of "Lonesomest Gal."

Nineteen forty-one was the last prolific recording year Ella was to have until after the war, with over twenty tunes waxed in twelve months. In January, she shuttled between "The One I Love Belongs to Somebody Else" and "Three Little Words" and such trifles as "Hello Ma! I Done It Again," "The Muffin Man" and "Keep Cool, Fool." While hindsight might tempt one to dismiss the latter three as throwbacks to her earlier novelties, they were notable for the band's vocal choruses (in which, at one point, they syncopatedly referred to her as "Sis-ter Ella").

Kalmar and Ruby's "Three Little Words," although very famous for its melody, has a lightweight lyric. A saxophone solo by Chauncey Haughton, a piano solo by Roger Ramirez, and Ella's spirited articulation made for a fulfilling recording, including yet another chance for vocal improvisation. "The One I Love" found Lady Time much more comfortable and confident in placing her personal brand on the song.

Among the best songs of 1941 was perhaps the torchiest of all torch tunes, "My Man." Made famous by Fanny Brice in the Ziegfeld Follies of the 1920s and later by Billie Holiday on wax in the 1930s, this was Ella's first (but certainly not last) crack at this song. Although taken at too fast a tempo to be fully effective, the treatment was both sensual and pretty; not as pathos-filled as Brice or as rock-bottom as Holiday, but impressive nonetheless.

Ella was beginning to bring her personal experience to her music, and most certainly she could relate to having loved and lost. Her accompaniment was accomplished by the rhythm section, with the full band rarely in evidence. For the first time, it was evident that Ella needed very little musical support to accomplish her aims; as good as her band was, she no longer needed them to provide her musical bearing.

The midsummer stint in the studio was a true point of demarcation in the Fitzgerald career. All of the recordings put primary emphasis on the vocals; the band was pushed into the background. Even where the band was featured, such as the piano solo on "When My Sugar Walks Down the Street," the solo smacks more of Bill Basie's one-fingered jazzercises than of a piano break with a big band. "Sugar," a Dixieland classic without any trace of Dixie in its arrangement, was the last Fitzgerald recording even to offer the band an instrumental break.

With "I Can't Believe That You're in Love With Me," Ella once again took great liberties with the melody, although the overall feeling was of a song that did not have enough rehearsal time to work out all the bugs (giving it the sound of an unused outtake). Another sensual experiment was "I Must Have That Man," a vocal fairly dripping with longing. While such attempts were not yet totally satisfying, the growth of Ella's style and confidence is a fascinating process to witness. This process paralleled the one in her personal life, as Ella the girl fought for supremacy with Ella the woman.

All of the elements she had been working on came together in the last two great songs she recorded with the band. "I Got It Bad and That Ain't Good" was a perfect example of a new, richer, and more mature ballad sound. It was also the beginning of Ella's recording love affair with the music of Duke Ellington, one that was fanned in the 1940s and exploded in the 1950s. Here at last was a proper tempo to display her wares. The singer was full-voiced, with her vibrato very much in evidence. It was Ella's best ballad up to that time. The lyric, "we gin some/pray some/and sin some" was an alternative bridge to the song, an unusual twist of words that Ella did not use in her later recordings of this number. "Can't Help Loving Dat Man" was the first example of the sound that would be familiar throughout the rest of her Decca career.

When several of the songs from this time were rereleased by Decca in 1947, the liner notes stated: "This Decca album contains many of Ella's most popular numbers. Among them are the haunting 'Cabin in the Sky' and 'Can't Help Loving Dat Man.' All these selections give the listener Ella Fitzgerald in her own inimitable style, a style which has been copied often but never equaled."

Unfortunately, Ella had very little chance to hone her recording craft with her band. Between the obvious storm clouds of a pending draft and the upcoming Petrillo ban on recordings, by July 1941 Ella and the band were kaput. But this, of course, served to set the stage for the next phase of her career, striking out on her own as a soloist.

Chapter Five

1941–1945

$\mathscr{M}$oe Gale decided that Ella still needed the structure of a group around her, and put Ella together with a vocal-instrumental group called the "Three Keys," comprised of the Furness Brothers who sang and played piano, bass, and guitar. The orchestra continued under the leadership of Eddie Barefield, a clarinetist from Des Moines, Iowa, who (like Ella) was under Moe Gale's wing. Although it was also announced at this time that Ella would have her own radio program on NBC, the show never materialized.

Ella's recording life with the "Keys" lasted from their first session (on October 6, 1941) until August of 1942, when the musicians' union started a strike that forced a ban on recordings. The Keys were later drafted, anyway. Strangely enough, her output during this period was free of the novelty tunes, concentrating on ballads (such as the outstanding "Jim" and "You Don't Know What Love Is"), including one chart topper, "All I Need Is You" (not to be confused, of course, with the Sonny and Cher hit several decades later).

Their recording schedule was not nearly as bounteous as had been with the Webb organization; between their initial recording marriage and subsequent parting, only thirteen sides were put to wax. Much of this was due, of course, to wartime shortages. Again, as with the latter days with her own band, it became obvious that Ella no longer needed any particular group of musicians to perform; any musicians would have done as long as they were good and so was the material. While the Keys gave her a transition from big band singer to chanteuse, they were simply not in her league. Certainly her songs still sold, for by this point she was a household name with the youth of America. Alas, the chemistry was simply no longer there.

While singing with the Keys brought to her a new dimension, it was not a boon to her career. Previously, the band played the larger ballrooms and nightclubs that could accommodate both the band and the dancers who came to see them. With the small group, and without any recent hits, she was singing in small clubs that carried less prestige.

In many ways, this time in Ella's career paralleled the lull that existed in Sinatra's career in the early 1950s. She was not recording much, and her popularity slipped in the polls. Wartime restrictions made gas scarce. Both the performers and the audience had trouble showing up. It was more difficult for Moe Gale to get her bookings and some thought her career was hitting a slide from which it would never recover. It seems unbelievable with the wonder of hindsight that the great Ella Fitzgerald could ever have had problems getting work.

"This was a low point for her," recalls a friend from those days, "she really didn't know how to take it. She started off being a winner right from the start. She just got more and more famous, although she still wasn't making any decent bread. Chick and [later] Moe tried to insulate her from the realities of show *business*, and when faced with them, Ella didn't like it one bit." To her credit, she never let up, just continued to learn and grow. Very soon, she would get to face a new challenge.

Hollywood beckoned, and Ella reported to Universal in the San Fernando Valley for her first big screen moments in an Abbott and Costello film, *Ride 'Em Cowboy*. Although released in 1942, the movie featured her (playing a maid in those unenlightened times) singing "A-Tisket A-Tasket" on a bus, with Bud and Lou hanging onto the back of the bus to join in on the "fills." The song pretty much followed the original arrangement, although the musical bridge was shortened. On the third time Ella sings ". . . no, no, no, no . . ." at the end, she performed a spasm of "no," with arms flailing and voice scatting "no" over many different notes. While the effect seemed odd in the film, it was perfect vocally for the song. She sang it that way ever since.

Not content just to have her warble on the bus, Universal gave her more to do later on in the film with the Merry Macs. "Rock 'n' Reelin' " was a rhythm song that came later on in the program, but it did not do much to add to her stature as a movie performer. The script had her appearing almost mentally deficient, with no place in the actual plot. Ella never appeared in the "soundies" of the 1930s and '40s, and she wouldn't appear on the big screen again until *Pete Kelly's Blues* in 1955.

With no backup group of her own, Ella began to tour as a special guest artist with other bands. In fact, her appearances began to greatly resemble those she would make for the rest of her life: the band opened the show with their set, there was an intermission, and a second set featured Ella doing songs from her repertoire. She then joined the members of the band for an impromptu jam session. It was during these performances that she truly began to hone her scat singing to an art form, and several of her scat hits were birthed out of these evenings.

The first band she toured with was that of Duke Ellington. While she did not record with them at this time, and in fact did not sing much out of the Ellington bag, it was once again a great growth process for her. She was surrounded by some of the finest musicians extant, her songs were being arranged in the Ellington style, and the great Edward K. Ellington was taking her under his wing musically.

After her last recording date in July 1942, Ella would not return to the recording studio again until the fall of 1943. Decca was the first label who came to terms with the musicians' union and began recording again, although at a much slower pace due to the war. By this time, pianist and arranger Bill Doggett had become her musical director.

On November 3, she recorded "Cow Cow Boogie," another big hit. Produced for Decca by Dave Kapp, this semi-boogie, semi-novelty, semi-offensive number has shown up in the soundtracks of several films, ostensibly to give the film the proper verisimilitude. "Boogie" was, in fact, yet another Decca novelty number, although there was no attempt to even try to make her sound young. It was recorded with the able assist of the Ink Spots, and her voice had gone through one of the first of its remarkable changes. She had developed a distinctive vibrato, and the female voice was definitely that of a grown woman.

At this time we must stray from Ella's story to other events within the jazz world that would affect her for the rest of her life. Norman Granz, the jazz promoter from Los Angeles who had paid Ella's sidemen $6 a piece for jam sessions several years earlier, had been arranging jazz concerts in the L.A. area since 1940. Born in Los Angeles on August 6, 1918 (sharing a Leo birthday with Lucille Ball, for astrology fans), Granz became a film editor at MGM while promoting his jam sessions. On July 2, 1944, he presented an all-star jam session at Philharmonic Hall. Appearing that fateful night were many legends, including Nat Cole and his trio, Illinois Jacquet, Joe Sullivan, Les Paul, J. J. Johnson, and others. The Armed Forces Radio Network carried the concert, the first such concert relayed to our fighting troops. The evening of jazz at the Philharmonic by the erstwhile "Sol Hurok of Jazz" quickly became known as Norman Granz's Jazz At The Philharmonic (JATP), touring yearly around the United States and, after 1952, all around the world. Almost all of these concerts would be recorded by Granz, issuing them on his Clef and Norgran labels in the 1940s and early '50s.

The year 1944 also saw the beginning of what would be a recurring theme in Ella's work—the use of her recordings in feature films, even though she herself would not appear. The first such vehicle was MGM's *Two Girls and a Sailor*, which featured Ella's vocalizing of "A-Tisket A-Tasket." In 1946, four years since its appearance in the Abbott and Costello romp, once again Ella's version of "A-Tisket A-Tasket" was released as part of the music for a film—*Il Bandito*, made in Italy. The movie, never shown in America, was the story of a returned ex-soldier from a camp in Russia after World War II.

Ella's recording work throughout this time had shown a woman still searching for an identity. Her personal life followed a similar pattern. There was little time for her family, who were increasingly turning toward dysfunction as she became (in their eyes) more a meal ticket than a relative. "It's a shame how they treat her," said one close companion confidentially. "They don't know she exists until they need a new car, or new furniture or money for schooling. Many times they've tried to squeeze her right before she went out on stage." Companionship came and went, but her schedule left little time for anything deeper than an evening's entertainment. With little satisfaction from either her relatives or companions, more and more Ella *was* her career.

Her popularity in the polls had slipped, from fourth in 1942 down to thirteenth in 1944. Her first recordings of the new year on March 21, 1944 (in fact, her first recording since "Cow Cow Boogie"), "Once Too Often" and "Time Alone Will Tell," did not set the world on fire. The war years did not treat her well. However, starting with "I'm Making Believe" on August 30, the second phase of Ella's recording legend began.

"Into Each Life Some Rain Must Fall," written by Allan Roberts and Doris Fisher and done in conjunction again with the Ink Spots, remains to this day a classic swing number, with the Spots and Ella easily trading time. She wasn't recording often, but she was scoring a hit almost every time at bat. Again on November 6, four sides were cut, one of which would remain in Ella's repertoire from then on. "I'm Beginning to See the Light" was rerecorded twice more during the Verve years, but here was the original, taken at an easier tempo than her later renditions.

It was during this period that Ella began to pay her dues in the clubs, working her way up from boîtes to smaller prestige clubs. She also embarked on tours with the bands of Count Basie and Dizzy Gillespie. The tours reinforced her jazz roots and reintroduced her to the growing world of bebop. As early as 1941, Dizzy Gillespie had been featured in her band, so she was no stranger to this kind of music. Her keen ear quickly grasped the new concepts, which held her in good stead with both bands. "Basie, he would just play the piano until he got the tempo real groovy," Ella reminisced, "then he'd just raise that finger and everybody would jump in. No one could get tempos like Basie." With Ellington, she had faced a different challenge. "That great Duke of Ellington, he'd have the band playing and he'd just point to me and I'd have to come in with them. I never knew where in the arrangement he was going to ask me to sing. He really kept me on my toes!"

Now she was a solo recording artist for Decca, but her studio output in 1944 and 1945 was meager at best. Certainly, she had winners but her recordings had almost nothing to do with what she was doing in the live arena. For the most part, this is how she spent the rest of her tenure at Decca: recording Tin Pan Alley pop during the day (with the exception of her scat solos) and being a jazz singer at night.

Chapter Six

1945–1946

There has been much written about vocalizing. Singing is an art. Singing is a skill. Anyone can be taught to sing. No one can be taught to sing. One must always take voice lessons. One should never take voice lessons. To quote journalist Linda Ellerbee, "And so it goes. . . ." One of the reasons Ella Fitzgerald is such a fascinating subject to write about is because, almost literally, year by year her vocal growth was obvious and measurable.

Her early years showed a voice with potential but little style or substance. Gradually, by constant exposure to a live audience and the critical ear of the microphone, Ella chose what was best for her vocally. The maturation of her talent was often a growth by making wise choices. She discarded what did not work and embraced what did.

In 1945 Ella turned a major corner musically speaking. While her career still faced many obstacles over the following ten years, the choices she made bore very lucrative fruit. The recording gem from this period (March 27, 1945) was "It's Only a Paper Moon," this time backed by the Delta Rhythm Boys. Besides their rich, clear harmonies, Ella's scat singing was featured, this talent obviously having progressed quite a bit since "(If You Can't Sing It) You'll Have to Swing It."

On October 4, 1945, Ella made recording history with her first totally wordless scat recording. Taking Lionel Hampton's arrangement of "Flying Home" and making it her own, Ella bopped her way through the entire song. She worked the arrangement out while on the road, using it as an encore to her set.

Scat singing has been a popular but little-used device employed by singers since the 1920s as a gimmick or "hook." One of the first recorded uses was by "Pops" Armstrong on his first big seller, "Heebie Jeebies." Bing Crosby, Judy Garland, and others had scatted for Decca in the 1930s, but theirs was either just tossed away or totally orchestrated by the arranger. What was fascinating about Ella's scatting is that it wasn't just mindless noisemaking like many of the early scat singers. Rather, she was following the arrangement, playing the various parts of the band and *improvising* with them at her leisure (and our pleasure). Needless to say, "Flying Home" was a monster hit. Thirty-two years later, Ella stopped the show at the Montreux Jazz Festival with an eight-plus-minute version of the same song.

Decca looked upon the song as just another novelty. They honestly didn't know what they had. "She was definitely the sweetheart of Decca," remembered Milt Gabler, who had entered her recording life as a producer with "Paper Moon." Having joined Decca in November 1941 just before the war started, he was already a well-known producer and jazz authority. A family-owned business turned into the Commodore Record Shop, a place Gabler established as a clearinghouse for jazz music, gossip, and records. He eventually began to record his own records to satisfy his eager customers, and the Commodore record label was born. Before coming to Decca, he had already recorded Lady Day. With a promise to make all of his hits for Decca, Gabler continued to produce for both labels for nine years. His nephew is comedian, writer, actor, and director Billy Crystal.

By the time Gabler began working with Ella, he understood her problems in being creatively fulfilled. "They kept her on a juvenile diet," he remembered. "After all, the youngsters buy the platters and learn every word of the songs on them. They still do. When you have a hit you have to make a follow-up. Most of the time the follow-up is not as big as the original smash, but it is still a profitable venture. The truth is, I hated to do this. I wanted to blaze new trails." It took Gabler to understand how to use Miss Fitz to her better advantage, and even then there would be the pop devil to pay to get what he wanted for her.

An even bigger hit (at the time) emerged with Ella's first attempt at calypso, "Stone Cold Dead in De Market." While this song smacks of the same kind of novelty Ella had been singing for almost a decade, her ear for the Caribbean accent and the fact that the lyrics told the first-person story of a wife killing her husband caught the taste of the nation. Strangely, Ella and Louis Jordan had stayed up all night working out an arrangement for this number; Decca nixed the arrangement and the number was done with little effort. A similar story would be told of the duo's work on "Baby, It's Cold Outside." Either way, her star was on the ascendancy again.

Like others in the profession, Ella cut "V-Discs," records intended especially for the fighting boys of the latest great war. Three of them were recorded on October 12, 1945 (even though the war was over by this time, many of our boys were still overseas), the most enduring being "I'll See You in My Dreams." Interestingly, though she recorded this song any number of times in her career, the song has mostly been pulled from release. As late as the 1980s, Ella was closing her concerts with it.

The new year, 1946, got off to a rousing start with the first studio pairing of two voices that would forever seem to have belonged together: Ella Fitzgerald and Louis Armstrong. Armstrong, arguably the greatest male jazz singer in history, had by then already reached a popularity unmatched by any other performer of color. While he was sometimes criticized in the black press for his seeming "Uncle Tom" demeanor, he had broken barriers in the recording, motion picture, and personal appearance arenas that opened doors for generations of others.

While neither "You Won't Be Satisfied" nor "The Frim Fram Sauce" were exactly showstoppers, both would be included in Ella's live concert appearances over the next ten years. The former was an easy-swing ballad, while the latter was a novelty number utilizing some of the African "jive talk" that had become popular during the swing era. (For the *classic* Ella-Louis duets, see The Verve Years.)

There were two more recordings during 1946 that tickled the public's fancy: Duke Ellington's "I'm Just a Lucky So-and-So," and the sweet ballad "(I Love You) For Sentimental Reasons." "So-and-So" was another of Ella's excursions into Ellingtonia, again with extremely satisfying results. And certainly, Ella's charm with a ballad at this point in her career had more to do with the use of her voice as opposed to her solid interpretation of the lyrics. That deep understanding of the words in a song did not come for another decade.

Though 1946 yielded only eight sides waxed, two band tours, and a chance for Ella to sing with Satchmo, the following year would bring big hits and a big romance.

Chapter Seven

1947–1948

*E*lla began 1947 with three new ballads added to her repertoire, which were to endure ("Sentimental Journey," "A Sunday Kind of Love," and "That's My Desire"), as well as an appearance on a local New York radio show, "The Saturday Night Swing Show," on April 5. However, the breakthrough recording from this late winter season (recorded March 19) was George and Ira Gershwin's "Oh, Lady Be Good."

"Lady" had been making the rounds of most of the big bands and many of the new bebop combos as a swing number, taken at double time. Ella had been doing the number while touring with the Dizzy Gillespie band, and sang it on Dave Garroway's radio show out of Chicago. "Dave Garroway, bless his heart, liked the song and encouraged us to record it," remembers Ella. "He began to play the song over and over until everyone was picking up on it." Relying mostly on a rhythm section to keep time (and a big band to occasionally accent the arrangement), "Lady Be Good" put Ella over the top of bebop.

Starting with a fast chorus of the actual lyrics to the song (well, close enough), Ella followed with two choruses of scat singing before ending the number with the closing lyrics. This was one of the biggest hits of Ella's entire career, yet it is one of the least rerecorded songs from her repertoire.

Ella was once again climbing the popularity polls, back up to fourth place in the *Metronome* listings by mid–1947. A special concert at Michigan University had Ella doing her usual concert of bop, swing, jazz, ballads, and nursery rhymes, with the student body voting for or against bebop as presented by Ella. While this type of appearance was probably part publicity, it is indicative of the regard young people had for Ella, and continue to have to this day, as an arbiter of good music and good taste.

Around this time, there started a public controversy as to why Ella was not given her own radio program, or at least a featured spot on a regular, major show. Crosby, Sinatra, Day, Clooney, Haymes, Boswell, Stafford, Whiting, Shore . . . all of them had been featured on their own shows or those of others when they had reached the popularity Ella had achieved. Yet, all signs pointed to Ella's ethnicity as being a stumbling block to a regular radio gig. African Americans did not host mainstream radio shows (remember, "Amos 'n' Andy" were white men portraying black stereotypes) for fear of sponsor reprisals. Although by this point Ella was earning over $2,000 a week for her live appearances (she was earning over $200,000 a year by the decade's end), Ella never did get her own show on radio or television.

There was an additional problem with Ella's image at this point. While she was an African American, many claimed she *sounded* European, and complaints of her being a female "Uncle Tom" (an Aunt Jemima?) were being heard from the African community. Also, she began playing many more venues that catered to "downtown" audiences as opposed to "uptown." It took years of working with Norman Granz to mixed audiences, and the addition of the soul idiom to her music in the 1960s, before these complaints would be put to rest.

Ella embarked on a tour of Europe in July 1947, her last American stop being Chicago's Ragdoll Club. Flying to London, the wire services picked up a local paper's account on her private life. The copy went as follows:

ELLA SILENT

LONDON—Secrecy was surrounding the name of the man who is bringing the big smiles to singer Ella Fitzgerald and whose engagement ring she is wearing these days.

Miss Fitzgerald wouldn't discuss anything about it, except to say, "All I am saying is that he is an American and not a musician. He has asked me to marry him and I have accepted."

Nowhere was it ever written who that man was, or even if he ever existed. It was not unusual for such puffery to appear, and in fact was often placed by press agents for celebrities to keep their names before the public. This helped to sell records and tickets. It still does.

Ella's next tour was with the Dizzy Gillespie band, a tour that not only reunited her with Diz but brought her face to face with Bird and introduced yet another of her hits, perhaps her greatest. It was during this tour that Ella began to swing the jazz classic "How High the Moon," albeit with much more of an easy swing than her later whacks at it. Thankfully, there remains a recording of this tour, an evening that also includes the great Charlie Parker.

On September 29, 1947, the Gillespie band featured Ella and Bird as special guests at Carnegie Hall. This was her debut, and she must have done well. She appeared there consecutively for forty-four years without one season missed. That first time, Ella did six tunes with the band, three with the entire ensemble, and three with the rhythm section and Dizzy.

"Almost Like Being in Love" was an early attempt at Ella swinging Broadway, and all of the elements that made her forthcoming Songbook series so successful were present: a top-flight arrangement, clear singing of the lyrics with a slight burlesquing of the tune, and her trademark vocal manipulations solidly in evidence. This she followed with "Stairway to the Stars," reaching all the way back to 1939 for one of her favorite ballads. Naturally, her rendition here is much more mature than the original, her voice showing a new richness and fullness. In fact, this early live recording shows a truism of Ella's talent evident even in 1947: a live audience contributed greatly to Ella's creative powers. Her energy level, even the beauty of her voice, was greatly increased by putting her in front of the audience she adored.

The other ballad that evening was "Lover Man," perhaps her most haunting rendition of this beautiful song. Dizzy joined in for a beautiful solo (with Ella's "play pretty for the people" encouragement to Dizzy). Also evident here is another of the "Ella-ments" that make her so unique: the use of the vocal coda at the end of a ballad. While quite often her Decca recordings did not include such codas, her live performances consistently featured them.

Ella followed this with her two recent scat hits, "Flying Home" and "Oh, Lady Be Good." The audience reaction to these tunes was phenomenal, with wild cheering between the numbers. Then Diz joined Ella for "How High the Moon," trading fours with her after the initial lyrics and scat chorus. Ella's "... we're singing this / because you asked for it / so we're swinging this / just for you ..." was already a part of the song. Ella began to do this number because bebop fans would yell requests at her to scat the number while she was on stage. Always a whip with a lyric quip, this is how Ella presented the song to her fans.

Ella's popularity was soaring not only with her fans but with the critics. With her placing fourth in *Metronome*'s poll for 1947, an article from November of that year in that magazine discussed her popularity:

> The Ella Fitzgerald cycle seems to be on the way back to the top. A recent record of "Lady Be Good," which is one of the good things that has happened to The Queen, represents her awareness of the Gillespie school of jazz (which will be still further exploited through "How High the Moon") and her intelligent musical progress. "Lady Be Good" may become another and more representative "A-Tisket A-Tasket" for Ella Fitzgerald. Believe me—and all the country's smart singers—it couldn't have happened to a more gifted person.
>
> P.S. The greatest pop singer of them all still ain't on the radio.

That last comment was all too true, and the article bravely put it on the line:

> Ella kills everybody–musicians, other singers, fans, hard-boiled recording men–but somehow or other she has been unable to get on the radio with a regular program of her own. ... Ella Fitzgerald, the greatest pop singer of them all by years of almost unanimous acclaim, cannot be heard on the great American wave lengths, while such obvious vocal foul balls as Milena Miller, Dorothy Lamour, Dorothy Shay, etc., etc. are to be heard all over this great free air. Need we draw any neon arrows to

lead you to the large and disgraceful spectre of Jim Crowism behind American radio? It's so and I throw this charge at every advertiser and network, along with the back of my hand. If you want one small example of the malodorous color line in radio today I will simply cite the answer I was given by one advertising bigwig when I suggested Ella for an opening on a big network show: "She wouldn't look so good for pictures." Television isn't that close, bud.

With the success Ella achieved later in her life, it is perhaps difficult to go back and ponder what might have been had she been white, or if the entertainment industry and its sponsors had been less race conscious. Ella, were she white, was still quite heavy-set and not terribly photogenic. However, Kate Smith, a stout lady with the voice of an angel, was the biggest female musical star on radio.

Around this time, a good-looking musician caught Ella's eye and remained a large part of her public life long after he left her personal one. Ray Brown was a gifted and handsome bassist from Philadelphia who was already a part of the Norman Granz group, playing their jazz gigs out in Los Angeles. He had sharpened his musical chops with the Gillespie band, where he met Ella. The two became an item, and in very short order fell in love. They complemented one another, both personally and musically.

On December 10, 1947, Ella married Ray Brown. The couple took up residence on Ditmars Boulevard in the East Elmhurst section of Queens, New York.

Ray knew music, and the two spoke the same language when it came to the presentation of Ella Fitzgerald. She had gotten used to being taken care of professionally, first by Webb, then by Gale, and then by Gabler, who had taken over producing her records. Brown did, for a while, fill a similar role, leaving her free to grow musically while her man would fight her battles. He continued to fight musical battles for her for over five decades, the de facto producer on her last Grammy-winning album in 1989.

Decca did not beckon Ella into the studio again until December 1947, as she was still on tour. But over three dates in mid-December, Ella finally recorded "How High the Moon" in the studio, as well as three more songs that would endure for the rest of her career. "That

Old Feeling" and "You Turned the Tables on Me" were two more of the easy-swing numbers that became staples of her later Decca years. While several other forgettable grade-B pop tunes were waxed at the time, few remember "No Sense," a novelty tune that followed Ella from label to label.

Fred Robbins was a DJ very important to the young hep-cats in New York. His daily show was heard by millions, not only in the New York area but wherever the radio waves could be heard. As a sop to this powerful broadcaster, Ella recorded "Robbins' Nest" (the name of his show). In later years, as the show became a faded memory, Ella rerecorded the song with different lyrics (see The Independent Years and The Pablo Years). Also recorded at this time, but unreleased, was "I Cried and Cried and Cried."

The year 1948 was a watershed year for Ella. Though she made very few recordings, two of them became huge hits. More important, Ella, now married to Ray, once again crossed paths with the man who at one point wanted no part of her, the inscrutable Norman Granz.

Chapter Eight

1948–1949

$\mathcal{O}$ne night, Ella went to see Ray at a Jazz At The Philharmonic performance, as she often did during their courtship. This time she was spotted in the audience of the concert hall. Her fans shouted for her to join the festivities, and Granz was forced to begrudgingly allow her on stage for one number. Ella traded fours on "How High the Moon" with almost everyone on stage, and the audience was blown away. So, finally, was Granz. Within a year, she was an integral part of Granz's shows; soon after that she was the main attraction.

Another pair of recording sessions on April 29 and 30 yielded solid gold with a tune Ella initially did not want to have anything to do with. "She was temperamental about what she sang," said Tim Gale, brother of Ella's manager in the 1940s and who served as her booking agent for many years. "However, she would sing *anything* if her advisors were insistent. One of her records was a thing called 'My Happiness.' She cut it under protest; I brought the dub backstage to her at the Paramount, and she said 'It's a shame. A corny performance of a corny song.' It turned out to be one of her biggest sellers."

Here's how Milt Gabler remembered it:

"Jon and Sandra Steele had a big success with a song called 'My Happiness' in 1948, during the second musicians' recording ban. Decca needed a 'cover' record. I figured that Ella could get a good piece of the business. What to do? I could not use musicians. I persuaded Ella to try it with a group called the Song Spinners, who could hum with the best of them. The beauty in the Steele waxing was in two-part harmony, so the Spinners were to hum in unison away from Ella, to make a similar sound only bigger. It worked fine, and the record became a hit. It didn't swing, but it had a commercial sound."

He continued:

"Shortly after that, Ella was working in London and at the end of each show asked the audience to request favorite numbers that had not been included. The most requested title was 'My Happiness,' and Ella didn't even have it in her act. Decca had shipped the master to their British affiliate, Brunswick, and it was issued in time for her appearance. Ella had forgotten all about recording it. She had to get the disc from our people in London and learn the song again. After that, she used it regularly as an encore."

The song is very straightforward and would most likely have not been a choice of Norman Granz. However, it struck a chord in postwar America, and became her largest seller for Decca at that time.

Always a pioneer, Ella made television history as one of Ed Sullivan's first guests on his new "Toast of the Town" show on CBS. Although she appeared only one month after the show's debut (July 18, 1948), her stint has been lost to time, and no one remembers what she sang. She was such a hit, however, that Ed asked her back only nine years later. So much for being a pioneer. But Ella was too busy to be concerned. She was a new bride, and personal happiness seemed within her grasp at last.

While the rest of her recording year consisted of more pap ("To Make a Mistake Is Human," "In My Dreams"), "It's Too Soon to Know" (recorded August 20, 1948) was one of the few pop songs she was given that really fit her style. Backed by a small group and chorus, Ella caressed the song with a tenderness and maturity that had been lacking in much of her studio work.

After Ella and Ray's romance culminated in marriage, more and more her live performances were backed by Ray's trio, when she was not backed by Granz's JATP groups or All-Stars. Ella was now a solid member of the JATP tours, and in fact became the star of these jam sessions within short order. Naturally, her career was not confined to the JATP tours, as Ella liked to work as often as possible.

While she now commanded gigs such as the Paramount Theater in New York, she still was working small clubs all over the country and of course on the famed Fifty-second Street in Manhattan. In the late 1940s, it was possible to walk down Fifty-second Street on a warm night and hear Ella, Billie, Dizzy, Bird, and Prez bopping through the open doors of various clubs. Norman steered Ella away from playing the joints, assuring her bookings into classier clubs while insuring that her style not change to suit the plusher (and flusher) audiences. It wasn't that Norman was hired and the Gale Brothers fired; Granz just slowly took over until he was her de facto manager. Surely he had no control over her recordings, a thorn that would stick in his side for the next six years.

It was also during this time that several bootleg recordings were made of her radio work with husband Ray Brown and his group. Today, variously released on two records and three CDs, these performances not only give examples of the wider range of what Ella was singing but provided the listener a chance to hear Ella in the nightclub settings of that time.

Most of these songs had been recorded from radio remotes at New York's Royal Roost Club in the late fall of 1948. Ella had spent the summer appearing at the Three Deuces Club on Fifty-second Street, before she toured and returned to New York in November. Ray's trio at that time was comprised of Hank Jones on piano, Charlie Smith on drums, and (naturally) Ray on bass. Additionally, Kai Winding on trombone and Allen Eager on tenor sax often rounded out the trio into a quintet.

On both November 27 and December 4, remotes from the Roost included such numbers as "Love That Boy," "It's Too Soon to Know," "Heat Wave," "Flying Home," "Old Mother Hubbard," "Mr. Paganini," and "Ool-Ya-Koo" (a Dizzy Gillespie tune alternately referred to as "Royal Roost Bop Boogie"). All of these numbers were done with the trio in support. Ella was not in great voice, and in fact seemed to avoid high notes whenever she could. Such were the exigencies of live performances. She was a human being, and sometimes the equipment didn't work. This has happened to any singer performing frequently in public.

Quite often, jazz musicians just showed up in clubs, unannounced, to jam. Among jazz players, perhaps more than any other kind of music, the joy was in the playing, wherever and whenever they could. If Ray Brown was playing at the Roost, then it was not uncommon for Lester Young to show up, and bring with him pals like Jesse Drakes, Ted Kelly, Fred Jefferson, and Roy Haynes. Such a combination of talent occurred during the November remote, when everyone took a slice of "How High the Moon." All the players took turns soloing through the number, with Ray trying to explain to the listening audience who was playing what. Ella brought up the rear, scatting to the end. It was not the famous scat of her recording, mostly because the song was not in her key. Staying to the lower part of her voice, she nonetheless held her own.

Three months later, similar radio remotes took place three weeks in a row on April 15, 23, and 30, 1949. Ella was in much better voice, and also a great deal more confident in her sound. Songs that were repeated from her earlier repertoire sounded more tuneful and were less forced in their swinging. New tunes, such as "There's a Small Hotel," "Someone Like You," "Again," "Robbins' Nest," "In a Mellowtone," and "Lemon Drop" also gave further evidence to the growth in Ella's artistry in just a few months. From this point on, the clear, confident sound of Ella Fitzgerald was evident, the one that stayed in evidence until the late 1960s.

To satisfy her "bop" fans, Ella had to include her hits of "How High the Moon," "Flying Home," and "Mr. Paganini," all of which were fairly honest to their original recordings. A bit of temperament can be heard, as Ella was given the wrong chord during "Paganini," stopped, asked for it again, and hissed "thank you" before continuing.

"Old Mother Hubbard" was one more attempt at swinging a nursery rhyme; in fact its style was very similar to "Tisket." Even the tag at the end of the song, "Mother Huzzard / Bring me some Buzzard," was reminiscent of Ella's "truckin' on down the avenue" from eleven years before.

Norman Granz had been recording all of his JATP tours since 1944, but always had to cut out Ella's part due to her contract with Decca. Deciding that her contract only covered her studio work, Norman decided he would release her live work on his Clef label. As it turned out, Decca was not amused, and the albums were never released. It's too bad, because they included four concerts at Carnegie Hall, two from 1949 and two from 1953. Bits of these ended up on a Verve reissue in the early 1980s, called *The Ella Fitzgerald Set*, and others on her seventy-fifth birthday retrospective CD set released by Verve in 1993.

From February 11, 1949, her set included "Robbins' Nest," "I Got a Guy," "Old Mother Hubbard," "Flying Home," "Lover Man," and "Royal Roost Bop Boogie" (or "Ool-Ya-Koo"). On September 18 of the same year, Ella's trio at Carnegie was Hank Jones, Ray Brown, and Buddy Rich. Her bag that night was "Robbins' Nest," "Black Coffee," "I'm Just a Lucky So-and-So," "Somebody Loves Me," "Basin Street Blues" (the audience went wild at her Armstrong impression), "Old Mother Hubbard," "A New Shade of Blue," "Lady Be Good," and "A-Tisket A-Tasket."

It must have been disheartening to someone of Miss Fitzgerald's enormous talents to be in her position professionally. Her records sold, but it had been ten years since her heyday with Chick Webb. She was a good draw in nightclubs catering to African Americans, and she also played some of the better mainstream clubs in large cities. She did not, however, play the best clubs.

Life was lived out of a suitcase, eating well but not always in places of her choosing. Marriage under these circumstances was difficult at best. While they would be together for JATP tours and club gigs, work often forced long separations. Ray and Ella decided to adopt a son to bring some family cohesion. They named him Ray, Jr.

There is some confusion over Ray's natural parentage. At the time of his appearance in the Browns's life, it was simply announced that they had adopted a baby. However, more recent reports place Ray as the illegitimate son of Ella's sister Frances. While this sounds plausible, it is also confusing, as Ella was fairly close to her sister. This means that there was contact between the natural mother and the child on a consistent basis. If this is true, it could not have been healthy for anyone concerned. At this time, Ella's Aunt Virginia joined the household to take care of Ray, Jr., just as she had briefly cared for Ella before her life on the streets. It has also been said she became the maid as well.

Unfortunately, Ray, Jr., spent as much of his time with other relatives and/or a governess as he did with Mom and Dad. This is not to say that Ray was not loved and wanted by the Browns, but Ella and Ray were busy touring the planet, the only way to stay ahead in the jazz world.

Speaking of being disheartened, it could not have done Ella's ego much good to have an embarrassing little calamity spread around in all the papers. On March 18, 1949, Ella was in an elevator in New York on her way to a recording date (although no sides would be waxed that day) when the elevator stalled between floors. Ella, in a desire to get to the date on time, endeavored to escape through the trap door in the top of the cage. Unfortunately, at 220 pounds she didn't quite fit, and got stuck in the hatch. It took three strong men to rescue the First Lady of Song. (There is a published report that this story happened in 1939, not 1949, and was repeated for the purposes of press agentry. However, in 1939 Ella was not yet hefty enough for the story to have happened.) Ten days later, beautifully gowned, she sang to full houses in an engagement at the Blue Note.

On April 23, 1949, Ella did double duty. She appeared at the Royal Roost, and between sets made her next excursion into TV land, appearing as a guest on a show that did not have quite the longevity of Mr. Sullivan's. "Eddie Condon's Floorshow" featured the guitarist on NBC, doing a show that had originated on local New York stations WPIX and WNBT during World War II, making it one of the oldest features on television. Jazz heavy, the show featured such talents as Ella, Louis Armstrong, Woody Herman, Gene Krupa, Patti Page, and Rosemary Clooney. The show finally petered out under the pressure from other, better-produced shows as television began to have some production values. The network run of this show was actually only nine months, with another CBS stab at the show the following summer. Condon was then joined by young writer and comedian Carl Reiner, who chatted with the guests between numbers.

Meanwhile, Ella was about to record with the first of the really great arrangers to work with her. Certainly, Van Alexander was no slouch, but that had been years before and Ella had been more often stuck with staff arrangers at Decca. Now, Ella had her opportunity to work with Gordon Jenkins. Decca put together an album of songs from the Broadway musical *South Pacific*, and Ella was given the task of warbling Bloody Mary's salute to sign language, "Happy Talk," along with Mary Martin's showstopping "I'm Gonna Wash That Man Right Out of My Hair." "Talk" was pleasant and fairly straightforward, but "Wash" was given an easy-swing treatment, and delightfully so.

It is this writer's opinion that her work with Jenkins (there would be enough recorded in the next few years to fill an LP) was some of the best in her long career at Decca, and certainly her best ballad singing. Jenkins provided for Ella what the best arrangers all did: arrangements in the jazz idiom with rich backgrounds and solid musicians to support her, yet enough room to allow for her style to show through. I know much has been written about the lack of meshing of Ella's jazz style and Jenkins's lush strings and chorus work. I heartily disagree. Many of the albums she recorded with Granz for Verve had huge orchestrations (although no chorus), and some of the albums were indeed more pop than jazz.

The songs she recorded with Jenkins were well-chosen ballads taken at tempos that allowed her to sing more freely, much in the style of her live ballads. Her vocalizing at this point was as satisfying stylistically as Sinatra's, someone who would also work with Jenkins in the coming decade.

Two more Jenkins cuts were recorded that day (April 28, 1949), and both are Ella at her jazzy, smoky best. "Lover's Gold" deserved better reception than it got, a story-song that combined poignant lyrics, lush violins, and a first-class vocal reading by Ella. Even better was "Black Coffee," one of the quintessential Ella ballads. With the exception of "Angel Eyes" in 1952, it is the closest Ella ever got to recording for Decca in the studio the sound of her ballads on the concert or nightclub stage. Also recorded on that fateful April day was the aforementioned "Baby, It's Cold Outside," which suffered the same fate as the Fitzgerald/Jordan predecessor "Stone Cold Dead in De Market" in its interference from Decca. Ella and Louis worked it up; Decca flattened it out.

Miss Fitz was the subject of an early *Ebony* magazine article in May 1949. The article was interesting not only for what it said but for what it did not say. *Ebony* was, at that time, the only national magazine aimed at the African-American market. Strangely, there was no mention of the problem with her being unable to land her own radio show. There was no discussion of a black woman's success in a white-dominated industry. Such comments as, "In the spotlighted circle of popular U.S. female singers, names like Peggy Lee, Jo Stafford and Dinah Shore vie hotly for top honors," only served to compare her with white performers. Names like Dinah Washington, Billie Holiday, Sarah Vaughan, and Lena Horne were not even mentioned. It was as if her success only counted when measured against white society. And this from a magazine like *Ebony*. Describing her as "copper colored," "matronly-looking," and "disliking makeup," the magazine certainly did nothing to glamorize Ella.

On September 18, 1949, there was a complete recording made of Ella's portion of the JATP concert at Carnegie Hall for Granz's Clef Records. The late show that night had also been recorded by Granz, and Ella's encores ("Flying Home," "How High the Moon," "Perdido") were finally released in 1992 on a Verve CD Collection *The Complete Charlie Parker on Verve.*

Over the next two days, Ella continued to record with vocal brilliance. Turning "Basin Street Blues" into a tour de force, Ella saluted Satchmo Armstrong in an uncanny impression that not only showed off a fantastic ear but also her sense of humor (when Ella did this song live, the audience would always burst into spontaneous applause, nudging her into growling "thank 'ya, folks" à la Louis; this always brought the house down). This song crept into Ella's life one night in Las Vegas when business was slow and Ella was bored. Kidding around with the band and drummer Lee Young, Ella began to impersonate Satchmo as Lee whispered the lyrics to her from behind. It murdered the four people in the club, and Ella kept it in. Sy Oliver was the arranger for this cut, as the two began a string of recording sessions that lasted until Ella left the label in 1956.

Four more Gordon Jenkins outings, including the romantic "I Hadn't Anyone 'Til You," "Dream a Little Longer," "Foolish Tears," and "A Man Wrote a Song" with the typical Jenkins background singers in close harmony behind Ella, were recorded the next day. These songs, as well as others recorded with Jenkins, made their way onto one of the first twelve-inch LPs of Ella's songs Decca released in the 1950s.

Milt Gabler chose to follow up this burst of brilliance with the deadly dull "I'm Waitin' for the Junkman." When Ella griped that the material she was given was not the stuff to set the world on fire, Milt explained, "Ella, some songs we do for the money. They pay for the swinging ones that we love and want to do. Not all of our choices make it." Gabler spoke to Ella, but it was Granz who listened and kept his eyes open.

Chapter Nine

1949–1951

*I*n his syndicated column, "Recordially Yours," of October 17, 1949, writer Will Davidson discussed Ella's then-recent work:

> They call Ella Fitzgerald the "first lady of song" and altho [sic] there will be many who have other candidates, the competition IS rather limited. No matter what song she sings, Ella is never at a loss for meaning. She has control, tone, beautiful timing and a great ability to project feeling and emotion without resorting to the clichés that are part of the working equipment of too many singers.
>
> In her current DECCA release, "A Man Wrote a Song"— "Foolish Tears," Ella gives one of her best, and simplest, performances. Strings set the background for "A Man" and in this rather unusual environment Ella tells her story with gently beautiful effect. "Foolish Tears" is of the "Jealous Heart" school, since Jenny Lou Carson wrote them, and that should give you an idea of what Ella has to contend with. That she makes "Foolish Tears" effective is a minor triumph. The choral background,

in revival style, doesn't hinder Ella's work. In fact, she stands so high above it that it enhances her stature.

Ella was finally getting some big press, and not all of it was positive. An incredibly shy woman who to the end of her life could not believe how big a star she was, her reticence was often taken by the press as arrogance. Her publicity agent in the 1950s, Virginia Wicks, observed:

"You will never meet a star more completely un-publicity-conscious than Ella. She can come over to the house and we'll exchange small talk and she's just as sweet and charming as can be. Then I'll gingerly try to ease the conversation around to say, a *Life* or *Time* man that wants to see her and her face will fall and she'll stomp her foot and say, 'Gosh darn it, Virginia! I can't do it—I have to go shopping!' And she'll stay crotchety, but finally, very reluctantly, she may say, 'Oh, all right.' " Ella never believed that anything she had to say was worth writing about, she simply wanted her music to speak for her—especially when so much of her past had been fictionalized. It wasn't easy to remember so many lies.

Ella's unfailing ear and sense of rhythm kept her in good stead at this time. On one JATP date, her regular pianist failed to appear by showtime. Ella marched herself out on stage, and with the accompaniment of Ray Brown on bass for pitch and Buddy Rich on drums for rhythm, she did her entire set.

Also at this time, fellow Decca artist Bing Crosby was riding a crest of popularity almost unmatched in show business history. It would be pointless to wax poetic about his career, but his radio show was one of the highest-rated efforts of the late forties and early fifties. Due to Bing's admiration for Ella and not a small amount of prodding by his record label, she was invited to appear on his radio show several times over the following few years.

The first appearance was on November 9, 1949, and had Miss Fitz plugging "My Happiness" as her solo, as well as duets with Der Bingle of "A Dreamer's Holiday" and "Way Back Home," the latter with the aid of the Mills Brothers. Quite often, Crosby would invite other African-American performers on his show the same nights Ella would appear. Rarely was she given much of a chance to talk. While Crosby's affection for Ella was genuine, she was often treated like the much-loved cook who was clumsily introduced to the guests after an exceptional dinner and then sent back into the kitchen.

The following year, 1950, started off with the release of Ella's first album collection released in the new 33⅓ rpm format then becoming popular. *Ella Fitzgerald's Souvenir Album* was not a greatest-hits compilation, but was the first of many albums released by Decca featuring previously released material. This one featured five songs she had recorded in the early forties. The new year also saw more collaborations with Sy Oliver, more sessions with Louis Jordan and Louis Armstrong, and the first of only two albums that were recorded by Decca as albums; that is, all the songs were recorded together and were meant to be released together.

It also saw months and months of touring, both with her husband and without. The signs of discontent were making themselves known even at this stage of the marriage, as the constant separations and Ella's total ignorance of what might be required of a wife made for rough riding. She was not alone in sowing seeds of disharmony; Brown was hard put to end the habits of years of being a touring musician. Additionally, while Ella was tops in the pops department, many say she lacked the maturity to keep a relationship going.

"Ella is like a child, and as long as you keep that in mind you'll get along famously with her," recalled one longtime friend and fellow musician. "If you treat her like a responsible adult and expect her to act like one, she'll pout, yell, or otherwise act out in her behavior. If, instead, you pat her hand and ask what you can do for her, she'll take direction and be the most cooperative person. But she won't take responsibility on her own." That must have been difficult for Brown to deal with, himself a man used to the free and easy life of the jazz musician. To have to deal with a spouse who was, essentially, a child-woman in temperament, and who was more famous, successful, and well paid than he was not easy.

However tentative her homelife, her music just kept prospering. "Doncha Go 'Way Mad" was a solid click for her on February 2, another of those songs she would sing forevermore. After a trip to Chicago to fulfill two weeks of theater appearances with Ray, on March 6, 1950, she cut "I've Got the World on a String" with the able assist of Sy Oliver's arrangement. Hank Jones, a longtime pianist for her and Ray, appeared here on wax in one of his earliest sessions with her. Once again, a gem was followed up with garbage, in this case "Peas and Rice."

Another radio appearance brought Crosby and Fitzgerald together. On May 3, she got to solo on "I Hadn't Anyone 'Til You" with the full Gordon Jenkins arrangement with violins and chorus, as well as a duet with Bing of the Jule Styne song "Stay With the Happy People."

Another Louis Jordan team-up yielded "Ain't Nobody's Business But My Own" on August 15. An obvious rip-off of " 'Tain't Nobody's Business If I Do," the song was cute and bouncy, but not much more. Another Louis, Armstrong, returned to the Fitzgerald music stand to duet "Dream a Little Dream of Me" the same day. A delightful product, this is the best of the Fitzgerald-Armstrong collaborations for Decca.

The magnificent pianist Ellis Larkins (who retired in the late 1980s to his native Baltimore) recorded with Ella her first collection of Gershwin songs, just voice and piano. While this collection does not have the depth or the breadth of her later Songbook Series for Verve, Ella is clearly at home both with the material and the intimate setting. The songs were recorded on September 11 and 12, and comprised her first long-playing record (although these songs were released in 78 rpm versions separately). Many of these were tunes that became part of the Fitzgerald recording mythos: "How Long Has This Been Going On?" and "I've Got a Crush on You" were rerecorded several times each, and appeared in literally hundreds of live appearances.

Perhaps the agony of her recording career at this time can best be illustrated by the fact that when Decca chose her *next* recording date, it was comprised of "Santa Claus Got Stuck in My Chimney" and "Molasses, Molasses." It was caviar (domestic, not imported) one day and Hamburger Helper the next.

Another NBC television appearance, July 23, 1950, on a program called "Summer Nights' Dream," is so obscure that no one even remembers the show, never mind what Ella did.

In 1950 there was a film made of one of Norman's JATP tours. In September, director Gjon Mili gathered Ella, Harry "Sweets" Edison, Charlie Parker, Coleman Hawkins, Flip Phillips, Hank Jones, Ray Brown, and Buddy Rich into his studio to produce a sixteen-minute film of them performing together. Recorded for posterity were such unusual nuggets as "The Boy Next Door," "The Hucklebuck," and "Don't Cry, Joe." For years it was assumed that the film had been lost, but in 1994 it turned up at the Swiss home of Norman Granz.

In November Ella returned once again to Bing Crosby's radio show. Readers not old enough to know better might assume that with the advent of television, radio immediately turned to top-forty DJ shows and sports. This was simply not so, as it took years for television to infiltrate the entire country. Performers such as Jack Benny, Ozzie and Harriet, and Eve Arden (on "Our Miss Brooks"), as well as others continued to broadcast weekly radio shows while appearing on television in completely different shows, some well into 1955 before giving up the "ether." Ella continued to appear on radio as long as it was viable. Crosby's show on November 29 was devoted to her, with Ella soloing on "Can Anyone Explain?" then dueting with Bing on "Silver Bells" (at the time a brand new Christmas song), "Marshmallow World," and then "Basin Street Blues" featuring Red Nichols on trumpet.

After producing an album of excellence with Ellis Larkins, it would be normal to assume that Milt Gabler would continue to produce sessions that would showcase Ella's ever-growing talents. Alas, the first half of 1951 was wasted with recording total drivel. Remembers an associate at that time: "Under Norman's direction, Ella was receiving standing ovations for her concert and club work, was singing some of the truly great popular songs, and then under Gabler's direction she would head for Decca's studios to record crap. Granz was very frustrated. Gabler was very frustrated. She was *very* unhappy." Her unhappiness spilled over to her marriage, which became more and more fragile. She and Ray were very good friends and musical companions, and that's what they remained for the rest of their lives.

CBS presented a salute to Bing Crosby on January 9, 1951, over their radio network that included such talent as Edgar Bergen and Charlie McCarthy, and Mary Martin (still performing on Broadway in *South Pacific* eight times a week) singing "I'm in Love With a Wonderful Guy." Ella's contribution was a second singing of "Can Anyone Explain?" within two months, a so-so ballad with a backup singing group lending no particular charm.

Unfortunately, 1951 did not see her shine in the recording biz. Although Decca released over twenty tunes throughout the year, only two (recorded on June 26) were worth collecting. "Mixed Emotions" was another ballad in the "Black Coffee" vein that managed to capture some of the magic Ella was able to generate onstage. Another in her series of scat hits, "Smooth Sailing," got three live recordings in future years (in fact, she always joked that "the record's still available" between scat choruses). Featuring Bill Doggett on organ and a quartet with Hank Jones on piano, Everett Barksdale on guitar, Ray Brown on bass, and Jimmie Crawford on drums as well as the Ray Charles Singers (that's the "other" Ray Charles, as he's known today), it was an easy-swing number with an infectious beat.

Rather than bore the reader with a listing of the poor material she was saddled with the rest of the year—two songs, for instance, were "Oops!" and "The Hot Canary"—check out the discography in Appendix Four. To be fair to Decca, this was the trend for many of the record companies in the early 1950s. Frank Sinatra left Columbia records because of the pop songs Mitch Miller chose for him. Rosemary Clooney was forced into "Come on A-My House" (as was Ella), a huge seller but a dumb song that even she admitted was awful. For every "Temptation" that Perry Como got from RCA, he had to "Hot Diggity" himself all over the place.

Writer Carter Harman devoted his entire column to Ella in September. Many of the things he wrote were simply reworded homilies that were printed time and time again:

> Band men who play with Ella Fitzgerald have been heard to say they tune up to her voice, so true is it.

> The remarkable thing about Ella is her ability to sing any kind of song and do it with more spirit, with more impact on her listeners and with more purely vocal personality than other performers who specialize in her style.

> As she prances into the spotlight, your impression may be of a large, cheerful child. Her smile is entrancing in her cherubic face; her eyes twinkle with more than a touch of mischief; her body—no longer sylph-like, you will agree—seems light and responds eagerly to the bouncing rhythms.

Harman did, however, add some insight into her performances and personality:

> . . . she might include a new favorite of hers, "Smooth Sailing,"

an arresting item which as yet has no words. Burbling syllables are used instead, and the melodic line grows into arabesques of instrumental precision and agility. Ella is supposed to have said that she "should have been a tenor man." She makes up for the error by singing the kind of music a saxophonist might play, and as easily as he would play it.

Sitting with her and her friends recently, watching her distastefully eat a box of ice cream because it soothed her sore throat, one got the impression that [she did not theorize too much about] other performers. When someone said that one style sounded like another, Miss Fitzgerald overcame her shyness long enough to object: "People are always talking about somebody sounding like somebody else," she complained.

A musician's spirit seems to be almost more important to her than his ability; she once complained mildly about a man who had accompanied her in an orchestra, not because he played badly, which he did not, but because she didn't think he joined in the fun.

Ella appeared again with Bing on November 28, 1951, along with good pal Louis Armstrong. Here her contribution was a modernized but recognizable bastardization of the original arrangement for "Undecided" from 1939. She also joined Bing and Louis for "Memphis Blues." She was in fine fettle, but obviously treated like this week's "girl singer," a frustrating situation for someone who had been a recording artist for sixteen years and was a veteran of Crosby's shows. Her radio appearances with Bing were "safe," that is, she sang her Decca repertoire and did not sing anything more sophisticated (or more connected to her JATP appearances with Norman Granz). She was given little or no chance to show her charm and sense of humor as a guest. She was generally introduced, she sang, and she was off. Rarely did she read lines, as she was not treated as the main guest star but as an extra added attraction. It took her forthcoming movie role, television, and her Verve recordings before she was treated like a star in the media, twenty years after she joined Chick Webb's band.

Chapter Ten

1952–1954

*A*s dry as her recording year was in 1951, that's how rich it was in 1952. Right off the bat, on January 4, Ella hit a double with "Air Mail Special" and "Rough Riding." Two more examples of Ella's skillful use of scat singing—"Special" followed her for years while "Riding" eventually got words for its rerecording on Verve—were backed by the Ray Brown Orchestra, which was really just Bill Doggett on organ, Hank Jones on piano, Ray on bass, Rudy Taylor on drums, and Dick Jacobs on percussion.

"Goody-Goody" got its first attention from Ella on February 25. Its syncopated rhythm was perfect for her swinging, and stayed perfect as she sang it with seemingly dozens of different arrangements over the next forty years. Again, Sy Oliver provided the arrangement.

Ella's video appearances began to pick up in 1952. On March 14, she was on local New York station WNET (now part of the PBS family) for the "New York Cardiac Hospital Telethon," starring Martin and Lewis. Yes, even back then Jerry loved a telethon, this one running from midnight until 4:30 A.M. The proceeds from this telethon were split with the Muscular Dystrophy Fund. Say what you will about Mr. Lewis, but he was a tireless worker for people with these related diseases for a very, very long time. Long before his career needed any boosting.

The stars must have been in exceptional coordination on June 26, for Ella not only rerecorded "You'll Have to Swing It" (can't we call this "Mr. Paganini?—everyone else does) with a modern arrangement (with Taft Jordan from the original Webb band repeating his effort on trumpet) by Sy Oliver, but gave her attention to one of the best "saloon songs" ever written, "Angel Eyes." With a simple arrangement by Oliver, she made enchantment. With all due respect to Mr. Sinatra, no one sang this song like Ella Fitzgerald. Two other songs, "Early Autumn" and "Preview," were recorded on the same day and achieved momentary popularity.

Mention must be made of the paths Norman Granz paved for jazz and racial equality during those years. He brought the best jazz musicians, according to his taste, that could be found and gave them an arena to play together. Granz refused to play to any segregated audiences. Quite often people were stunned to find themselves sitting with folks from other races for the first time in their lives. Granz had a clause in all of his contracts that demanded equality in the selling of tickets and seating. If the clause was broken, Granz was legally entitled to have the contracted fee and refuse to play. More often than not, the JATP troupe won the day.

However, there were times when thousands of dollars in bookings went by the wayside in the promotion of equality. And there were some hairy experiences. Once, while JATP toured in the South, patrons in a Charleston, South Carolina, club were so startled to find themselves integrated in their seating that they forgot to applaud. When they caught their breath, they ran the troupe out of town.

The concert halls and nightclubs were not the only places the JATP-ers had problems. Nor was it only in the South. On a tour of the Midwest, an Ohio hotel manager refused to allow black and white musicians to room together. Granz contacted the local chapter of the NAACP, and the next morning's newspaper headlines got that manager fired.

Fitzgerald and company once tried to board an airline to sit in their first-class, reserved seats. They found that they were bumped, despite their reservations. Granz won a large out of court settlement from the airline. Ella would later comment: "Regardless of where you go, you're going to find people who are like that and you can't stop a person's thinking."

Comedian Jerry Lester had become big news with his pre-"Tonight Show" "Broadway Open House" for NBC, the first such late-night network program. He was rewarded with a summer-replacement show in 1952 for the network's prestige variety offering, "Your Show of Shows." Called "Saturday Night Dance Party" (can you imagine a network executive going into a meeting and actually being paid to suggest such a title?), it had an Ella appearance on June 28, 1952.

Ella did more video charity with an appearance on the "Damon Runyon Memorial Fund," subtitled the "Milton Berle 4th Annual Telethon." It was Berle who coined the term "telethon" back in 1948, and named the first telethon after the perennial and productive Broadway raconteur and writer, whose stories were the basis of such shows and films as *Guys and Dolls*, *The Big Street*, and *Sorrowful Jones*. The 1952 version ran on NBC on June 7 through 8, and Ella made her appearance in the later hours of the show.

August saw Ella back on the tube in another summer-replacement show. NBC's "All Star Revue" had been garnering good ratings, another in the series of early variety shows headed by a rotating cast of big-name stars. Danny Thomas, Bob Hope, Ed Wynn, Jimmy Durante, Martha Raye, and others had all had numerous turns hosting. During the summer of 1952 there was no regular star and the program adopted the look of a straight vaudeville show. On August 16, Ella made her contribution to the program, which folded its vaudeville tents the following spring. Within two weeks of her appearance, Ella's marriage would fold, too.

As with many performers, the roller-coaster ride of their industry rarely makes for a successful relationship. "It was a good marriage, but it's hard for two people in show business," Ella recollected. "You have to learn to really understand somebody."

Ella and Ray divorced on August 28, 1953, in Juarez, Mexico, with Ella receiving the custody of Ray, Jr. Remaining close friends with her ex, she also remained Ray's close performing companion, with dozens of concerts and albums to their mutual credit. It was also around this time that Ella bought her first home, on Murdock Avenue, in the St. Albans section of Long Island, New York. Ella would keep close to New York as long as she recorded for Decca.

Years later, Ella spoke of her unhappiness after the divorce:

"When my husband and I broke up, I got a little despondent. I cried and cried, and my cousin said, 'Oh, take her to a bar. I can't stand her crying.' So I went into this bar and there was this pleasant bartender. 'What'll you have?' he asked. I jumped and said, 'I'll have a Manischewitz.' The whole bar said, 'Manischewitz?' The bartender said, 'If she wants it, she'll get it!' That's how much of a drinker I was."

On November 23 and 30 Louis Armstrong appeared one last time on the Fitzgerald/Decca horizon. This time, the two artists recorded a quartet of songs. While "Would You Like to Take a Walk" was popular for a while, none of these songs shook the world.

The unhappy year was closed out with yet another Crosby radio appearance. There was no duet with Bing, just a medley of "Trying," "My Favorite Song," and "Between the Devil and the Deep Blue Sea." A few weeks later, kicking off 1953 with Bing for a New Year's Day show, Ella was featured with Joe Venuti. This time she was permitted another medley, consisting of the Gordon Jenkins arrangement of "I Hadn't Anyone 'Til You" (including the vocal chorus), "If You Should Ever Leave," and an uptempo version of "I Can't Give You Anything But Love." Bing joined her for "Chicago Style," a song from his, Hope, and Lamour's *Road to Bali*.

While both "Careless" and "Blue Lou" (recorded on February 13, 1953) weren't all that bad, most of Decca's plans for Ella throughout 1953 had to do with rereleasing her songs on LPs, which had quickly overtaken the old 78s, making the 78s primarily obsolete (much in the way CDs assassinated LPs thirty-five years later). Ella's on again–off again recording career was once again off, with five LPs released of old material before year's end.

Norman Granz brought his JATP troupe to Japan in the fall of 1953. The Granz gang had toured America five times and had been to Europe twice. This was the first time that American jazz artists would be playing before a civilian audience in Japan. Previously, Gene Krupa had toured army camps there, and had come back with such glowing stories of the Japanese love for jazz that Norman Granz decided to take his troupe there, after first touring North America and Hawaii.

Appearing at the Nichigeki Theater in Tokyo on November 18, 1953, this time around the group included Ella, Roy Eldridge, Charlie Shavers, Bill Harris, Willie Smith, Benny Carter, Ben Webster, Flip Phillips, Oscar Peterson, Herb Ellis, Ray Brown, J. C. Heard, Gene Krupa, and Raymond Tunia. Ella was surrounded by her quartet of Tunia (piano), Ellis (guitar), Brown (bass), and Heard (drums), and her program was a mixture of rhythm tunes and ballads.

Ella's announced entrance was met by huge, cheering crowds as she stepped up to the microphone to sing "On the Sunny Side of the Street." Done in easy-swing time, the audience again cheered as Ella bopped her vocal at the line ". . . crossed over and I'm walkin' in clover. . . ." At the close of the number, the zealous Japanese audience already began screaming titles for her to sing, but she ignored them to settle into the luxurious ballad, "Body and Soul." Her performance of this number, which remained almost completely intact for the next ten years, will be discussed later. Suffice it to say that this would have been an almost perfect rendition, save for an eager photographer's light bulb exploding, the sound of which caused Ella to stifle a laugh at the third verse.

"Why Don't You Do Right?" was a then-current Peggy Lee hit that Ella did right. "Oh, Lady Be Good," "How High the Moon," and "Smooth Sailing" were faithful to their original, familiar renditions. The last included Ella's famous "the record's still available" toward the end. "I Got It Bad and That Ain't Good" and "My Funny Valentine" were two more examples of Ella trying to break away from the bop mode and apply her beautiful voice to the classic songs of the century. She succeeded magnificently. "Frim Fram Sauce" gave her a chance to use her Louis Armstrong muscles in impression of him, while "Perdido" was a JATP free-for-all, one that was used countless times in jam sessions by Granz artists.

There were two additional songs recorded during the week-long stay in Tokyo, both of them at after-hours jam sessions, but they were not included when Norman Granz belatedly released this concert in 1977 on his Pablo label. It would have been interesting to hear these greats of jazz just noodling together in their spare time on "Sweethearts on Parade" and "Dixie." There's always a chance for a future release.

The aforementioned *JATP: The Ella Fitzgerald Set*, recorded in

1949 and reissued by Verve, also features two songs from a Carnegie Hall concert on September 19, 1953, and four from September 17, 1954. The bag here was ballad-heavy, with "My Bill" and "Why Don't You Do Right?" (both from 1953), "A Foggy Day," "The Man That Got Away," "Hernando's Hideaway" (redone in the studio a few years later), and "Later" featured.

She closed out the year back in the studio, and the now-usual assortment of dross and beauty yielded such winners as "Moanin' Low," "Taking a Chance on Love," and "Empty Ballroom" with zonkers like "Somebody Bad Stole De Wedding Bell." Ella recorded some wonderful songs for Decca, but after almost twenty years, it was becoming obvious that even Milt Gabler's attentions were not enough to find her a musical identity that could be true to her talent and be commercial at the same time.

Around the same time, Ella made back-to-back appearances with Crosby on radio. December 13 found Miss Fitz doing "Moanin' Low" and then joining the crooner for "White Christmas." The following week had her paying attention to Gershwin with "Someone to Watch Over Me" and "Looking for a Boy" before dueting on "Istanbul" with a trumpet solo by Ziggy Elman.

It was during December of 1953 that Norman Granz officially became her manager as her contract with Moe Gale finally expired. In order to show his loyalty to Ella and prove that he would take care of her properly, Granz reached into his own coffers to settle an IRS debt for her.

As early as 1954, Ella was beginning to publicly complain about her recording lot with Decca. Not that she didn't have plenty to complain about, but 20/20 hindsight reveals that Norman Granz was beginning a publicity push to rid Ella of her Decca contract in order to fully take over her career. In *Metronome* magazine, she talked of wanting to do more small group work and more ballads, being pleased only with her recording of Gershwin songs as a project that really fit her ideas of music. Throughout the next year and a half, Ella more and more often took the opportunity to knock Decca's musical decisions on her behalf.

Ella's final Crosby radio appearance took place on February 14, 1954. "Taking a Chance on Love" was the solo, with "That's A-Plenty" the dueter. Television had finally taken its toll, and big-budget radio variety series were just too expensive to continue. Within the year, only such stalwarts as "Ma Perkins," "The Lone Ranger," and "Amos 'n' Andy" were still heard on network radio.

Soon after the Crosby appearance, Ella was taken to the hospital for surgery for a node on her vocal chords. Naturally, there was distress in the Fitzgerald camp. What would happen to that pristene voice? Ella literally didn't talk for six weeks. When she finally opened her mouth to sing, she actually sounded better.

Strangely (or perhaps ironically), 1954 saw the beginning of her best work for Decca. Four more Gordon Jenkins tunes recorded on March 24 (including the beautiful "I Wished on the Moon"), as well as a spate of songs with Ellis Larkins. This time there was no theme to choice of repertoire, with such standards as "Stardust" (Ella's only studio recording of what had been called the best pop song ever written), "My Heart Belongs to Daddy," and "People Will Say We're in Love." The overall effect was not as good as the original Fitzgerald/ Larkins collaboration, but extremely satisfactory nonetheless.

Pollsters were once again taking notice of the Fitzgerald magic. Ella won the *Metronome* poll as Best Female Singer in 1954, as well as the *Down Beat* poll and the *Down Beat* Critics poll. The roller-coaster ride of her career was once again on the upswing.

Chapter Eleven

1954–1955

The first of the great Ella fetes took place on June 1, 1954, when the nineteenth anniversary of her first recording was celebrated (although the celebration was thrown to celebrate her twentieth; someone couldn't count). The extravaganza was held at the Basin Street East, the famous New York nightclub devoted to jazz where Ella was about to open. With Steve Allen as master of ceremonies, the other talent included Pearl Bailey, Eartha Kitt, Dizzy Gillespie, and Harry Belafonte. Cables and telegrams poured in from Paris (Lena Horne), London (Billy Eckstine), and the United States (Benny Goodman, Fred Waring, Rosemary Clooney, Ray Anthony, Guy Lombardo, the Mills Brothers, Lionel Hampton, Louis Armstrong, and others). Ella was showered with sixteen awards and plaques, and flowers from both foreign and domestic jazz publications. Decca awarded her with a special plaque for her 22 million records sold for them. This number would be significant twenty-six years later when Ella sued Decca for misrepresentation of records sold.

At the time, Ella was quoted as saying, "I guess what everyone wants more than anything else in the world is to be loved. And to know that you people love me and my singing is too much for me. Forgive me if I don't have all the words. Maybe I can sing it and you'll understand." Sing it she did, and enchanted the star-studded audience with her voice. Certainly she survived with all that love, for what with the divorce, she and Ray, Jr., were living alone in that house in St. Albans (when she was home).

It was also around this time that the First Lady got her only chance to meet up with the Chairman of the Board in the recording studio. Long before Fred Astaire lensed it for the big screen, an animated version of the Broadway show *Finian's Rainbow* was planned as a feature. Frank Sinatra, Louis Armstrong, Red Norvo, Oscar Petersen, Ray Brown, and others, along with Ella, pre-recorded some of the songs for the film. While the project was scrapped before it got under way, Frank and Ella recorded a duet of "Necessity." They both were in great voice and swung tunefully, although the arrangement didn't embellish the song. The cut was later released on LP, and much later on CD, with little fanfare. What might have been one of the great moments in popular recordings remains an interesting footnote.

The JATP tour in 1954 added someone new in the form of Louie Bellson. The drummers for the previous tours had been Gene Krupa and Buddy Rich, but in 1954 Norman Granz called Louie and asked him to join the tour. "Buddy and I had been very close," according to Bellson, "and we were extremely pleased to be working together." For this six-week tour, Ella was the star, with Oscar Peterson, Ray Brown, Herb Ellis, Buddy DeFranco, Bill Harris, Lester Young, Flip Phillips, and Roy Eldridge gigging together. Ella followed the drum battle, doing seven or eight tunes plus three or four encores. The audience wouldn't let her off the stage.

Her sense of swing made it easy for musicians to follow her, especially with the head arrangements used in many of the JATP concerts. She was just that good at time. In fact, Bellson says, "The greatest drum solo I ever heard was done by Ella at this time doing her scat choruses. She had such a strong pulse, the musicians just *had* to swing."

The only other contributions Ella made to the recording world in 1954 were spare, to be sure, but choice. Recorded on June 4, "Later" was yet another swing number that was popular enough to follow Ella throughout the rest of the decade. However, "Lullaby of Birdland" was a rare opportunity for Ella to swing jazz in the studio. Starting off with the moaning saxophone, this cut sounded more like her work for Verve than for Decca. In fact, all of her forthcoming recordings for Decca were more mature, had better arrangements, and were generally much more satisfying all around. Unfortunately, with more of her old stuff being rereleased, Decca didn't allow her to record for another ten months.

Ella did more complaining in print in an article featured in *Down Beat* magazine on February 23, 1955. The entire interview is infiltrated with Fitzgerald digs at her parent company, Decca:

> . . . it's been so long since I've gotten a show tune to do, or a chance to do a tune like "The Man That Got Away." . . . I never do get a chance at the songs that have a chance. They give me something by somebody that no one else has, and then they wonder why the record doesn't sell. . . . I'm so heartbroken over it. . . . I don't know what they're doing at the record company . . . the disc jockeys claimed that the company doesn't give them the record [to play] . . . it's because the record company is mainly interested in pictures now that they don't give as much attention to the records.

Clearly, Ella (and Norman) were paving the way for her eventual departure from the Decca fold, a move that came within the year. She also chose this opportunity to pitch for a television show of her own:

> . . . even if it was just a local New York program. So I could stay home a little. I can dance, you know, if I get a show. I'd like to do a program that was like inviting the audience into my home.

Most interviews at that time were written with the help of agents and publicity men, so it is unknown if Ella actually uttered these words herself. Alas, that television show never materialized.

Unhappy though she and Granz may have been with Decca, there wasn't one false step in her recordings for that company in 1955. With Ella working with the likes of Sy Oliver, Tutti Camarata, André Previn, and old friend Benny Carter, those cuts were as good as any of her early Verve work. The sound was crisp and clear, the arrangements first class, the song choices inspired.

On April Fool's Day, Ella warbled "You'll Never Know," "Thanks for the Memory," "It Might As Well Be Spring," and "I Can't Get Started" for André Previn. Previn at the time was leading a dichotomous professional life, spending half his time in jazz and half his time in classical music (much like Wynton Marsalis in the 1980s).

These were followed on April 27 by "That Old Devil Moon" and three more songs that Ella would sing forever: "Lover Come Back to Me," "Between the Devil and the Deep Blue Sea," and "That Old Black Magic," brought to her via Benny Carter. All three were swingers, each giving Ella the opportunity to loosen up and let go.

Producer/director/deadpan actor Jack Webb decided to pour some of his "Dragnet" profits into a big-screen effort. *Pete Kelly's Blues*, based on an old radio series of his, purported to be a realistic story of jazz and gangsters in the roaring twenties. Produced by his Mark VII production company for Warner Brothers, the movie starred Webb, Janet Leigh, Edmond O'Brien, Andy Devine, Lee Marvin, and two very popular songbirds, Peggy Lee and Ella Fitzgerald. The story, set in 1927, revolved around Webb's character Pete Kelly, a jazz coronetist who takes on a vicious ganglord in Kansas City. Ella played a honky-tonk singer, whose offerings in the film included the title song, as well as "Hard Hearted Hannah." The Decca versions were recorded on May 3, released along with Peggy's songs as a pseudo-soundtrack album. Backed by a trio consisting of Don Abney, Joe Mondragon, and Larry Bunker, "Hannah" proved to be a favorite of Ella's. By the 1970s, she was singing the number with the accompaniment of symphony orchestras.

Ella's acting talents weren't really featured, but her musical presence was definitely felt in the film. To promote the movie, the entire cast appeared on "The Colgate Variety Hour," an offshoot of "The Colgate Comedy Hour," with the same basic format as the aforementioned "All Star Revue," in fact sharing some of the same hosts. In the summer of 1955, Colgate began a tie-in with Paramount Pictures and the Brothers Warner, and it became a practice to show scenes from upcoming films, and then have the stars come on to chat or perform. On July 24, Ella was among many from the cast of *Pete Kelly's Blues* who appeared to "plug away" its release.

Ella made her final records for dear old Decca on April 1 and 5, 1955. This last gasp again had Ella giving wonderful versions of great songs like "My One and Only Love" and "(Love Is) The Tender Trap," while murking her way through such forgettables as "Soldier Boy" and "The Impatient Years." While Decca rereleased Ella's music in a myriad of LP forms over the following twenty-five years, it was not until 1993 that the company would begin to release her music on CD. Well produced by Orrin Keepnews, these collections put her career with Decca in perspective and highlighted just how much good music she really did record for them over that twenty-year period between 1935 and 1955. While arguments can be made that she was not handled properly, it is easy to pick out at least forty outstanding cuts made for Decca. Not many singers can claim to have forty outstanding cuts *anywhere*.

Scandal had hardly touched Miss Ella, with respect to her career or her personal life. Possibly the closest she ever came was on the night of October 8, 1955. Sitting in her dressing room in Houston, Ella was having pie and coffee and entertaining her fellow JATP performers before the first show. Ever the lady but one of the boys, she was daintily sipping tea while her cronies were shooting craps on her dressing-room floor. The local vice squad burst in, and the First Lady of Song was carted off to the local pokey, along with Dizzy Gillespie and Illinois Jacquet (among others). Ella dissolved in tears, crying, "I was only having a piece of pie and a cup of coffee." Her fellow "inmates" found her distress hysterical, that she could psychologically remove herself from a situation that was part and parcel of touring with jazz musicians, something she had been doing since she was fifteen. Ella was *always* a lady, even when she was hanging out with the boys.

Sergeant W. A. Scotton of the vice squad was kind enough to wait until the first show was over before removing the gang to jail. Norman Granz came and paid the $10 bond for each arrestee, and the group returned in time for the second show. The troupe left Houston at eight the following morning, and the bond was forfeited. Local officials did admit that Ella had not been actually shooting or holding any dice when they raided her dressing room.

It is not known if such a fuss was made because they were in the Southwest and were African Americans, or whether this was a planned publicity gimmick. Since Dizzy Gillespie told this story in his auto-biography with much glee, it is doubtful that it was born out of the imagination of any publicity men. Besides, such notoriety would not be good for a troupe looking to play the biggest concert halls in the world. Granz eventually returned and cleared everyone of all charges.

Doing double duty in December of 1955, Ella appeared in almost back-to-back programs for television. Tennessee Ernie Ford had her as a guest on his television "spectacular" (they weren't called specials back then) broadcast on December 9, that was a precursor to his long-running NBC variety show on Thursday nights. Ella returned to TV eight nights later for CBS, this time doing a color program for the series "Ford Star Jubilee," subtitled "I Hear America Singing." "Jubilee" was the first regularly scheduled color program airing on CBS (appearing as a "spectacular" about once a month). Such names as Judy Garland, Mary Martin, and Noel Coward had already lent their efforts to make this series a success. Joining Ella on December 17 were MGM dancing star Bobby Van and comedian Red Skelton, along with singers Nat "King" Cole and Eddie Fisher, and actress Debbie Reynolds.

Her acting talents weren't any more featured in her next film, *St. Louis Blues* (released in 1958). In this "story" of W. C. Handy, Ella anachronistically appeared as herself—before she was born—a saloon singer heard by Handy (Nat "King" Cole) as she sang "Beale Street Blues." For the recording of the song, Ella was joined in the studio by Don Abney on piano, Joe Mondragon on bass, and Larry Bunker on drums, with an arrangement by Nelson Riddle. This was the first time she worked with Riddle, who was to loom large in her recording future. "Beale Street Blues" was recorded by Verve, her new recording company as of January 1, 1956.

The Verve Years

Chapter Twelve

1956

$\mathscr{S}$he and I have no contract," remarked Norman Granz in the
1950s, "just a handshake, and we can afford the luxury of telling each
other off." The beginning of the Verve years brought immense change
to Ella's career. Like many artists, Ella needed the right arena to
display her talents. Joan Crawford had a long career in movies, but
truly blossomed as the queen of the soap operas at Warner Brothers
in the 1940s. Lucille Ball had made almost seventy movies before she
and television spawned an entire industry. By 1956, Ella had more of
a career than most successful recording artists could hope for, but
with her recording marriage to Norman Granz she entered rarified
territory.

   With Granz already handling her career as a manager for several
years, and with him now at the studio helm, she began an outpouring
of recording, both studio and live, unmatched by any other artist. It
is significant that in the early 1990s, Ella had more CDs in general
release than any other artist, yet only a fraction of that material pre-
dated 1956. Her twenty-one-year association with Decca, which
yielded quite a few pop hits (both as a singer with Chick Webb and

as a single), became a long, fondly remembered footnote to her recording career with the release of her first Verve album, the legendary *Ella Sings the Cole Porter Songbook*.

However, there was more to this story than just Ella's jumping from one record label to another. Granz had tried and tried to get her released from her Decca contract in order to record her himself. Proprietary Decca always refused. Sometimes, parent companies make strange bedfellows. MCA, which now owned Decca, also owned Universal Pictures. With the success of *The Glenn Miller Story* in 1954, Universal decided to mine for gold again in '55 with *The Benny Goodman Story*.

Starring Steve Allen and Donna Reed, the film also featured many of the artists then under exclusive contract to Norman Granz. Naturally, Decca wanted to release a soundtrack album featuring those jazz greats. Granz had Decca right by their platters. No Ella for Granz, no album for Decca. With the grit of teeth and the sign of a pen, Decca released Ella from her contract. It is significant that Decca prized one album over its relationship with Ella. Such poor decision making spelled the end for Decca as a major recording company by the 1960s.

At this point, mention must be made that there are a multitude of opinions regarding Granz's influence on Ella. Many interviewed for this book painted Granz strictly as a money-handler, that is, he didn't know beans from music but had a genius for presenting it. There were complaints of his interference in Ella's music, and his inability to properly run a recording session. One person described him as like a taxi-driver, always aware that the meter was running and forcing the recording of songs with inadequate rehearsal time. Some claimed that Granz really has no taste for music involving more than six musicians at a session. Said one old Granzite, "He never was able to grasp properly the concept of using orchestras and big bands, and the development and rehearsal time required for such projects." Still other objectors said Granz worked Ella into a stupor, booking and touring her to exhaustion in order to earn money.

But there was also much praise for Norman Granz. He freed Ella from recording pop garbage and allowed her to perform in the finest places with the finest musicians. Ella always gave Norman credit for the Songbook series, and for pairing her with people like Louis Armstrong, Oscar Peterson, and Joe Pass. Many true jazz stalwarts claim that Norman was just being true to the jazz idiom, where musicians get together and play off of inspiration instead of charts. Surely, his management of Ella was significant in making her independently wealthy, and her career certainly was rescued from possible mediocrity or early windup by his decisions. More on this aspect of their relationship will become evident.

Ella began her recording career on Verve (the name Granz gave to his new company; his other labels of Clef and Norgran would soon be history) not with the Songbook series, but with four sides recorded on January 25, 1956. With the band under the baton of Buddy Bregman, Ella sang "Stay There," "The Sun Forgot to Shine This Morning," "Too Young for the Blues," and "It's Only a Man." Bregman was given this assignment as a warmup for the upcoming Cole Porter collection recorded two months later. Strangely enough, none of these songs hit the charts or were ever reissued on albums, and today they are only represented on Verve CD reissues. The arrangements for these songs were actually better than the ones Bregman would came up with for the Porter songbook. Most sources inaccurately list Ella's first Verve recordings as those on the Porter albums.

Ella credited Norman Granz for both the Songbook series and for opening new vistas in her artistry. "I always have to thank Mr. Norman Granz for the idea for the Songbooks, and so many of the things I sing," Ella told audiences in concert. Like many singers that were weaned on the big bands, Ella sang in a style that complemented the orchestration of whatever song was put in front of her. Neither the songs nor the orchestrations always did Ella right. Now, however, Ella only sang the best of what has now become "the standards" of pop and jazz, written by the best composers, backed with orchestrations that suited both the songs and her incredible voice. Director of engineering Val Valentin ensured that Ella's voice did not get lost in lush orchestrations, or sound as if she were singing in an echo chamber. Each of her Verve albums was impeccably recorded, and followed state-of-the-art trends from hi-fi to stereo in 1957. The albums were crafted to a theme, and each theme was treated with its own set of guidelines. Compare and contrast the arrangements and choices of material on such albums as *Like Someone in Love, Rhythm Is My Business*, and *Clap Hands, Here Comes Charlie*. The first was a collection of standard ballads set to Frank DeVol's lush arrangements; the second was a collection of rhythm tunes backed by Bill Doggett's swinging big band; the third a collection of jazz and pop tunes backed by Ella's quartet led by Lou Levy. Each album was completely different in mood and texture, the only constant being Ella's enormous understanding of how best to present a song. In each case she was totally true to her style, never trying to be anything but Ella. Yet, she flexed musical and artistic muscles that in lesser hands would yield preposterous recordings of infinite ego and tastelessness.

The Cole Porter Songbook, recorded in February 1956, was originally released in two single-record albums, and then rereleased as a two-record set. The songs were Porter's best, with only a few classics ("My Heart Belongs to Daddy," "Down in the Depths," "Blow, Gabriel, Blow," "Friendship") conspicuously missing. Buddy Bregman was brought in to arrange the tunes, having previously adapted several Porter classics for two Ethel Merman television outings of *Anything Goes* and *Panama Hattie*. That both Fitzgerald and Merman could sing the same songs, each in a style totally unlike the other yet totally true to Porter's intentions, reflects not only on the phenomenal artistry of both ladies but on the musical foundations Porter laid in each song he wrote.

Bregman's orchestrations for Ella were the least satisfying of any done for her under the Verve label. "It was no small coincidence that Jule Styne, who produced the two Merman outings, was Bregman's uncle," recalls one musician who played on the album. "He made his name with that album. Hell, anyone would have been made with that album."

Controversy surrounds this collection. Bregman and Granz both claimed credit for the idea. "Buddy said the idea was totally his," claims one recording executive. "He said he came to Norman with the idea to do an all-Porter album, and that he picked the songs himself. In fact, he said the reason he stopped working on the Songbooks after the Rodgers and Hart outing was that the concept was all played out." Considering that everyone interviewed for this book claims that Granz was close to a tyrant about choosing all of Ella's songs himself, it is unlikely that Bregman would have had such a free hand.

While Bregman's arrangements weren't bad, the best cuts were those featuring the small group led by Paul Smith. "Too Darn Hot" was a rouser, but many of the others were simply pedestrian orchestral efforts, with Ella's vocals making them sound a lot better than they were.

This is as good a time as any to talk about the multitalented Paul Smith. Paul worked with Ella as pianist on all of her Songbooks for Verve (except for the Kern and Mercer collections), and was her now-and-again pianist/conductor in the late 1950s and early 1960s, and then again from 1978 until 1989. In the late 1940s, he had been the arranger and pianist for the post-Sinatra Dorsey band, as well as staff pianist at Warner Brothers Studios. All during the 1950s and early 1960s, Paul was the staff pianist at NBC Television in Burbank, shifting his responsibilities between live jazz performances and TV work. Red Skelton, Dinah Shore, Nat "King" Cole, Bing Crosby, Carol Burnett, Jo Stafford, Gordon MacCrae, and Tony Martin utilized his talents on their network shows and specials. Pat Boone, Steve Allen, and Sammy Davis, Jr., enjoyed Paul's stints as conductor all through the sixties and seventies. Two of Bing Crosby's 1970 albums featured Paul's arrangements, and Paul has recorded over fifty solo albums for various major recording companies.

To this writer's ear, the best cuts on this collection were the ones that showed Ella's amazing versatility. Porter's "Too Darn Hot," from *Kiss Me Kate*, was sung in broader strokes than her previous work, yet was true jazz nonetheless. This ability to broaden, and yet remain true to the roots of jazz, was one of the surprising and welcome aspects of the collection. Both "All Through the Night" and "Miss Otis Regrets" (a song not written for any particular production; it just came to Porter) were saved from almost total obscurity by Ella's interpretations. Over thirty-five years later, audiences still screamed for Ella to sing the latter in her concerts.

Although not a hit in the United States, "Everytime We Say Goodbye" was such a smash success for Ella in the United Kingdom that audiences there would thereafter not tolerate an appearance without it. And although Ella later brightened these songs with more modern arrangements (Bregman's sound "fifties" dated), "Let's Do It," "It's Alright With Me," "I Get a Kick Out of You," "Love for Sale," "Just One of Those Things," and "Night and Day" were still staples of Ella's concert appearances until the 1990s.

Also recorded at this time was "Beautiful Friendship," a single that eventually found its way on to one of the Verve compilation albums. A pretty ballad, it also suffered from the tiresome arrangement which dragged it down. Curiously, there was also an obscure song, "I Had to Find Out for Myself," which was recorded but not released.

Within one month of its issue, *The Cole Porter Songbook* sold over 100,000 copies. By today's standards, where albums are *shipped* gold and platinum, it doesn't sound like much. However, this was a tremendous amount of sales for 1956. Especially for a two-record set. By year's end, it became the eleventh best-selling album of 1956. Not bad for someone who, just a year earlier, complained that her recording career was in the dumps.

Steve Allen had always been a big fan of jazz, and when he got his "Tonight Show" on NBC, he was happy to include the talents of Ella Fitzgerald. On April 2, 1956, she appeared with her trio, which at that point included Don Abney, Gus Johnson, and Bennie Moten.

Ella's next two recording projects were further proof of the new direction Norman Granz had implemented. *Metronome* had named Ella and Count Basie as its All-Stars of 1956. Such an honor could not go by without a brief recording marriage of Granz's two stars. *Metronome All-Stars 1956*, recorded June 25, was an unusual album in that it had no real theme. Ella and the Basie band swung through "April in Paris," a Basie hit from the album of the same name on Verve. Ella's added vocal to a slightly altered chart from the instrumental version was a gem, making it curious that the entire album was not cut along the same line. Basie's famous coda at the end of the song, where he stated "just one more time," was followed by a singing coda by Ella, making for a clever and humorous ending to the song. The rest of the album featured the Basie band doing instrumental solos, along with some Joe Williams vocals and two Fitzgerald-Williams duets, "The Party Blues" and "Everyday I Get the Blues."

A second album, comprised of unused songs recorded at the same time, later received limited distribution under the title *One O'Clock Jump—Ella Fitzgerald, Count Basie, Joe Williams*. Ella's main contribution here was a laid-back duet with Joe of "Too Close for Comfort," a song that in later years proved to be a showstopper for her.

Wisely, Norman Granz decided to break up Ella's year with non–Songbook assignments, and her next steps up to the microphone were truly inspired. On August 15, 1956, Norman Granz produced a jazz concert at the famous Hollywood Bowl. While concerts such as this one are standard fare today, it was only the second one of its kind back then, the first to feature all music and no narration. It was also the first recorded jazz concert in the history of the Hollywood Bowl.

Entitled *Jazz at the Hollywood Bowl*, the concert boasted a lineup of a veritable who's who of jazz at that time: Buddy Rich; Ray Brown; Herb Ellis; "Little Jazz" Roy Eldridge; Illinois Jacquet; Flip Phillips; Harry "Sweets" Edison; Oscar Peterson; Art Tatum; the father of jazz, Louis Armstrong; and Miss Fitzgerald, who came on at the end of the evening, accompanied by Paul Smith. Ella gave live treatments of some of her recent Porter recordings, a glance at her soon-to-be-released Rodgers and Hart album, a reprise of "Too Close for Comfort" as recorded with Basie and Williams, and two special material pieces that were with Ella for years.

"I Can't Give You Anything But Love" had been around since the twenties, but Ella invigorated this song, not only with swing, but with choice impressions of Rose "Chi-Chi" Murphy and the great Louis himself. One can only imagine the electricity of Ella's graveling of Louis's voice, with the Great One there in attendance. This was followed by an adaptation of Ella's hit "Air Mail Special," released for the first time with a live interpretation. This song again emerged in two other live albums, *Ella and Billie at Newport* and *Ella in Hollywood*. Each is interesting, as Ella changed her vocal doodles everytime she swung into this classic. The Hollywood Bowl recording ended with Ella and Louis dueting on "You Won't Be Satisfied," a Decca pairing of the two, and "Undecided," from the days when Ella led her own band. Strangely, none of the songs from her upcoming album appeared here.

In the 1940s, Ella and Louis Armstrong had recorded some 78s for Decca, but hardly anyone had noticed. With *Ella and Louis*, recorded on August 16, 1956 (the day after the Bowl concert), not only did people notice but wondered what the pair had been waiting for. The collaboration, backed by only a rhythm section comprised of Oscar Peterson, Ray Brown, Herb Ellis, and Buddy Rich (along with Louis's horn), produced some of the best recordings of either of their careers. This author truly believes there has been no greater jazz vocal duet than Ella and Louis's "Can't We Be Friends?" due to the easy tempo started by Oscar, the good-natured kidding back and forth between the singers, the interplay between the musicians, and Louis's "oh, yeah!" at the tag.

Each song was taken as an individual piece, with Ella and "Satchmo" swapping vocals back and forth depending on the song and the mood. Louis punctuated several cuts with his timeless trumpet solos. The easy fun of the participants, each egging the other on to do their best, practically gave the album an audio smile. The contrast of the two voices, sometimes singing in different keys, swapping verses or singing together like sandpaper on velvet, brings jazz that is mellow, rewarding, and swinging. Check out "Moonlight in Vermont" for a contrast in styles. Both Ella and Louis caress this song, but with such individuality it seems almost impossible for the two interpretations to fit together. But fit they did.

This album also inaugurated another unusual facet to Ella's recording career: the recutting of songs already recorded, even if they had been recently recorded, to fit an album's theme. "April in Paris" was given a new treatment here, as it did again nineteen years later in the album *Ella and Oscar* (see The Pablo Years). Every single song from this collection has been given further treatment by Ella elsewhere, many of them within three years of this recording. Yet, every time she stepped up to the microphone, the treatment was different, fresh, and interesting.

Since her divorce and "marriage" to Granz, Ella hardly had time to breathe. When she wasn't in the studio recording at breakneck speed, she was touring all over the world. Frequently, months would go by without a day off. Having a personal life was now out of the question, as her nights were filled with performing and her days were spent traveling and recording. The success of the Porter albums brought her a celebrity she hadn't enjoyed since her salad days with Chick Webb. The time of playing joints or dives were over. However, there was always a piper to be paid. As she had no time for men, she also had no time for Ray, Jr., who only got to see Mommy on the fly as he was in school. Granz saw to it that Ella depended only on him, fueling rumors that the two were involved romantically.

Nothing in my research substantiated anything like that. If anything, their relationship was of the love/hate variety, with Ella alternately needing Granz for his direction and then resenting him for it. Their affiliation became a delicate game of manipulation, as each tried to have the upper hand. Granz almost always succeeded.

Chapter Thirteen

1956–1957

*W*ho could possibly follow Cole Porter? Granz's answer was Rodgers and Hart. *The Rodgers and Hart Songbook*, recorded just two weeks after *Ella and Louis* between August 27 and 31, was produced along the same lines as its predecessor. Again featuring Buddy Bregman's arrangements, the album treated the urbane, witty, and touching lyrics of Larry Hart much the same way it had embraced Cole Porter's. Richard Rodgers's tunes, much more lyric in nature than Porter's beguines, showed once and for all that no one could sing a ballad like Ella. In cut after cut, "Bewitched," "My Funny Valentine," "Dancing on the Ceiling," "I Didn't Know What Time It Was," and others, Ella displayed the rich warmth in her voice, her gentleness with a phrase, and her understanding of a lyric. The album showed that Ella did have not only a voice but a true feeling for the maturity of the material at hand. Once again, Paul Smith's piano was featured, and once again it is the small group sessions that really did shine.

August also saw the first of two appearances in 1956 on "The Ford Show," starring Tennessee Ernie Ford, although the name of the show did not refer to the star but to the sponsor, the Ford Motor Company. On August 31, Ella did a prerecorded spot with Ernie, videotape having just come into use. A second appearance on December 27 was similarly on tape, and both of Ella's segments may have been made at the same time to accommodate her heavy touring schedule.

Frankie Laine, that "Mule Train" man, had a summer series that year, and Ella helped him wind up his stint on September 8, 1956. The appearance was an odd one, both due to the choice of material and Ella's performance. Clearly, Ella either was not feeling well or was just plain uncomfortable. Her voice quavering, her tone unclear, and her manner not showing the least bit of ease, Ella was brought out to sing "Beautiful Friendship" (Frankie incorrectly introduced it as being from her latest album). Sitting in a mock living-room setting, Ella had trouble manipulating her voice in the Fitzgerald style to the simple arrangement. The second half of the show found Frankie saying Ella picked out the next song herself, which coincidentally was the other side of the record, "The Silent Treatment." The song was a light swinger, the title referring to "the weapon of a woman in love." Its clearly sexist lyrics are now extremely dated, and even then appeared unseemly for someone over the age of twenty-five (or over the mentality of ten).

Frankie joined Ella on those then-standard old stools for "You're the Top," with Frankie (who began to sport glasses on the TV screen) handing Ella a pair of her own to wear for their duet. This was unusual in that Ella would not wear glasses in public for over fifteen years. Ella forgot the special material words, even got lost in the meter of the song, and screwed up the special ending. It may have been that she was trying to read the lyrics from cue cards or a TelePrompTer, something she never did again as she always had her songs for television down cold. An interesting footnote to the appearance was the use of a Verve promotional ad (for "The Silent Treatment" and "The Sun Forgot to Shine This Morning") as a billboard for Ella's appearance at the opening of the show.

Her recent successes also spilled over into her live performances. In his November 28, 1956, syndicated article, writer John Tynan addressed Ella's new-found achievements:

> Ella contends the main reason for this triumph is that for the first time in her career she's got a best-selling album package

working for her, Verve Records' *The Cole Porter Songbook*. In support of this reasoning is the fact that during the last stint [at the Mocambo, where she had recently appeared] early this year business was clearly disappointing. More often than not, she sang to a room half full, a clientele more of noisy bon vivants than admirers. Then, this summer, her album of Cole Porter tunes was released by Norman Granz, the artist's first LP since leaving Decca. Since then it's been near panic wherever she appears.

Returning to the subject of recording, Ella spoke of her just-completed *Rodgers and Hart Songbook*. "It's so pretty," she said. "I did it mostly with strings [not true], and I've always wanted to sing with lots of strings [what about her work with Gordon Jenkins?]. Then, I think the average layman knows the songs better, so it should sell more than Cole Porter. Another thing is that we didn't have to rush it like we did the first album, so I think the whole feeling is more relaxed." Of the Rodgers and Hart songs, she especially mentioned "Spring Is Here" ("I *like* that") and "Bewitched" ("I got real sexy on that one") as evoking particularly warm feeling.

As conversation reverted to in-person performances, the topic of audiences naturally predominated. "In ten years of making concert tours [she'd been doing them for over twenty] I think the audiences have matured quite a lot," she observed. "Particularly the JATP audiences. This year I believe we had the nicest houses so far, and a great deal of credit must go to Norman. You know, he even wrote a little instruction on the JATP program this year on how they should behave. And it worked. Oh, you'll always get a few loudmouths. Guess it can't be helped. I think the Modern Jazz Quartet, too, helped make them quiet this year. When they play, people just have to listen."

While such interviews did give some penetration into Ella the performer, once again there was no public awareness of Ella the woman. Still young, divorced, and the mother of a small boy, nowhere did she discuss the exigencies of her life. This wall between her personal life and her audience remained to the end of her career. Sadly, by the end there wasn't much to tell.

Ella closed out her recording year with another single, this time arranged by Nelson Riddle (the first of many pairings of the two with a full orchestra). "Everything I've Got Belongs to You" was an out-and-out swinger, an arrangement she used for years in concerts that featured a full orchestra. Alas, this song never saw the light on an album.

For a very short time, Ella began to play the harmonica on stage. THE HARMONICA? Ella chuckled to John Tynan:

> More people have been asking me about that darn harmonica. Well, here's the true story. Oscar and "Herky" [Herb Ellis] bought one in Europe to tease Norman. They'd play it hillbilly style to rile him. I used to play in school and one day I got a hold of theirs and started blowing. Then, for a gag I played it at a concert one night. In Europe, I mean. Norman thought it was a pretty good bit, and he'd have me play on our tour back home. And that was that. It was something a little different. A bit of fun, you know. But then, I'd like to learn the vibes, too. . . . That'd be a ball."

Another interview at that time still featured Ella as the shy performer. Speaking backstage at the Apollo Theater during a JATP tour, Ella revealed:

> I know I'm no glamour girl, and it's not easy for me to get up in front of a crowd of people. It used to bother me a lot, but now I've got it figured out that God gave me this talent to use, so I just stand there and sing.

The new year, 1957, proved to be a banner year for Ella, with six of her most classic performances on wax and her continued live performances all over the world with the Jazz At The Philharmonic. The studio year started with a short trip to the microphone with Russ Garcia. Garcia, who would soon helm a major project for Ella, was brought in to do two sides, "Hear My Heart" and "Hotta Chocolotta." The first was a straightforward ballad, the second a novelty number with a Latin beat. These were issued as a single, but never got album coverage.

That year would continue the beginning of Ella's classic appearances on television. She was seen on home screens several times in 1957: first on "The Ed Sullivan Show," and then twice on "The Nat "King" Cole Show." However, the year almost immediately got waylaid with a hospital stay.

On January 28, 1957, while Ella was appearing at the Paramount Theater, she began to experience pains while onstage, cutting short her set. Backstage, a doctor was called in, and she was immediately rushed to New York Hospital where she was admitted for observation and treatment of an acute abdominal condition. Three days later, she suffered through a seventy-five-minute operation to remove an abdominal abscess. While recuperating in the hospital for an additional two weeks, she had to cancel out any plans to finish her Paramount stint.

Ella was nursed back to health by her Aunt Virginia. In an article by Sidney Fields in the June 21, 1957, issue of the now-defunct *New York Mirror*, the wall to her highly guarded private life was cracked, ever so slightly. Talking of her aunt, Ella said:

> I call her mother. She's a believing woman, and she raised me and my sister and her own son and daughter and all our eight children. When I woke up in the hospital she was the first face I saw. She'd take care of the kids all day and then come to sit with me in the hospital all night. She just loves you back to well.

Why did Aunt Virginia have to raise all the eight children? Where were the parents? Oh, well.

Remarking about Miss Fitz's other family members, Fields said:

> Ella has profound pride in her family: her remarkable aunt, her cousin who's a preacher, her niece who just won the chief oratory prize in all the high schools, and the others for their quiet, steady decency.

Certainly, while the information was interesting (this was the first mention in print that Ella even *had* a sister), the only true mention of her *personal* life came at the end of the article:

> "I guess I pick them wrong," Ella admits. "But I want to get married again. I'm still looking. Everybody needs companionship." That's the missing note in her song. Ella is just lonely.

The critiques of Ella's work with Granz kept pouring in. A March 16, 1957, review of *The Rodgers and Hart Songbook* included this observation:

> What Ella Fitzgerald can now do with a melodic line is a treatise on self-improvement, in which thought and taste (plus a considerable amount of intuition) have given one-time baby band-singer rank with the by-gone Mildred Bailey. If there is higher praise in this area, someone else will have to think of it.

Her second stint with Sullivan (the name of the show had been changed from "Toast of the Town" to "The Ed Sullivan Show" in 1955) on March 24, 1957, was nine years after the first, but it certainly wasn't the last. Ella's newfound position as the queen of popular music ensured seven more appearances after this one. She only sang one song, "Oh, Lady Be Good," but spent some extended time talking to Ed, discussing how this was Bing Crosby's favorite song. This kind of exposure helped to make her more acceptable to the mainstream public, who in 1957 still did not eagerly invite African Americans into their homes. A handshake or arm around the waist from Ed could do more for a career at that time than a hit record.

Ella returned to the JATP for a European tour, one night of which (in Stockholm on April 28, 1957) was belatedly released in CD form on the TAX label in 1991. Ella's set reflected her current recording status, with Porter, Rodgers and Hart, and Basie represented. A little Ellingtonia, a preview of the album Ella and the Duke would record over the summer and fall of the year, cropped up, along with Decca chestnuts "Angel Eyes" and "Lullaby of Birdland." "You Got Me Singing the Blues" was the only sop to current pop tastes. This melange of songs, ever changing from concert to concert depending on Ella's mood and her latest recordings, was a staple of the Fitzgerald concerts. If you came to see Ella three times in a year, you would have heard as many as forty different songs.

An historic filmed account of Ella in concert at this time "just standing up there and singing" was released in 1993 by Green Line Video. Before a standing-room-only audience in Bruxelles in May 1957, Ella was seen joined by her quartet (Don Abney, Herb Ellis, Ray Brown, and Jo Jones) to do many of the songs found on the TAX CD. Of special interest are live versions of "Roll 'Em Pete" (which Ella would turn into "Joe Williams' Blues" in a few years); "Air Mail Special" (Ella couldn't hear her introduction so she started the song by herself and then apologized to the quartet in her lyrics as she sang); and a jam session with Herb, Ray, Jo, Oscar Peterson, and Roy Eldridge on "It Don't Mean a Thing. . . ." Wearing a satin sheath covered by empire overlays, Ella looked slimmer than she had in years, and clearly her recent rise to the top of the heap was wearing well on her. Ella was no longer *a* singer, she was *the* singer.

With the success of her many Verve albums and Norman Granz's expert management, Ella was found playing the premier nightclub in the country, the Copacabana. During the week of June 19, 1957, she appeared with Buddy Hackett, in an unusual arrangement where both performers got equal billing. Jules Podell had been cautious in booking Ella, fearing folks wouldn't pay his $5.50 minimum (believe it or not, a lot of money in those days) to see her unless they were a sophisticated, hip crowd. Ella totally won the engagement, opening with "This Can't Be Love," followed by "Angel Eyes."

Remember, ten years earlier African Americans were not allowed *into* the Copa, so this was quite a triumph. Even lovers of Ella's music in print never failed to mention that she was "a Negress," "colored," or "black." It must have been annoying to constantly have your incredible talent always be qualified by your skin color. Only performers who have been there could possibly understand what this meant.

Independence Day brought Ella to the famous Newport Jazz Festival in Rhode Island. Her set, along with that of Billie Holiday, was recorded and released on an album called, not surprisingly, *Ella and Billie at Newport*. Her program here was typical for that time, with a haunting version of "Body and Soul" the standout number. In my evaluation, Ella's versions of this song were the quintessential examples of a jazz ballad. The pure voice, the plaintive lyric, the interpretive reprise of the bridge and final chorus, and the trademark coda that is pure Ella made for the most perfect jazz ballad ever recorded. Her pianist was Don Abney, who traded chores with Paul Smith, Oscar Peterson, and Lou Levy during this phase of her career. Also of note was "I've Got a Crush on You," a holdover from her Decca album of Gershwin tunes with Ellis Larkins, also rerecorded for *The George and Ira Gershwin Songbook*.

One of the strangest public appearances Ella would ever make was four days later on July 8, 1957, in Atlantic City. In a gig with Louis Armstrong and the Lionel Hampton band, Ella was in the middle of a number when a twenty-nine-year-old man (who happened to be African American and also surnamed Fitzgerald, but no relation), leaped onto the stage of the Warner Theater, screamed, "You've got another man!" and punched Ella in the jaw. As she reeled back, musicians and police caught the man, a narcotics addict who had been treated for a mental disorder at a local veteran's hospital. Ella did not finish the show. She also did not press charges, as the man was sent to the Ancora State Hospital mental ward.

In the midst of all this activity (and breadwinning), Ella sold her house in New York and built one in Los Angeles for her and Ray, Jr. By this point, Ella was working so much (as was Ray, Sr.) that the boy was left to the care of relatives and household help while both Mom and Dad toured almost continually. Ella's income by this point had topped almost $400,000 per year, a fortune in those days (in fact, it's pretty damn good today).

Much was made in print around this time of Ella's "loneliness," this time changing the story of her success to include Chick Webb as coauthor on "Tisket," as well as adding in several more blood relatives to the supposedly "orphaned Ella." This was pretty lame stuff even for those days, the truth being that her life was in her music. Newspapers and magazines needed juicy stories, and while Ella was at the top of her field she just did not make for good press. There simply wasn't any gossip except for some of Ella's romances, and little was said about these (after all, people are allowed to date). As she would say in later years, "It's not that I loved too much, just too easily."

More was written about her love of ballads, and the effect that the Porter Songbook had on popular music. In the year since its release in the summer of 1956, Ella had become a pop icon, a gleaming banner in the fight for culture and "good" music that both she and Sinatra were to be identified with for the rest of their lives. Time has not embellished the words spoken about her work; the same words were being said in 1957 as they were in 1967 or 1977 or 1987.

Murray Kempton simply titled his *New York Post* column "She" in the summer of 1957, as he tried to define her special brand of musical sorcery:

She is by now a cultural force, a permanent tradition, a great river, if you please. She stands, remembering everything, anticipating everything, younger than any child, older than Robert Moses. Her audiences are indescribable. They look like people in from Scarsdale [a New York City suburb]. Do people in Scarsdale know about anyone of the truly first class except Ella Fitzgerald? They come, I suppose, because Ella Fitzgerald sings ballads and they buy the albums and, because of her and, of course, Sinatra, they know about Cole Porter and Larry Hart.

She remembers everything, absorbs everything, uses everything. She has become the propriatrix of the ballad; yet she will not let one set pass without singing a long jump tune, all interior reference, all parody, none of it possible to appreciate altogether without having heard every jazz record since Clarence Williams . . . she performs this miracle, one has finally to decide, because she never knows who may be listening. She sings for musicians.

Three eventful projects were worked on that summer. With the idea that success breeds success, Norman Granz got Ella and Louis back in the studio July 23 and August 13, 1957, to record *Ella and Louis Again*. With only a slight change in personnel from the original (Louie Bellson replaced Buddy Rich on the drums), this was one case where a follow-up album was just as good as the first. While Ella gave fuller treatment to each of the twelve songs on this album elsewhere (except for "Learning the Blues"), the collection was as charming and enchanting as their earlier project.

As with *Ella and Louis*, there were just head arrangements with the key and pattern worked out in advance. "Each musician felt his place in the pattern," said Bellson, "such as Herb Ellis knowing exactly what to do so as not to disturb the line by comping too much." "Stompin' at the Savoy" was a rare gem, in that it was a rehearsal cut that Granz decided was so clever he included it as the album version. Armstrong had to leave before the session was over, so three additional songs were recorded by Ella as solos. They were included on the LP release, but deleted from the CD version. It would be a waste of space to further describe the magic of Ella and Louis; get yourself a copy of one of these two albums.

Chapter Fourteen

1957–1958

*T*he only one of Ella's Songbook projects where the central figure was actually involved was *Ella Fitzgerald Sings the Duke Ellington Songbook*. Recorded on various dates in June, August, September, and October of 1957, this most ambitious of Ella's projects at that time involved the Duke, his band and entire working company. Almost all of the great Ellington tunes were given their due, although there were enough leftovers for yet another collaboration eight years later. Some were done in the big band setting, others with a small combo. The various solos contributed to the feeling of the album having been recorded in a jazz club instead of a studio. Thirty-eight numbers were treated (released on two double-record albums), two of them specially written for the album.

"Portrait of Ella Fitzgerald" was a sixteen-minute salute to Ella by the Duke and Billy Strayhorn. The piece is in four movements: Royal Ancestry, All Heart, Beyond Category, and Total Jazz. The other original piece was called "The E and D Blues" (E for Ella, D for Duke), an almost five-minute treatment in a blues tempo by two of the greatest exponents of jazz.

Many of the songs on the album followed Ella into the concert hall. No other Songbook gave Ella so many gems, many of them rerecorded on studio albums in later years. It is difficult to choose favorites from such a classic collection, but listen to "Sophisticated Lady" for a truly interesting treatment of a ballad, with featured jazz violin. "I Got It Bad (And That Ain't Good)" had been part of Ella's live repertoire for quite a while, but was treated here with a seldom-heard verse and throbbing saxophone solo after the first chorus.

As with any project, there were a few bumpy moments. The Duke had begun a popularity resurgence following his appearance at the Newport Jazz Festival in July 1956. His label, Columbia, was thrilled to be able to capitalize on his refound popularity. It was less than thrilled to have to loan him out to Verve. Once again, Norman Granz prevailed. How? He simply owned an exclusive contract on Johnny Hodges, Ellington's number-one sax man. Columbia's George Avakian got Hodges, and Granz got the Duke. Also, the Duke's Columbia contract restricted the time he was available to record. Almost half of the Songbook was done with small groups, without his involvement. And although he was asked to produce fresh arrangements for Ella, Ellington showed up at the sessions with the same old stuff. For the most part, Ella sang along with slightly altered versions of the band's standard arrangements.

Critical reaction to the Ellington collection was positive, to say the least. Jazz critic and historian Leonard Feather had this to say in the November 1957 issue of *Playboy*:

> Today's world of jazz is fat and sassy. So great is the embarrassment of riches served up in night spots, at concerts, on LPs, that the good performance is rejected as commonplace, the exceptional as merely acceptable. Rarely, then, does an event take place that can boost the pulse-beat of the jaded jazzophile. But such an event is the current release of Verve's *Ella Fitzgerald Sings the Duke Ellington Songbook*, a four-platter package that brings together—for the first time—two of jazzdom's greatest talents. That such jazz royalty should merge on LPs is as logical as serving caviar with champagne. During the series of recording sessions necessary to produce the four LPs, perfectionist Ellington was heard to complain that this had turned into one of the

most demanding tasks of his life. "With Ella up front," Duke
declared, "you've got to play better than your best."

Another sign of her growing stardom was the evening of July 20,
1957. With the 102 musicians of the Los Angeles Philharmonic led
by Frank DeVol, it was "Ella Fitzgerald Night" at the Hollywood
Bowl. This was the first of many such nights at the Bowl over the next
thirty-five years. They were all sellouts; 17,000 people per performance sat in the cool California evenings to listen to Ella Fitzgerald.

Norman Granz decided it was time for Ella to record some pop
tunes with no special theme, just great songs done with a top arranger
à la Sinatra. Talented Frank DeVol was brought in for a session on
July 24, 1957 (the day after the first session of *Ella and Louis Again*
was being recorded, and during the time the sessions for the Ellington
albums were done; one needs a scorecard to keep track as Ella so
frequently recorded).

These recordings shared a strange evolution to album form. Three
songs were never issued on wax. One song, "A-Tisket A-Tasket" (done
to a pseudo-Latin beat and recorded in the studio again for the first
time since 1938), was released as a single, and appeared later on a
compilation LP. Four songs later were included on *Get Happy*, a
compilation album released in 1959 (although the four were released
as singles first). Three more were held for *Hello Love*. This was a
collection of songs done that were recorded with DeVol at various
points in the late fifties, and released in 1960.

Though Ella was growing musically by leaps and bounds, personally
she repeated the same romantic mistakes again and again. Much in
the same way she had taken up with her first husband, so had Ella
gotten involved with a Norwegian named Thor Larsen. While the
New York Post had her married to the man, their romance was
thwarted when it was revealed that Larsen had been convicted of
stealing money from a former fiancée. He spent five months in Sweden serving prison time, and then was banned from the United States
for several years. It was her first husband all over again, except this
time his true colors were revealed before the wedding. There were
to be several more such "romances" in Ella's life in the coming years,
especially with Scandinavian men.

By 1957, *Porgy and Bess* had stopped being just an opera and became a show business legend. Written by George Gershwin, with lyrics by DuBose Heyward and Ira Gershwin, the original production had several shaky starts, with problematic writing, casting, and critiques. However, production after production all over the world, along with the untimely death of its composer, ensured that the opera would live in the annals of American music. Samuel Goldwyn was planning a splashy, Technicolor film version of the story, and Norman Granz grasped the opportunity to bring Ella and Louis back into the studio to record their version beginning on August 18, 1957.

Obviously, the two had to sing all the parts, so Ella sang all of the female roles and Louis the male (with the exception of "The Buzzard Song," also sung by Ella). The orchestration by Russ Garcia, himself very familiar with the Gershwin catalogue, provided the proper jazz-tinged but full-blown arrangements.

The obvious favorite from the album was the duet of "Summertime"; each took a chorus and threw in an extra one for Louis's horn. My personal favorite, however, was "I Wants to Stay Here," also known as "I Loves You Porgy." The lyrics were loosely lifted from the original play, and the melody was one George Gershwin pulled out of his trunk, having written it several years before. This arrangement of the song was reprised thirty years later by Barbra Streisand in her *Broadway Album*. With all respect to Ms. Streisand's enormous talent (perhaps second only to Ms. Fitzgerald's as a female vocalist), no one could sing this song like Ella. Only she was able to combine the jazz idiom, the girlish innocence that belied the deeper understanding, along with a total understanding of how the music and lyrics fit together. An additional song, "They Pass By," was recorded at this same session, but went unissued.

Ella's television appearance with Nat "King" Cole on September 10 was as much out of loyalty as a desire for exposure. Cole's show, an excellent variety series on NBC-TV, was floundering in the ratings. Middle America still would not accept an African American into their homes as the host of a show. Many show business greats came on to help Nat boost his ratings and gain wider acceptance, and Ella was no exception. The show was done as a live remote from the Copa Room of the Sands Hotel in Las Vegas. Guests who were acknowledged in the audience included Victor Borge, Vivian Blaine, Art Mooney, Spike Jones, Joey Bishop, and Milton Berle. Ella started her part of the show with the full orchestral arrangement of "Goody-Goody," then segued into "Bewitched" (without the verse) before she sang a duet with Nat on "It's All Right With Me." Ella's segment finished with another rendition of "You're the Top," this time with special lyrics used to allow Nat to compliment Ella with superlatives above and beyond Cole Porter's. The two worked together so well, and had such obvious respect and affection for one another, it was too bad contractual differences kept them from ever recording together.

One would think, with all this activity, that Ella would take a break. She certainly deserved a rest. However, the autumn of 1957 took her all over the United States, and back into the recording studio. The fall tour of the JATP was the last regularly scheduled one, as it became a once in a while thing thereafter. Ella performed with the JATP at the Chicago Opera House, which Granz recorded and released as *Ella at the Opera House*. Actually, this stereo album received very scant distribution, and was generally superseded by *another* album recorded on October 7 at the Shrine Auditorium in Los Angeles. Released with the same cover and title, this mono album (which also featured the Oscar Peterson Trio) had the same song lineup as its predecessor, with the elimination of "Them There Eyes" and the addition of an extemporaneous version of "Oh, Lady Be Good."

The rest of the lineup reflected Ella's recent recordings, as well as such recently recorded but unreleased jazz standards as "Don'cha Go 'Way Mad" and "Goody-Goody." The album was ballad-heavy, with beautiful renditions of "Bewitched," "These Foolish Things," "Ill Wind," and "Moonlight in Vermont." The highlight of the album, however, was Ella and the JATP All-Stars swinging a seven-minute "Stompin' at the Savoy." This was some of Ella's best scat singing on record, and a pleasure to hear with a big band backing her up.

"Oh, Lady Be Good" was interesting, for it did not follow the charts of Ella's hit recording. As an unrehearsed encore, the arrangement was pure head, played by ear with Ella and the jazz greats at hand. Strangely, there were no further recordings of Ella doing her up-tempo version of this song, while all the rest of her Decca bop songs were reprised more than once.

Up to this point, Ella's released albums had been Songbooks, live concerts, and duets with Louis Armstrong. On October 15 and again on October 28, Ella went into the studio to record an album of love

Ella by Bruno, 1941. *Courtesy Institute for Jazz Studies at Rutgers University.*

A 1942 glamour shot. *Courtesy Institute for Jazz Studies at Rutgers University.*

Ella in a glamorous
performance.
*Courtesy Institute
for Jazz Studies at
Rutgers University.*

A plaintive, expressive
face sans makeup, 1943.
*Courtesy Institute for
Jazz Studies at Rutgers
University.*

The Carnegie Hall debut with Dizzy Gillespie, 1947.
Courtesy Institute for Jazz Studies at Rutgers University.

The Sweetheart of Decca Records, 1950.
*Courtesy Institute for Jazz Studies at
Rutgers University.*

Singing her thank-yous at Basin Street East, 1954. *Courtesy Institute for Jazz Studies at Rutgers University.*

Miss Fitz, tunesmith Sammy Cahn, arranger Ray Heindorf, and Jack Webb on the set of *Pete Kelly's Blues*, 1954.
Courtesy Institute for Jazz Studies at Rutgers University.

Publicity shot with Steve Allen before her first *Tonight Show* appearance.
Courtesy Institute for Jazz Studies at Rutgers University.

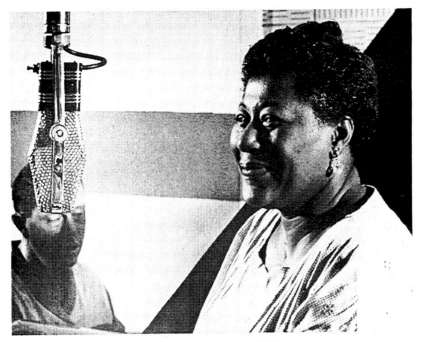

Recording *The Ellington Songbook*, 1956.
Courtesy Institute for Jazz Studies at Rutgers University.

An attempt to hide Ella's
more-than-ample figure, 1956.
*Courtesy Institute for Jazz
Studies at Rutgers
University.*

The beginning of a
long-time love affair:
Ella and Grammy, 1958.
*Courtesy Institute for
Jazz Studies at Rutgers
University.*

Each song was well done, but taken as a collection they were not as interesting as some of the other Songbooks. Once again, Norman Granz chose the tunes to be included, which seemed to rely heavily on songs pushed for popularity as opposed to reflecting the best of the Berlin catalogue (as both the Ellington and Gershwin Songbooks did for their composers).

While thirty-two songs were recorded, the obvious exclusions were peculiar. The overlooking of such Berlin classics as "They Say It's Wonderful," "My Walking Stick" (which Ella had recorded with Chick Webb), "The International Rag," "Easter Parade," "White Christmas," and "There's No Business Like Show Business," among others, is confusing, as one can imagine how well Ella could have made them her own.

Several of Ella's favorite musicians made appearances here, including Paul Smith, Harry "Sweets" Edison, and Jack Sperling. There were standouts, such as the driving "I've Got My Love to Keep Me Warm," and the Fred Astaire songs. Rarely heard Berlin songs like "Russian Lullaby" and "Now It Can Be Told" were trotted out and given new life with Ella's vocalizing and Weston's charming charts. "Get Thee Behind Me Satan," sung by Harriet Hilliard in the film *Follow the Fleet*, was a personal favorite of Weston's. He had harbored a huge crush on the future Mrs. Ozzie Nelson before meeting the future Mrs. Weston (singer Jo Stafford and a good friend of Ella's).

Overall, the album was pleasant and fun, several notches above the Bregman arrangements previously used in the Songbook series but pedestrian in comparison to the Ellington Songbook. Perhaps this is an unfair comparison, and certainly not a reflection on Paul Weston (a top-flight arranger who had gotten his start with the Dorsey organization and whose albums with Doris Day, Dinah Shore, and wife Jo are classics), or Ella's talent in the least. Ella was her usual gracious self, and had no say in the choosing of the material. She heard the arrangements for the first time in the studio. She was also a little nervous working with Weston, because as she told him the first day, "... If I hit a klinker you'll go home and tell your old lady." One additional cut, "Swinging Shepherd Blues," was recorded but was unused until the release of the CD *First Lady of Song*.

Interesting to note is a remark made by Paul Weston: "I never had a moment's trouble with Norman Granz in the studio. I did not feel rushed or hurried, and had all the time I needed to get the sound I wanted from the orchestra." It is fascinating how different people in the same circumstances see things in a different light. None of the other arrangers interviewed for this book were as generous in describing Granz's allowance of rehearsal time.

Time magazine liked the Berlin collection a lot better than some. In their October 6, 1958, issue, here is how they described it:

> En route Ella proves again that she is mistress of more moods than anybody else in the business. She bends her remarkable voice with sighing ease around tortuous, voice-trapping lyrics ("I want to peep through the deep, tangled wild wood/Counting sheep 'til I sleep like a child would"). Best of all, she takes the faded material and gives it a fresh emotional gloss.

In my opinion, it would have been better if she had given *great* material a fresh emotional gloss. Douglas Watt, in *Show* magazine, agreed:

> The least of [the songbooks], to my way of thinking, is the one concerned with Irving Berlin's product. The master of simplicity is here revealed as perhaps too simple to be taken in such a large dose. Then, too, a particular facet of Berlin's writings—his long preoccupation with two subjects, the weather and dancing—is likely to induce monotony. . . .

Also of note is Ella's quip to one of the beat generation upon the release of this album. When asked if it meant that Ella was going square, she simply answered, "I'm not going square, man, I'm going versatile!"

Chapter Fifteen

1958

$\mathcal{N}$orman Granz kept broadening and broadening the arenas in which Ella was presented. Booking her into the Los Angeles nitery the Moulin Rouge was a gamble, as it wasn't a regular gathering place for jazz aficionados. Ella's thirty-minute set won everyone, the entire packed house, as she and the Lou Levy Trio (along with Dick Stabile's orchestra) pulled the repertoire mostly from the Songbook albums.

In April, Ella contributed to a delightful special, "Swing Into Spring," hosted by Dave Garroway on NBC-TV and sponsored by Texaco. Garroway, an avid jazz fan, was in his element with the likes of Ella, Benny Goodman, Harry James, Red Norvo, Jo Stafford, the McGuire Sisters, Bambi Lynn, and Rod Alexander. The musicians were given a fairly free hand by producer/director Charles S. Dubin in choosing what they felt like performing, so they put their collective heads together to come up with the music.

Benny and Ella paired for a loose version of "Ridin' High," but the highlight of the show was a jam session with the entire cast. "Hard Hearted Hannah," from *Pete Kelly's Blues*, was given fresh treatment here by Ella, along with "I Got a Right to Sing the Blues" and a wild duet with Jo of "St. Louis Blues." This particular version was Jo's idea, as the assembled cast could not come up with an ending to the medley. "I had recently recorded 'Blues' with a swinging arrangement and a special material tag," recalls Mrs. Weston. "I sent for the arrangement from my home, and it and especially the tag were used on the show." Rehearsals were minimal (Norman Granz probably liked that) and limited to only four days for almost fifty-six minutes of continuous music. Both Ella and Jo were in superior voice and sparkled together, as they did three years later in London.

After completing the Berlin sides and the "Swing" show, Ella toured Europe. She spent her supposed fortieth birthday doing a concert in Rome. Later released as a CD on the Verve label, *Ella in Rome* showed her in peak form. Not only was she in magnificent voice, but for the first time the CD gave the listener a chance to hear her in an entire, full-length concert. Much of the material on the album was from the then-recently recorded Songbooks. Many of these songs were all available on other live albums as well, but the combination of them all together made for an exciting concert.

There were songs recorded here for the first time, such as "When You're Smiling," along with reprises of Decca classics "Angel Eyes" and "That Old Black Magic." The beautiful but seldom-heard verse was included in Ella's rendition of "These Foolish Things."

While the entire collection made for the most satisfying of albums, the highlight here was the live version of Gershwin's "I Loves You Porgy." While "Body and Soul" was a more perfect example of a jazz ballad, Ella's total control, use of nuance, and timing made this one of the most intriguing live ballads ever recorded. One almost held one's breath, waiting for Ella to falter, not being able to believe this level of perfection in a live environment. This effort was a good example of what made Ella's live albums such enjoyable experiences: the excitement of on-the-spot improvisation, along with such skill that if the applause were cut out, one would think the recordings were made in a studio, under perfect conditions.

"Sunday Night at the Palladium" was England's answer to the Ed Sullivan variety show. About her appearance, London's *Daily Mail* wrote (May 5, 1958):

Relaxed and carefree, the fabulous Miss Fitzgerald put a new gloss into every number she handled. For her opening, she took a fast, old Louis Armstrong number, "When You're Smiling," switched into a fluent version of "Midnight Sun" before paying Britain the compliment of singing Jack Strachey's lovable ballad, "These Foolish Things." Eyes shut, sometimes smiling to herself, Miss Fitzgerald put over the song in just about the greatest way it has ever been sung in this country.

Also at this time, Ella learned about the famous British press. And the British press learned about Ella's temper. While being asked such piercing questions as who her favorite singer was, zingers and barbs were hurled at her by reporters. Flashbulbs (one of her pet peeves) exploded in her face. All of this while she was trying to eat dinner at the Dorchester. She lost her cool. "I can only do one thing at a time," she called. "I can't look at all directions at once and answer questions at the same time. And you [turning to one persistent reporter], let me finish one question before you ask the next!"

Returning to California, Ella got an offer she couldn't refuse: guesting on "The Frank Sinatra Show" on ABC, May 9, 1958. It was the first of several classic appearances the two made together through the years; Frank and Ella were born to sing with one other. At the top of the heap and at the top of their forms, both their duets and solos were pure magic. Without creating too much commotion, here were two great singers enjoying the hell out of themselves. Audio of their duet was released on a bootleg LP from Retrospect records called *F.S.—The Television Years.*

Ella entered 'toon town with the release in 1958 of director John Hubley's seven-minute cartoon *The Tender Game.* It's simple boy-meets-girl plot featured Ella, along with the Oscar Peterson trio, doing "Tenderly." This is the only known example extant of Ella having lent her voice to a cartoon release, although her singing was featured in many films through the years for mood, background, or over the titles.

On July 1, 1958, Granz recorded Ella with a small group for two sides, "Your Red Wagon" and "Traveling Light." With Lou Levy on piano, Gus Johnson on drums, Max Bennett on bass, and Dick Hyman on organ, the sides were released as a single but remained primarily obscure until the 1993 CD release of "Wagon" on a Verve compilation, *The Essential American Singers*. "Wagon" was very different from the type of song Granz had Ella doing in those years, an almost straight-out rhythm-and-blues tune with a heavy emphasis on organ. It sounded more Ray Charles than Ella Fitzgerald in arrangement and meter, but it was pure Ella on the vocal. The phrase "your red wagon," by the way, was used as slang to mean "your problem."

On August 10, Ella began a week-long engagement at Mr. Kelly's, one of Chicago's premier nightclubs in the 1950s. Granz decided to record her sets there (mostly on opening night) for release as her next live album. He decided to call it *Ella Live at Mr. Kelly's*. The recorded output was tremendous, yet for reasons known only to Norman Granz, none of the recordings were ever released. More's the shame, for Ella was in top form, and many of these songs were never recorded by her again, live or otherwise. As this book went to press, there was a slim chance that Verve put some of this material on their release schedule for the mid-1990s.

Grass never grew under Ella's feet. When she wasn't recording, she was playing clubs or touring with the JATP. The tour that year (and many times thereafter) took her to Toronto to play Massey Hall. *Daily Star* writer Stan Rantin devoted his September 16, 1958, column to her concert costarring Oscar Peterson:

Musical seasons come and musical seasons go and so does jazz impresario Norman Granz. He has brought so many seasons into Toronto's Massey Hall in the past ten years, it looks as if we were in a permanent rut.

But last night Norman justified his existence with what was probably the best concert of jazz music this city has heard in several decades.

The great Ella Fitzgerald—and we mean "great" . . . put on a performance of such polish, such refined taste and such solid, swinging, happy high-class jazz they completely obliterated the memory of those sordid honk-and-squeal orgies that Granz once inflicted on Toronto audiences.

Even when she garbled up the lyrics on "Let's Do it," her quick sense of humor was able to turn the goof to advantage. With a casual, "I've done it," she broke the audience into peals of laughter.

One of the reasons that Ella became Granz's number-one star, besides her obvious talent, were reviews like the one just quoted. While Granz was always a respected producer of live jazz, with Ella's continuing ascendancy he became one of the top musical entrepreneurs in the world. Additionally, he was a major records producer, and owned his label outright. Both Ella and Granz had worked for years to solidify their reputations. Now that enormous success entered their lives, they both guarded it fervently.

Ella helped Dinah Shore see the USA in her Chevrolet for the first time on October 12, 1958, when she joined Peter Lawford, Jimmy Durante, and Julius LaRosa on "The Dinah Shore Chevy Show" in color on NBC. Dinah's hour-long music extravaganzas were an outgrowth of her three-times-per-week fifteen-minute program. These shows had filled out the half hour that the then–fifteen minute evening news appeared in. Dinah had the top guests on television (save for Ed Sullivan), and did her show three weeks out of every four.

Much of the set and costume design was used to promote color television, then still very new. Very few homes had color televisions, but NBC was gearing up to be the all-color network, with Dinah, Perry Como, Howdy Doody, and several daytime shows broadcasting in color so that RCA dealer showrooms had something to show on their color sets for sale.

Marty Paich picked up the baton for the next "swing" session, *Ella Swings Lightly*, recorded in Los Angeles on November 22 and 23. The marriage of Ella's swing and Marty's zing made for perhaps the most mature Fitzgerald album to date. There was the beginning of a change in Ella's voice, a more mature, smoother, and self-assured sound that began to exhibit itself, especially in this album. Eighteen songs were recorded at this session, all to be later released in the 1992 CD version on Verve. A wonderful melange of swings, ballads, Broadway, and bop, *Ella Swings Lightly*, more than any other album up to that time, showed Ella's versatility, jazz roots, and ability to swing *anything*.

By that point, it was obvious that Ella's dominance as a singer was second only to Sinatra's, yet even the Chairman of the Board could not bop. Outstanding are "You Hit the Spot" and "Little Jazz," Ella's tribute to Roy Eldridge (both the master and alternate cuts appear on the CD). "Blues in the Night" and "If I Were a Bell" were both

later rerecorded in other collections, but I prefer these Paich arrangements. There are so many gems here, it is difficult to give an impartial
analysis without simply listing all the songs and saying "marvelous."
Several were almost totally unrecorded except for Ella's versions in
this album.

Paich, whose "dektette" brought a new sound to the world of jazz,
was an arranger and musician who really understood Ella's approach
to music and recording. "Norman chose the songs and brought them
to me; Ella had no part in it," says Marty. "I went to her house in
Beverly Hills to check the keys of the songs and generally discuss the
approach. She was very open to my input and direction. She never
heard the actual arrangements until we were in the studio, and thankfully she fell right into it because Norman didn't give us a lot of time
to rehearse. He never understood the need to work things out in the
studio, that what worked on paper might need some fine tuning with
the singer and the musicians at hand. Ella became queen of the one-
take singers."

Frank DeVol reentered the scene the following day, November 24,
1958, with the recording of *Sweet Songs for Swingers*, a studio album
featuring ballads and easy-swing tunes. One can only imagine the
impact Frank Sinatra had on the entire recording industry at this time,
with the inclusion of the word "Swingers" in the title. It was the
second of several times Ella would use the word "swing" in the coming years, but in Ella's case it referred mostly to her music. While my
personal favorites were "Gone With the Wind," "Let's Fall in Love,"
and "I Remember You," there was an infectious giggle in "Makin'
Whoopee" and "Lullaby of Broadway" that added extra zest to the
collection. Some seldom-recorded tunes such as "Sweet and Lovely,"
"Moonlight Serenade," and "East of the Sun" were given their fair
due. How many songs has Ella snatched from obscurity simply by
including them on albums like this one?

Ella finished her year with a video visit with Mr. Television himself,
Milton Berle. Berle had lost his landmark show "The Texaco Star
Theater," later called "The Buick Berle Show," in the middle fifties,
and was hosting "The Kraft Music Hall." On December 3, 1958, Ella
was paired with vaudeville's George Jessel on the Kraft show which
would become the domain of Perry Como the following year.

Chapter Sixteen

1959

*T*he year 1959 was a big year for Ella on television.

It started with her first of several appearances on "The Garry Moore Show." Moore was a busy man, with a very popular evening variety hour on CBS, as well as a daytime show and the hosting chores of Goodson-Todman's panel show, "I've Got a Secret." Among Moore's sidekicks on the evening hour were Durward Kirby, Marion Lorne ("Bewitched's" Aunt Clara), and a young Carol Burnett. On January 13, 1959, Ella shared guest duties with Andy Griffith. Griffith at that time was negotiating with Danny Thomas to film one of his shows in which Andy played the sheriff of a small town where Danny gets arrested. This eventually became the pilot for "The Andy Griffith Show." This was an exciting era in television, as legends rose from vacuum tubes at a dizzying rate.

Ella made her first appearance on the then extremely prestigious "The Bell Telephone Hour" on February 10, 1959. The "Hour" was a full-color, highbrow variety program produced and sponsored by the Bell Telephone Company and appearing approximately twelve times a year. Appearing on the program was considered a coup, for it was always lavishly produced in great taste. Each program was different from the next; one month it was Wagnerian opera selections from the great voices of the world, and the next Ethel Merman, Ray Bolger, and Beatrice Lillie shared memories of the Broadway stage in comedy and music. Ella's first show was entitled "American Festival," and featured the New York City Ballet and Rise Stevens, with Ella and the Duke Ellington Orchestra doing a medley of Duke's tunes. It was extremely well received, with no hint of the problems surrounding her next appearance on the program.

The major recording project for 1959 would be Ella's greatest challenge to date: a five-record tribute to the music of the Gershwins. *The George and Ira Gershwin Songbook* (recorded January 5, 7, and 8; March 18 and 26; July 15–18; and August 20) carried a long list of firsts: the first of many album collaborations between Ella and Nelson Riddle as arranger, the first (and only) of her Songbooks to be released in five separate albums, the first of her projects to be released in a deluxe boxed set, the first of her albums to have special artwork created for the cover (by Bernard Buffett), and the first of her projects to have extensive liner notes written for it in booklet form. A total of fifty-three Gershwin songs were treated here; some were classics and some had been little heard since their original Broadway or Hollywood productions.

Perhaps we should start with the principals, Fitzgerald and Riddle. "Ella sings *The George and Ira Gershwin Songbook*. That was the big thing for me," remembered Nelson in the early 1980s. "André Previn picked up on that. He heard it and he was amazed that I was able to approach fifty-nine [sic] sides with such a variety of ideas. Ella was a doll. She's so sweet."

During this same period, Ella recalled (in a radio interview):

"I remember that there were songs in there that I just felt, 'My gosh, I can't sing that type of song,' and then on the other hand I felt like it was a challenge. The first one that they [the Gershwins] wrote ["The Real American Folk Song"], that was a lot of fun, but I mean I said, 'Oh my gosh, what am I gonna do singing that song?' But then after we did it I liked it because [humming a few bars], well, I really liked that. Norman loved Ira Gershwin. They were very good friends, you know, and he could find songs. [Ella had wanted to sing that first song, but could not find music for it. Norman Granz called his friend

Ira Gershwin, and Ella had her music.] 'But Not for Me' is one of my favorite songs, both the lyrics and the melody. We've done that number three times, with two pianists [Larkins in the 1940s and Previn in the 1980s] and Nelson."

Riddle also had some insight into the complicated Fitzgerald-Granz relationship, once remarking:

"She and Norman have had a longtime relationship, sometimes stormy. I think she leans on Norman a great deal. I know that he has considerable affection for her. Whatever comes out of his mouth is not necessarily a true reflection of his feelings. He becomes irritated with her occasional petulance. They quite often battle about the type of songs she should do. Norman wins more often than not. It so happens that it's his [Verve and later Pablo] record company. But she's his prime client. I think that the relationship between them has an undercurrent of affection and mutual respect which perhaps is even hidden from them."

"Oh, Lady Be Good" was another inspiration of Norman Granz. Rather than rerecording Ella's up-tempo romp, Granz wisely had Ella sing the song as originally intended as a sweet, innocent ballad, including the verse. (A word about verses: Ella almost always sang the verses to songs in her Songbook series whenever possible, leaving an audio legacy of songs as they were originally presented.) With reference to this number, Ella once said, "We've always done it fast. I love the way we did it in the album, did it slow. And the first time we tried it somewhere, it was surprising. The people said, 'Oh, we never knew it was so pretty.' " She also giggled at the lyric to "Who Cares" (. . . who cares what banks fail in Yonkers . . .). "I'll never forget the lyrics because I *came* from Yonkers."

For "I Got Rhythm," Ella and Nelson wisely chose to swing easy and bright, and not compete with Ethel Merman's signature belt and extended notes. Sweet but low-down renditions of "Sam and Delilah," "My Cousin in Milwaukee," "The Half of It Dearie Blues," "Treat Me Rough," and "Lorelei" once again showed how Ella could take a sophisticated but ever-so-slightly risqué ditty and keep the sophisticated, keep the risqué, but envelope the entire thing in good-natured humor and even innocence. It was a very fine line to walk, and Ella balanced it expertly.

"Love Is Here to Stay," the last song George Gershwin wrote (from

The Goldwyn Follies), was given pure jazz treatment, with big band brass and muted trumpet solo by Roy Eldridge. This arrangement was a huge winner, one that Ella used when she sang with a swing orchestra or symphony. "How Long Has This Been Going On?," "S'Wonderful," and "A Foggy Day" all followed Ella into the live arena, each approached in a completely different manner. "S'Wonderful" was often done with a full symphony orchestra; "How Long" was usually reserved for voice and piano or trio; and "A Foggy Day" was sung and swung by everything from Joe Pass's guitar to the San Francisco Symphony.

"The Man I Love," perhaps Gershwin's most simple but effective ballad, was treated just that way by Ella: simple but effective. It became a permanent part of her live repertoire, as did "They Can't Take That Away From Me," which appeared on three live albums as well as her Gershwin album with André Previn (see The Pablo Years for complete details). The first time through Ella gently swung through the song, then picked up the power on a second burlesque through the song. Once again, Paul Smith's piano accompanied Ella.

As far as working with Riddle was concerned, Ella was quoted as saying:

". . . He's a singer's arranger and a gentleman. When you see him you'd never even think he was a musician. He's everything combined. He should be in the Hall of Fame because what he's done for so many artists is just unbelievable. He has made a lot of people—people you don't even think can sing—he can make them sound good. He gets better and better. I just love him. I think it's like two people just jell."

Of Riddle (and Ella), singer Linda Ronstadt (who recorded three Riddle-arranged albums in the 1980s) recalled, "I listened to Ella because my father was a fan. I noticed the difference between Nelson's charts and other arrangers of that time was that Nelson really understood what the jazz part was doing so he was able to deliver these arrangements that were a synthesis between jazz and orchestra."

The George and Ira Gershwin Songbook sold more than 100,000 copies in its first sixty days. That was an amazing number for a five-record set. In the 1960s, after the collection was pulled from general release, Norman Granz offered it through a special mail-order promotion. It, too, sold very well.

Taking out time for television, Ella again guested with Dinah Shore on March 8, 1959. Fellow performers Tony Randall and Betty Grable joined Ella and Dinah in a rousing musical comedy sketch satirizing what television would have been like in the Roaring Twenties. This gave Ella the opportunity to sing snatches of many twenties torch songs. The finale of the show also featured her in a production number based on the song "Alabamy Bound." Ella journeyed across the hall at NBC Burbank to do "The Eddie Fisher Show" on March 17. Again appearing in color, the usual stools were there to provide a place to sit while Ella and Eddie munched their way through a duet.

On March 25, 1959, Ella returned to the studio with Frank DeVol, recording the rest of the songs that would be included on the *Hello Love* album the following year. "You Go to My Head," "Willow Weep for Me," and "I'm Through With Love" were lushly arranged ballads that went well with the already recorded songs for use on the album. Also recorded at the same time, but unissued, were "I've Grown Accustomed to His Face," "Spring Will Be a Little Late This Year," "Pennies From Heaven," "Great Day," and "Detour Ahead."

Ella then appeared on a companion program to the earlier aired "Swing Into Spring." This time Benny Goodman hosted the show which was aired in April. Besides Ella and Benny, the other stars included Peggy Lee, Lionel Hampton, Shelly Mann, and the Hi-Los. Ella's contributions included Gershwin's "S'Wonderful" along with "Mountain Greenery," "The Gentleman Is a Dope," and "I Must Have That Man." She sang some duets with Peggy Lee, but most of the Texaco-sponsored hour belonged to Benny. The following month Ella returned to New York to appear on Garry Moore's program, where she shared vocalizing with Mel Torme and Jean Carroll.

The rest of Ella's year was taken up with touring, television, and recording. On May 4, 1959, the very first Grammy awards were handed out for excellence in the recording industry. Ella won two awards, one for Best Vocal Performance—Female, for *The Irving Berlin Songbook*, and one for Best Jazz Performance—Individual, for *The Duke Ellington Songbook*. Naturally, Ella was the first person to win two awards in one year, a record that was to stand until she did it again the following year.

Once again, Ella's voice was heard on the soundtrack to a film in 1959. Director Walter Lang came out with *But Not for Me*, the third screen adaptation of Samson Raphaelson's stage hit *Accent on Youth*. Ella's voice was heard under the credits, using the singles version from the Gershwin Songbook.

Frank DeVol and Ella again teamed up on July 11, 1959, for a recording session that would fill out the forthcoming *Sweet Songs for Swingers* album, as well as the forthcoming *Get Happy* compilation. The winner here is "Gone With the Wind," an easy snapper that Ella swings at a brighter pace than most singers allow this number. A morose number done at ballad tempo, the extra finger-snap allows the energy of lost love to come through without a desire to slash one's wrists.

On September 3, 1959, the studio again beckoned Ella, this time to work on several projects at once. With Russ Garcia at the baton, she recorded "Beat Me Daddy, Eight to the Bar." "Beat Me Daddy" was pure swinging boogie-woogie. Although credited to Garcia, Marty Paich arranged the next two songs, "Like Young" and "Cool Breeze." "Like Young" was an André Previn song done with a "cool jazz" feel that was becoming very popular in the late 1950s and early '60s. "Cool Breeze" was Ella's first bop song with a big band arrangement since her Decca days, and it simply blasted off. She still did this arrangement into the 1980s.

All of these songs found their way onto the *Get Happy* melange, along with "Blue Skies" from the Berlin album, and two songs recorded for the Gershwin Songbook but not used because someone finally figured out that the lyrics were not by Ira Gershwin. "Somebody Loves Me" was a Ballard MacDonald–Buddy De Sylva–George Gershwin collaboration, while "Cheerful Little Earful" was a Harry Warren–Ira Gershwin–Billy Rose effort. Both had arrangements by Nelson Riddle, but were withheld for *Get Happy* when the mistake was realized. *Happy* also saw the beginning of the Granz use of "candid" pictures of Ella to grace album covers. This one, a color photo of Ella in a polka-dot dress, did not flatter her. One also wonders why the album was called *Get Happy*, when that song does not appear on the album.

Recorded at the same session (with arrangements by Garcia) were "The Christmas Song" and "The Secret of Christmas." The version of the former was much different from the version Ella recorded the following year on her holiday album. Neither was on an album until the 1990s, when Verve released a Christmas CD compilation containing both of these cuts.

More and more, Norman Granz focused his energies on Ella Fitzgerald. Not all of the Granz "family" was happy with this ever-increasing focus on Ella. Some of his JATP All-Stars began to leave the fold, searching out managers and record labels that gave them more artistic freedom. Those who stayed weren't exactly thrilled, either.

"It soon became obvious that Ella was Norman's main girl," reminisced Anita O'Day in her autobiography, *High Times, Hard Times*, written with George Eels. "She wasn't going to get most of the good stuff, she was going to get it all. I was an afterthought, a tax write-off . . . was it chance to put me with (Paich, May, Garcia) first, listen to the results and then pair the goodies with Ella? . . . I don't think there's any question Norman respected Ella for more than her talent. She is a straight cat who doesn't drink hard liquor, take drugs or make waves. That made her one of the few easy people to handle around Verve."

Further evidence of Granz's concentration on Ella was his decision to start featuring her as a solo attraction. He built entire concerts around Ella, with no other musicians present except for her trio or quartet. Morris Duff, staff writer for the *Toronto Daily Star*, wrote of her first solo concert there on September 25, 1959:

Norman Granz unveiled a mystifying jazz concert at Massey Hall last night. It was offered as a piece of pioneering which would demonstrate that one artist—in this case Ella Fitzgerald—was sufficient for one full evening's jazz entertainment.

Many jazz fans were frightened off by the prospect of a full night with even so great an artist as Ella. The result was a hall obviously less than half full.

But the size of an audience is not of the greatest importance when one is out to prove a theory. It may only show that Granz is ahead of his time. And by intermission, it seemed that as long as the singer was Ella Fitzgerald, the Granz theorem would hold.

With the passage of time, it seems incredible that an evening of Ella Fitzgerald had been deemed an experiment. However, this was the beginning of Ella's pulling away from her JATP roots. While there were more JATP tours, more and more often Ella appeared alone. The small clubs were a thing of the past. Ella only appeared in the top supperclubs, hotels, concert halls, and, finally, Las Vegas. Her Songbooks gave her a repertoire that enabled her to perform "pops" gigs in Vegas and with symphony orchestras, leaving her traditional jazz numbers at the door. In four short years, Ella and Norman made Ella a millionaire. Ella would have been able to answer that heckler who, so many years before at the Harlem Opera House, had shouted, "What's *she* gonna do?" By 1959, she could have answered, "I'm a superstar."

Chapter Seventeen

1959–1960

Get Happy was finally released, and the reviews were surprisingly excellent. For a hodgepodge of songs, arranged by different people and recorded at different times, the album received four-star ratings. The following review appeared in the *London Times* in early 1960:

Using strictly popular material, Miss Fitzgerald takes complete control here and swings delightfully throughout this album.

She is characteristically adept with the carefully turned phrase and tempo elasticity, as in "Feel So Young." Her scatting is clever, even breathtaking. "Blue Skies" and "St. Louis Blues" contain her most interesting passages. In "Blue Skies," Miss Fitzgerald hits the opening notes with startling accuracy. "Goody-Goody" is another technical showcase for the vocalist as she carries the tune from one key to another with effortless grace.

The album contains its most effective quiet moment in "Moonlight," in which the vocalist treats the tune with tenderness and simplicity.

A representative album by one of the great jazz singers.

Ella must have truly enjoyed doing television shows sponsored by Chevrolet, for besides the numerous appearances with Dinah Shore, Ella visited "The Pat Boone–Chevy Showroom." Taped on October 8, 1959, and broadcast on October 29, Boone's other guest was John Zackerly. "Zacherly," as he was known, was an actor who hosted a local New York television show on WOR-TV on Saturday nights. Dressed like a ghoul, he hosted his late-night horror movie from a coffin, and began a fad that would sweep local stations in every major market. His contribution was a "ghoul" sketch as the show saluted Halloween. "But Not for Me" and "Beat Me Daddy, Eight to the Bar" were Ella's solo contributions. At the break during "Beat Me Daddy," she danced and got spontaneous audience applause twice.

Pat and Ella's medley viewed what they called the five stages of love. While the two stools were not used for the duet this time, the songs were "Riding High," "When I Lost My Baby" (Ella implored, "Sing pretty for the people"), "Making Whoopee," "I Wish I Were in Love Again," and "It Don't Mean a Thing (If It Ain't Got That Swing)." Mort Lindsey, later to be Judy Garland's conductor and arranger, put this medley together.

Ella soon made several more TV appearances, with old friends. A week after taping the Boone show she returned to Garry Moore, on October 13, sharing the spotlight with Carl Ballantine (*McHale's Navy's* Gruber) and the Dukes Of Dixieland. In November Ella was honored at the second annual Grammy awards, even though it had only been six months since the last awards were handed out. Again, Ella copped two trophies, one as Best Vocal Performance—Female, for "But Not for Me" from *The George and Ira Gershwin Songbook*, and one for Best Jazz Performance–Soloist, for *Ella Swings Lightly*. The proceedings, held in Hollywood on November 29, were shown on NBC as part of a program called "Sunday Showcase," actually a varied series of Sunday night specials

In between television dates Ella played various concerts in Europe that fall of 1959, into early winter 1960. The only released example of her live work at this time appeared on a Japanese CD on the Denon label, *The Best of the Jazz Singers*. Along with Sarah Vaughan, Carmen McRae, Ruth Brown, and Dakota Staton heard doing a song or two, a portion of a 1959 Ella concert in Italy was featured. Here Ella harked back a bit more to the old days, with reprises of "Lover Come Back to Me" (including the updated lyric of "you cooled on me and I'm drugged as can be"), "Angel Eyes," and "My Heart Belongs to Daddy" from her album with Ellis Larkins. Also remembered were a Porter standard and an Ellington ballad, both on other live albums, as well as the perennial "Air Mail Special."

Controversy reared its head when Ma Bell beckoned for the second time in 1959 on November 20 with a "Bell Telephone Hour" entitled "The Music of Gershwin." Appearing with such other fans of good music as Polly Bergen, Vic Damone, and André Previn, Ella and pianist Teddy Wilson did "Oh, Lady Be Good" as their contribution to the festivities. There was, however, a problem.

Ella's earlier visit required the services of the Ellington organization, an African-American singer backed by an all African-American band. For this gig, Ella had Teddy Wilson and the rest of her regular combo, which at that time (and at various points through her career depending on which top musicians were available) was racially mixed. The folks at Bell Telephone got nervous, worrying what the people at home might think about ethnically mixed musicians playing together. NBC didn't care, as their orchestras had been mixed for years (and usually off-camera), but this was back in the days when sponsors still ruled the airwaves. Today, it is inconceivable that this issue would even be brought up, but in 1959 this was still common practice. Until the early seventies, network logs consistently kept records of African-American performers appearing on their broadcasts by putting an X or a C next to their names.

The producers requested that the quartet be all one color or the other, but preferably the other. (What would folks think if Ella had all white musicians behind her?) Ella was incensed, and Norman Granz threatened to pull Ella off the show and let everyone know why. With only one day until live air time, with a show already rehearsed and the prestige of the Bell Telephone Company on the line, a compromise was negotiated. Ella and Teddy appeared in front of a translucent curtain, while the rest of the group was behind the curtain in silhouettes. The audience couldn't tell if it was Ella's trio or the Nairobi Trio playing behind her. So much for NBC being the full-color network. Granz was beside himself. He took out a two-page ad in *Variety* that read partially as follows:

I manage Ella Fitzgerald. A few months ago I was approached by the representatives of Henry Jaffe, who packages a show called *The Bell Telephone Hour*. I was asked if Ella Fitzgerald could appear on that show's "Tribute To Gershwin," and of course I readily assented. . . . I was asked if I would approve of Teddy Wilson's Trio appearing with Ella Fitzgerald, and I agreed to that. . . . About a week before the show began its rehearsals, I was called by Al Lapin, the contractor for the show, and was asked if I would approve of Ella's bassist and drummer appearing with Teddy Wilson in place of the two regular members of Wilson's trio. . . . I also suggested that Teddy could use Ella's guitarist. . . . [that] when the Wilson Trio backs Ella it will have to be a quartet because the guitarist must appear with Ella. He said he would get back to me.

An hour later I received a call from Barry Wood, the producer, and his opening statement was, "If you insist on using the guitarist, okay, but it will have to be a Negro guitarist instead of a white one. . . ." I said that if that was so, I would pull Ella off the show, and after further argument he finally consented to the white guitarist. . . .

I submit that [NBC-TV] concern itself with the principles of human rights and human dignities rather than the fixing of quiz shows. They must concern themselves with sponsors' policies which foster racial prejudice—the worst kind of prejudice in America. It isn't even a question, as is often put, of the eyes of the world upon us; it's simply respect for our fellow man. . . . Signed, Norman Granz.

In an unusual invasion of Ella's desire for privacy, she consented to appear on CBS's "Person to Person." For those too young to remember, Edward R. Murrow began this program as a live, informal chat with a famous person in his or her home. Many of Ella's contemporaries and the greats of show business and other fields had appeared, including Frank Sinatra, Ethel Waters, Ethel Merman, Groucho and Harpo Marx, and Grandma Moses to name just a few. By this point, Murrow had retired from CBS to work for the government, and Charles Collingwood had taken over.

Ella was naturally ill at ease (as many of "Person" 's guests were), but did give some sage advice on what she felt was wrong with young singers: "They package young singers without slowly building up their careers. Folks come to see them in a club and all they've got is that one song." The living room and den of Ella's Beverly Hills home got television coverage, as well as her four Grammy awards and auto-graphed pictures from such friends as Sinatra, Dinah Shore, Nat Cole, and manager Norman Granz.

Frank Sinatra also asked her to appear on his television special, "An Afternoon With Frank Sinatra." Having lost the ratings war with his series the previous season, Sinatra now was appearing in intermittent specials. This one was supposed to be produced live from Frank's new base, Palm Springs, outdoors on the sand. The show was telecast December 13, and the only pretaped number was done by Juliet Prowse, who required video magic to change her costume several times during a dance to Cole Porter music.

As often happened in live television, problems arose: a freak rain-storm hit the desert, and the cast and crew had to quickly scramble into a studio and reblock the action. The only set pieces were black wooden chairs as might be found in a nightclub, stacked up to rep-resent tables, bridges, or other things that might make the bare stage look interesting. Ella was found sitting in a chair, and simply sang "There's a Lull in My Life" from the DeVol album. Frank joined her for a special material duet of "Can't We Be Friends." Ella looked a little self-conscious, as she always did when performing this kind of material on television. She was also featured in the finale of the show, as Frank announced the release of the Gershwin albums, and the cast plus Ella sang a medley of songs from the collection.

Ella inaugurated 1960 by making an appearance on "The Dinah Shore Chevy Show." Broadcast live and in color on NBC, the show featured Ella joined by the Limeliters, Howard Duff, and Ida Lupino on January 10 for yet another standout video gig. Ella's solos were "Misty," done with a trio plus strings, and the big band blast of "Cool Breeze." While the audience made its pleasure known with quite a bit of applause, they went berserk after Ella and Dinah dueted to a medley of blues songs. This cleverly arranged medley, which included snippets of such songs as "Memphis Blues" and "St. Louis Blues" was done with such good spirits, such high energy, and with both ladies in such good voice, that it was truly spectacular. With all her years as a television hostess, one sometimes forgot what an outstanding singer Dinah Shore was. (Both she and Ella had started in the business at the same time.)

On February 13, 1960, Ella was booked to open the JATP's next season at the West Berlin Deutschlandhalle. Appearing in front of an estimated 12,000 people, Ella sang a usual concert: a compendium of songs from her recent albums. With the accompaniment of Paul Smith and his quartet, the eventual album began with "Gone With the Wind" from *Sweet Songs for Swingers*, followed by "Misty," "The Lady Is a Tramp" from Rodgers and Hart, "The Man I Love," "Lorelei," and "Summertime" from Gershwin, and "Too Darn Hot" from Porter.

Ella was in excellent voice, and her choices alone would have made for a good concert and enjoyable album. However, she decided to spice the concert with a request for her to sing the brand-new pop hit, "Mack the Knife." "There was no sense that this night was going to be anything special," says Paul Smith. "We were starting a very draining tour. It wasn't long, but Norman had double-booked us, and sometimes we would do a 7 P.M. show in one city, race to the airport, and land to do an 11 P.M. show in another city. There was certainly no thought to making recording history."

"Mack the Knife" was originally written for the show *The Threepenny Opera* with music by Kurt Weill, and both Bobby Darin and Louis Armstrong had recently recorded hit versions of the number in a pseudo-pop, pseudo–rock 'n' roll arrangement. Ella, being in good spirits, thought she'd take on the challenge, and what followed was recording history. She started off by saying ". . . We'd like to try to do something for you now, and we've never heard a girl doing it. We hope we remember all of the words." With the tape rolling and in front of a capacity audience, Ella simply forgot the words.

She got to the first chorus all right, but when the lyric came to "on a tugboat / down by the river . . ." Ella blanked out. Other performers would have frozen, or stopped the song altogether. With a twinkle in her voice, Ella's next sung lyrics were "What's the next chorus / to this song now? / this is the one now / I don't / But it was a swinging tune / and a hit tune / so we tried to do / Mack the Knife." The audience just exploded, both at her daring and at her honesty. Ella then used the song as a vehicle, singing the lyrics when she could remember them, making up her own when she couldn't. One chorus started "Bobby Darin and Louis Armstrong / they made a record / oh, but they did / And now El, now Ella / Ella and her fellas / we're making a wreck / of Mack the Knife." Few can imagine anyone with enough fast thinking, good humor, self-assurance, and talent to carry that off except Ella.

(And this wasn't the first time Ella had pulled this kind of trick out of her bottomless vocal bag. "She once played a club in Omaha when Frankie Laine's 'Mule Train' was a tremendous hit," recalled Tim Gale. "One of the biggest spenders in Omaha came in consistently and demanded that she sing it. She kept ducking it until finally the club boss begged her to please the money guy. Ella said to herself, 'I'll sing it in such a way that he'll never ask for it again' and proceeded to do a burlesque so stupendous that on leaving town she kept it in the act and scored riotously with it everywhere—even at Bop City.")

It is unimaginable what could possibly have followed this number, except for Ella's high-speed, extended scat of "How High the Moon." She lengthened the perennial showstopper to more than eight minutes, throwing in snatches of "Stormy Weather," "Smoke Gets in Your Eyes," "Ornithology," and other songs as she scatted at a tempo that could make the listener dizzy. On one extended section, Ella did not even have musical accompaniment, only drummer Gus Johnson helping her keep time. Yet, Ella never lost her beat, never lost a note, never fumbled, paused, or hesitated even for a second. The sheer genius of this talent is astounding.

These last two numbers, along with the rest of those mentioned, were released by Verve as *Ella in Berlin*. The album won her a Grammy as Best Vocal Performance Album–Female, and another Grammy for Best Vocal Performance–Single or Track, for "Mack the Knife." A best-seller, this remains perhaps Ella's best live album.

Several other numbers were also recorded at that time, but were cut to fit onto one LP. A special CD reissue of the concert, released by Verve in August of 1993, included four previously unreleased tracks. "That Old Black Magic" followed the same course as the cut from her 1958 Rome album. "Love Is Here to Stay," from the Gershwin Songbook, was the only released example of Ella doing the song in front of a live audience. Two more songs, "Love for Sale" and "Just One of Those Things," were taken from the original Dutch Masters release of the Porter album in Holland. The liner notes from this special reissue seem confused as to the exact running order of the show. Conflicting reviews and running times made it uncertain whether all these numbers actually came from one show. Actually, there were two shows that night, but not in Berlin. For the second show, Granz flew his cast to a now-forgotten second European city.

Max Jones, in his column in England's *Melody Maker*, did not rave about the album upon its original release:

> The songs are those we have heard at most of her British concerts. The accompanists are the same, the performance is, as ever, highly professional . . . for the same reason . . . though the singing is technically good—sometimes superb—we are sometimes conscious of the effort, which is unusual for this personification of vocal perfection . . . one point must be made: the majority of these songs have been recorded by Ella before.

Mr. Jones may have missed the point. Ella always mixed up her bag of songs to include the old and the new. Riding high on a tremendous output of recordings, Ella was doing a sampling of what had made her such a success. Her repertoire in Europe always rested heavily on Cole Porter, due to the incredible impact of that album there. As a jazz album, it was tops. If Mr. Jones was looking for a pop album, he should have bought Peggy Lee.

Upon returning to the states, Norman Granz got Ella busy on television, and in the recording studio on three special projects. She made her last appearance on "The Garry Moore Show" for quite a while on March 29, 1960. Guesting on the show with Mel Torme, Ella fulfilled her four contracted shows and was not invited back on the show for four years. This was fairly common in those days, where performers would often do several stints with just one or two variety shows one year, then move to another the next.

On March 5, 1960, the newspapers were again full of reports that Ella was involved in a new betrothal, wearing an engagement ring from a non-musician American. Nothing much came of this. Ella never did get married again, nor was this person's identity ever revealed. More importantly, it had no impact on her career or her music. A publicist's idea? This was the same type of subterfuge that press agents had been planting for years about Ella. In fact, this exact story had been printed while she was dating Ray Brown. When Ella had a discrete romance, it did *not* make the papers.

At this point in her career, there was virtually no personal life. While she would occasionally bemoan her schedule and wish she could stay home a little more often and spend time with Ray, Jr., the fact is that no one was putting a gun to her head. Norman Granz booked her, but he couldn't *make* her perform.

She was aware that she was Norman's pet project, and eventually became his only focus. Perhaps she worked hard in order to get his approval, for although she was a woman in her forties and spent a great deal of her time fighting with him, Norman Granz was for all intents and purposes the man in her life. Certainly she dabbled with men, even keeping an apartment in Denmark to spend time with a local sweetheart on the short vacations Granz allowed her during her European tours. But Granz was the one she looked to: daddy, friend, companion, director, boss, brother, and antagonist. He wanted her to work, and by now she knew no other life. The die was cast.

Chapter Eighteen

1960–1961

$\mathcal{O}$n April 4, 1960, Ella sang on the annual Oscar telecast (after all, she had made three major motion pictures in five years). It was a humorous experience for her and conductor André Previn. The previous year, Previn had won the Oscar but could not attend in person as he was conducting for Ella at the Americana Hotel in New York. That year, he won again and got to accept in person. As he walked offstage he ran into Ella, who said, "Where are you going? You have to get out there and conduct for me now." "Again?" he grinned as the two laughed and went onstage as she was announced. Ella did a medley of nominated songs, with Previn and his orchestra providing the musical accompaniment.

Let No Man Write My Epitaph was a dark movie, very typical of the so-called social movies of the late fifties and early sixties. Costarring with Burl Ives, Jean Seberg, and Shelley Winters, Ella portrayed a junkie who supported herself by singing and playing the piano. Not much of Ella's singing was heard in the movie, just snippets of songs behind dialogue and action in the bar where she played (the most noticeable of which was "Reach for Tomorrow," by Jimmy McHugh and Ned Washington).

Cliff Smalls played the piano for Ella in the movie, but when Norman Granz decided to do an album in connection with the release of the film, Paul Smith was brought in. He and Ella rerecorded the songs she had either sung or had considered doing in the film. Originally recorded on April 14 and 19, 1960, and released with the title of the film, the album, in its liner notes, suggested that Ella had recorded these songs first, then the studio decided which were to be included in the film. In the much later CD release as *The Intimate Ella*, the liner notes indicated that this album had little to do with the music in the film, and was soon forgotten after the film did poorly at the box office (Paul Smith supports this version).

Either way, this was a beautiful album of ballads taken at a very melancholy tempo. Several of the songs, such as "Black Coffee," "Angel Eyes," and "I Hadn't Anyone Till You" were old Decca favorites; "Misty" had been featured on *Ella in Berlin*; the others were standard ballads given a somber but gentle touch by Ella, with only Paul Smith's piano in support. Ella's previous efforts at voice and piano had only been with Ellis Larkins; she repeated the pattern of voice and single instrument again and again in later years. Paul Smith's playing gingerly supported her tender vocals, once again underlying what a topnotch pianist he was and how little adornment Ella needed to succeed.

It was during this time that Ella was gearing up for a Las Vegas appearance, and she and Paul went to see Teresa Brewer's show—a smash, with numerous costume changes and dancing boys a-plenty. Ella turned to Paul and said, "Gee, maybe we oughta get me some chorus boys to dress up the act. This *is* Las Vegas, after all." Paul turned to her and said, "Yes, you *could* appear with dancing boys like *she* does, but could Teresa appear with just a trio and pack them in like *you* do?"

Miss Fitz's recordings for the year were rounded out by *Ella Wishes You a Swinging Christmas*. Recorded on July 15, 16, and August 5, the mood here was not religious but joyful. Ella concentrated on such seasonal songs as "Sleigh Ride," "Jingle Bells," and "Let It Snow!" "What Are You Doing New Year's Eve?" was the album's ballad (strangely, this sad torch song was thrown in the middle of holiday merriment), and "Good Morning Blues" was a delightfully humorous attempt at swinging the Christmas blues. Along with other yuletide standards, this album contained a very fulfilling dose of ho-ho-ho. "The Christmas Song" and "White Christmas" were the ones redone on August 5 ("White Christmas" was taken at a brighter tempo, with vibes and a larger orchestra filling out the same basic arrangement), while two additional songs were taped but not used. The carols "We Three Kings of Orient Are" and "O Little Town of Bethlehem" were released only in Europe on His Master's Voice, and have not yet seen the light of day in America on record or CD.

Of much importance was her receipt of the first New York City Cultural award at the New York Coliseum on December 1, 1960. She was honored by Alpha, Kappa, Alpha, the nation's oldest and largest African-American sorority, and was made an honorary member. The Award was presented for exceptional achievement in the performing or creative arts. Ella was performing at the Americana Hotel at that time. During the late fifties and sixties, the Americana was a first-class hotel and had a policy of presenting major entertainers in its showroom. Ella appeared there frequently, sometimes more than once a year.

Not completed but begun in 1960, the next of the Songbook series brought Ella's only major musical marriage with Billy May. May, who got his feet wet with the original Glenn Miller Orchestra, was a prime choice to arrange *Ella Fitzgerald Sings the Harold Arlen Songbook*. This was different in texture from the other Songbooks because Arlen had worked with so many different lyricists. The songs, recorded in Los Angeles on August 1 and 2, 1960, and January 14, 15, and 16, 1961, due to Ella's busy schedule, were from nightclub reviews, Broadway shows, and movie musicals. Featuring such lyricists as Ted Koehler, Johnny Mercer (who got his own Songbook in a few years), Ira Gershwin, "Yip" Harburg, and Leo Robin, the albums did not have the flavor of a unified whole as do the Porter, Rodgers and Hart, or other Songbooks. This was not necessarily bad, as it allowed Ella to sing pure jazz, pop ballads, torch songs, and pseudo-blues. Once again, Norman Granz decided to grace the covers with art, this time by Henri Matisse. The sound quality was excellent, attributable to Val Valentin's careful engineering. Remember, stereo was only four years old, and some stereo albums from this era sounded like they were mixed in a closet.

"I called Ella at home to discuss the various keys of the songs Norman had chosen, but the first time Ella heard any of the arrangements was in the studio," recalls May. "[She] heard it once and always had it." The songs included several Ella retreads, as Ella had always been a fan of Arlen's.

"The Man That Got Away" was introduced by Judy Garland in the film *A Star Is Born*. Ella had sung it as early as 1954 at Carnegie Hall, but was not allowed to bring it into the studio. This Songbook version, while not as dramatic as Judy's, demonstrated Ella's ability to make a song her own, even when someone else had recorded the definitive version. "That Old Black Magic," originally recorded in the last days at Decca, had been done live on Verve already, and so was given a slightly altered treatment. While not totally abandoning the previous versions, Ella did alter the vocal line enough to give it a different flavor. This is one example where the original Decca version was better.

The opposite was true for "I've Got the World on a String," its easy swing and good-hearted emotion just perfect for Billy May's arrangement. May changed his original charts of several songs in order for Ella to use some of the vocal line with which she was comfortable, having already recorded them. "Right in the studio we changed some of the endings to make Ella happy," says May, "it was no trouble." "One for My Baby" had just been recorded the previous year with Paul Smith on piano, but was given more of a heartthrob feeling here, with the original carrying a smokier verisimilitude.

"Blues in the Night," "Stormy Weather," "When the Sun Comes Out," and "Come Rain or Come Shine" were unusual; torch songs that almost every other female singer of Ella's class (Garland, Streisand, Horne) treated with quite a bit of belt. Ella's versions were just as valid, but without the seemingly prerequisite shouting of her contemporaries. Two additional songs were released on the CD version, "Ding Dong the Witch Is Dead" and "Sing My Heart." They weren't released at the time because they were not the best Arlen songs, and the album was already full.

One song they *did* have trouble with was "Over the Rainbow." While several satisfying versions of this song have been recorded in more recent times, in 1960 Judy Garland was very much alive and owned it lock, stock, and vibrato. Ella simply did not want to record it, and her lack of enthusiasm showed in the studio as she vocally walked through the bridge of the song. Norman Granz booked the studio space on a very tight schedule, forgetting that an album with a huge orchestra does not go as quickly as jazz. Granz called Billy May into the control booth, and told him he was going to ask Ella to record it again and blame a problem with the drums. He wanted her to improve her lackadaisical performance. Billy was instructed to go talk with her until Granz was to make the announcement over the intercom. Billy walked up to Ella, who stopped him short with, "I know what Norman told you. He didn't like the take, and he's gonna blame the drums or something to get me to sing it again!" Just then, Granz made his announcement about the drums, and both Billy and Ella burst out laughing. The song was done again, and Ella did it beautifully. "Heart and Soul," recorded with May on January 14, 1961, was not released until the 1990s on CD.

When I interviewed Billy May, he made several comments about working with Norman Granz that he asked remain off the record. However, since he repeated some of them in an interview for the boxed CD set *The Complete Ella Fitzgerald Songbooks*, I feel I no longer have to hold back. Billy told me:

> I would never work with Norman Granz again. I loved working with Ella, but Norman's the reason I never did another album with Ella. He was a total pain in the ass. He didn't understand orchestras or rehearsal time. He never gave me the time to develop arrangements or work out details in the studio. His eye was always on the clock. In fact, so little time and thought were given to me that I couldn't even be there for all the sessions to conduct, and farmed out at least one arrangement to Walter Sheets. It's not that I dislike Norman personally, and I just adore Ella, but as a producer he really pissed me off.

One of the singers *Ella* listened to was Dinah Shore, and on December 11, 1960, she joined Dinah again for one of her Chevy shows. By that point, Ella was almost a semi-regular. The program was subtitled "The Blues and All That Jazz," and also featured Al Hirt, Andy Williams, and Perez Prado and His Orchestra. Having joined Dinah and Andy in the opening for a blues medley, Ella, dressed in a stun-

ning off-the-shoulder sequined gown and boa, then was featured on
"Joe Williams' Blues." This was a shorter version of a number she did
in concert over the following year. Taking time out for ads for "The
'61 Chevy With the Jet-Smooth Ride," Ella and Dinah returned for
a medley of "Mood Indigo," "Sugar Blues," "Wang Wang Blues," and
"Bye Bye Blues." The program was well produced and thoroughly
enjoyable. Dinah was to remain an important part of television for
yet another thirty years, an incredible accomplishment when one con-
siders she had been making regular appearances for ten years at that
time and had been a stalwart on radio for ten years before *that*.

The concentrated amount of work during the previous five years
could not help but take its toll on Ella. There were tremendous weight
fluctuations, as gowns had to be let out and taken in. She suffered
frequent headaches as it became obvious that she was having problems with her eyes. At times her temper would flare, either with
Granz or others who worked with her. Since joining Verve, she had
recorded more songs than in the fifteen years previous to 1956. Her
family became ever more burdensome, with their demands for financial assistance growing with her substantial ability to earn money. She
was a very secure millionaire, and could have sharply cut back on her
schedule without feeling a pinch. Perhaps her health problems in later
years could have been avoided had this been the road traveled, but
despite the signposts up ahead things only got busier.

It was around this time that Granz finally decided to unburden
himself from the actual running of Verve by selling out to MGM for
nearly $3 million. The only proviso was that Ella's contract would be
secure through 1966, and that all of the controls and perks she enjoyed would continue. Norman would remain her recording producer.

After all this studio work, Ella plunged into rehearsals for John
Kennedy's inauguration. Frank Sinatra coordinated the talent, the
best this country had to offer at the time. Besides Ella and Frank, the
talent included Pat Suzuki, Joey Bishop, Louis Prima, Keely Smith,
Nat Cole, Harry Belafonte, Ethel Merman, Jimmy Durante, Alan
King, Gene Kelly, Milton Berle, Janet Leigh, Tony Curtis, and Sir
Ralph Richardson. Broadway producer David Merrick closed both
Gypsy and *Becket* so the stars could perform. The day of the inau-
guration, a blizzard hit Washington, stranding the talent on their specially chartered bus after rehearsals so that those who had not brought

their costumes had to perform in their street clothes. Ethel Merman sang "Everything's Coming Up Roses" to the handsome president's face. Following her own appearance, Ella left for Europe to begin the next JATP tour.

Norman Granz wisely chose to bring her back to her place of triumph the previous year. Belatedly released on CD, *Ella Returns to Berlin* was recorded on February 11, 1961, at the same venue as her previous appearance. The only change in personnel was Lou Levy spelling Paul Smith as pianist. In fine voice and great spirits, Ella started the evening by swinging, for the first time on a recording, "Give Me the Simple Life." She used this number as an opener for over thirty years, and this disc showed why. It was uptempo and infectious, and gave both Ella and the audience a chance to get comfortable. There were reprises here from earlier live concerts, of "Caravan" and "Misty," but much of the material was new in live versions. "Witchcraft," with a truly wonderful arrangement that took nothing from Sinatra, was done with its clever verse. "Take the 'A' Train," "Anything Goes," and "Cheek to Cheek," from various Songbooks, got the live attention they deserved. An Oscar Hammerstein medley of "Why Was I Born," "Can't Help Loving Dat Man" (both later recorded on *The Jerome Kern Songbook*), and "People Will Say We're in Love" was the first of many medleys that appeared on Ella's live albums. Bossa nova and rock 'n' roll were represented by "You're Driving Me Crazy" and "Rock It for Me," respectively.

The true highlights of the album came at the end of the concert. "Mr. Paganini" had originally been recorded by Ella in the thirties as a novelty song; a bopped-up version was recorded in the later Decca days. Always a crowd-pleaser, this song topped the list of Ella's best, and in many venues had to be performed before fans would let her off the stage. Ella followed this with "Mack the Knife." While she had a better grasp of the words, much was still extemporaneous. She even inserted a bit of self-deprecating humor. The lyrics "we're making a wreck of the same old song" gave a nudge at how often even then Ella had to perform this number. A bluesy scat of " 'Round Midnight" followed, while the next number was a wild phantasmagoria of vocal doodles, "Joe Williams' Blues." Not unlike the previous year's "How High the Moon," the paean to Joe went through five-and-a-half minutes of lyrics, scatting, and fast rhythms before it ended

Ella's set. The CD also included Ella's encore with Oscar Peterson's trio, "This Can't Be Love."

While in Europe, Ella taped a television special for Granada TV in England on April 12. Appropriately titled "An Evening With Ella Fitzgerald" (and simulcast on BBC radio), the show featured Ella, the Oscar Peterson Trio, and the Johnny Dankworth Orchestra. The highlights of the hour were " 'Round Midnight," "Mr. Paganini," the slow version of "Oh, Lady Be Good" with the orchestra, "Mack the Knife" with the trio, and everybody carrying on through "Stompin' at the Savoy." Naturally, Norman Granz was the executive producer.

On April 17, 1961, it was Grammy time again, and naturally Ella did not walk away empty-handed. Two more of those little statuettes adorned her Beverly Hills den, as she won for Best Vocal Performance, Single Record or Track–Female for "Mack the Knife," and Best Vocal Performance, Album–Female, for *Ella in Berlin*.

Ella returned to Los Angeles for another studio set, and to fulfill a nightclub engagement. While the album (as it was released) was recorded after the club date, the songs had first been recorded in January in New York and then rerecorded in Los Angeles with a different rhythm section.

All of Ella's live albums to this point were recorded "in concert," with large crowds in attendance. In May, she fulfilled a nightclub stint at the Hollywood Crescendo, where she performed for a comparatively small crowd of two hundred people. *Ella in Hollywood* continued the "Ella In . . . " series. Repeating "You're Driving Me Crazy," "Take the 'A' Train," and "Mr. Paganini" from her earlier concert in Berlin, Ella's set was once again ballad-heavy.

Almost all of her sets from several days were recorded, and Norman Granz chose a hodgepodge of tunes to string together as if they were done in one set. A big winner was "Stairway to the Stars." Performed with more feeling than the original, this was the only live recorded version of that classic Ella big band ballad. During "Satin Doll," the house mike failed (although the recording mike did not), which made for a humorous moment when the sound came on and the audience heard what Ella was singing as she vocally thanked the sound man (". . . what happened to the mike? / Thank you . . .").

"Blue Moon" would appear, on paper, to come from *The Rodgers and Hart Songbook*, but here Ella threw a large pop curve. The song was then currently appearing on the charts as a rock 'n' roll song, doo-wopped (as they say) to the max. Tongue planted firmly in cheek, Ella also doo-wopped, although she lyrically complained about doing this to such a beautiful song as "Blue Moon." Norman closed the vinyl set with the sweet but sunny "Baby, Won't You Please Come Home," and the de rigueur "Air Mail Special." For this last time on wax, Ella bit her tongue during the number, and gave both herself and the audience a good giggle. "A-Tisket A-Tasket," done with the same Latin feel as her studio recording with Frank DeVol, remained unissued until the 1980s, when Verve released it on one of its CD compilations. See the Discography in Appendix Four for all the songs recorded at this time.

Clap Hands, Here Comes Charlie!, recorded January 23, June 23 and 24, 1961, in Los Angeles, is the only example of Lady Time going into the studio to record with just her regular rhythm section—a quartet of piano, bass, drums, and guitar. Lou Levy led the musicians for what was an extremely satisfying album of jazz. Norman Granz again covered the album with art, this time *Tête d'une Femme* by Jean Dubuffet.

A key favorite cut from this collection is that most torchy of torch tunes, "Good Morning Heartache," made popular by Billie Holiday. With Ella's reading, there was no better example of the combination of song, arrangement, and artist. The opening bars, where Ella and company invited both heartache and the audience to sit down, was done in a very slow, modified jazz waltz, the rest of the song following in normal time and tempo. A second version of the bridge, followed by the looser second chorus (a pattern Ella followed in many of her ballads), was ended in the same tempo as the opening, and gave the song a definite beginning, middle, and end. Only a live, uninhibited version of this arrangement could have been better, and one can be found on *Ella Fitzgerald at Carnegie Hall*.

While there were no bad cuts on this album, the other truly inspired numbers included "Night in Tunisia," "I Was Born to Be Blue," "Stella by Starlight," "Cry Me a River," and "This Year's Kisses." Once again, several numbers were rerecorded in later years, including three versions of " 'Round Midnight," two versions of "Spring Can Really Hang You Up the Most," and one of "The Jersey Bounce."

Three additional numbers, recorded on January 23 in New York but not released with the final version of the album, can be found on the CD version. The best of these is Steve Allen's "This Could Be the Start of Something Big." While Granz used the song to open Ella's *Hollywood* live album, this version included a different set of lyrics in the second chorus, and was a great romp for everyone concerned. "I Got a Guy" deserves to have been released with the original album, and "The One I Love Belongs to Somebody Else" was given better treatment when Ella and Joe Pass soloed it in later years (see The Pablo Years). "Slow Boat to China" was also recorded at the New York session, but remained unissued.

Life could have been very sweet for her at this point, but a close associate who traveled hundreds of thousands of miles with her sadly remembers life on the road:

"She was working her ass off. Sometimes, Norman double-booked her in two different cities on the same night. She always did two shows a night, and then she went off with her musician buddies to jam and try to relax. Even at dinner, she'd be talking about songs, trying them a capella this way and that, worrying that the show wasn't good enough, that the audience didn't like her.

"She wasn't a doper, she wasn't a big drinker, maybe she'd split a bottle of good champagne with someone's wife after a show. Her traveling companion [Granz always had someone travel with her, make sure she got where she needed to go and even tuck her in bed if desired] would get her back to the hotel, put her to bed, get her up in the morning, and off we'd go to the airport and on to the next show. No shopping, no movies, no television, no friends, no contact with family (unless they needed money), just hard, hard work until she dropped. Don't get me wrong, she loved it, but everyone deserves to have a life."

Chapter Nineteen

1961–1962

$\mathcal{A}$t the invitation of Jo Stafford, Ella flew to London in the summer of 1961 to appear on television. Stafford had been signed by London's ATV to do a series of specials, ones that would also be broadcast in the United States in the fall and early winter of 1962. Once securing Ella, Paul Weston (Jo's husband and arranger of *The Irving Berlin Songbook*) got together with a young music team, Alan and Marilyn Bergman, to come up with some original material for Jo and Ella to do together. With rehearsals lasting only a few days, there wasn't time in London to work out any complicated arrangements. These were done in Los Angeles in the late spring.

Ella was given a solo spot to sing three songs of her own choosing (or, more correctly, Norman Granz's choosing). Wearing a chiffon gown with a pleated skirt and a flowered trim bodice, Ella sang three ballads in her spot: "I Got a Right to Sing the Blues" and "The Man That Got Away," from her then recently released *Harold Arlen Songbook* with Billy May; and "What Is This Thing Called Love," with Buddy Bregman's arrangement loosened up from the stiff album version.

Ever since Ethel Merman and Mary Martin did a medley on two stools for "Ford's 50th Anniversary Show," it became simply the thing to do. Ella did these "stool" medleys with such people as Dinah Shore, Bing Crosby, Carol Burnett, Perry Como, Andy Williams, Karen Carpenter, Nat "King" Cole, Frankie Laine, and Toni Tennille through the years, and the results were mixed.

The de rigueur medley was brilliantly conceived: over ten minutes of songs in debate, with Jo taking a pro-love stance, and Ella providing the position of the devil's advocate. With Ella sitting in a three-quarter sleeve brocaded dress, she and Jo covered their musical debate with such songs as "Love Is the Sweetest Thing," "Love Is a Simple Thing," "I'm Through With Love," "The Glory of Love," "But Beautiful," "Falling in Love With Love," "Without Love," "They Say It's Wonderful," "Love Is the Reason," "Something Wonderful," "I've Heard That Song Before," "For Every Man There's a Woman," "A Good Man Is Hard to Find," "There Must Be Something Better Than Love," "Alright, OK, You Win," and finally ending with "Yes, Indeed!"

Jo Stafford recalls, "Although Paul [Weston] had worked on these arrangements, Jack Parnell directed the orchestra as the British show only allowed so many Americans on the staff, and the Bergmans took up the quota. So, while Ella and I sang, Paul played golf."

Paul and Jo did a series of albums featuring an inept pianist and his always off-key vocalist called "Jonathan and Darlene Edwards." I defy anyone not to double over in laughter at these purposely musically awful albums. Only great musicians could make music this bad on purpose!

While in Europe, Ella did a recording in Copenhagen on August 25, 1961. "Mr. Paganini" was backed with the local "Ich Fuhle Mich Crazy" ("You're Driving Me Crazy"), with Knud Jorgensen on piano, Jimmy Woods on bass, and William Schiopffe on drums. The recording only received Scandinavian release, but Ella at least got to spend some time with her boyfriend and relax.

The Fitzgerald recording year finished up with a one-two punch by Nelson Riddle. Two back-to-back albums were recorded in November and December of 1961, with Ella swinging to Riddle's rhythms. The first, appropriately titled *Ella Swings Brightly With Nelson*, was recorded on November 13, 14, and 15. It featured finger-snapping tempos to several classic songs, again showing the new maturity first evidenced in *Ella Swings Lightly*. The standout songs in this collection were two Ellington numbers not appearing on the Songbook, "What Am I Here For?" (which was rerecorded four years later with the Duke) and the breezy "I'm Gonna Go Fishin' "; and Jerome Kern's "I Won't Dance." "Dance" had been recorded a few years earlier with Louis Armstrong, but this time the full orchestra and syncopated arrangement made for a truly superior cut.

"Don't Be That Way" was given a fine arrangement by Nelson, but the definitive performances of this arrangement appeared on the collection *The Greatest Jazz Concert in the World* and on the television special "A Man and His Music Plus Ella Plus Jobim."

"When Your Lover Has Gone" (also rerecorded by Ella in later years) had an arrangement very reminiscent of the one Riddle did for Frank Sinatra with "I've Got You Under My Skin." "Call Me Darling" was another in a series of songs that was only released in the United Kingdom. Then, there was the song for the United Nations.

The United Nations? The United Nations High Commission for Refugees asked actor Yul Brynner to produce an album, the benefits of which would go to help the world's refugees from various wars, plagues, and political struggles. The artists chosen for this endeavor were an international cornucopia of some of the best; it is no wonder Ella appeared there. All the songs were produced especially for this project and appeared nowhere else, so this was the only place to find Ella's studio version of "All of Me" until the CD reissue of the Riddle albums. Backed by his brassy big band, she sang two choruses and then scatted two more, making for one great, big, joyous noise.

The second leg of Ella's 1961 Nelsonmania was called *Ella Swings Gently With Nelson*. Recorded on December 27, 1961, and April 9 and 10, 1962, it was an album of easy-swing ballads, fine interpretations of such standards as "Darn That Dream," "Imagination," and "The Very Thought of You." Ella rerecorded "It's a Blue World" from her Chick Webb years and "I Wished on the Moon" from her side with Gordon Jenkins, and finally gave us a studio version of "Body and Soul," although without her trademark coda at the end. The most enduring recordings were those of "I Can't Get Started" (which, while not a commercial hit, was much requested at concerts) and "Street of Dreams." The string introduction to the second, Ella's full understanding of the implications of the lyrics, and Riddle's gentle swing that restrains itself from just swinging hard made this a real gem, and my personal favorite of all of his arrangements for Ella.

It is also noteworthy that Ella tried her hand at Ray Charles's hit, "Georgia on My Mind," although she scored much better a few years later with his "I Can't Stop Loving You." All of the unissued cuts were released with the CD reissues in 1993. Riddle was forever linked with both Fitzgerald and Sinatra, and continued to loom large as her recording life began to change.

The next two years did not follow the pattern Norman Granz had previously set for Ella. In 1962 and 1963, there would be no released live albums (Granz constantly recorded Ella's concerts and they pop up more and more often on CD, but none were actually released in those two years) and only one Songbook, a single-record edition at that. The albums over the next few years had less of a jazz feel and leaned more to the "pop" sounds that adult music then embraced. With the popularity of rock 'n' roll, the coming British invasion the following year, the crossover successes of such young artists as Bobby Darin and Connie Francis, and the rising careers of singers like Barbra Streisand and Johnny Mathis, adult pop was becoming a hodgepodge of rehashed standards, *very* easy rock 'n' roll, and instrumentals featuring such artists as Ferrante and Teicher, the pianists. Bop vocals were once more not at the top of the vogue, as belting ballads, show tunes, and easy listening filled the airways.

Nat Cole and Dean Martin were recording country; Ray Charles and Johnny Mathis were getting into R&B. Streisand, Garland, and Horne were belting Broadway. Sinatra, Clooney, Bennett, and Day were still doing business as usual; however, Sinatra and Bennett would soon embrace the new generation, Day would stop recording altogether, and Clooney would have to wait until the jazz resurgence of the 1970s to have a big career on wax. To that end, Norman Granz sparingly used the jazz idiom in Ella's studio albums over the next few years. He also sprinkled in R&B and easy rock into her repertoire as tastes changed. With less time in the studio, she was now traveling the world on a constant, nonstop tour that took her everywhere humans had ears.

Ella's television year began with an appearance as the "mystery guest" on "What's My Line?" For the uninitiated, the entire concept of panel shows must be foreign. The production team of Mark Goodson and Bill Todman had landmarked the television panel show with "What's My Line?" in 1950. The simple game featured four urbane celebrities in dress clothes as they tried to guess the occupation of contestants with questions that could be answered yes or no. A Sunday night staple on CBS for seventeen years, the highlight of the show was the appearance of the "mystery guest." The panelists would be asked to put on elaborate blindfolds (the women hated them because it made their mascara run), and a big-name celebrity would come out and, as host John Daly used to say, "sign in please" at a large blackboard. It was great cachet to appear on the show, for it meant that you were indeed a true star who would be instantly recognized by anyone not blindfolded. The mystery guests used all sorts of vocal disguises to try fooling the panelists.

On January 21, 1962, Ella signed in on the show. Using her little-girl voice, she tried to stump the panel, and even though it was guessed that the mystery person was a singer, none could zero in on her then-current Basin Street East appearance. She looked lovely, with a chic gown and elbow-length gloves, which got stained by the wet chalk used for signing in. Everyone had a great time.

Rhythm Is My Business was the first recording of 1962 (not begun in 1961). Recorded on January 30 and 31, 1962, the arrangements here were by Bill Doggett, the only time he and Ella worked together on Verve. The major differences between this work and the previous albums with Nelson Riddle was in both the musicians at hand and the choice of songs. Doggett's band was just that, not an orchestra, with no strings, harp, or vibraphone. The brass of the band matched the rhythm numbers Granz chose, with no apologies for the sound that harked back to the glory days of Sweet's Ballroom as well as the new sounds coming from Motown.

The songs chosen were not all well-known; several were downright obscure. The album opened with "Rough Ridin'," another holdover from the Decca days. Here the treatment was brighter and more spirited, and Ella sang the lyrics instead of only using the tune as a scat vocal. Doggett playing organ was featured, along with a fine trumpet solo. All of the songs in the album highlighted the band, while each cut took a vocal break to include the big band arrangements. "Broadway" was a fast-paced finger-snapper, this time featuring the sax.

"Halleluja I Love Him So," with its gospel organ opening, allowed Ella to really shine here with a fun, loose, and mature sound that she used more and more frequently in the following years. While she didn't break good grammar by rhyming "know" with "do'" (she pronounces the hard r in door), this cut probably had more of an R&B sound than any of Ella's previous efforts.

The standout cut was "After You've Gone." Given a full big band treatment, Ella sang one chorus through in an even swing, then double-timed a second set of lyrics as she traded time with the band. Therein followed a third full chorus, with Ella and the band trading fours as she scatted and they wailed. For a hugely wonderful live version of this arrangement, get a copy of *Ella and Basie: The Perfect Match* from the Pablo years. Ahh, what sounds! Two additional songs were recorded at these sessions and remain unissued: "If I Could Be With You" and "Taking a Chance on Love."

Once upon a time, the major variety and comedy shows of television did not show reruns in the summer. The best of the shows were rerun in the month of June, then the show went off the air until September to be replaced by a different, usually lower-budget program. Broadcasters thought audiences would tire of shows if they were seen more than once. How times have changed! Although performers of Ella's stature rarely did "summer replacement" shows anymore (albeit Ella got her video legs on such programs), she did agree to appear on two episodes of "The Lively Ones," 1962's replacement for "Hazel." On August 2, she came on to sing "Body and Soul" and "Lady Be Good" in a Greenwich Village setting. The show was a prestige effort, and Ella's contribution came off beautifully. She returned four weeks later on September 6, but her contribution has been lost to time.

Another "single" session came on October 1, 1962, as Marty Paich arranged and conducted "Desafinado" and "Stardust Bossa Nova" for Ella. "Desafinado," with an arrangement that sounded almost exactly like the one DeVol did for "A-Tisket," was the first of many Fitzgerald attempts at the music of Antonio Carlos Jobim. Many singers, such as Sinatra and Vaughan, also toured South America, and like Ella found the Jobim melodies and tempos fascinating.

Next out of the studio (on October 1–4), an album that has been erroneously referred to as a Songbook, was *Ella Sings Broadway*. The tunes of Lerner and Loewe and Frank Loesser were featured, as well as two cuts from Rodgers and Hammerstein and a couple of nods to Adler and Ross. Writers have referred to Lerner and Loewe or Frank Loesser Songbooks having been vocalized by Ella; this was it. Done much in the style of the previous Songbooks (perhaps that's where the confusion lies), this was a much lighter album than her previous efforts. Recorded with a full orchestra, a wink, and a smile, the album was bright, bouncy, and a lot of fun.

Many of the inclusions were novelty songs, such as "Steam Heat," "Hernando's Hideaway" (truly wonderful), "Whatever Lola Wants," "Dites-Moi," and the title song from *Guys and Dolls*. Much attention was paid to *Guys and Dolls*, with "If I Were a Bell" (rerecorded from her album four years earlier with Marty Paich), "Warm All Over," and "Somebody Somewhere" added to the list. "Almost Like Being in Love" was a song Ella had featured on tour with the Dizzy Gillespie Orchestra in 1947; the version here swung just as brightly. "Show Me" was a finger-snapper from *My Fair Lady*, along with "I Could Have Danced All Night" from the same show. Also recorded was "A Felicidad," but it remains unissued.

This might be a good time to mention something that was also a trademark of many of Ella's albums: the liner notes. Many of her albums had extensive liner notes, taking up the entire back cover. Usually written by Norman Granz, Benny Green (as they were for *Ella Sings Broadway*), or Leonard Feather, these notes waxed poetic on Ella's talent, the composers and arrangers involved, or (all too occasionally) interesting sidelines about the album. Sometimes the information presented was erroneous, sometimes self-serving or laced with puffery, but often it included valuable material on Ella's career and music in general. Ella never wrote any of the liner notes for her albums.

Rhythm Is My Business and *Ella Sings Broadway* are probably the least popular of all of her Verve studio albums. They are the ones Verve never rereleased on vinyl, and are not scheduled for CD release any time before the late 1990s. While they are not bad albums at all, they lack the inspiration and chemistry that made her other collections such winners. Also (with the exception of "After You've Gone"), there weren't any songs that Ella embraced for her live work.

The other new album, released in 1963, was a compilation album much like 1959's *Get Happy*. Titled *Verve's Choice: The Best of Ella Fitzgerald*, the album featured singles of recent years, some of which had appeared on albums and some which had not. At least this collection did not pretend to be anything more than a compilation.

Ella's recording path had definitely changed, and perhaps some of it had to with Norman Granz's sale of Verve to MGM Records. While Granz refused to explain why he made the sale, there are two main areas of speculation. One is that Verve had shot its load, so to speak. Seeing that the recording business was changing, Granz wanted to make big money off of Verve before its worth was diminished. Then, there is the more interesting version. Granz fancied himself to be quite a business brain, so it was not surprising that he found himself in the company of Jerry Rosenthal, an attorney who specialized in dealing with show business types. His specialty was business investments, and his list of clients was impressive: Kirk Douglas, Billy Eckstein, Gordon MacRae, Van Johnson, Irene Dunne, George Hamilton, and Zsa Zsa Gabor. Musical friends of Granz like Gogi Grant and Frank DeVol also put their money into Rosenthal's money-making schemes.

Rosenthal's investment situations usually involved bilking his clients by such tricks as phony oil investments, cattle ranches without any cattle, and hotels that overbilled for their services. Rosenthal himself took a large retainer for his services, then sometimes billed his clients hefty fees for services already paid for. He put his clients in the position of investing extra funds in projects, supposedly to protect the money already invested. He dug his clients into deeper and deeper holes, until he literally controlled their finances. He also broke state bar rules by investing and co-mingling his money with that of his clients.

Perhaps Rosenthal's most famous clients were Doris Day and her husband, Martin Melcher. In Miss Day's successful lawsuit against Rosenthal, she was awarded $22,835,646 in damages. Also listed as one of Rosenthal's clients who had been bilked was Norman Granz. If Granz had been pulled into the same downward financial spiral as had Doris Day, he might have needed the money from the sale of Verve to keep himself afloat. Or, it might explain why, in 1966, he abandoned Ella's recording career altogether for several years.

Chapter Twenty

1962–1963

*W*hile Granz no longer owned Verve, he still produced Ella's recordings and remained her manager. Another set was recorded at the Crescendo on June 29 and 30, with Paul Smith replacing Lou Levy on piano and the elimination of the guitar altogether. The stand-out here was the cut "Bill Bailey, Won't You Please Come Home." This infectious song was intended to be used for recording at the live session, as was evidenced by Ella's lyric, "Who knows like Mack the Knife / you may play this song all of your life."

There were a number of songs done at the Crescendo, but with the exception of the "Bailey" single, none of this material was released. See the Discography in Appendix Four for the complete listing of songs.

As in the previous year, Ella had three albums recorded in 1963. However, they were completely different from one another, and began a resurgence of originality that followed Ella through the end of the Verve years. After a two-year absence, the Songbook series was revived with *The Jerome Kern Songbook*, recorded January 5–7, 1963, in Los Angeles. Nelson Riddle once again took up the baton for Ella, this time for a single-album Songbook.

For the first time, Norman Granz did not commission two albums to cover the work of the artist. While the most glaring omission was "Smoke Gets in Your Eyes" from *Roberta* (and Ella had recently recorded "I Won't Dance" with Riddle), there were many Kern gems that were not big hits but could have been included, just as Granz had chosen little-known songs from other tunesmiths to use in their Songbooks. None of this detracts, however, from what *was* recorded.

"A Fine Romance" was as good an example as any of the right song with the right arrangement sung by the right singer. "Why Was I Born" and "Can't Help Loving That Man" harked back to the old Helen Morgan/Libby Holman days on Broadway, with Ella able to conjure up much of the charm of these magnetic ladies. Both "All the Things You Are" and "I'm Old Fashioned" were taken a bit too briskly to really show off the songs, but Ella's vocals and included verses made for some of the best singing on the album. Most of Ella's Songbooks included a wide smile, and "You Couldn't Be Cuter" provided the humorous bounce here. Overall, the album was lush and enjoyable, but did not carry the weight of many of the other Songbooks, ranking, despite Ella and Riddle, at the bottom of the list.

Dinah Shore was now doing occasional specials, and on January 23, 1963 (aired April 17, 1963) taped a truly special one with Ella and opera diva Joan Sutherland. Taped in color in Dinah's original New York television studio, the show was a tour de force for all three. Ella got three solos, "Body and Soul," "Running Wild" (from the *Rhythm Is My Business* album), and "I Got It Bad (And That Ain't Good)." The three later joined forces for two unusual segments: one in which they did Gilbert and Sullivan's "Three Little Maids" (Ella would later giggle and question, "I wonder who picked the key for *that* one?") and "Lover Come Back to Me." Each did that song in the style and tempo which suited her best, and then trioed to finish the song in harmony. Dinah and Ella had to use a special boom microphone lowered to mouth level to ensure that they would not be drowned out by Sutherland's soprano.

Naturally, Ella and Dinah did a medley, this time standing *behind* the prerequisite stools. The songs were "Sentimental Journey," "The Gypsy in My Soul," "Far Away Places" (with a rock beat), "Keep

Moving On," and "Kansas City." The arrangements were done by Harry Zimmerman and Marty Paich.

Stopping over again in New York, Ella once more joined Ed Sullivan on May 5, 1963. She sang two songs this time, "I'm Old Fashioned" from the recently recorded Kern album, and "Stompin' at the Savoy," scatting her brains out on national television. There was always a schism between Ella's television appearances and her live concerts. While her concerts could be raucous, her video gigs were generally tamer, with Ella dipping more into her conservative Songbook bag than into her jazz milieu.

Not so conservative was her first visit to "The Tonight Show," which Johnny Carson had taken over from Jack Paar the previous October. On May 13, Ella joined Johnny in New York, appearing live to sing a few songs from her recent recordings. NBC, in a moment of great stupidity, erased all of the "Tonight Show" tapes prior to 1972, so the exact contents of Ella's performance are unknown. Even more a mystery, Johnny's own Carson Productions does not have a reference to this appearance in its records.

Ella stepped up to the Grammy plate again on May 15, 1963. This time, she won for Best Solo Vocal Performance–Female, for *Ella Swings Brightly With Nelson*. Strangely enough, after Ella had been given seven Grammys, the recording academy did not see fit to honor her again until the 1970s (with the exception of a special award in 1967, see The Independent Years).

After returning to the West Coast, Ella did an appearance on Steve Allen's syndicated show, broadcast on July 3, 1963, but shown at different times of the day in different parts of the country. Allen's show by this point was not the variety type of the late fifties but much more in tune with his stint as host of "Tonight." Appearing on talk shows seemed less than comfortable for Ella, as her natural shyness precluded her enjoyment of the question-and-answer format of such shows. This show was no exception, so Ella just sang. The studio audience was so jacked up to hear her sing that Steve was drowned out when he tried to first introduce her musicians (who included Tommy Flanagan and Roy Eldridge). She did two numbers not in her usual repertoire, "You're Nobody 'Til Somebody Loves You" and a medley of "You Make Me Feel So Young" and "Like Young." Allen came out to join her, and with the audience cheering and stomping asked her to sing again. Naturally, Ella asked Steve to join her. In an unusual spirit of honesty (for television), he admitted he hadn't attended rehearsal and had no idea what was next. So Ella started to bop " 'A' Train," with Steve accompanying her on bongos to augment the quintet.

What can you say about an album that was nearly perfect—one that had so many gems that more than half of them ended up in Ella's permanent live repertoire? One that shuffled the greatest singer of the era (Ella), the finest musicians of the era (the Basie band), and one of the most imaginative young arrangers of the era (Quincy Jones, who himself ended up being one of the biggest arranger/producer/ writers of any era)? *Ella and Basie!* may well have been the best studio album Ella ever recorded. Put to wax July 16–17 in New York City, there wasn't a wrong step or a wrong breath. The collection was lovingly recorded with great sound quality. The relaxed cover photo by Jay Thompson featured Ella and Basie in a pleasant outdoor setting with "modern" graphics.

The twelve songs themselves were all familiar, some tracing back to the earlier days of both principals. It is difficult to pick standouts in such a glorious piece of work, but if pressed, the following are my personal favorites. "Shiny Stockings" followed the pattern set by the earlier collaboration on "April in Paris." Using a modified chart from the Basie band's instrumental version, she added lyrics provided by that well-known lyricist, Ella Fitzgerald.

"Them There Eyes" was a dream of a swinging arrangement, as Ella sang one fast-paced chorus, scatted through the next, gave space to the Basie band for a third, and everyone wailed into the final chorus. This was perhaps Ella's most innovative scatting in the studio.

"Satin Doll" was an Ellington redux; recorded on his Songbook as a wordless bop, the song was given grander treatment here with full orchestra and lyrics. This was probably one of Ella's most performed numbers in concert, although her live version was taken at a more lively tempo, whether performing it with a band or just her rhythm group. "On the Sunny Side of the Street" had the distinct flavor of Motown, as it would, remembering that Jones arranged it. Excellent!

Both "Ain't Misbehavin' " and "Honeysuckle Rose" were rerecorded by Ella and Basie in 1979 (see The Pablo Years), and while their efforts with Jones are noteworthy, I do prefer the Benny Carter arrangements of the later recordings. Ella also rerecorded "My Last Affair" and "Dream a Little Dream of Me" in her *All That Jazz* album in 1989 (see The Pablo Years), but their treatments here were much more full-bodied and interesting, including the seldom-heard Basie touch on the organ.

Billie Holiday had always been labeled a blues singer and Ella a jazz or pop singer, but on October 28 and 29 in New York, Ella did what Billie never did: recorded an entire album of classic blues. Surrounded by Wild Bill Davis on organ (no piano was used for these sessions), "Little Jazz" Roy Eldridge on trumpet, Ray Brown on bass, Herb Ellis on guitar, and Gus Johnson on drums, *These Are the Blues* is one of the most unusual albums Ella ever recorded. With a cover painting of Ella by David Stone Martin and extensive liner notes by jazz historian Frederic Ramsey, Jr., the album owed almost nothing to anything Ella had previously recorded. The only rerecorded tune was, of course, W. C. Handy's "St. Louis Blues." Ella's version here was choice, with no up-tempo swings or bops, and included many choruses not found on most recordings of this song. Ella sang this song many times, with three live cuts released in the following sixteen years. This one was the purest, the closest to Handy's original intent.

The other songs on this album listed like a who's who of blues, written by such greats as Bessie Smith, Ma Rainey, Joe Turner, Alberta Hunter, and Louis Armstrong. The only problems with this collection were that some of the songs were corny, such as "Jail House Blues" (with its spoken opening, "This house will surely be raided, yes!"), and the blues can get tedious if listened to for forty-one-and-a-half minutes nonstop. Remember too that, even in 1963, some of these songs were over fifty years old. Ella's voice, by the way, evidenced even more maturity here. The deepening of her quick vibrato at this point only seemed to have improved the quality of her singing. The album was a wonderful remembrance of an era in music long gone, performed by some of the best jazz musicians around. There was, however, no album, "These Are the Blues, Two." An extended blues jam session by all concerned was recorded but unreleased.

Chapter Twenty-one

1964

*I*n 1964 Ella returned to the pattern of her recordings in the late 1950s: a pop album, a live album, and a Songbook. And naturally, she was appearing everywhere: Las Vegas, Europe, Japan, South America, Carnegie Hall, Lincoln Center, the Copacabana, the Americana Hotel, the Fairmount Hotel, the Hollywood Bowl, everywhere. If possible, she was even busier than she had been, and folks, she had been crazy busy!

Norman Granz was, of course, everywhere, too, prodding, producing, and manipulating behind the scenes. One night, Granz came backstage to announce, "Ella, Drake Brown is in the audience tonight." "Who?" inquired Ella. "Drake Brown," Granz intoned. "You mean you've never seen his picture in the papers?" Ella, embarrassed and nervous, did an extra-special show that night for the nonexistent Mr. Brown. Norman just wanted Ella up on her toes.

While Norman was totally in charge, their relationship could get stormy when Ella didn't think she was getting her due, or wasn't being listened to. A musician who worked with her at this time remarks, "You have to deal with Ella as you would a young girl. Listen intently, be very sympathetic to whatever she says, and you'll get along with her fine." The quality of Ella's performances was almost never in question: just the quantity and content. "I'll ask her to do two ballads in a row to set a mood," Granz once said, "but some kid in the back row will yell 'How High the Moon' and off she'll go. Or I'll say I want her to do eight tunes and she'll say 'Don't you think that's too many? Let's do six.' And she'll go out there and do the six and then if the audience wants fifty she'll do forty-four more. It's part of her whole approach to life. She just loves to sing."

Ella made another television foray on "The Ed Sullivan Show" on February 2. This was an extended visit, as Ed saluted Ella all during the show. "I Love Being Here With You" was done with the full orchestra, as was "My Last Affair." According to the Sullivan people, trumpeter Roy Hilton joined Ella for her next two numbers, but my guess is they mean Roy Eldridge, as she did "Perdido" and "Them There Eyes." Ed joined Ella onstage for an extended talk about her career, both past and present, and looked to the future as she plugged upcoming appearances and album releases.

Also appearing on the show that night was Sammy Davis, Jr. Like most of us, he was an Ella fan from way back, so a duet was arranged of "S'Wonderful." Both were obviously enjoying performing together, and were nonplussed when Ed joined them after the selection and began singing the song back at them. Ella exclaimed through her laughter, "Look at him! He's singing!"

Hello, Dolly!, recorded in the spring in both New York and London, was a refreshing pop album for Ella. It was a collections of songs, both new and old, that she wanted to sing. With the New York recordings, done first on March 3 and 4, 1964, under Frank DeVol's baton for the first time since the Christmas album (and the last time with her), she hit her stride here vocally. At forty-six, Ella sounded twenty years younger. "Miss Otis Regrets" was rerecorded from her first Verve album eight years before, and the treatment was special enough to deserve it. More knowing than innocent, this version allowed Ella to give deeper meaning to the lyrics, backed by the full orchestra. It is this version that Ella sang in her concerts for the rest of her career. Three additional songs were also recorded at this session, "There, I've Said It Again," "I'll See You in My Dreams," and "There Are Such Things." Sadly, they remain unissued.

The biggest plus of the album (with no offense to Mr. DeVol) was the session done on April 7 in London. "Hello, Dolly!" had been made into a pop hit by "Pops" Armstrong, and was covered by every other singer in the business. Henri René arranged it for Ella, with a band led by a man known mostly in the United States as Tom Jones's musical arranger, Johnnie Spence. Bright and bouncy, it was a good cut, but what really sold was the other side of the 45 rpm record on which it originally appeared, "Can't Buy Me Love."

No one dared cover the Beatles' songs, as the originals were played constantly on the radio and were, indeed, *the* versions, the only versions. Also, mainstream music saw the Beatles as the enemy, and pretended that the mop-tops didn't exist and had no effect on American music. Ella knew better, and Spence arranged a swinging big band version of "Can't Buy Me Love," which Ella wailed to pieces. Not only was it good, it didn't detract from her style or the original intent of its creators. It was a smash for Ella, in fact her last hit recording on the popular charts. She sang this song several times on television in the coming years.

Ella loved the score from *Funny Girl*, and sang "People" from this album as part of her live repertoire from then on. Also recorded around this time (on March 23, 1964) was a single that was released in Europe but not in America. "Ringo Beat" was backed with "I'm Falling in Love," both obscure songs that remained, well, obscure songs. The personnel on the sides is unfortunately unknown. Another (equally, alas, unknown) TV appearance on May 26, 1964, was recorded for posterity with Ella joining the Duke Ellington orchestra for "I'm Beginning to See the Light" and "Satin Doll." Neither was ever released.

Miss Fitz continued with her tour of Europe, which always brought her to the jazz festivals at Montreux, Juan-les-Pins, Antibes, and the Côte d'Azur. A television crew filmed Ella's performances on July 28 and 29, 1964, at Juan-les-Pins, France. Released as *Ella at Juan-les-Pins*, this live collection was unusual for several reasons. It was the only live album done with the leader of the quartet being a trumpeter, in this case her close friend, "Little Jazz" Roy Eldridge. It was also the first album teaming up with a man who became very familiar to Ella Fitzgerald fans: Tommy Flanagan.

Tommy, who would be important in Ella's later career, was a superb pianist who pushed her live performances to even greater heights of perfection. One of six children born to a musical family in 1930, by 1945 he'd already made his professional debut in his hometown of Detroit. Appearing at the Bluebird with other future heavyweights Milt Jackson, Thad Jones, Elvin Jones, and Kenny Burrell, it didn't take long before Flanagan hit New York. His first gig was subbing for Bud Powell at Birdland. Recording dates soon followed, with his first solo album, *Tommy Flanagan Overseas*, recorded in 1957. His gifts are amazing; his quiet, almost self-absorbed demeanor and obvious intelligence front a fountain of talent and energy. He can play almost anything in almost any style, and can switch keys, meter, or rhythm with breathtaking speed and efficiency. Once he learned Ella's musical bag, he never even read her charts. He knew it, he breathed it, so he played "without a net," no music. He was the perfect accompanist for Ella Fitzgerald, a walking textbook on how to play jazz piano.

The original liner notes to *Ella at Juan-les-Pins* indicated that Ella was unaware of being recorded, although I would imagine the television camera crew might have aroused her suspicions, as the concert was taped for a European special. They also mentioned a chorus of crickets being heard in the background, but they were almost inaudible on the vinyl version. Strangely, almost no mention was made of the program or its performance, and probably for a good reason.

The vinyl version was a little strange. There was little scatting (evidenced by one song, "Honeysuckle Rose" from the previous year's album with Basie) and few hints of her recent studio work. Even this cut had an uncomfortable feel to it. The best cut on the album was the opener, "Day-In, Day-Out," a foreshadow of her next Songbook. It swung, Ella was in good voice, and her interplay with Eldridge and Flanagan served everyone well. The next cut, "Just A-Sittin' and A-Rockin'," did well, but Ella's voice sounded forced for the first time on record. Over the following few years, a husky gravel found itself in Ella's voice, sometimes adding to the performance and sometimes not. A slowed-up version of "The Lady Is a Tramp" (with Ella mispronouncing Sidney Poitier's name) was followed by another live oldie, "Summertime." Neither was as good as the original, and the listening audience might have wondered why these choices were included on the album.

"St. Louis Blues," a sop to her blues album, followed, along with the previously mentioned "Honeysuckle Rose." Ella sounded as if she were ending the concert here (she sang, ". . . come back tomorrow night and we'll sing 'Lady Be Good' ") due to the impending rain. Yet, there was a side two. "You'd Be So Nice to Come Home To" was the other winner on this album, coming from the Cole Porter collection along with "I've Got You Under My Skin." Ella covered a television theme song, "Somewhere in the Night," which she recorded twenty years later with Nelson Riddle in the studio (see The Pablo Years).

The lineup of these songs did not seem right for one of Ella's concerts, kind of unbalanced and uninspired. She ended the album with a cute idea, singing an on-the-spot creation to the unheard crickets that were interrupting her, and a ballad version of "How High the Moon."

What the record-buying public could not know is that these were just snippets from several much longer concerts, and they would not know the truth until the release of the concert on CD. The recording sound did get a little uneven on some cuts because it was extremely humid and about to rain on both nights, with the thunder much more audible on the disc. Poor "Little Jazz," the humidity made him really strain for his high notes, and he just didn't make it on many of the cuts. Weather problems not withstanding, what *doesn't* appear on the album version is what makes the CD a great listening experience.

Add the outstanding cuts from the album version to such rare live gems as "People," "Someone to Watch Over Me," a wild "Can't Buy Me Love" duet between Ella and Roy, a wilder "Them There Eyes" interplay done in an incredibly fast tempo, a novelty song "Cutie Pants," Ella and Roy's seven-minute-plus swinger of "Perdido," "Goody-Goody," "The Boy From Ipanema" (Ella's first live Jobim cut, not to be confused with her Jobim medley of later years), and Ella and Roy both trying hard to fight the thick air on "Shiny Stockings," and you had a most satisfying treat. True, the album did not make Roy sound good, and even Ella showed signs of not being perfect. But that is jazz, and this was a great jazz concert.

The tour continued to Japan, where Ella, the trio, and Roy made a television special *there* as well. The show was divided into three parts: Ella with Tommy, Roy, Wilfred, and Gus plus an orchestra of

Japanese musicians; the quartet by itself doing instrumentals; and Ella with the quartet. The first section showed Ella, in a dark sheath and a slightly disheveled wig, starting off with "Everything I've Got Belongs to You." As there was no audience, Ella just went from one number to another, no talking and no stopping. Holding a hand mike with a twelve-inch cord attached to nothing (an early Japanese wireless mike?), she next swayed with "Ain't Misbehavin' " followed with "My Last Affair," both from her album with Basie. Peggy Lee's "I Love Being Here With You" was excellent special material, with many "in" references of the day. "Perdido" closed the orchestral part of the show.

The second stint showed just how wonderful her musicians were, with the virtuosity of Tommy Flanagan being even more evident than that of Roy Eldridge. Tommy was almost mesmerizing in his use of the keyboard, much the same way Joe Pass was in his control of the electric guitar. After two numbers, Ella rejoined the group, wearing a black sequin and lace gown. "Cheek to Cheek" got the set started, the same arrangement as from her second Berlin album. "Dream a Little Dream of Me" again harked back to the Basie album. This was followed by a steamy and sexy version of "Whatever Lola Wants," and then "Misty."

Ella and Roy really got down on back-to-back versions of "Shiny Stockings" and "Them There Eyes," both following the same pattern as the version on the present *Juan-les-Pins* CD. Roy sounded in much better shape on this special than he does on the CD. The special ended with "Bill Bailey," Ella adding an extra impersonation of Dinah Washington at the end to make this version better than her 45 rpm single. Much more was recorded during her time in Japan, intended for an album scheduled to be called *Ella in Nippon*. Although there was much post-production work done, none of the material has been released to date.

The last Songbook Ella recorded for sixteen years was *The Johnny Mercer Songbook*. Once again, Nelson Riddle conducted and arranged in Los Angeles, on October 19–21. This was a superbly well-done album with Ella in peak form. Once again a single album, it could have been double simply by rerecording all of Mercer's collaborations with Harold Arlen. Only one, "This Time the Dream's on Me," was revisited, and with all deference to Billy May, it was a much more satisfying version.

The album swung open with "Too Marvelous for Words," a typical Nelson Riddle arrangement very reminiscent of his best work with Sinatra. This cut set the standard for what followed: precise, swinging, and sharp. The ballads were lush and lavishly produced, beautiful not only for Ella's voice but for the sound of the whole as a concept. "Midnight Sun" was a redux from both the *Like Someone in Love* album and the live album in Rome. The treatment here was even more luxuriant, with the strength and maturity in Ella's voice giving the song an even greater depth.

October of 1964 also saw many songs recorded in the studio but not released. Many of these songs later found their way onto Ella's last Verve studio album, *Whisper Not*, in 1966. These versions, recorded October 22, 1964, were not used. Additionally, two cuts ("When Sunny Gets Blue" and "Melancholy Serenade," Jackie Gleason's theme song) were never again recorded or released.

Daytime television was not an area most seasoned singers performed in, especially since it required them to be *awake* during the day, with all of their shows performed at night. However, the "Today" show invoked the name of Duke Ellington, and on November 5, 1964, Ella could not resist being a part of "Today Salutes Duke Ellington." More and more in the middle sixties, Ellington was revered as more than just a bandleader, and his enormous musical gifts were recognized for their genius.

There was yet another Sullivan show for Ella, this time on November 29, 1964. By this time, she had become part of the Sullivan family, performers who were booked whenever they were available and needed little supervision from the showman himself. Ed was into every part of his productions (as were other giants such as Milton Berle and Lucille Ball), but where his "family" of players was concerned (Ella, Alan King, Frank Gorshin, Joan Rivers, Totie Fields, Sammy Davis, Jr., and others), he gave them the opportunity to present themselves as they thought best. Ella did three songs this time: "Day-In, Day-Out" plugging the Mercer album; "Thanks for the Memory," and "Old MacDonald."

Ella's albums were no longer selling as they had been in the late fifties and early sixties. Slowly, her musical life was moving from recording star to performance star. There were no more hit records, and the albums were released a lot more slowly. Unbeknownst to Ella, the Verve years were beginning to wind down.

Chapter Twenty-two

1965–1966

*T*here were only four more released albums during the Verve years, two each in 1965 and 1966. The recording industry had changed immeasurably over the previous few years. Artists who once released as many as seven or eight albums in one year found themselves without contracts as the inroads of rock, rhythm and blues, and country pushed what used to be pop music into an "easy listening" category. Dinah Shore, Doris Day, and Rosemary Clooney were no longer regularly recording. Sarah Vaughan and Carmen McRae were jumping from label to label trying to get their work released. Sinatra was still Sinatra, and he still had hits on the pop charts ("That's Life" and "Strangers in the Night" were yet to come), but even his recording schedule was cut back. Elvis was making movies, not records.

Everything was British, British, British; the war in Vietnam was heating up as the country was still reeling from President Kennedy's assassination; innocence had been lost and a sexual revolution, along with those for African Americans, women, and gays, was threatening to burst on the public. Even Ella was affected, putting more contemporary sounds in her sets, wearing wild-colored wigs (blond, red,

frosted) and flashier gowns in her personal appearances. She was always immaculately dressed in the latest styles, but those styles
changed considerably, almost by the month.

The change in Ella's appearance in the four months between her
last Sullivan and the next were proof of how fast things were changing.
Appearing with Duke Ellington and orchestra on March 7, 1965, to
kick off their two-year world tour and recording sessions, Ella wore
a much teased wig with a heavy eye makeup and a glamorous but
modern styled dress.

The tunes were a frantic "It Don't Mean a Thing (If It Ain't Got
That Swing)" and "Do Nothing 'Til You Hear From Me," but the
highlight of the appearance was a medley of Ellington songs done
without words as Ella scatted through much of the Ellington Songbook ("I'm Beginning to See the Light," "Don't Get Around Much
Anymore," and others). This Sullivan television appearance was recorded by Norman Granz, but was never released. While Ella's studio
album with Duke and world tour were still a few months away, this
appearance set the pace for much of the next two years in Ella's life,
a pace that would make her an even looser live performer, but at the
same time would begin to take a serious toll on her health.

Each of these next two years had one studio album and one live
one, and all four were well done. On March 26, 1965, Ella did a
concert in Hamburg, Germany, at the Musikhalle. For the first time
on record, she was accompanied by the Tommy Flanagan Trio, which
included Keter Betts on bass and Gus Johnson, her drummer for
many years.

This was Keter's first time recording with Ella in an association that
continued for the rest of her career. Like Tommy, Keter had a sixth
sense with Ella, instinctively knowing what she needed and when.
Most singers are driven by the drummer, but Ella got driven by Keter.
Drummers and pianists have come and gone (the best being Louie
Bellson and Tommy), but Ella got Keter whenever she could. Keter
also spent much time in Washington, D.C., working with young people and introducing them to jazz.

The cover of the album featured many shots of Ella in performance
in small squares, her blond wig glistening with sweat as she smiled,
laughed, sang, and breathed from shot to shot. It was actually very
effective, and very cool for Ella to go blond in Germany. The set

started with "Walk Right In," an ersatz rocker that brought to the forefront the change in Ella's attitude and voice as the sixties rolled on. The voice was strong and sure, but got raspy as Ella began to belt her notes. This attraction for Aretha Franklin–like sounds permeated much of Ella's work in this period. "Body and Soul," for the fourth time on wax since 1953, followed the Nelson Riddle arrangement recorded in 1961, and was not as satisfying as her previous live attempts. Ella continued to sing this song in her concerts, changing arrangements with her moods from slow to fast and jazzy to soulful.

"Here's That Rainy Day" was a pop song that everyone at that time was covering; Ella skillfully handled it here, with one of her best codas at the end. "And the Angels Sing" was a big band number, with lyrics by Johnny Mercer. Starting off with a modified, slow Charleston tempo, it swung in the second chorus with Ella at full throttle. Again, the rasp in her voice was evident as she hit loud, high notes, but this added rather than detracted from her performance.

Ella surprised her audience next with a tune that meant a lot to natives of Hamburg. The Beatles had appeared there very early in their careers, and Hamburg was one of the first cities to really notice them. They sort of claimed them as their own, so it was no surprise that when she started in with the lyrics "It's been a hard day's night . . ." the audience went crazy. Ella had real feeling for the song, which was as well done as her earlier "Can't Buy Me Love." She could not help injecting a little humor, throwing in "you'd better believe it" before wailing the last "hard day's night." As she said on the album, she liked Fab Four's music and wished she had a hit one fourth as big.

An Ellington medley followed (one she would do for years), along with "The Boy From Ipanema." The show *Funny Girl* was heard from again, this time with Ella doing "Don't Rain on My Parade." There are certain songs that don't do well as jazz numbers, and this is one of them. Ella also included the published verse and alternate lyrics, even though these were not used in the show or movie. Another version of "Angel Eyes," surely Ella's most recorded ballad, followed. This was perhaps the best one, very tight, with an extended high note at the end not found on other versions.

"Smooth Sailing" was her bop finale in Hamburg, with an unusual encore afterward. Ella had given a concert for children, and began to use one of those numbers in her sets for adults. "Old MacDonald Had a Farm" was as unlikely as any number for Ella to sing, but she handled it in a way almost impossible to describe. Fast paced, it got one Ella chorus after another with a musical break, with the list of things found on the farm (including a Ford that went clunk, clunk) getting longer and longer until she said, "Oh, the heck with it/how 'ya gonna keep them down on the farm/like Old MacDonald did!" The arrangement was by Marty Paich. Ella returned vocally to the album to say thanks, that she and the band had done everything they knew (obviously there was more to the concert than contained on the album) and it was like Christmas. A wonderful album, different than any of her previous live efforts in texture and program. A busy spring was capped off on May 14 when she received the first ASCAP award in recognition of an artist, in New York.

Ella made a quick trip to the studio on June 25 and 26 to record and then discard seven more songs that would end up on the Paich album (one, "Don't Rain on My Parade," never made it). Again on July 7, 1965, she recorded two more European goodies unheard west of London ("She's a Quiet Girl," "We Three").

After the unfortunate circumstances of her last appearance, the Bell Telephone Company waited almost six years before inviting her on the show again on September 26, 1965. Joining hostess Ginger Rogers, Nancy Dussault, and John Davidson on an all–Jerome Kern show, Ella was given much to sing from her *Kern Songbook*, all with Nelson Riddle arrangements. "Yesterdays," "Can't Help Loving That Man," and "You Couldn't Be Cuter" were much like they were on the album. One song, "Till the Clouds Roll By," wasn't on the album, but the arrangement was by Riddle nonetheless. Ella did get her chance to sing with Ginger, as all three women giggled through "She Didn't Say Yes."

In October, Ella returned to the studio to record with one of the stalwarts of her career, Duke Ellington. This album, entitled *Ella at Duke's Place*, was the beginning of a two-year world tour for Ella and Ellington that culminated with a syndicated television special early in 1968. On vinyl, the songs were divided by side, with the ballads (or as it said on the album, the pretty, the lovely, the tender, the hold-me-close side) on one, and the swingers (the finger-snapping, head-shaking, toe-tapping, go-for-yourself side) on two.

The ballads, all arranged by Jimmy Jones, included some over-looked beauties such as "Something to Live For," which opens the album. Ella's voice was warm and full as she sang the lovely verse with Jimmy on piano, followed by the moan of the orchestra as she began the chorus. Rarely do a song, an arrangement, and a singer blend so well, especially in a ballad with long extended notes such as this. Plain and simply, no one can sing this song like Ella, as was evidenced by the live version that would follow in 1966. "A Flower Is a Lovesome Thing," cowritten by Ellington and Billy Strayhorn (as was the previous number), was a strange and ephemeral salute to, well, flowers. The jumps of the notes in the melody at the bridge were haunting; Paul Gonsalves's tenor sax played well with Ella's interpretation.

"Imagine My Frustration" started the finger-snapping. The story of a wallflower, this Gerald Wilson arrangement featured Johnny Hodges, who won many kudos for his work at the 1965 Monterey Jazz Festival with the instrumental version of this song. Following a pseudo-blues/pseudo-rock beat not unlike "Don't Get Around Much Anymore," the song incorporated much of Ella's new sound as she got in the groove with a wail. "Duke's Place" was a reworking of the jazz classic "C Jam Blues." With new lyrics by Ruth Roberts and Bill Katz, the song frolicked as Ella sang the praises of the imaginary nightclub featuring Duke at the piano. Ella's scat coda fit right in with the horns, once again placing her in the position of being another instrument in the band.

"Brownskin Gal in the Calico Gown" was one of the first examples of Ella singing lyrics obviously meant to be sung by a man. She did not adapt the lyric, but sang it as if there were nothing incongruous. In later years, Ella performed "Have You Met Miss Jones" in concert and apologized to the audience saying, "The author did not want me to change the lyrics. Now, you know I don't go around with . . ." as the audience hooted and laughed at her timid reference to the lesbian implications.

The album ended with "Cottontail," the only number repeated from the Ellington Songbook. Speeded up here, Ella was used even more as an instrument, as both Ellington and Jimmy Jones traded turns on the piano. Ella's scatting here was magnificent, surpassed only by the two live versions to come.

Tenor Andy Williams had Ella as his guest on November 15, 1965. Ella was in good company, along with her longtime friend André Previn and television star Sid Caesar. Ella's contribution was a solo of "Sweet Georgia Brown," and a scat duet with Andy of "Let's All Sing Like the Birdies Sing"

Another video stopover found Ella as one of the early guests on Dean Martin's new television variety show. In color on NBC on December 16, 1965, Ella was beautiful, wearing a stylishly long wig and a black velvet gown with fur trim and pearls. Against a simple background, she wailed through "Can't Buy Me Love" and "Time After Time." As Dean joined her, the set flew all over the place, and suddenly they were in a corral to do country songs. Joined by fellow guests Gordon MacRae and George Gobel, they did a medley of "Jealous Heart," "A Roomful of Roses," "Bury Me on the Lone Prairie," "If You Loved Me Half As Much As I Loved You," "Red River Valley," "Tumbling Tumbleweeds" (actually very effective in three-part harmony), and "You Are My Sunshine."

During a stopover between Martin assignments, Ella again made a single for European distribution on April 5, 1966, and this time it really was too bad it was not released in America, for the "A" side was the haunting, "The Shadow of Your Smile." A lush Nelson Riddle arrangement underscored Ella's sensitive vocalizing, and even the raucous "You're Gonna Hear From Me" on the flip deserved album presentation. Five days later, Ella returned to NBC Burbank and Dean Martin to share guest billing with Johnny Mathis. She featured one of her best swingers, "That Old Black Magic," then balladed with "Mean to Me" from the Riddle album. The Dean-Ella duet this time was a Gershwin medley, including such songs as "S'Wonderful," "Nice Work If You Can Get It," and "They All Laughed."

Kraft Music Hall had Ella back on the tube a month later, to join host Perry Como. On that April 25 broadcast, Ella had more to do than the typical variety-show appearance, even though other guests included the comedy team of Burns and Schreiber and singers Caterina Valente and John Davidson. Ella soloed on "Let's Do It" (featuring sax man Phil Bodner) and "Cottontail." Perry and Ella kidded their way through "A-Tisket A-Tasket" (one of the few times Ella ever actually sang this song on television), then Ella, Perry, and Caterina played around with "Avalon," with Perry singing the lyrics while the ladies scatted around him.

Ella toured the world with the Ellington Orchestra during 1966 and 1967, going back and forth to do television projects and record albums. At this point, the demarcation line between the Verve and Pablo years becomes blurred. A live album was released by Verve, featuring Ella and the Ellington Orchestra, Ella and the trio, and the orchestra by itself. The two-record set was called *Ella and Duke at the Côte D'Azur*. Many years later, Norman Granz belatedly released an album on Pablo called *The Stockholm Concert—1966*. Recorded during the same tour, this album concentrated more on the numbers Ella did with the orchestra. Two more live albums from this period were also belatedly released.

In July, Ella made her final studio album for Verve. It was called *Whisper Not* and recorded in one day on July 20, 1966, the songs were arranged and conducted by Marty Paich, sadly the last time he worked in the studio with Ella. The songs featured more Broadway show tunes, several numbers Ella had been doing live in her concerts, a couple of oldies from the big band days, and two Billie Holiday ballads. This is the album that the folks at Verve point to as having been tried and aborted by two other arrangers over the previous eighteen months, but there is clearly not enough information to make even an educated guess. As Marty said, "I might have done them myself. I was writing so much material for Ella's club acts that I might have done these also. Then again, maybe not. I simply don't remember."

Paich had already arranged some of the numbers on the album as early as two years before (for Ella's concert work). "Sweet Georgia Brown" had been featured in the Fitzgerald concerts for a couple of years, but appeared here on record for the first time. Starting with a brass bite, the first chorus went through swinging, with a second chorus slightly burlesquing the first. A third chorus featured special material lyrics, with changes in tempo at various places to spice up the arrangement. The ending, with its mixed tempos and extended notes, was very special, and the entire arrangement was a staple of Ella's concerts from then on.

"It was Ella herself who filled in all those special lyrics, making them up on the spot after rehearsing the arrangements with me," recalled Paich. "It was quite a kick to see a talent at work like that." This album was also one of the tightest musically Ella had done in the studio, for Norman Granz allowed several hours of rehearsal time for the orchestra, which usually was not part of his recording equation. Again Marty recollected, "The arrangements were complicated and swinging, and Ella needed to do some work in the studio. This album would not have been nearly as good if Norman had stuck to his usual desire to be in and out as quickly as possible."

"Old MacDonald" appeared here again, the same arrangement with a big band instead of a trio. "I've Got Your Number" and "Matchmaker," from *Little Me* and *Fiddler on the Roof*, respectively, were two more examples of songs that every singer of that era covered. Both were fun and pleasant but not terribly exciting in terms of arrangement or vocal line. "Wives and Lovers," a pop waltz, was another example of a male-oriented song that Ella chose to do battle with. Ella won.

Quite often, music publishers pleaded with Granz for Ella to record numbers from shows and movies, or to include them in her live performances. Some even offered gifts or financial inducements. More than likely, that is how these previous three songs ended up on the album.

The surprise of the album was a new arrangement of "Spring Can Really Hang You Up the Most," originally featured on the *Clap Hands, Here Comes Charlie!* album with just the rhythm section. Ella's version was richer this time, with the Marty Paich's octette behind her. She used a different set of lyrics for this project, and as was true for much of her performing during this period, gave a much more developed performance than ever before.

Marty Paich was an excellent arranger for Ella; more of his arrangements can be heard on the *Jazz at the Santa Monica Civic '72* album, discussed in The Pablo Years. This was not only Ella's last studio album for Verve, it was, for all intents and purposes, her last pop album. All of her recordings after this were tailored to a specific audience, the bulk of which was the jazz listener. Rarely did Ella "cover" contemporary adult music; her material was mostly the standards of the previous fifty years done in a total jazz environment. Only those albums produced during the Independent Years, soon to be discussed, strayed from that vision.

Ella's last original release for Verve on vinyl was the live *Côte D'Azur* album, recorded July 27, 28, and 29, 1966. Norman Granz detoured from his usual practice of presenting Ella as if the audience were listening to an entire set; the album only featured applause to fade in and out of songs as necessary. The two-record set interspersed the Ellington Orchestra doing solo cuts with Ella singing, both with the Jimmy Jones Trio and with the band. While Ella's vocals were wonderful, the album did not work because it had no direction. It would have worked better as two live albums, with Ella and the Duke each getting their own due.

When her sister passed away during the jazz festival, Ella flew home to Los Angeles for the funeral, but turned right around and flew back to the Côte D'Azur for the following night's performance. Ella gave herself no time for mourning or embracing the emotions she was feeling. She simply rushed back to work. There was also no consoling her son, who not only lost his aunt, but possibly (as mentioned earlier) his birth mother.

The three cuts with Ella and the band were uncommon. "Squeeze Me" was a head arrangement that obviously had no rehearsal, with Ben Webster's ill-fated attempt to share the vocal with Ella. "It Don't Mean a Thing" was probably the finale or encore to the evening; Ella bopped and traded time with the band. The thrill of the three cuts was a big band version of "Mack the Knife," a heavy swinging chart that included a driving scat chorus. While the earlier live versions had much more of an air of spontaneity, this version was hard-driving jazz, and extraordinarily gratifying. The trio cuts were extremely varied: a samba, a rock song, an old Decca favorite, a Gershwin song, a reprise of an old ballad, and a sop to pop.

George Shearing's "Lullaby of Birdland" received its most swinging treatment here, with scat intro and tight arrangement played well by the trio. Errol Garner's "Misty" was revived, with much the same vocal line as in its previous incarnation. Miss Fitzgerald tried her hand again at the youth culture with her version of "Goin' Out of My Head." As with her Beatles treatments in recent years, she chose well and made her adaptation smooth without being campy or condescending. "The Jazz Samba" was a Jobim favorite that Ella repeated all through this tour, a combination bossa/vocal/scat that was heavy on rhythm and Latin atmosphere.

Ella's appearance also included two songs with piano and voice, "The More I See You" and Gershwin's "How Long Has This Been

Going On." The former had a strange, loose arrangement, going in and out of the written pattern with special lyrics and melodies woven through. The latter was another example of an almost perfect live performance; take out the applause and one would swear this was a studio cut. Her questioning "okay?" at the end of the song revealed that this was a request from the audience with which she felt compelled to comply. When she was in the right mood, Ella often added songs into her program as they were shouted out by enthusiastic audience members, often without rehearsal. Sometimes she may not have sung the song in years or ever done it live, but she always made the grade.

Much more material was recorded at this time (see the Discography in Appendix Four), and Granz choices for inclusion are at the very least odd. He simply was no longer paying attention. He knew the contract at Verve was not going to be renewed, and had pitched this album to Columbia. John Hammond would have been happy to get Ella, but did not want to record Ellington again. Granz was stubborn. No Ellington, no Ella. Ella paid dearly for his decision.

There was a film made at this time, ostensibly for a television special that was never aired in this country but is now available in Japan on laser disc. Ella's part included three numbers (after she was introduced by narrator Rod Serling), "Satin Doll," "Something to Live For," and "So Dance Samba." While the filming was amateurishly done, it was an excellent example of Ella in concert at the top of her form. The year 1966 was a watershed for Ella; never again was she to be at this height of her vocal powers.

Chapter Twenty-three

1966–1967

*A*s 1966 progressed, Ella's career and health began a roller-coaster ride. Norman Granz, occupied with his own problems, left Ella in the recording studio in the hands of people who didn't know how to deal with her. Yet, there were some splendid items that were recorded.

Ella and the Duke took their concert tour to Sweden, where *The Stockholm Concert—1966* was recorded. Jimmy Jones was again the pianist; Joe Comfort replaced Jim Hughart on bass; and Gus Johnson returned to the fold to replace Grady Tate on drums. This time Norman wisely chose to present the music in order, featuring much of the work of Duke Ellington. The collection opened with "Imagine My Frustration" and "Duke's Place" from the album of the same name. The performances here were much the same as on the studio set; Ella was extraordinarily unbound and in good voice as she wailed them.

"Satin Doll" from the Basie album got its first live exposure, with a quicker tempo that better suited Quincy Jones's arrangement. Ella always introduced the pianist at the bridge of this song, and as the years passed only the names changed. It was always "Jimmy Jones at the piano, ladies and gentlemen, Jimmy Jones at the piano," or Tommy Flanagan, or Paul Smith, or whoever. "Something to Live For" rated with "I Loves You Porgy" and "Body and Soul" as perfect examples of a live jazz ballad done to a T. As good as her studio version was, this performance far excelled it.

New breath was pumped into "Wives and Lovers" from the Paich album; the good nature and excitement of the evening made even this pedestrian song a winner. A shortened version of "The Jazz Samba," referred to here as "So Danco Samba" in its native Portuguese, was then followed by Cole Porter's "Let's Do It." With a Marty Paich arrangement, this version featured the verse not included in *The Cole Porter Songbook* ten years earlier. This was a lively arrangement, with Ella vocally mugging her way through, ending the song with topical references to Sonny and Cher, Elizabeth Taylor and Richard Burton, and James Bond before belting a socko ending. This arrangement was repeated time and again on albums and in concerts.

It was also during this tour that Ella was forced, for the first time, to deal with the exigencies of the pace she was keeping. During one concert, Ella lost her breath and could not continue. After she was helped off the stage by Gus Johnson, the concert was canceled and, in fact, the rest of that leg of the tour was cut short. Much was made of this in the press, with Ella being written of as having "a nervous breakdown," "nervous exhaustion," or it being the "end of her touring career." The simple fact was that Ella had toured for almost a solid year, traveling or performing seven days a week, doing outdoor concerts in high heat and humidity with no rest. Her system simply had enough and told her to slow down.

This was the beginning of years and years of health problems for Ella. Many people feel she would have had years more of good health if not for the schedule she had been keeping since the late fifties. The years of an up-and-down career during the forties and early fifties hurt her deeply. When the opportunity presented itself during the Verve years to ride the crest of a huge career wave, she grabbed it. Certainly, either her associates or Norman Granz himself could have seen the storm clouds and insisted that she take better care of herself. It was also true, however, that by this point she had no life except for her music. Consistently, for the rest of her life, she defied doctors who insisted she retire or at least slow down, and continued working when it wasn't, in George Bush's favorite word, prudent. It must be considered, too, that not only can a person not be happy if he or she is ill, but a singer *needs* to be healthy in order to function at all. Ella's voice suffered greatly as her health declined; in fact, she would never sound as good again as she had previous to the Ellington tour.

Also at this time, purported remarks by Frank Sinatra implied that Ella did poorly with her breathing and phrasing, and Ella was quoted as saying she was so upset, she couldn't sing for a week. All of this made for a lot of magazine fodder, but Frank and Ella were friends, remained friends, and continued with their friendship and respective careers long after the newspaper pages had turned yellow.

On June 1, 1966, *Variety* reported that Ella had signed to do a half-hour color television series with the Ellington band to be taped in Great Britain. Taping was supposed to begin on September 13 at ATV in London, with several "live" recordings to be made from the television shows and released on Verve. Unfortunately, this never came to pass, and the closest Ella ever came to her own show would be the syndicated special she was to have with the Duke in 1968.

Ella flew to Burbank in July to tape "The Andy Williams Show" along with the Smothers Brothers, Jonathan Winters, and Roy Rogers and Dale Evans. It aired on September 11, 1966, and Ella soloed on "Lover Man," while she and Andy sang a medley that included "Without a Song," "Talkin' Blues," and "If You Haven't Got a Song." The finale featured a country fair theme, but Ella did not join in the fun.

A week after "The Andy Williams Show" was broadcast, she taped "The Danny Kaye Show" on September 17 (it aired on November 16). Danny had been a major motion picture star in the 1940s and '50s, but his star had begun to wane as he aged. He began working with UNICEF in the late 1950s, as much to give himself something to do and be in the public eye as it was for charity. As he was a longtime fan of jazz and Louis Armstrong, several of his films had backstage musical themes. Although his hidden gay lifestyle and long-time relationship with Lord Laurence Olivier would not become public knowledge for more than two decades, the "fey" side of Kaye was becoming more apparent as he got older. Finally, he was talked into doing a series of television specials that could utilize his talents, and these led to his variety show (1963–67). He remained a much-loved star until his death.

Buddy Greco and Brazil '66 were the additional help, with all appearing in the opening production number "It Don't Mean a Thing
(If It Ain't Got That Swing)." Danny, Ella, and Buddy did a picnic at
the beach scene (Ella had very few lines; she did *not* do skits), with
the three singing "We Like Each Other." The three then sang Ellington's "Mood Indigo." Ella's solos followed, with Ella caressing
Nelson Riddle's arrangement of "Body and Soul" followed by a swinging arrangement of "The Moment of Truth." Buddy joined Ella for
a special-material arrangement of "My Wild Irish *Kaye*," then Ella
and Danny finally got to their medley of jazz songs.

While Ella was in New York appearing at the Americana, she once
again was a guest with Johnny Carson on his late-night gabfest on
October 25, 1966. The contents of this show, too, have been lost by
network suits with an itchy finger on the erase button.

On December 12 the *Los Angeles Times* named Ella their Woman
of the Year for 1966. This award topped off a year that saw the end
of her recordings for Verve, the beginning of her changing style and
vocal quality, and several years of recording disarray.

Bing Crosby played host to Ella on "The Hollywood Palace" (taped
November 5, 1966, and aired February 18, 1967). This show, an ABC
copy of "The Ed Sullivan Show," had the same mix of jugglers, ac-
robats, singers, comedians, and actors, but the hook was that a different big-name star hosted every week. Such stalwarts as Elizabeth
Montgomery, Adam West, Raquel Welch, Jimmy Durante, Martha
Raye, and Judy Garland took turns, but the show was most identified
with Bing Crosby, who hosted approximately once every four weeks
and did his Christmas shows as part of the series. Der Bingle introduced Ella as "The Sandy Koufax of Song, the Brooks Robinson of
Rhythm, the All-Star of Timing—the Peerless One." This was their
first professional pairing since the old radio days, and they were obviously enjoying one another.

Ella wore a heavily frosted wig and black strapless gown with a
chiffon sheath and bow at the back. Her solos were "So Danco
Samba" (this time done with the entire orchestra and strings) sung to
a boom mike, and then "How Long Has This Been Going On?" as
she stepped to a mike stand. The obligatory medley had Ella and Bing
discussing that the best way to get started in singing was to do children's songs. Bing joked that he knew *every* children's song (alluding

to his late-in-life second family), leading into the medley that included "London Bridge," "Row Your Boat," "Three Blind Mice," "Frere Jacques," and then the two songsters' theme songs, "When the Blue of the Night Meets the Gold of the Day" and "A-Tisket A-Tasket" (Bing whistled as Ella scatted). How ironic that so many years after her Chick Webb days, she was still doing children's novelties for adults.

Andy Williams lured Ella again for her third visit on his show. At this point she was doing more consistent television work than she had in years. On the January 1, 1967, broadcast, Ella soloed this time on "Midnight Sun"; her duet with Andy was "The Lonesome Road." The arrangement was rather original and frenetic, boasting quite a feat for Ella, whose eyesight was already so troublesome that she could not see the cue cards with the bright lights. All of Ella's television work during the 1960s (and thereafter) was rehearsed and memorized, with no relying on cue cards at all since she couldn't see them. For all those medleys, all those turns with stars on stools to sing duets, Ella rehearsed for hours like a true professional, learning the words (always a problem for her anyway) and the intricate musical patterns to perfection, while others only had to look to the cue cards if they were lost. That is why Ella was always able to look her costars in the eye, close her eyes for high notes, or move around. Often her cohorts were stuck looking into the camera, or off to the side to glance at those cards. Ella's efforts were seamless.

In the maelstrom of change, Ella still leaned heavily on her recent past. On the last of her visits to "The Dean Martin Show" on March 16, 1967, her solos were excellent versions of "You've Changed" and "Hallelujah I Love Him So." While her mandatory duet with Dean was a pleasant medley of "For You" and "I'd Climb the Highest Mountain," the finale was almost embarrassing. With the entire cast dressed in children's clothing, Ella and Dean sang children's songs in yet another medley.

An unusual album was released in 1988 on an Italian CD from Stradivarius Records featuring Ella's work from this period, teaming her with two other "divas," Elisabeth Schwarzkopf and Cathy Berberian. Just how Ella got mixed into this formula no one is quite certain, but a portion of a concert done at the Teatro Lirico in Milan on April 30, 1967, was featured. Ella was mostly backed by her trio, but the Ellington band came in for one number. The liner notes stated that it is the Duke himself at the piano, but upon listening that seems highly suspect. From style alone, the most likely candidate is Jimmy Jones. The sound quality is poor, not even up to vinyl standards, but certainly listenable. Besides retreads of such already recorded live cuts from this era as "Cotton Tail," "Lover Man," and "So Danco Samba," the focal points here were "new" live versions of "How High the Moon" and "Mack the Knife." This CD is available in larger classical music stores, or directly from the distributor, Qualiton Imports, Ltd. It is not really necessary for a good collection, but it remains a must for die-hard fans.

There was one more live recording made of Ella and the Duke in this period, also released by Pablo many years later. *The Greatest Jazz Concert in the World* was released as a boxed set of four albums ostensibly featuring a concert with a tremendous cast of performers. Actually, this was a compilation of the best from several concerts done in the summer of 1967 in New York, Los Angeles, and Oakland. The stars of the collection were Duke Ellington and his orchestra, Ella, Oscar Peterson, Coleman Hawkins, Clark Terry, Zoot Sims, Benny Carter, Bobby Durham, and others. For Ella's part (with the Jimmy Jones Trio and Duke's Orchestra), the opening song was obviously cut out, with Ella welcoming the audience to her part of the show, something she almost always did after the first number. She was hoarse, which limited both her range and her ability to manipulate her voice. She sang around her hoarseness, and in doing so made many of the arrangements even more inventive and original. The trio took over for four numbers Ella rarely sang live. The set ended with "Between the Devil and the Deep Blue Sea," a wild cut with added trumpet that was delightful as Ella used her genius to get past her problems. Most likely, there was more to Ella's part of the program, probably repeats of songs appearing on the last several live albums.

These albums put together probably made up the entire part of Ella's contribution to these concerts. They also spelled finis to the Verve years, bringing tremendous change to her career and her life.

The Independent Years

Chapter Twenty-four

1967–1969

*N*orman Granz decided to leave Ella's recording side and take a much needed breather from producing records. No one interviewed seemed to know the exact reasons for his departure at this sensitive point in her career, but some have mentioned the constant friction between them coupled with Granz's growing legal, financial, and tax problems as some of the causes. He began to spend more and more time in Europe at homes in Switzerland and Italy. Both Granz and Fitzgerald were millionaires many times over by this point, and both could have cut back and lived an easier life. However, Ella wouldn't and Norman still had his fingers in too many pies to simply walk away from his commitments altogether. While the actual sale of Verve had actually occurred several years earlier, Granz now gave up the control that had still been contractually his.

For the first time since *The Cole Porter Songbook* in 1956, Ella was without Verve and Granz's direct supervision of her recordings, though he was still her manager. Music was changing on an almost monthly basis, with someone like Frank Sinatra being on the charts one week, the Who the next. One needed only to watch "The Ed

Sullivan Show" to see the immediateness and quick change of popular music in this country. Taking all of that into consideration, Ella and Granz made a strange choice here, signing her with Capitol records in a deal that would have her albums produced by Dave Dexter, Jr.

Capitol, home at one time to Frank Sinatra, Dinah Shore, and other faithfuls of the genre, pooled its corporate brain trust to come up with the perfect debut album for La Fitzgerald. Granz had agreed to give Dexter total creative control over the Fitzgerald product, a move he would later regret. Decisions had to be made. Should Dexter get Nelson Riddle or Marty Paich, or maybe should he continue the Songbook series? Perhaps a new arranger, such as Peter Matz, would work. Maybe a salute to the songs that got her started? How about a contemporary album featuring songs of the Mamas and the Papas; the Beatles; or Peter, Paul and Mary?

Any of these fantasies would have been preferable to *Brighten the Corner*, a collection of gospel songs that was so dull it seemed that Ella must have been dragged into doing it. With the Ralph Carmichael Choir and Orchestra backing her up, Ella sang such traditional Christian music as "Abide With Me," "God Be With You Till We Meet Again," and "That Old Rugged Cross." Ella was a very religious woman, and no doubt these songs meant something to her, but the presentation here was inept.

The cover featured a stiffly wigged Ella in a blue satin wrap with a frozen smile on her face. The orchestra and chorus totally drowned out her voice, which was poorly mixed by John Krause; Ella missed Val Valentin's expertise here. This was hardly the album to debut with on a new label, and an album that, at best, should have had a limited Christmas or Easter release.

One can only imagine the great thinking that went into *Ella Fitzgerald's Christmas*, her next great Capitol splash. Recorded July 19 and 21, 1967, once again Carmichael's chorus and orchestra failed to give Ella the room she needed to be creative. While this album differed from her classic holiday album on Verve in that she sang religious favorites, one wonders why it was released on the heels of another religious album. Why wasn't Ella backed by a more lush orchestration that would have featured her voice rather than having her be, for all intents and purposes, one of Ralph Carmichael's choir? Why try to compete with her holiday album still on the market? For lesser talents than Ella's (and if MGM and Decca weren't still releasing her old albums), these decisions could have very successfully ended her recording career.

Capitol then decided Ella needed to be put into the Nat Cole/Dean Martin mold. Surrounding her with a chorus and orchestra led by Sid Feller, she was asked to be a country singer for *Misty Blue*. Actually, this was not a bad album per se, only unusual in its presentation of Ella. The cover featured chrysanthemums and lettering tinted blue, with a small picture of Ella in the upper right hand corner. She did quite well with the title song, and this time her voice was not mixed into the background. The Roger Miller tune "Walking in the Sunshine" was too cutesy to really suit Ella's maturity in style, and "Turn the World Around" might have done well with Ella's trio instead of all the extra voices and instruments that led to incredible overproduction.

Again it is curious that none of the musicians or arrangers familiar to her were let in on these recordings, which were totally in contrast to her live concerts. This situation was not unlike her Decca years, except that Ella was no young, up-and-coming singer. She was at the top of the heap and should have been presented that way. Additionally, the changes in her voice were making themselves evident in these recordings. While she was universally revered, these unfamiliar presentations did nothing to protect her vocal quality.

While the religious albums never had a chance at a great place in the Ella legend, the *Misty Blue* album actually just missed. Some of the songs suited her well, but not enough came together to make this a keeper. Around the time of the release of this album, Ella did a radio show with Skitch Henderson of "Tonight Show" fame. A recorded version was released on Joyce records as part of their "Greatest Vocalists" series, as Skitch plays songs from both *Misty Blue* and Ella's Verve catalogue. The big find on this album is a song Ella wrote and performed to express her grief when Dr. Martin Luther King, Jr., was assassinated. "It's Up to You and Me" was one of the last songs to which Ella wrote lyrics, and deserved wider release than it got (Capitol released it as a single).

Ella's last effort for Capitol should have been her first effort: an album of jazz with her mentor, Benny Carter. A fine musician, arranger, and composer, Carter was essential in the launching of the career of the teenage Ella Fitzgerald. Now they performed as peers, in a clever concept album, *30 By Ella*, featuring thirty songs performed in six long medleys, each constructed with loose head arrangements and one additional instrumental solo. Jimmy Jones was back with her on piano, and old pals "Sweets" Edison and Georgie Auld joined in the fun. The album was well produced, creatively arranged, and highly spirited.

It is also interesting that here, because of the jazz milieu, for the first time the average listener can hear the perceptible change in Ella's voice. It was huskier, with a deeper vibrato and some rougher edges. The metamorphosis of Ella's voice came gradually over the next few years, finally settling into the voice that was familiar all during the Pablo years. It wasn't that her voice wasn't good, but it was different. And perhaps more interesting. At the same session that produced this album, Ella recorded a single of "The Hawaiian War Chant" with Benny Carter's group, backed on the "B" side by "It's Only Love" from the country album. "Chant" is the only real scat singing Ella did for Capitol, and it was too little too late. Ill-used, Ella and Capitol parted company.

There is, however, more to this story, as told by Dave Dexter, Jr. Before he passed away, Dexter wrote and published his memoirs, which he titled *Playback*, published by Billboard Publications in 1976. His impression of Ella was extremely negative, and he wrote of her as a recording has-been who had not sold well for many years. He remembered her as being a cold, thoughtless woman who never sent him a Christmas card or thanked him for his lovely gifts while he was producing her Capitol albums. He wrote of begging Capitol to take her on as a client, and that it was a struggle to get her signed. He praised his own efforts to turn out Fitzgerald product that the public would buy.

In all of the research done for this book, not one person, on or off the record, had even one picayune thing to say about Ella as a co-worker that was in any way negative. Time after time, the comments were "elegant," "ladylike," "totally cooperative," "a thorough professional." Yet, Dexter remembered her as cold in the studio, uninvolved and unmotivated.

Although Mr. Dexter had a long and successful career as a producer of records, he failed miserably with Ella. Rather than admit that he didn't have the foggiest notion how to produce an album for the world's greatest female vocalist, he simply degraded Ella and blamed her for lagging sales. That Norman Granz could and would produce almost thirty albums (successful albums, winning many Grammy awards) after this time while he could not; that Richard Perry could produce a revolutionary and inspired pop album for Ella while he could not—these facts tend to indict Mr. Dexter's ability as a producer *for* Ella, not Ella's ability to vocalize a successful album.

While Mr. Dexter was rationalizing why he couldn't sell Ella, on May 24, 1967, she appeared on NBC-TV's "Best on Record." In the days before the Grammys got their own show, this was an hour-long look at the best of the winners. Pat Boone presented Ella with the Bing Crosby Lifetime Achievement award, and then she sang "Satin Doll" and "Don't Be That Way" backed up by Les Brown and His Band of Renown.

Salle Records (Ella's spelled backwards) released a single of two live cuts with Jimmy Jones leading an orchestra. The "B" side here is a cover of "The Moment of Truth," done in typical Fitzgerald swinging style. The "A" side features yet another attempt at Ella's trying to tap the youth market with the Nancy Sinatra hit "These Boots Are Made for Walking." Ella planted her tongue firmly in cheek for this one, not taking too seriously what she was doing. She was campy because this song was pure camp, not comparable in quality to the Beatles songs or "Goin' Out of My Head." The song was amusing, nonetheless, and the record was slightly disappointing in that the length of the single required the song to be faded out before it was quite finished.

On November 13, 1967, Ella joined Antonio Carlos Jobim on the television special "Frank Sinatra—A Man and His Music Plus Ella Plus Jobim." In this follow-up to Sinatra's first special of the same name, Ella was a much featured player. Soloing with Nelson Riddle arrangements of "It's All Right With Me" and "Body and Soul," Ella joined Frank at the piano for a medley of tunes ending with a driving duet of "Goin' Out of My Head." Again, one could see her straining to hit notes, although hit them she did with complete accuracy.

This medley alone would have been worth the price of the show; however, in the second half the two performed a legendary piece before an onstage audience in the round. Stepping out in front of the crowd to a brassy Riddle intro into "The Song Is You," Ella and Frank sang "They Can't Take That Away From Me." Frank and Ella munched on distant relatives to the lyrics of "Stompin' at the Savoy," then Ella exploded with a scat that was one of the most vivacious of her career. Sinatra breezed through "At Long Last Love," then Ella put her all into Riddle's arrangement of "Don't Be That Way." The Dynamic Duo next bopped into "The Lady Is a Tramp," tearing it up so much that they had to do an encore, with Frank holding extended notes against Ella's furious bop. They repeated this performance twenty-three years later for Frank's seventy-fifth birthday, neither losing much in the translation.

Carol Burnett had Ella join her for the first Christmas show of the former's long-running variety series that had its premiere in September. Aired on Christmas Day, 1967, the show also featured Jonathan Winters doing Carol's cold opening while she mugged behind his back, and Sid Caesar doing his "Professor" bit with Carol. Ella then appeared in a black strapless gown with a sheer chiffon chemise. She sang the Nelson Riddle arrangement of "A Foggy Day" from the Gershwin Songbook in an elegant setting with crystal chandeliers, along with a Marty Paich chart of "Always True to You in My Fashion" (including the unrecorded verse) from *The Cole Porter Songbook*.

Ella seemed a little stiff in this outing, and was not asked to move much. Unbeknownst to the audience at that time, Ella's eyesight was already bad, and her appearances on television limited her choreography.

She later loosened up when, wearing a red sequined dress appropriate for the holiday, she joined Carol on those obligatory stools in front of lights set up as a Christmas tree. Ella and Carol did a medley of songs arranged by Artie Malvin, with Ella throwing in a holiday coda, ". . . deck the halls with lots of fellas" at the end. Harry Zimmerman and his orchestra gave the ladies their musical support.

The final leg of the Fitzgerald-Ellington tour was a television special that was syndicated in early 1968. This was the only special on American commercial television that featured Ella as the star. The hour-long, color show featured the Ellington band doing several of its standards, but the rest of the hour was pure Ella. Using simple backdrops and several costume changes, the show was simply and inexpensively produced, punctuated by filmed lead-ins provided by Ella at and around her home.

Opening with "People," Ella went directly into an up-tempo, big band arrangement of "Just One of Those Things." This arrangement does not appear on any album, unfortunately, because Ella really went to town. At the second chorus, Ella changed keys and inserted ". . . one of those bells that now and then rings / jingling, jingling, jingling, jingling / one of those things . . . ," ending on a high note that was totally pure. The pace was changed when the strings came in and she crooned "Street of Dreams" from her album with Nelson Riddle. "I Can't Stop Loving You" was heard here for the first time, crooned, belted, shouted, and blown apart as Ella interpreted the song so unlike Ray Charles one forgets that anyone else but her sang it. "Summertime" was given life here again, with appropriate billowing smoke for effect.

A section featuring a trio had Ellington on piano, Keter Betts on bass, and Louie Bellson on drums, with Ella repeating her original Decca arrangement of "Oh, Lady Be Good," as well as the Duke's "Don't Get Around Much Anymore." The years of constant touring were saluted, with both "A Foggy Day" and a jazzed-up "Loch Lomond" sung while posters and pictures of Ella's concerts in Europe were superimposed in the background.

A final section had Ella jamming with the big band, giving excellent renditions of "Lover Man" and "Sweet Georgia Brown" before socking out perhaps the very best version of "Mack the Knife." This special clearly showed Ella in good spirits and at her very top, although her discomfort in appearing on television never completely disappeared.

The same week that Ella played Toronto's Massey Hall with Oscar Peterson, she accepted the honorary chairmanship of the newly formed Martin Luther King Foundation in Washington. She always did her charity work very quietly, shunning publicity. Almost no one knew of her work with inner-city youth in Los Angeles, or of her help to children everywhere. Many of her hundreds of concerts per year were done either gratis or at greatly reduced fees.

Ella's voice once again graced a film in 1968, *A Place for Lovers*, directed by Vittorio De Sica. The following year, to record "Lovers," Ella went back into the Verve studio, although she no longer had a contract there (she no longer had a contract anywhere). She also cut another song, "Lonely Is," though neither song was released. Ella included both these songs in upcoming concerts over the following eighteen months.

Pat Boone invited Ella to be on his syndicated talk show in the fall of 1968. Although she was currently appearing at the Coconut Grove at night, she agreed to show up if she could do her turn and leave at the commercial. Making her entrance after the introduction of cohost Louis Nye (others appearing included Pete Barbutti and Kenny Rogers and the First Edition), Ella was chic in a short black dress with lace bodice and onyx tear-drop earrings. However, she looked very tired, and was having obvious problems dealing with the studio lights. She hardly opened her eyes while she sang, and even when she talked with Pat her eyes remained mostly closed. Dipping into her Verve bag for songs, she performed "Time After Time" and "I Remember You" with a full orchestra. The deepening of Ella's vibrato was evident, with her throat muscles straining as she held sustained notes. This throbbing of her throat would stay with her for the rest of her career, along with a slight wobble of her chin as her larynx would vibrate. The musical director for the show was old friend Paul Smith.

There followed an interview with Pat, with Ella talking about the college campuses to which she had made tours. When asked how she felt about being liked by young people, she replied, "When *they* like me, that way I know I'm in." Pat brought up the story of her amateur-night debut, and Ella rejoined, "If I had stayed a dancer, I'd have starved!" Pat then spoke about her being a legend and being perfect, and her answer to him was unusually insightful. "Being at the top is a strain," she said. "The first time you get hoarse or aren't up to par, you think you're slipping. Any time you think that you're at the pinnacle, that you've made it, then you're nothing." She was speaking from her heart, as both her health and confidence would begin a downward spiral over the next few years.

After years of late night supremacy, Johnny Carson was challenged around this time by Joey Bishop on ABC. Trying to get the best possible guests, Bishop invited Ella to be on his show the night of October 24, 1968. Singing "Shiny Stockings" with the Bishop house band, Ella was in good spirits but still uncomfortable in the talk-show setting.

After the Bishop show, Ella continued to tour as she'd done in the past, sometimes doing extraordinarily long concerts. A good example was an evening she spent at Paterson State College in New Jersey. Performing to a sold-out crowd on November 23, 1968, Ella sang for almost two solid hours. Her appearances at this point became more than just concerts; they were happenings. One never knew what Ella would sing; anything she had ever recorded or was currently popular was fair game.

This night she opened with a rhythmically tricky version of "Cabaret," followed by her collaboration with Basie, "Shiny Stockings." Ella played to her young audience, singing favorites from her catalogue, such as "Sweet Georgia Brown" and "Just One of Those Things," with the more current sounds of "Sunshine of Your Love" or "Sunny." Ella performed a medley of songs from *30 by Ella* and then followed with Burt Bacharach's "A House Is Not a Home." Many songs appeared in her repertoire at this time that would never be released on record, such as "Three Little Words," "Lonely Is" (that beautiful ballad really deserves to be heard), and "A Place for Lovers." She seemed consumed by the love she was receiving, and would do encore after encore, even after the break for the first half of the show when everyone knew there was much more to follow.

Ella wore the latest in "mod" fashions in exquisitely designed gowns and wigs that belied her age and fluctuating weight. Her voice was strong and amazing in its scope, as she switched from the little girl sounds of "Old Devil Moon" to the raucous shouting of "Sunny." Jobim's "One Note Samba" also made one of its first appearances here, done in double time at a tempo that was breathtaking to listen to. Toward the end of the number, the trio stopped playing altogether, and for more than two minutes Ella scatted totally unaccompanied, never losing her timing or a note while the audience sat there with their hearts in their throats, marveling at the wonder of it all. While her later recorded versions of this song were wonderful (there were three in all), this version was a true masterpiece.

Ella taped another "Hollywood Palace" while on the East Coast on January 7, 1969 (the show aired four nights later), an unusual turn for the normally West Coast–based variety series. This time Jimmy Durante was host and Marvin Gaye was the other musical guest. Her contribution here was a swinging version of the then currently popular "Hey Jude." She sang this song several times over the next two years, both in concerts and on television. Sometimes it worked, and sometimes it didn't. This time it worked.

Ella was noticeably heavier than she had been in recent years. In good voice but with a much deeper vibrato than had been displayed in earlier video appearances, Ella was again squinting into the lights and blinking frequently. Her second solo was also a surprise, as Ella warbled a haunting "Melancholy Serenade." Durante seemed genuinely in awe of Ella, and his demeanor during their duo turn showed his high admiration of her talent. Jimmy sat down at the keyboard and began "Bill Bailey" as Ella walked behind the piano and picked up a hand mike. At the second chorus, the orchestra kicked in while the two principals each grabbed "Durante" hats and began to strut, with Ella scatting while Jimmy sang. This was one of the few examples of Ella doing "choreography" for a number on television.

While in New York, appearing at the Americana, Ella also visited Ed Sullivan on January 12, 1969. This time, however, she was one of the celebrities whom Ed invited to take a bow. Sadly, Ella did not sing that night, for there would not be many more opportunities for her to appear with Sullivan as both their careers would change significantly in the coming year.

Chapter Twenty-five

1969

$\mathscr{N}$orman Granz reentered Ella's recording life to produce a live album in May of 1969 at the Fairmont Hotel in San Francisco. The Fairmont had been a yearly stop on Ella's touring schedule for many years, and this booking also brought Tommy Flanagan permanently back into the picture. Flanagan had worked with Ella in the middle sixties before her tour with Duke Ellington, but had been supplanted by Jimmy Jones since then. Jones had tired of touring and settled down in Los Angeles. Tommy returned, and was Ella's only pianist for the next ten years. With all due respect to all the other fine pianists Ella worked with through the years (with major regard to the incredible talent of Paul Smith), Tommy Flanagan was simply the best *for her*.

The album was originally called *Watch What Happens*, with a cover photo by Audrey Franklin. The album was eventually withdrawn and rereleased as *Love You Madly*. Again it was withdrawn and rereleased, this time with a picture of a high-rise apartment building on the cover and titled *The Sunshine of Your Love* on the MPS label.

It was around the time of this recording that Ella made another change in her performing career: the use of the hand microphone. For years, she had stood center stage, singing into a mike (or several for simulcasts and recordings) on a stand, her hands free to snap her fingers and wipe her perspiring face with a handkerchief. Now, Ella freed up her movements, and picked up a hand mike from the grand piano as she entered, moving it from hand to hand as she sang.

Granz once again broke up the songs on the album, presenting them out of order and with as little applause as possible. In the original liner notes, Granz stated that he felt audiences were tiring of all the applause on live albums. He must have changed his mind, because he produced Ella's next eight live albums as he had the early ones, with much of the applause intact. As for the songs themselves, Norman divided the big band cuts on one side, and the trio cuts on the other. The trio those days consisted of Tommy, with Ed Thigpen on drums and Frank de la Rosa on bass.

The trio's turn gave us a peek at some of the new material Ella had been performing since her last released live album in 1966. She always liked to add new songs to her list, but without albums for new material, she was turning to pop, rock, and bossa nova. Only "Don'cha Go 'Way Mad" was a retread, this time with an updated arrangement. "A House Is Not a Home" showed Ella using a technique unique for her style: the purposeful rough edging of a note as if she were out of breath as she slides down the musical scale to the note of the next word. This was one of Ella's favorite ballads, and she sang it often in concerts for years. Amusingly, in 1992, Ella sang this song at the Hollywood Bowl. She began to introduce it by saying, "We sing this song because . . . just why *do* we sing this song, anyway?" Alec Wilder's mysterious sounding "Trouble Is a Man" was Ella's best ballad from the late sixties, with one of her remarkable codas making the song even more than it was.

It is said careers are made of decisions, and making the right decision can make or break a career. Norman Granz would still not return to record producing full time, and Ella did not want to stop recording, despite her failing health and changing vocal quality. She had made five albums in three years since leaving Verve and needed both a new home base and a shot in the arm to her recording career. For years Frank Sinatra had wanted her as part of his stable of stars at his Reprise label, and without Norman Granz an active part of the picture, Ella decided to join the Reprise team.

After flying to Great Britain, Ella first appeared with Canadian entertainers Sandler and Young on their summertime variety show for Kraft. On May 26 through 30, 1969, she recorded in London a unique assortment of songs produced and arranged by Richard Perry. Perry was a rock 'n' roll wunderkind, whose specialty was to make contemporary albums for singers who were not particularly known for that kind of music.

"I had been a staff producer at Reprise for two years at that time," asserts Perry, "producing music for Tiny Tim and Fats Domino, among others. I was looking for interesting and original projects, and when Ella was signed, I knew it was the opportunity of a lifetime." He got the okay from Warners (Reprise's parent company) to go ahead and record her, but ran into an interesting logistical problem. Norman Granz had booked Ella on an extensive three-month European tour that had begun shortly after her gig at the Fairmont. The only open time she would have was one week in May while she was taking a short vacation in London. If Perry did not take advantage of this time, he would have to wait until the following year before Ella's time would free up and they would be able to record, mix, and release the album. He decided to do the entire album in one week, including choosing the songs, finding British musicians he had never even met, and booking time in the studio.

Richard Perry met with Ella each day and went over three of the songs they were to record each evening. All of the songs were new to her. Learning the words so quickly was a huge accomplishment, for her cataracts were causing severe vision problems. When performing onstage and on television, Ella wore specially made contact lenses which not only helped her vision, but also blocked out the painful rays of the high-wattage lighting necessary in those arenas. Privately, she wore thick glasses, and was having great problems even in getting around. Perry rehearsed Ella briefly considering she had never heard the songs before, but by recording time she had them down pat. Nicky Hopkins, pianist for the Rolling Stones, played keyboard on this album, because Richard liked him and because the Stones were in the same studio mixing the *Let It Bleed* album at that time. Both the Stones and George Harrison were regular attendees at the Ella recording sessions, taking advantage of the chance to see a legend record.

Although the album was recorded live—with the musicians present and playing as Ella sang—the cuts were eventually the result of studio magic. Occasionally, Ella did stumble on a word or musical phrase. Richard used all the various takes to come up with the best vocal line for Ella. Only one song, "Knock on Wood," was totally redubbed in the last session of the week, as Perry thought Ella could do better (and she did). He took the tapes back to Los Angeles, and decided that much of the instrumentation would have to be redone.

"Keeping Hopkins's piano licks as well as all of the strings, I rerecorded and remixed the drums, brass, bass, et cetera in Los Angeles and shuffled them together with what I kept from London," says Richard. "Knock on Wood" kept only Ella's vocal from the original session.

As he would for Barbra Streisand the following year, Perry put together an amalgamation of songs and sounds that not only suited Ella's style and voice, but touched the heart of the easy rock/rhythm and blues charts of the day. Simply titled *Ella* with a brown cover and a pencil drawing of The Lady, the album featured songs by Randy Newman, Lennon and McCartney, Bacharach and David, George Harrison, Harry Nilsson, and Smokey Robinson. Other performers who came up with Ella tried similar stabs at "relevant" music, and usually fell right on their faces. Sinatra usually (and successfully, to be sure) included one or two of these rock endeavors on his albums, but never devoted an entire album to this kind of music. Tony Bennett tried it, and one of the best male jazz singers extant didn't record again for almost ten years. Andy Williams tried it, and I am sure he is greatful to be remembered for other marvelous recordings. Sarah Vaughan tried an entire Beatles Songbook, and practically had to change record companies. Ella, however, embraced these sounds, stretched her talent, and became one with the music.

While a commercial flop at the time of its release, this album was a creative victory and definitely deserves a place of honor in the Ella legacy. "Ooo Baby Baby," "Knock on Wood" and "Get Ready" were especially good, without a trace of hesitation on Ella's part to just dig in and do it. The arrangements were brass and electric, and neither drowned Ella out nor avoided offering the support she needed to carry this project off. There was never a sense that Ella was self-conscious about the material at hand; her ease with this music was apparent. Nilsson's "Open Your Window" was electronically interesting in the way Ella's voice was mixed and faded by engineer Gene Shiveley, especially during her scat at the bridge. Ella was very pleased with the final results, calling Perry on the phone to tell him he was a genius. It takes one to know one.

Ella was not so pleased, however, with the promotion the record received. While a big billboard was put up on the backside of the Whiskey A-Go-Go on Sunset Strip, the album got little promotion in record stores, newspapers, or radio ads. Both Perry and Ella were surprised, but looked to the future. This was the nadir of Ella's recording career, as she hadn't had a successful album in three years, with seven misses gathering dust in record stores. Again, she could have stopped recording and just lived off of her live appearances and backlog of Decca and Verve albums still available. But, again, she chose to persevere.

Richard wanted to take her to the next step of rock, and begin work on a second album that would push Ella even farther away from her jazz roots. Several sessions were done in late 1969 that yielded four never-released cuts plus one instrumental that Ella never even got a chance to sing on. "Try a Little Bit," "Lucky," "Timer," and "The Flim Flam Man" (Perry would have better luck at getting Streisand's version of this song released but prefers Ella's) showed Ella in good voice, having a ball rocking out. All were recorded with a total electronic feel, without the heavy brass or strings of the earlier effort. Before more work could be done, Reprise pulled the plug because Norman Granz did not like, and could not relate to, the direction in which they were taking his superstar. For no matter what, she was *his* superstar, an attitude of practical ownership that would continue for the rest of their relationship, much to the consternation of those who tried to work with her.

Also during this period, Ella lent her talents to an unusual project. A multinational production of *Uncle Tom's Cabin* was mounted in Europe, with a modernization of the story not only to make it palatable for contemporary audiences but also to stress the theme of racial harmony that was so needed in those troubled times (and in these troubled times, as well). Eartha Kitt was featured as a singer, and her voice was, for some reason, dubbed by Ella. This 170-minute film never received wide distribution, and while it is not available in video stores, copies are available through some small distributors.

Ella did get to perform two of Richard Perry's arrangements on television, visiting both Carol Burnett and Ed Sullivan for one last performance. Sojourning to Burnett for a second time on November 10, 1969, Ella was also reunited with Bing Crosby, the last time the two would sing together in public. Surrounded by four African-American male dancers in silver lamé jumpsuits and fringed vests, Ella danced around in a chiffon dress with a sequined bodice as she rocked to "Get Ready." The number was preposterous, kind of like Pat Boone hosting "Soul Train." Ella's "mod" dancing was spirited, but not becoming for a woman of obvious weight and age. She fared much better in her two other outings on the show: a duet with Carol of "I'll Never Fall in Love Again" (also from the Perry album) with Ella in an orange satin jumper with lace blouse, and her duet with Bing.

The camera found Crosby and Ella sitting on stools, Carol noticeably missing as she gave these two superstars the room they needed to work together. The theme of the medley this time was songs from pictures made by Paramount, which included "Moon River," "Buttons and Bows," "In the Cool, Cool, Cool of the Evening," "Swinging on a Star," "Call Me Irresponsible," and "Thanks for the Memory." Both were in excellent voice, obviously enjoying working with one another. This segment was preceded by a skit in which Bob Hope made a surprise appearance, and Hope and Crosby bounced extemporaneous jibes at one another to everyone's delight. Bing was energized for his tuning with Ella, a highlight of any television season.

Sullivan's show was winding down its twenty-two year run, but Ella came back on November 23, 1969, one more time. After the host did an Ed Sullivan-ism and introduced the Rolling Stones singing "Gimme Shelter" from their latest album *Let It Be* (he meant *Let It Bleed*), Ella came out next. In a sequined and beaded gown with a satin scarf carefully thrown over her shoulder and down the left side of her dress and wearing heavy eye makeup, she sang "You'd Better Love Me" (with an arrangement by Marty Paich and never recorded), and followed that with a live version of "Open Your Window." While the studio version of the song needed a little doctoring for Ella to sing it live (the fadeout had to be replaced with an actual ending and the extra echo at the scat chorus could not be repeated with the same effect), this version was wonderful, gentle and sensitive, with orchids deserved (as Walter Winchell used to say) by both Ella and Richard

Perry. Ed called Ella over for a brief chat, where they discussed such earth-shattering topics as what her first big hit was and where she was born. Norman Granz was also careful to provide Ed with information so he could plug Ella's appearance the following night at the Latin Casino in Cherry Hill, New Jersey.

Chapter Twenty-six

1970–1971

*T*he first year since 1935 that Ella did not go into the studio to record was 1970. She did go to Television City in Hollywood to tape "The Glen Campbell Goodtime Hour" on February 2, 1970 (the other high-ticket guests were Raymond Burr and Neil Diamond). She looked wonderful in a short, "Lucy"-like wig, brown gown, and gold and brown bolero jacket. Featured in a boudoir-type setting, Ella cuddled "Watch What Happens." She clutched onto the back of a chair for support and did not use a hand mike. Glen then joined her for "Hey Jude" (a testament to then-current tastes melded a jazz singer and a country singer dueting to a rock song). This time it worked. Ella was obviously having fun as Glen strained to sing in her key—and succeeded. At one point, she tossed off a "show-off" to him as he hit a high note. The two sang in harmony beautifully, and it was the most satisfying television appearance she had had for quite a while. The musical conductor for the show was her old comrade Marty Paich.

The ongoing problems with her eyes forced her finally to cut back sharply on her career, taking time out for treatment to try and save her eyesight. These treatments and operations continued for almost two years. The blanks in Ella's touring and recording were filled in by hospital stays and convalescence. Due to her weight, high blood pressure, and early stages of diabetes, any operation was dangerous. Most people did not know that some of these conditions were potentially life threatening. Diabetes, heart disease, and hypertension were very serious for an exhausted woman who was extremely overweight. Privately, some people wondered if this wasn't the end of an illustrious career.

She still had an album left on her contract with Reprise, and Decca, Verve, and Capitol kept her albums in record stores. Financially independent, Ella did not need to work, but it was her whole life. She fought back courageously (as she always had when anything interfered with her singing), and in the fall was well enough to do several variety shows.

Two were taped in October, and the first was aired on October 17, when she once again visited Andy Williams. This time she not only sang but appeared in a skit for the only time in her career (she gave Andy's "bear" a cookie). On November 26, 1970, Ella was seen appearing on the then-popular Flip Wilson variety series. Wilson was the first African American to host his own variety show (Bill Cosby and Diahann Carroll were first with a drama and a situation comedy, respectively), and Ella was still a much-sought-after guest. Appearing in a beige gown with a sequined bodice, she wore a long, brown "flip" wig. Her eye problems were taking an obvious toll, for Ella, still not wearing glasses in public, looked ten years older than on her stint with Glen Campbell just months before.

Ella sang the Beatles' "Something" with a full orchestra, and while her voice was strong, her vibrato caught in her throat and she did not look at all happy. "Lady Be Good" was done with the trio of Flanagan, Ed Thigpen, and Frank de la Rosa; Ella changed to a green blouse with a green and purple lamé skirt. Her version here was the original scat, and Ella wailed as only Ella could. She and Flip did a non-duet duet, with her crooning "The Glory of Love" while him tried his best to get through "Makin' Whoopee." Ella's video Christmas was spent with Tom Jones, but it was again obvious she was not feeling well.

By 1971, she began to try to put her career back in order, much to the shock and surprise of her doctors. She completed her commitment to Reprise that year with *Things Ain't What They Used to Be*. This was a musical potpourri of different styles, whose title said a lot about the state of Ella's career at that point. Gerald Wilson arranged the songs, the styles of which jockeyed for supremacy. "Willow Weep for Me" (recorded for the second time) and "Black Coffee" (recorded for the third time) were juxtaposed with "I Heard It Through the Grapevine" and "Sunny." There was a lack of cohesion and continuity from one cut to another, although each worked well individually.

Norman Granz returned to Ella's recording life to produce this album, and never left again. The album was not pure easy rock as was her previous, but the standards and the pop were given a "mod" treatment. This was particularly true for "Tuxedo Junction" and "Things Ain't What They Used to Be," as the big band style musically fought with the rock idiom almost schizophrenically.

More changes were evident in Ella's voice, as all the anesthesia and weight fluctuations took their toll. Quite often, in the days when gas was used as a general anesthetic, the vocal chords were traumatized. The speaking voice was sometimes left lowered and gravelly, so it is no wonder that a singing voice might have been affected. Ella was not quite as sure in her higher register, and her vibrato developed a quiver. Her legendary breath control wasn't really affected, but she paused to breathe more often and in more conspicuous places.

Her versions here of "Mas Que Nada," "A Man and a Woman," "Days of Wine and Roses," "Don't Dream of Anybody But Me," and "Manteca" were all winners, as was much of the album, as a whole. "Just When We're Falling in Love" had an interesting footnote for Ella fans: it was a reworking of her old "Robbins' Nest." Ella rerecorded this song again on her Grammy-winning *All That Jazz* in 1989.

When it came time to release the two Reprise albums on CD, Warner Brothers decided to combine them both on one (the cover featuring an old picture of Ella that had been originally used for the *Like Someone in Love* album back in the fifties) and chose this project for inclusion in their "CD + G" catalogue. CD + G, which means compact disc plus graphics, enabled the consumer to view lyrics, pictures, and other visual accompaniment on a television screen while listening to the compact disc. When Philips and Sony originally published their world standard for the compact disc, they included specifications not only for sound, but for graphics that could be generated out of CD data and displayed on a home TV monitor. In the rush of the great CD explosion, not much attention was paid to this aspect, except for the Japanese karaoke machines, where it was used to put song lyrics on TV screens while fledgling Sinatras tried out their scooby-dooby-doos.

After audio is encoded onto a CD, there is a five percent space left over. That's where the graphics are encoded. These graphics can come in the form of pictures, song lyrics (which can be translated into other languages), and other liner-note type information. Warner New Media, a sister company to the Warner Brothers/Reprise record conglomerate, used this new technology on dozens of contemporary, jazz, and classical titles. The graphics of CD + G discs could be seen using any CD + G player hooked up to a television set. The music would play on all CD players. CD + G players included JVC's CD + G machine, CD-ROM–based game machines such as NEC's Turbo-Grafx-CD System and Sega's Genesis CD-ROM Game Player, and other interactive CD players, among them CD-1 and Commodore CDTV. Naturally, technology changes faster than the time it takes to read this book, so check with your local dealer to see if your CD player can accommodate this CD's graphics capabilities.

Tracy Bader was the designer in charge of Ella's CD, working with others at Warner New Media like Mike Damm, John Dennis, and Larry Israel. The graphics they designed for the albums were basic but suited the music, interweaving song lyrics with graphics of the era in which they were recorded and pictures of Ella (supplied by Salle Productions). Looking at the graphics, there was no mistaking that these albums were a product of the late sixties and early seventies. There was creative tongue-in-cheek with the pictures of flowers, desserts, and other visual stimuli that followed the literal flow of the lyrics without taking into account their actual context. This was all very well done, and did enhance the enjoyment of the music.

Ella was feeling better enough to travel, and wanted to play again (both literally and figuratively) in New York. Norman Granz arranged for Ella to do a free live concert in Central Park on July 12, 1971. More than 200,000 people packed the Wollman Rink of the park as part of the Schaefer Music Festival to hear her perform again. Oscar Peterson opened the evening, and Ella filled out the second half. In the audience that night was Benny Goodman, so Ella introduced him and then sang "Goodnight My Love," the song they had recorded together so long before. Ella was in fine voice, opening with a swinging "St. Louis Blues" and including such favorites as "They Can't Take That Away From Me," "Hello, Dolly!" and "Night and Day."

It was the first time New York saw Ella with her glasses on, and the first time Ella had (literally) seen New York in years. Feeling well, she traveled to Europe, but unfortunately did not get very far. On July 21, nine days later, Ella performed at the Theatre de Verdure in Nice. Norman Granz had the tape recorder rolling, the result of which was released many years later on Pablo as *Ella a Nice*, complete with French liner notes. The sound quality of the album was poor, having an empty, tinny sound that had an eerie "buzz" when Ella sang loudly. The songs were again rearranged out of order, although the applause was mixed together to present them smoothly. Despite the fact that Ella wasn't well, she was in good voice on this recording, an album that in my opinion should never have been released. No less than six of the entries had been released on previous live albums, with such goodies as "Something," "Close to You," and "Put a Little Love in Your Heart" recorded with such muddy sound that they were difficult to enjoy.

With unreadable liner notes (in French), hope was held that the CD version would be clearer. While the notes *were* translated into English for the CD version, the digital remixing brought out the worst in the recording. Any sounds louder than a whisper had distortion; the entire CD was unlistenable on any good sound system. This was a shame, one that Norman Granz could not avoid, as by the time the CD was released, he had sold Pablo to Fantasy, Inc., and *they* had sold the recording to Original Jazz Classics.

Ella was so ill by the end of the concert that she was hastened by private jet back to the United States, and then rushed to the Massachusetts Eye and Ear Infirmary on July 30. She was operated on for the removal of a cataract from her right eye and a hemorrhage from the left. She was released on August 14. Once again she fought back, but not without scars. Her once pudgy face now had prominent cheekbones and dimples when she smiled, and her voice developed a rougher edge to it. However, with thick glasses or without, Ella was still the best jazz singer in the world, and she was about to begin a series of recordings and concerts to prove it.

There was one more false start at a recording contract before the Pablo years started, and it involved two old friends: Nelson Riddle and Cole Porter. Granz arranged for Ella to record for Atlantic Records a new collection of Porter songs to be called *Ella Loves Cole*. Riddle was brought in to reorchestrate the numbers to make them different from their original recordings on Verve. A couple of songs, such as "My Heart Belongs to Daddy" and "Down in the Depths on the Ninetieth Floor," had been overlooked on the Verve album. The release of this set, originally recorded on February 13, 1972, was timed to coincide with the ten-year commemoration of Cole Porter's death, although it was released two years before the anniversary. The cover featured an older-looking Ella, her wig in a topknot, wearing a modern knit dress. The album was released, and then Norman Granz pulled it, severing both his and Ella's ties to Atlantic Records. The album was rereleased in 1978 (with two added songs) as *Dream Dancing*, and will be discussed in its entirety when we get there. For now, though, the Independent Years were over, and Ella and Norman once again made recording history with another Granz label, Pablo.

The Pablo Years

Chapter Twenty-seven

1972–1973

$\mathscr{T}$he early seventies were a very strange time in music. Everything was in a state of constant flux. The Beatles had broken up, Elvis was beginning his downward spiral into self-destruction, and rock 'n' roll had metamorphosed into rock. The British invasion was over, and in its wake a whole battery of singers, groups, and songwriters had emerged. Janis and Jimi exploded themselves into Eternity, and the order of the day was sex, drugs, and rock 'n' roll. Young people turned away from television in droves, and the television variety show was all but extinct. Even Sinatra had a short-lived retirement, and Streisand was recording "Stoney End," not "Second Hand Rose." Many of Ella's contemporaries found themselves without recording contracts; some were forced to retire. Others spent their time playing state fairs, retirement villages, or other venues of nostalgia, trading in on the fading memories of their glory. Even dyed-in-the-wool rockers were having a tough go of it, with record sales at an all-time low, and the recording industry keeling over from the withdrawals. Mom-and-Pop record stores closed down all over the country, and the days of going into a private booth to hear a sample of what you wanted to buy had long passed.

Into this tenuous atmosphere strode Norman Granz, once again ready to champion the cause of "good music." Jazz would lose two of its greats in quick succession: Louis Armstrong and Duke Ellington would not live to see Granz's new label become the preeminent place for the greats to record.

Pablo Records was named for Pablo Picasso, a good friend of Norman's, and the label's symbol was Picasso's little minimalist horse. Granz began recording Ella before he even had a studio or a distribution deal. Her strength had returned sufficiently to do a concert on June 2, 1972, at the Santa Monica Civic Auditorium outside of Los Angeles. The show required no long travel and Ella was in good spirits. She gave what is arguably one of her best concerts on vinyl. On a bill that also included Count Basie and his band, Oscar Peterson, Stan Getz, Roy Eldridge, Eddie "Lockjaw" Davis, Harry "Sweets" Edison, and Al Grey, Ella was inspired to be in peak form. She always got an extra boost out of performing with musicians who turned her on musically, and this night was no exception.

Backed by the Basie band and her trio (Tommy Flanagan on piano, Ed Thigpen on drums, and Keter Betts returning on bass in a job he would hold on and off for more than twenty years), Ella came out swinging.

Beautifully recorded with just enough echo to balance her voice against the huge hall (Val Valentin was once again at the engineering controls), Ella opened with a Jim Hughart arrangement of Nat Cole's "L-O-V-E" (Hughart had bassed for Ella during her Ellington tour), a swinger that set the standard for the evening. Cole Porter's "Begin the Beguine" was next, with the best marriage of standard song and special material I have ever heard. Marty Paich's arrangement was lively and rhythmic, driving itself into a special piece where Ella remembered the great bands and ballrooms of her youth. At the end of the song, Ella swooped through one more "begin the beguine," scooping up on "the" and hitting, a split second in rhythm before the band did, an extended high note on "guine." That this sound came so easily was a testament to her art, and her continued growth as a singer. The practice of ending songs on an extended high note had been done by other singers (Eydie Gorme, for example), but none so cleverly and with so much accuracy in pitch and timing. Ella did this more and more often, developing yet another trademark that distinguished her work in this period from that of her previous efforts.

A Nelson Riddle version of "Indian Summer" followed, showing once again that Ella's voice had taken some changes, and that she was using those changes in her art. Her voice was less smooth, but somehow stronger, much like many people who mature and grow as they get older. While Ella was always able to inject that little-girl quality into her ballads, now she folded in huge amounts of deeper understanding, maturity, and wisdom into her singing and her voice. It made for a more interesting if somewhat spicier dish.

Still looking to incorporate the sounds of the younger generation into her performances, Ella gave a double-barreled shot of Carole King's "You've Got a Friend" and Marvin Gaye's "What's Going On?" The former, with a chart by Marty Paich (who arranged several of the songs she performed at the concert), showed Ella in full command of the song. She made it totally her own while respecting Ms. King's intent. Ella continued to sing this song for years, often using it as her encore. Even more respectful was Gerald Wilson's arrangement of the latter, taken at a faster tempo than the original. Ella sang the lyrics once through, using the rest of the song to do an unbelievable rock scat. The energy, the use, and understanding of the rock and soul idioms and the total musicality of this number put the original to shame.

As was her usual practice when appearing with a large group, she took some time out to feature the trio. Ella had long since abandoned using a quartet. Except for the brief time in the following two years when Joe Pass joined the group, a trio it remained. Tommy Flanagan was so skilled at accompanying The Lady that you almost didn't miss the other instruments; he could sound like an entire brass section or one reed if need be. "I just decide which instruments would sound best with the song," Tommy told me. "If I need brass, I think brass, and my playing comes out brass."

"Night and Day" opened the trio's portion of the program. This set ended with yet another wonderful bossa nova, "Madalena." These bossa numbers became a steady part of any Ella appearance, and justifiably so. Time after time, she took these Brazilian rhythms and shuffled them with pure jazz that was delightful.

The band blasted back in with "Shiny Stockings," a romp made even better by the participation of many of the original performers. Keter set the pace for "It's All Right With Me," pounding out the beat as Ella first fooled the audience with a snippet of "Big Noise From Winnetka" and then dived into a line from "Too Darn Hot" before finally settling into the song. Ella did all she could to wring the song out of rhythm and melody, taking it on a lyrical ride (no scat here) to the crescendo at the end.

Paich also arranged a number Ella used for years, always to the delight of the audience. ASCAP lyricist Ella Fitzgerald put words to Quincy Jones's melody for the television theme from "Sanford and Son," performed here for the first time on record. Ella's set ended with Ray Charles's "I Can't Stop Loving You," with Paich's arrangement done much the same as it had been on her television special with Duke Ellington.

All the participants in the evening jammed together for a ten-plus-minute finale of "C Jam Blues." As with many of these jam sessions, Count Basie set the rhythm with his piano, while Ella came in to bop several measures, followed by the various JATP All-Stars who traded fours with her. The entire performance was a tour de force for everyone concerned, as each one prodded the next to do a little better until Ella sang "I'm not gonna blow my voice on *that* note."

This album had an unusual history. Originally a mail-order item through a record club, it was released by Norman Granz in a condensed version in the late seventies, with five of Ella's songs edited out. The final, full concert was released on CD in 1989. Granz has been quoted as saying that his recording of the concert was a whim. Considering he then started a major record label, more likely he needed the extra income to offset his tax problems. Just a hunch.

In July, Ella flew to New York to appear on a Timex-sponsored special called "All Star Swing Festival." On a bill with Basie, Ellington, Benny Goodman, Dave Brubeck, and others, this was Ella's first television appearance in two years. She looked a little tentative at times, for this was her first time on the tube wearing glasses. Her weight had trimmed down quite a bit, and she looked glamorous but older, every bit her fifty-five years.

Host Doc Severinsen first introduced Basie and Ella as they bopped a big band chart of "Oh, Lady Be Good." Later in the program, Ella and the trio went through standard arrangements (for Ella) of "Body and Soul" and "Goody-Goody." The finale of the show was a salute to "Pops" Armstrong. The horn players took turns at Louis's hits, and Ella came out to sing "Hello, Dolly!" and then jitterbugged as the salute ended.

Europe was next on her itinerary, but on July 27, 1972, Ella suffered a hemorrhage in her left eye while singing in Verona, Italy. She immediately saw Professor Miller Berliner of New York University, who happened to be vacationing there. All of her concerts through November 20 were canceled to give her eye time to heal. However, upon returning home, she was taken to the Massachusetts Eye and Ear Infirmary where cataract surgery was performed on her left eye.

Ella rested through the summer in Beverly Hills, and resumed her career in late autumn. Now, however, it was no longer possible to disguise how ill she had been, or the toll it had taken on her vocal equipment.

Starting off the new year with fairly good health, Ella made her next appearance with Johnny Carson on "The Tonight Show" on January 11, 1973. She spoke little with Johnny, preferring not to answer too many questions about her health (or appearing on television with glasses). Ella sang "Sweet Georgia Brown," "Love for Sale" (the Nelson Riddle arrangement), and "What's Going On?" She was in good voice but seemed a little frail. As the year wore on, time was again taken out of her career for medical attention for her eyes. When she was well enough to perform again, a very special concert was planned at New York's Carnegie Hall.

Ella had performed there since the late 1940s, a groundbreaker with Granz's JATP concerts for playing jazz at serious music venues. On July 5, 1973, many of Ella's musical loved ones joined her for a concert that celebrated not only a great career in music, but the return of its full-time glory. Norman Granz put together a spectacular show, reuniting Ella with a re-formed Chick Webb Orchestra. It featured many of the original sidemen Ella spent her musical youth with, such as Eddie Barefield, Pete and Arthur Clarke, Taft Jordan, Dick Vance, and George Matthews. As always, Ella did several numbers with her rhythm section, this time including not only Tommy and Keter but also Freddie Waits on drums and, as the start of a long-running musical partnership, the great Joe Pass on guitar.

Pass had been making quite a name for himself all through the mid- and late sixties, but was brought to international prominence on Pablo records as both part of Ella's musical family, and on solo, duet, and group albums with other jazz musicians. Joe traveled with Ella only for about a year, at the end of which he was a Pablo star in his own right. Ella and Joe recorded and appeared in concert dozens of times after that, but as equals, partners in music.

Another virtuoso that night, although much more unsung, renewed a musical collaboration with Ella that was over twenty years old. Ellis Larkins was a well-known jazz pianist, having gigged on many sides with Ella for Decca. Other vocalists had relied on his generosity and individual musical style, the most unusual being an album with Julie Wilson of songs done in the style of Billie Holiday.

Since Granz still had not made a distribution deal for Pablo, he agreed to let John Hammond produce a live album on the Columbia label, for which Ella was paid a $25,000 advance. With the title *Newport Jazz Festival—Live at Carnegie Hall*, July 5, 1973, the double-record set featured Ella and the Chick Webb band, Ella and the quartet, and Ella soloing with both Pass and Larkins. Hammond rearranged the music on the album, as the concert had featured many entrances and exits of the different musicians and groups.

He assembled several of her songs with the small group first, although her small-group work had actually been featured in the second half of the evening. Introduced on Broadway by Steve Lawrence in the show *Golden Rainbow* and made popular on record by Sammy Davis, Jr., "I've Gotta Be Me" was a typical Ella opening swinger. Her rendition showed that she had lost none of her ability to manipulate a rhythm or a melody. The wobble in her vibrato was evident but not damaging. Tommy Flanagan wisely chose to play many of the newer selections in lower keys. This gave Ella more room to play vocally in a comfortable range. Joe Pass's guitar gave the group a deeper, sharper sound. Ella ended the song hitting a high note (as had become her custom).

Billie Holiday's "Good Morning Heartache" was next, the arrangement from the *Clap Hands, Here Comes Charlie!* album. Ella introduced the song referring to both Billie and the recent release of *Lady Sings the Blues*, but some of this introduction was shortened for the album. Frank DeVol's arrangement of "Miss Otis Regrets" was next, the best Ella put to record. Unfortunately, the CD version of the album distorted this song so that it seemed as though Ella's voice went off-key and cracked; it was a digital remastering problem not found on the vinyl version.

Rather than feature all of the quartet's numbers at once, Hammond cut to the duet between Fitzgerald and Pass. For the first time on record, Ella and Joe ran a musical duologue, with a medley of "Don't Worry 'Bout Me" and "These Foolish Things." The interplay between the two was fantastic. Each knew when to pause and when to fill in the pauses, a sort of musical mental telepathy. "Any Old Blues" ended the first side, with a lighthearted salute to Joe Williams, and the blues in general.

The second side started with the big band cuts, beginning with Ella's trademarked "A-Tisket A-Tasket." Undoubtedly this was an encore number for her set with the band, but was chosen to start this portion of the collection. Done here without the usual introductory bars, the arrangement followed Frank DeVol's from 1962. "Indian Summer" was a repeat here from her concert at the Santa Monica Civic the previous year. The coda was taken a little slower, and Ella's voice went just slightly off its mark at the last note. The trio of band cuts ended with "Smooth Sailing," on record for the fourth time. This was a lively and thrilling version, different from the others, but with the requisite "the record's still available" toward the end. The Ella/Ellis songs ended the side.

Side three was an all-music side, featuring Al Grey, Eddie "Lockjaw" Davis, Tommy Flanagan, and Roy Eldridge but no Ella. The last side returned Ella to the quartet: a medley of "Taking a Chance on Love/I'm in the Mood for Love"; "Lemon Drop" was a reworked scat number showing that, if anything, Miss Fitz had become even more creative in her bop singing as the years passed; "Some of These Days" was a fun special-material number; and "People" closed the album, a looser version than previously recorded but sung from the heart.

At this point it is interesting to note that Ella was embarking on a wave of creativity matching her best work for Verve. She could have relied on her Decca and Verve recordings for a huge catalogue of songs to do in her live concerts and still have had hundreds to pick from. Not only did she choose to record many new studio albums, but she often featured new songs in her concerts, material which never made it to the studio (and, unfortunately, sometimes never made it to live albums, either). Her live appearances were a careful crafting of old favorites from her albums and new songs; however, the "new" were not contemporary songs but classic standards and jazz. Ella pretty much gave up doing cover versions of rock songs, especially as rock began to fade into heavy metal and disco. Jazz was Ella's main focus for the rest of her life, and her Pablo albums were much more focused into the jazz milieu than many of her Verve albums had been, and certainly more so than the independent albums. Granz was no longer concerning himself with reaching the entire world, or putting Ella on the charts. Yet, as Ella's focus narrowed she was even more revered, more celebrated and awarded, and busier than ever.

Immediately following her Carnegie Hall concert, Ella did gigs with two symphony orchestras, one taped for television. Arthur Fiedler invited Ella to appear with the Boston Pops for a concert that was televised midsummer. This was Ella's second television appearance since returning to work, and a very successful one at that. Making her entrance midway through the program in a pink gown with feathers at the sleeves, around the hips, and at the hemline, she looked stylish in a short, curly wig and horn-rimmed glasses. She received an extended standing ovation; she was received that way at every concert.

Ella thanked the audience and expressed nervousness at working with the great Mr. Fiedler. One part of Ella's personality that did not change from her very first appearance at the Harlem Opera House was the extreme nervousness she experienced before each performance. She was quite aware of her audiences, and was terrified that she would let them down. She even kept track of what songs she sang in what city; she was careful not to repeat the same selections the next time she played in the same venue. As the years went by, often the first couple of numbers in her concerts showed her nervousness, until she caught her breath and regained her confidence.

Her trio, working with the symphony and by themselves, consisted of Tommy Flanagan, Keter Betts, and Freddie Waits on drums. While she did not do a full set due to the limitations of the television time slot, several of her symphony favorites were included here. She opened with a symphony version of "That Old Black Magic," taken at an even faster pace than before. Ella favored an old Cole Porter song from her defunct album *Ella Loves Cole* called "Down in the Depths on the Ninetieth Floor," and used it in her symphony concerts for years, as well as in her regular concerts over the next several months. "Good Morning Heartache" was simply beautiful with strings added to its usual arrangement. Switching to the quartet, "Alone Too Long" was one of those beautiful songs that never found its way onto an album. Her standard Ellington medley and "Lemon Drop" were given their due, with Ella self-consciously stopping Flanagan long enough to try and explain to the Boston audience what her "scat" was all about. At this point she mistakenly called Arthur Fiedler "Mr. Freed" when asking for a moment to explain "Lemon Drop"; Ella's nerves were troubling her again. The set ended with "S'Wonderful," lifted in toto from the Gershwin Songbook.

Ella repeated much the same concert several days later at the Waterloo Music Festival, lengthening her set with some of the Songbook tunes, "Some of These Days" and "People." Ella continued to tour North America all during the fall of 1973 and early winter of 1974, stopping only to record her first studio album for Pablo.

Chapter Twenty-eight

1973–1974

*I*t seemed inevitable that Fitzgerald and Pass would come together to record in the studio. Ella had previously devoted albums to
just voice and piano (with Ellis Larkins and Paul Smith), but this was
the first time she tried recording an entire album with just a guitar.
The choice was inspired; it not only successfully launched Pablo (Norman Granz had made a distribution deal with RCA), but started a
decade of innovative recording ideas that ensured Ella's place as the
prima jazzarina.

Norman Granz had taken hold of Joe Pass's career at this point,
and carefully pointed him toward not only working with jazz greats
but making a name for himself as a solo jazz virtuoso. Born Joseph
Anthony Passalaqua in New Brunswick, New Jersey, in 1929, Pass
was raised in a Pennsylvania steel town. Inspired by crooning cowboy
Gene Autry's six-string guitar, Joe was gifted with one by family
friends, and by the time he was nine years old he was practicing seven
or eight hours a day. After several false starts at a career in his early
adulthood, Pass recorded his first album, *Sounds of Syannon*, in 1962.
Having done studio work with the likes of Julie London and Frank

Sinatra, Pass was soon gigging with Gerald Wilson, George Shearing, and others. His impressive, individualistic style, where he played bass, melody, and chords all at the same time as if he had five hands, began to bring him notice. So did his simplistic showmanship. Joe simply walked on stage, nodded to the audience, plugged in his guitar, and played. If he was really jacked up, he actually announced a few of the tunes over the microphone. When he was finished, he nodded to the audience again, unplugged his guitar, and exited stage left. And when he was done, very few people could follow him. While George Benson, Barney Kessel, Wes Montgomery, or Charlie Christian might have been better showmen, there was simply no one who could touch Joe Pass on the guitar. His sense of tempo was on a par with Count Basie, his rhythm on that with Buddy Rich. Harmonically, he was a trio unto himself, and while he would never say so, he was one of a small handful of musicians who were on a par with Ella Fitzgerald.

Take Love Easy, their first studio collaboration, was recorded in Los Angeles on August 28, 1973. The entire album was done in one day, with some of the cuts accomplished in a single take with no rehearsal. This was to hold true for much of their work together, as four more such efforts would be in the can by the early nineties. "I really hardly knew her when we began," says Joe. "I came early and I was nervous. She and Norman showed up with a whole bunch of sheet music and we just started going through it. Norman picked all the songs and Ella and I picked the keys. Occasionally, Ella would pass on something she didn't like, but mostly it was Norman. I had no input on the songs that were chosen. Once they picked the tunes and we settled on the keys, the album was recorded very quickly."

It was an album of ballads and easy tempos, each punctuated by a Joe Pass solo before Ella returned to finish the final chorus. Joe never liked to take full choruses between Ella's warblings, because, "I felt the audience was there to hear Ella, and I was there to support her, not supplant her." Ella was eager for Joe to play, and their style together was formed by simply going out to the stage or studio and diving in without stopping. Once the songs were chosen, Joe found Ella's best key for each, sometimes suggesting a more unusual key to give a song a different slant. Ella enjoyed his input and took his suggestions.

"Take Love Easy" was an Ellington song that had been overlooked in both the Songbook and later studio album with the band. Ella's laid-back but full-bodied voice, ambling in and about the melody, set the pace for the entire album. Both "Don't Be That Way" and "A Foggy Day" had been given more full treatment by Ella in the past but were treated here with a light touch and much looser feel. "You're Blase," "Lush Life," and "I Want to Talk About You" were the torch pieces here, performances of superb nuance and sensitivity, making the songs both simple and sophisticated at the same time.

While this was not the best of the Ella/Joe collaborations (the album was done hurriedly at the request of Norman Granz, and it was mixed a little flat), it was a most satisfying first attempt, marred only by the cover. Most of Ella's Pablo albums had a bleak, black and white feel to them, rarely featuring a flattering picture of her. Miss Fitz had an expressive, pretty face, and a touch of glamour or color might have made for a more pleasing presentation in record stores.

The new year barely got under way when Ella was back in the studio to record her best album since leaving Verve eight years earlier. Again avoiding use of a full orchestra, Norman Granz surrounded Ella with many of the best jazz performers she had been appearing with in concert (and who, coincidentally, were all featured Pablo players). With Tommy on piano; ex-husband Ray Brown on bass; Louie Bellson on drums; Joe (of course) on guitar; and Harry Edison, Clark Terry, and Zoot Sims providing the brass, *Fine and Mellow* was a great romp for all concerned. Recorded on January 8, 1974, Ella tore into each number as if it were steak and she had been starving.

As with several of Granz's earlier small-group efforts, only the key and pattern was predetermined; the rest was left to improvisation. "The entire album was recorded in slightly more than three hours," remembers Louie Bellson, "with Norman wanting it to be recorded as if it were in a jazz club, with no baffles between the bass and drums. Ray Brown was excellent at working these things out in the studio, patterning songs with musicians and ensuring things coming out right musically." Granz much preferred working with these small groups as opposed to big bands or orchestras (with the exception of Count Basie) because he felt formal orchestrations inhibited the jazz milieu. Each song was given a different treatment and musical mood, served up with a little extra dressing so that each was something special.

The album was belatedly released in 1978. Granz was famous for

recording Ella and releasing the sessions one month later or sometimes twenty years later. The cover was the worst of Ella's career; she
looked like Garrett Morris doing a bad impression of Ella Fitzgerald.
Many of the songs contained here became staples of her live concerts.
Several of them had been done before but with completely different
approaches.

"The Man I Love" was extraordinarily original, starting the first
chorus with just a piano accompaniment by Tommy. At the end of
the first chorus, Louie began to beat out a steady, syncopated rhythm,
sharing the beat with Ray Brown until the release, with everyone
joining in for a rousing third chorus. The entire thing was worked out
(amazingly) in a matter of minutes by Ray. "I Can't Give You Anything
But Love" was spared the special material of Ella's version from the
late fifties, and was treated as a straight-out swinger. "I'm Just a Lucky
So-and-So" was a third time retread for Ella, the original going back
to the Decca days in 1946 with Billy Kyle at the piano. Here she
started at the bridge, going through to the end of the song with a
legato feel. The group came in behind her in a pseudo-rock rhythm
as she started the song again, this time rollicking her way through
until she reached an extended coda. Typical Ella.

" 'Round Midnight" was originally recorded in 1961 for *Clap
Hands, Here Comes Charlie!* (see The Verve Years), but this time the
treatment was more mature, with Ella not only conquering the difficult melody but amending it after the sax solo until she wound down
to yet another wonderful coda. "I Don't Stand a Ghost of a Chance
With You" was treated much the same way, with Zoot Sims and Joe
Pass shining as featured players. "Polka Dots and Moonbeams" was
another example of Ella not allowing gender to get in her way of
singing a good song. Starting with Ray Brown's slide on the bass, the
song was treated with much of Ella's innocent, little-girl quality, cra-
dled in her voice as she musically waxed poetic about love found at a
country dance.

The title song, made popular by Billie Holiday, gave Ella an all-
too-little-used chance to flex her blues muscles. " 'Rockin' in Rhythm"
was another tune from the Ellington catalogue given a fresh look.
Starting in a high key, this pure scat number offered Ella a chance to
bop out using almost every part of her still quite flexible vocal range.
Rounding out the nine tunes (only nine because each cut was espe-

cially long) was "I'm in the Mood for Love." Recently featured as part
of a medley with "Taking a Chance on Love," the song was a solo
feature this time. Starting with Ella's bop refrain, it moved into a
steady, finger-snapping rhythm featuring all the lyrics.

Ella returned to New York to appear at Lincoln Center's Avery
Fisher Hall on January 18. This concert was notable for the songs she
chose. "There Will Never Be Another You" was another swinger that
she used quite often as an opening number, but unfortunately never
appeared on any of her albums. Ella once again used her songwriting
talents to memorialize her recently departed friend in "I Remember
Johnny Hodges," also never recorded. Featured at this concert was
an Ella oldie not often repeated in her later years, "Stairway to the
Stars."

Ella also videotaped an appearance on a local New York NBC-TV
affiliate at this time, called "Harlem Homecoming," and broadcast on
February 10, 1974. The stellar cast included Ella, James Brown, Tony
Bennett, Dizzy Gillespie, the Edwin Hawkins Singers, Roscoe Lee
Browne, and The Dance Theatre of Harlem.

With two Pablo albums in the can and one recently recorded for
Columbia, Ella embarked on her first European tour (from February
1 through April 20) since being forced to fly home from Nice in July
of 1971. London was her first recorded stop, and rather than appearing in concert, Granz chose as her venue a nightclub, Ronnie Scott's.
Norman Granz distributed an album ostensibly from her April 11
appearance, calling it *Ella in London*, and returned to the pattern of
releasing a live Ella album on the average of every two years. She
appeared with the quartet, this time featuring Tommy, Joe, Keter,
and a new drummer, Bobby Durham. Like the others, Bobby (who
had the unfortunate penchant for arriving late for both rehearsals and
performances, causing him to be alternately hired and fired through
the years) would work with Ella on and off for more than two decades.
The acoustics at Ronnie Scott's were not terribly good for a live recording, so the sound quality of this album was not up to the usual
Norman Granz standards (but nowhere nearly as bad as those in *Ella
a Nice*).

The album was not all the liner notes said it was in that it was a
recording that took the best parts of more than one performance.
About half of the album was taken from the second show at Ronnie

Scott's that night, the rest taken from other sets at the club. BBC-TV recorded that second show for a television special, and that video revealed precisely how the gig went. Roy Eldridge opened with the quartet for the first part of the show, and Ella came out after a short interval. Wearing a gold lamé dress with a high brocaded collar and matching belt, she looked healthier than she had in years. Unfortunately, her vocal quality could not match her presentation. Scratchy and wobbly, she was quite aware of her limitations that night and studiously avoided any high notes after her first number.

Ella was not in top form vocally, but the gig at Ronnie Scott's did produce an interesting and worthwhile album nonetheless. It was fascinating to hear a small-group version of "Sweet Georgia Brown," as Ella greeted her audience with a quick "Hello, me loves." This selection was taken directly from that second show. This time the performance had a spirit and energy that belied the repetition, or Ella's garbling of the extended note on "away" toward the end. Even though not perfect, it was a wonderful, spirited cut with a spontaneous "live" feel. The actual second number that evening was "Good Morning Heartache," with La Fitzgerald having to belt out the notes in order to avoid cracking her voice.

It was interesting how different countries, and sometimes different regions or even venues, had special favorite songs that Ella had to sing for them. In England, the song was "Everytime I Say Goodbye." *The Cole Porter Songbook* had an immense impact on the British, and although Ella apologized for not knowing the lyrics (she sang them perfectly), the end result was touching and poignant. Again, this was from an alternate performance. Ella then moved deftly into an extended version of "The Man I Love" from the *Fine and Mellow* album. While this cut pretty much followed the arrangement from the album, the ending was played up to the audience, adding more of a "Vegas" feel than a jazz feel. While the effect worked very well in person, with the audience howling for more, the charm was lost on the album. On video, she turned to Tommy Flanagan after a particularly harsh note and said, "Doesn't seem like it's coming out tonight!" She played the audience like a violin, dancing, talking, and generally whooping it up for her eager fans.

Tommy, Keter, and Bobby left the stage for her solo with Joe Pass. Before singing (this vocal was on the album), she told the audience,

"This is my first time playing in a club in many, many, many years—my first time in a club in London. I played one a long time ago—a little place in Manchester!" After getting her laugh, she swiftly changed gears to croon "The Very Thought of You." It was here that Ella lost the words, but as you must know by now, this was never a problem for Ella. She knew the tune, she knew the intent, and nothing was lost in the translation. Suddenly, her throat opened up and here was the Fitzgerald voice of old.

With the release of this album, the general public knew that the Fitzgerald voice had gone through great change, although over the next few years it actually "settled out" and improved. While the video included the "Boy From Ipanema" medley, the album did not, and more power to it. The arrangement required several high notes, and she couldn't hit any of them. Her voice cracked whenever she tried. Both the album and the video ended with one of Ella's original vamps, "Happy Blues." Ella did this often throughout her later career, having the pianist vamp a rhythm while she spontaneously wrote and performed an original composition on the spot. The result here was marvelous, a happy, bouncy ending to an unusual album.

The year was not without other problems for Ella. In May, she lost her close friend and working companion, Duke Ellington, and was much grieved. Ella sang "Just a Closer Walk With Thee" at Ellington's funeral. The lyrics were printed for her in giant-size letters on a music stand so she could see them. CBS News did a special report, called "A Salute to Duke," on May 24, 1974. She was the final guest on the report, interviewed about her feelings for Duke. Dressed in a gray suit, white blouse, and short wig, she was noticeably distressed by his passing. When asked her feeling on having known and worked with him, she sang (a capella) "Just a Lucky So-and-So."

Also during this time, Ella filmed the first of her memorable Memorex commercials. The original one featured a stiffly wigged Ella, sans glasses, doing a modified scat of "Lemon Drop." As she hit a high note, a crystal glass perched next to a speaker shattered. Next, they played the tape of Ella's singing, and another glass shattered. The catch-phrase, "Is it live, or is it Memorex?" swept both continents, and for the next ten years Ella was asking that question on television. Small children, who did not yet know her music, would see her and shout, "There goes the Memorex Lady!" (or in the United Kingdom, "The Memorex Lydie"). There was, however, a trick.

"I shouldn't tell this, but each of those glasses were blown to a certain pitch," recalled Ella many years later. "All I had to do was hit that pitch, then they amplified my voice to make it shatter. We had all kinds of lawyers all around to make sure everything was on the up-and-up." Many years later at a concert for children in the Watts section of Los Angeles, one of the little ones was asked what they thought of her. The reply was simple: "She's okay, but she didn't break no glass!" Those commercials eventually netted Ella hundreds of thousands of dollars.

Ella also began a second, although much shorter-lived, association with a commercial product. In the August 1974 issue of *Ebony* there appeared an ad featuring Ella extolling the pleasures of drinking Jim Beam whiskey. It was a highly unlikely marriage of celebrity and product, as she was not much of a drinker and her image was not that of a hipster. While people immediately embraced the alliance between Ella and Memorex, this one did not pan out and was quickly dropped.

By now, Ella's career was fully back in swing. She was healthy and happy, thrilled to be returned to the spotlight and making her music. She was touring almost forty weeks a year, sometimes doing two shows a night. The honors began to flow in as her career resumed its momentum. On October 29, 1974, the University of Maryland dedicated the $1.6 million Ella Fitzgerald Center for the Performing Arts, a 1,200-seat theater and concert hall. After a performance by the Earl Brown Quartet and remarks by then-governor Marvin Mandell, Ella thanked the attendees by improvising "You Are the Sunshine of My Life." A full year took Ella around the world, with Granz getting more requests for her appearances than she could possibly fill.

Chapter Twenty-nine

1975–1976

$\mathcal{O}$n April 27, 1975, Ella was back at Ronnie Scott's, this time appearing with a trio as Joe Pass left the group to tour with Oscar Peterson. Since they were all managed by Granz, no one had hurt feelings. Ella sang several songs that never made it to a live album, like "I Only Have Eyes for You," which became a frequent live entry, sung in finger-snapping rhythm, usually as the second song in the show. "Jim," made popular by Dinah Shore and recorded by Ella over thirty years earlier, was a beautiful ballad that fit very well—her voice was much stronger than it had been a year earlier.

At one point, Ella joked with the audience that her voice was getting as gravelly as Louis Armstrong's. It was an interesting statement. It showed that Ella was aware of the changes. However, she was being much too hard on herself. In truth, she was in excellent voice that night, and her vocal quality over the next five years was consistently higher than it had been in the previous five years.

Oscar Peterson had been working with Ella since the late 1940s and accompanied her on the JATP tours. By 1975, he was considered a virtuoso giant, and had long since stopped accompanying singers.

Trying to make lightning strike twice, Norman Granz coaxed Ella and Oscar together for another album featuring her and a solo instrument. Recorded in Los Angeles on May 19, 1975, the album *Ella and Oscar* did not have the same magic as *Take Love Easy*. Not that this was a bad album, with its choices of interesting songs and both performers being in good form (Ray Brown bassed the second side), but where Ella and Joe had a psychic give and take, Ella and Oscar were two tremendous talents each used to the limelight. This album had both vying for it. While many of the tunes here should have paid Ella rent because they lived on so many of her earlier albums (the only new song was "I Hear Music"), they were given fresh outlooks in style and tempo.

"April in Paris" took a much different turn here from its four earlier Fitz readings. "Street of Dreams" borrowed nothing from the Nelson Riddle arrangement, with a faster tempo and meter. "More Than You Know" (called here, for some reason, "More Than You Ever Know") and "There's a Lull in My Life" harked back to the *Like Someone in Love* album, each taken with more ferocity and drive than the original. "How Long Has This Been Going On" and "Midnight Sun" had been recorded for the *Love* album, and several times each since. These ballads were all taken at slightly faster than ballad tempo, with ample breaks for Oscar's piano solos. The album was padded out with "Mean to Me" and "When Your Lover Has Gone." While all these songs were certainly worthwhile, one wonders why there was so much dependance on songs already recorded. At this point, there were at least a dozen songs Ella was doing live that did not appear on any albums.

A few days later, Ella was involved in a car accident in Nashville. On May 21, her limousine was hit while she was on her way to do a concert at the Grand Ole Opry. While not seriously injured, she was shaken up enough to require the services of a nurse, Beverly Cheek, to be with her after the accident. Pictures taken after the accident showed Ella hunched over, walking with difficulty. She had that difficulty for the rest of her life.

It didn't keep her down long, with live gold being mined again as Ella appeared on television. On July 8, 1975, she made her first appearance on Mike Douglas's successful syndicated talk-fest. With co-host George Kirby, the comedian, and Mercer Ellington's orchestra, Ella was in fine fettle, doing "Satin Doll" and "Roxy" (from the Broadway musical *Chicago* and recorded with "My Own Best Friend" as the only single she released for Pablo) before stomping through " 'A' Train" while Mike and George looked on in amazement. Ella and the band bopped through "C Jam Blues" as the credits rolled.

The following week, Ella jetted to Europe to appear at the 1975 Montreux Jazz Festival. She often appeared at the jazz festivals that proliferate in Europe during the summer months, and this year was no exception. With her trio once again comprised of Tommy, Keter, and Bobby, Ella appeared on July 17 with the cream of jazz at the festival. Her program was excellent, with much of it released on *Ella at Montreux*.

Opening with "Caravan," Ella and the trio set the pace for the rest of the concert by coming out swinging. The arrangement was a fast-paced, jazzed-up version of the original from the Ellington Songbook, featuring incredible piano work by Tommy Flanagan. His fingers seemed to be everywhere, yet he did not intrude on Ella's vocals. "Teach Me Tonight" started as a pop song in the early 1950s; Ella and the guys made pure jazz out of it, with a Benny Carter arrangement.

Jobim got two shots in this concert, the first with his easygoing "Wave." Ella dispensed with the words, bopping her way through and using every part of her still incredible range. She was in glorious voice that July night, pacing her program like a race-car driver. "It's All Right With Me" was the Marty Paich arrangement, even tighter than the one done at the Santa Monica Civic. The trio performed as one, and the band was not missed.

"How High the Moon" traveled back to 1948; here was a version that was worth having the song recorded yet again. Ella performed a songlover's phantasmagoria, interpolating within the song such selections as "Ornithology," "Heat Wave," "Dardinella," "Idaho," "Matchmaker, Matchmaker," and, of course, "Smoke Gets in Your Eyes." The last was served up as a reference for Ella's penchant to perspire heavily under the bright stage lights; she changed the lyric to ". . . sweat gets in your eyes" as she wiped her brow with the color-coordinated handkerchief she always carried with her onstage.

Ella's bossa medley followed, inaccurately titled "The Girl From Ipanema" on the cover and label. Jobim's "The *Boy* From Ipanema" started the medley after some initial scatting, followed by smatterings of "Oh Nosso Amor," "Cielito Lindo," "Agua de Beber," "Fly Me to the Moon," "Moonwalk," "Temptation," and ending back again where she started with a high swoop on "Ipanema." Olé, indeed! As her encore, Ella chose Billie Holiday's " 'Tain't Nobody's Business If I Do" (spelled "Bizness" on the cover and label). More than half the song followed a piano and voice duet between Ella and Tommy; the rest of the trio came in to bring the evening home to a most successful conclusion.

A cut not released with this album, but performed at the same concert, was "The Man I Love." Done along the same lines as the versions on *Fine and Mellow* and *Ella in London*, this was the superior version. There was no pretense of pop leanings or pandering to a nightclub audience; no special material here. This was pure jazz, served up hot and spicy. Again Ella went through the first chorus with just Tommy; again Keter set the tempo through the second chorus. At the third chorus, Ella threw everything to the wind and scatted through a magnificent panorama of sounds and melody. This cut appeared on an LP called *The Montreux Collection*, featuring songs not on the other albums released from the jazz festival. Had the song not been released twice within the past year, it most certainly would have been included on the original album.

Returning to the United States soon thereafter, Ella did what Ella always did: toured and appeared on television. Always looking for something new, her next project finally made her a Broadway Baby.

In a huge change of pace, she appeared for a two-week, sixteen-performance stand on Broadway (billed as simply *The Concert*), sharing the spotlight with the Count Basie Orchestra and Frank Sinatra, starting September 8, 1975. The occasion was used to open the newly completed Uris Theater (since renamed the Gershwin), the first of several new Broadway theaters built in the 1970s and '80s. The stand grossed $1.08 million, the highest gross for any Broadway attraction over a two-week period up to that time. The top ticket was $40, with the theater seating 1,900 people. Although there was a musicians' strike at the time, an agreement reached between the international parent body of the musicians' local and the management allowed the shows to go on.

Ella's numbers were typical of the time. For the finale, Ella and Frank reprised their medley from his 1967 television special, ending the evening with their free-for-all of "The Lady Is a Tramp." This New York run was followed by one-night stands in Philadelphia, Cleveland, and Chicago, as well as longer stints in Westbury, Long Island, as well as Las Vegas.

Constantly changing the lineup of songs she sang, it was not always possible to include them on albums. With literally dozens of new songs added to her repertoire every year, it would have taken three or four annual albums to record them all. Appearing in Hackensack, New Jersey, at the Orrie de Noyer Auditorium (Ella went *everywhere*), on September 27, Ella included live versions of such album favorites as "Love Is Here to Stay" and "The Jersey Bounce." "Easy Living" didn't appear on an album for another decade, but was included in this concert. The surprise of the evening was a medley from the current Broadway musical, *The Wiz*. Based on the movie *The Wizard of Oz* (music written by Ella's old friend and Songbook mate Harold Arlen) and featuring a talented young black cast including Stephanie Mills, the show provided Ella with a medley of the title song with "Ease On Down the Road." Although a little corny in presentation, it was actually quite good and deserved to be released to the public.

Ella began 1976 with a bang by returning to both Los Angeles and the studio. Norman Granz wisely planned a follow-up album to *Take Love Easy*, and as soon as Ella and Joe got back from their holiday gigs, record they did. *Fitzgerald and Pass . . . Again* ranks with *Ella and Basie* as an almost perfect album. Ella's voice was smooth and controlled in every part of her range; it sounded as if she'd had a larynx lift. Joe played a gut-string acoustic guitar instead of his usual electric. The songs were recorded on January 29–30 and February 8. Featuring a smiling Ella in dark glasses on the cover, the album boasted fourteen songs that are surely some of the best jazz releases ever.

Starting at the top, "I Ain't Got Nothin' But the Blues" had been showcased on the Ellington Songbook. Here it was taken a mite slower, with Joe setting the tempo and then breaking for Ella to join him. Much of what Ella had gleaned during the years she was recording rock and rhythm and blues showed in her comfort with the tempos and approach here. " 'Tis Autumn" was a little gem, with unusual internal rhymes and uses of language. A pair of "old" songs followed, the first being "My Old Flame."

Joe's performance in this number provides a good point to mention his genius. He had the uncanny ability to know not only what to play but *when* to play. Joe kept the pace and definitely had his moments when his virtuosity shone, but he had a sixth sense when to leave the musical holes for Ella to fill, and when to give her only the most minimal of accompaniment. Other greats might need to play throughout, thrusting their talent to the foreground. Joe had enough confidence to be a part of the musical whole, knowing his contributions wouldn't be overlooked and, in doing so, was true to the jazz idiom. "That Old Feeling" was taken at a breezy pace, not mired down in sentimentality. Ella's repeat of the "o" in "old feeling" at the end of the choruses was a wonderful example of using rhythm as well as melody to express an emotion.

Three more touches of Ellingtonia graced the album, all with interesting results. "I Didn't Know About You" was much different from the Songbook version, more world-weary and mature in attitude. However, "Solitude" was coincidentally done in the same setting as the original, with voice and guitar. Ella was in such good voice that the only things setting these two versions apart were Joe's expert handling of the guitar and Ella's maturity with the lyric. "All Too Soon" was given fair due, although it probably was not one of the better Ellington efforts. "You Took Advantage of Me" (from *The Rodgers and Hart Songbook*) was done with tongue slightly planted in cheek, as Ella grinned her way through lyrics that would be too naïve for anyone over eighteen. "I've Got the World on a String" had been through the mill with Ella: on Decca, on the Arlen Songbook, and done live with a quartet. Ella sang it as though she had nothing to lose and allowed the song to take her along. This approach worked well, and gave the evergreen a new lift.

The last three songs on the album show how phenomenally diverse the combination of voice and guitar can be in the right hands. Nat Cole's hit "Nature Boy" was caressed as though it were crystal and might break. Pass was given the first part of the song to establish the parameters, with Ella gently joining in to fill in the words. The result was graceful, engaging, and captivating. An unlikely song for Ella or this environment was the Patti Page success "Tennessee Waltz." Alternately taking turns fighting the inherent waltz time, Ella and Joe turned this song rhythmically inside out, rendering it their own and perfectly suitable for this collection. The final cut was an old Ella favorite, Jobim's "One Note Samba." The pace here was not the frenetic speed of her earlier live versions from the late sixties. Joe set the tempo with a more standard Brazilian rhythm.

Ella followed without the words, scatting through two choruses before she began trading fours with Joe, a sort of voice-and-guitar jam session. As with their previous album, the recording for this album was flat engineering-wise. The CD version was much enhanced by the digital remastering. This was Ella and Joe at their best, an album that should be in everyone's collection.

Jumping at a chance to be on the same stage with Fred Astaire and Gene Kelly (cohosts plugging *That's Entertainment II*), Ella once again graced Mike Douglas's show in Philadelphia on February 19, 1976. Ella triumphed them with *The Wiz* medley, "Smoke Gets in Your Eyes," and "Manhattan." This show was so popular that it was repeated again the week of July 10. Later in the month, Ella turned up at the Grammy awards as a presenter (with Mel Tormé) in the category of best jazz performance by a group. The winner was Chick Corea, but the award was accepted by Ella's old friend Louie Bellson.

Constantly touring, Ella returned to New York's Lincoln Center for another Avery Fisher Hall appearance on March 19. This concert was a treat, for not only was she in excellent voice but she had two big surprises. The first was her program, which was laced with songs not found on any of her albums. She opened with "Sugar," an easy-swing number that Ella and the trio managed to turn into an opening delight. The audience was aware that Ella was in a playful mood as she then swung "Thou Swell" (from *The Rodgers and Hart Songbook*) with a rousing rock beat, getting thunderous applause at its conclusion. Reaching back to *Ella Swings Lightly*, she breathed fresh life into Marty Paich's arrangement of "Little Jazz." She was so pleased with the reception for this song that she mistakenly told the audience that she ought to record it. The audience heartily agreed.

Shifting gears, she started to talk about a current pop hit she liked and wanted to do for them. The audience audibly gasped when Ella started to sing "Feelings." Remember, this was before the song was so overdone that people used this song as a comedy parody of overdone pop (and pap). Like "You've Got a Friend" before it, Ella obtained every nuance and subtlety from the song, rescuing it from banality and giving it deep meaning and beauty. Breaking the spell, Ella ripped into Rodgers and Hart's "Mountain Greenery," unsure of the lyrics but no one cared. By this point in Ella's career, it was a ritual in her concerts that during at least one of her efforts she would falter with the words of a song. She even introduced the evening by saying, ". . . We've got some old ones and some new ones, some we know, some we don't. . . ." And when the audience would applaud at the prospect, Ella countered with ". . . we hope you feel that way when we're *finished!*"

The second surprise of the evening followed. Ella told the audience she wanted to change her usual program and sing some numbers from her new album with Joe Pass. She waited a beat and then introduced the man himself, who came out on stage to do three songs with her. Pass often was a surprise guest after this; he sometimes opened the second part of the show with several solos before Ella joined him. Ella and Joe chose to do "Solitude," "Rain," and "One Note Samba" that night, and the audience was enthralled. Joe often felt intrusive appearing with Ella in what were basically her concerts, but he only needed to hear a recording of that concert to know how pleased the audience was to see him.

After taking her final bows, Ella looked to the wings as if expecting something. When she didn't see what she was expecting, she told the audience she was going to change her plans, and asked if she could do a ballad written by Mel Tormé. "Born to Be Blue" was a delightful surprise, and then Ella left the stage to a standing ovation, one that went on for minutes. And minutes. Even Ella was taking too long to come back on, and when she did, she was noticeably disturbed. The trio vamped into "Caravan," the introduction going on for almost a minute until she finally started to sing. It was its usual success, and finally Ella apologized to the audience. "We were supposed to do a jam session now," she explained, "but I just learned that Joe Pass had to go to Florida [audience laughter]. We didn't know what to sing and they were afraid folks would start to walk out. Now, nobody walks out on me [much applause]. What would you like to hear?" Three thousand people screamed three thousand different songs. Very few performers would have had the confidence, the talent, or the showmanship to do this, and Tommy Flanagan began to play "Mack the Knife." Ella stopped him, saying, ". . . You don't really want to hear that again. . . ." And Tommy segued into "You've Got a Friend." Ella started to a smattering of applause, and asked the audience "No?" with the crowd screaming their approval. The First Lady of Song turned the song into a revival meeting. The entire audience on its feet clapping in time and singing along. Once again, Ella turned what could have been a disaster into total success.

By 1976, Dinah Shore was doing a daily, syndicated talk show, ninety minutes in some markets and sixty minutes in others. This was a fairly common practice for these shows in the seventies, as both Merv Griffin and Mike Douglas similarly programmed their shows. On April 7, 1976, Ella visited "Dinah!," and much of the show revolved around her. She opened the show by singing "Sweet Georgia Brown" with the trio, and then joined Dinah for a coffee klatch. Ella had recently dined with the Queen of Denmark, and shared some Danish phrases she had learned while over there. Also discussed was her dream of owning her own place in which to sing when she felt like it. Obviously, this was not scintillating dialogue, but Dinah wisely steered the conversation away from anything personal or controversial.

Before the talk got *too* small, Raymond Burr walked on as a surprise guest. Bringing her orchids that he had grown himself, Burr then reminisced about his longstanding friendship with both ladies. Ella surprised "Perry Mason" back by singing "I Only Have Eyes for You." Roger Miller, a scheduled guest, came out to duet with Ella a song simply called "Scat." At the close of the show, seen only in the longer version, she did her bossa-nova medley and talked about the Center for Performing Arts at the University of Maryland that was named for her.

Doctors warned her to slow down. Her blood pressure was high, and it became more difficult to get around. Between her bad eyesight, advancing arthritis, and excessive weight, performing took everything out of her. She was not ill, but her health was not keeping pace with her spirit.

Chapter Thirty

1976–1978

$\mathcal{E}$lla kept up a frantic pace of touring; ignoring medical advice she still performed two shows a night, as many as six nights a week. Major cities, colleges, Las Vegas, symphonies, Europe, Japan—Ella was everywhere. April 11, 1976 was proclaimed "Ella Fitzgerald Day" in Los Angeles because Women at Work chose her as their Bicentennial Queen. She was honored at a dinner at the Century Plaza Hotel, which benefitted the Southwest Christian College and Pepperdine University.

On April 28, 1976, Ella made her final appearance on "The Tonight Show," a woman whose health was the only fly in the ointment as she rode another high crest in her career. She sang "Too Close for Comfort," "Thou Swell," and, as a change of pace, "Feelings." As always on these types of shows (and on television in general), Ella was nervous, and she spoke about it. She gave some advice to young singers (". . . just keep singing . . .") and answered non-threatening questions ("What is it like to write songs?").

As she did often in concert, Ella also apologized to the audience for having a runny nose. She was sensitive to air conditioning, smog, and other irritants and quite often she got the sniffles. Her audiences never noticed, but Ella was so sensitive to not doing her best that she felt the need to apologize. She was always terribly concerned about what people thought of her. This was the underlying cause of her shyness and her reluctance to discuss anything personal in public.

Also of note was Carson's having to escort her to the couch, as one would for someone who was sightless. Her eyesight was never as good as she claimed after the numerous operations. Cue cards were out of the question, as was reading sheet music. More than once she walked into the proscenium arch of a theater upon attempting to exit a stage. Ella couldn't see well enough to find the wings.

On May 4, she did a concert with Joe Pass, Oscar Peterson, and the Count Basie Orchestra to benefit the Neighbors of Watts charity. On June 2, she sang at another benefit for the Retire Association with Arthur Fiedler and the Boston Pops, singing only songs by Ellington, Porter, and Gershwin. Dartmouth College honored her with a Doctorate in Music on July 20. Ella received her diploma at a concert in front of 3,000 people in Hanover, New Hampshire. The National Association of Sickle Cell Diseases awarded Ella their second annual Award of Distinction on October 17. Ray Charles hosted the gala at the Beverly Wilshire Hotel.

The managers of Carnegie Hall must have sometimes felt like keeping an Ella Fitzgerald Room, for she appeared there so often. Besides the prestige of playing that auditorium, it was always a good booking because of the large seating capacity. There was very little overhead. All Ella and the musicians had to do was show up. In the later years, Granz often booked her into large forums like Carnegie Hall, the Hollywood Bowl, and the San Francisco Symphony Hall.

Appearing at Carnegie Hall on November 26, 1976, with the trio, Joe Pass, and the Count Basie Orchestra (without Bill Basie, who was recovering from a heart attack), she did many of the same numbers from her appearance on Broadway the previous year. More of her Memorex commercials began to appear, this time with Melissa Manchester unable to tell the difference between Ella and the sponsor's product. Both Nelson Riddle and Count Basie had previously joined Ella in these commercials. Her voice could also be heard on commercials for American Express, and soon she was pitching Kentucky Fried Chicken.

Benny Goodman, Peggy Lee, and Lady Time together for the second
Swing Into Spring special, 1959.
Courtesy Institute for Jazz Studies at Rutgers University.

Ella and the Duke: Jazz royalty out on the town.
Courtesy Institute for Jazz Studies at Rutgers University.

Still hiding her
figure for Verve.
*Courtesy
Institute for
Jazz Studies
at Rutgers
University.*

ELLA FITZGERALD

Singing "Time After Time" on *The Dean Martin Show.*
Courtesy Institute for Jazz Studies at Rutgers University.

No, that's not Dionne Warwick. A slenderized (and retouched) Ella in 1969. *Courtesy author's collection.*

Is it live, or is it...well, you know, 1974.
Courtesy author's collection.

Rehearsing with Marty Paich, 1975.
Courtesy Marty Paich.

In concert, 1975. *Courtesy author's collection.*

Oh, those awful wigs, 1978. *Courtesy author's collection.*

No, that's not
Pearl Bailey, 1979.
*Courtesy Institute
for Jazz Studies at
Rutgers University.*

Riding the last great crest of her powers, 1980.
Courtesy author's collection.

Surprised on-stage with a cake for her (supposedly) 65th birthday, 1983.
Courtesy Institute for Jazz Studies at Rutgers University.

Ella, in concert, toward the end of her career.

After a very long wait between drinks, the folks who give out the Grammy awards remembered that Ella was still around. On February 19, 1977, Ella received the Grammy (presented by Richard Pryor and George Benson) as Best Jazz Vocal Performance for *Fitzgerald and Pass . . . Again*. It was the reblossoming of the love affair the recording academy had with Ella, and she won several more awards over the next fourteen years.

Ella had retooled her repertoire for 1977, touring the country before heading to Europe. In April, she did a concert in New Orleans that was broadcast over National Public Radio. She ended the set with "Mr. Paganini," and was about to launch into another song when Stevie Wonder was brought out on stage as a surprise. The two dueted an unrehearsed "You Are the Sunshine of My Life" to the great delight of the Louisiana crowd. Also included in this concert was a song that Ella later omitted from her tour, "I Never Knew." Momentarily not familiar with the lyrics, Ella bopped through most of it, but this song was superseded in her repertoire by "Day by Day" (she didn't know *those* lyrics, either).

On July 14, 1977, Ella once again performed the jazz festival in Montreux. Norman Granz recorded much of the evening as *Montreux '77: Ella Fitzgerald With the Tommy Flanagan Trio*. That Tommy was given equal billing on the cover showed just how much Ella held him in esteem. The festival was even bigger that year, providing a spate of live albums for Norman Granz's Pablo records. The cover featured no picture, but a generous graphic salute to Tommy Flanagan, who by this time was Ella's pianist of longest standing. The trio had been consistent for several years, and Ella was more than pleased at their musical companionship. This was her final live album with Tommy, and it more than did both of them justice.

She came out like a commando who wasn't taking hostages, bursting through "Too Close for Comfort." This number, arranged by Bill Holman, was very important in the Ella mythos. It was repeated countless times, both with the trio and larger groups. It was a favorite of Ella's and Basie's, and Ella sang it at the drop of a hat. In fact, she often used this number in appearances (both in person and on television) when she was not doing an entire set and had little rehearsal. Ella was one with this number, an obvious fact on that July night in Montreux. She was hotter than the summer evening, going from "Too

Close for Comfort" to the steamy "I Ain't Got Nothin' But the Blues" from the last album with Joe Pass.

Ella found a song in Paul Williams's *Bugsy Malone* (a gangster musical played entirely by children and teenagers) that deserved not to languish in the pool of forgotten songs. "Ordinary Fool" (which Ella mistakenly called "Only a Fool" when she introduced it) was an exquisite torch song which she molded to her style, and added her trademark coda at the end. When Karen Carpenter later recorded the song for her last album, she very much followed Ella's vocal line. Tommy took Joe's place for a six-and-a-half-minute version of "One Note Samba," played at a slightly faster pace than the original. A new song to her repertoire, "Billie's Bounce" was a syncopated scat that owed as much to Dave Brubeck's era as it did to Chick Webb's. Its range, with sweeping high notes and searing low notes, would be a nightmare for almost any vocalist. Ella not only turned the nightmare into a daydream, but took to it like a dog to a bone, gladly devouring the song without caring about table manners. The encore here was Stevie Wonder's "You Are the Sunshine of My Life." Fantasy, Inc., also sold these Montreux albums for CD releases to Original Jazz Classics, who redid the covers.

Dinah and "Dinah!" coaxed Ella back for a show called "Dinah and the First Ladies." It was taped October 5, 1977. Joining Ella on the show was top company indeed: Lucille Ball and Elizabeth Taylor (by satellite). Lucy said, ". . . You know, Ella, you're incredible. My daughter says every time you make a mistake, they release it as a hit song. . . ." Ella discussed listening to Sarah Vaughan records at home, then she and Dinah sang a medley together, including "I Got Rhythm," "Buttons and Bows," and "My Heart Belongs to Daddy." Ella finished the show by doing "Ordinary Fool."

There was one more trek to Philadelphia to tape a Mike Douglas show on November 11, 1977. Ella's solos this time were Harold Arlen and Johnny Mercer's "Come Rain or Come Shine" and a number soon to be recorded, Cole Porter's "Dream Dancing." Mike asked Ella who her favorite singers were, to which she charmingly replied Sarah Vaughan, Gladys Knight, Natalie Cole, Frank Sinatra, Tony Bennett, Mel Torme, and Mike Douglas. Deciding Ella couldn't go it alone, guests Tommy Lasorda (L.A. Dodgers manager) and Gavin MacLeod (in between "MTM" and setting sail on "The Love Boat") joined Mike and Ella to sing "Heart" from *Damn Yankees*. This was Ella's last talk-show appearance.

Norman Granz took his shelved album *Ella Loves Cole*, and decided to rerelease it in early 1978. He reassembled the musicians who had appeared on the original album with Nelson Riddle, replacing Tommy Flanagan with Paul Smith. Ella recorded two additional numbers, "Dream Dancing" and "After You" on June 9, 1978. Taking its title from the former, *Dream Dancing* was a splendid album, making it obvious that its premature withdrawal had nothing to do with art. The title cut was wonderfully arranged. The first chorus was done with just the rhythm section, and the orchestra joined them for the second. "After You" allowed Ella to play in her lower notes, then swoop up and finish the song. The rest of the tunes, harking back to 1972, were done with the full orchestra to a jazz/rock beat. Riddle did not use strings, xylophones, or saxophones in the arrangements, relying instead on trombones, bassoons, clarinets, oboes, flutes, and trumpets to augment the rhythm section—an unusual arrangement of instruments that fit the attitude of the album perfectly.

Ella's 1972 cuts showed a voice that was strong, but she occasionally ran out of breath at the end of phrases. As a whole, the album was extremely successful in both its intent and execution, and was a fine companion to the original Porter Songbook. The CD version mistakenly noted that the disc label listed only twelve of the fifteen songs. It was only the first pressing that had had this problem.

Chapter Thirty-one

1978–1979

By the late seventies, Ella and Granz were pretty much used to each other, although there was still constant friction over what she would sing. "The idea was, get him to do the talking for me and I'd do the singing. I needed that," she once recalled. "Sometimes we'd argue and wouldn't speak for weeks on end, and he'd give messages through a third party, but now I just accept him as he is, or I may just speak my mind. We are all like a big family now—Norman and I and Joe Pass and Oscar Peterson and Basie—that's another thing that makes life so pleasant."

Life wasn't so pleasant for some of the members of the "family." More than one musician made the complaint that some members of the family were more equal than others. "It's hard enough to make a living as a jazz artist, but Norman was so cheap he cut his nose to spite his face," recalls one member who wished to remain anonymous for obvious reasons. "We'd play a concert, and he would come back-stage and say, 'Well, I think I might release this one [he recorded almost every concert he produced, just in case gold was mined], so here's an extra two hundred dollars for the record.' The record would sell tens of thousands, but we were expected to go along and take it because we were 'family.' "

When musicians didn't "go along," they might find some other guy gigging on the next tour. By the middle 1980s, much of the family would have left the Granz coalition.

Additionally, Granz was still in total control of Ella's musical choices. "We were touring Europe in the early eighties," recalls Paul Smith, "and she had worked out a smashing version of 'Send in the Clowns' with the trio during rehearsals. She had sung it successfully in several venues, until Norman came to see the show one night. After the show, he came backstage fuming, 'What the hell was that?' referring to the song. It seems that he had decided that Stephen Sondheim would never be sung by Ella, that his songs didn't lend themselves to jazz. She never sang the song again."

Ella flew back to Los Angeles to record her next studio album, a truly unusual and creative endeavor that produced novel and superior results. Even the title was singular, taken from Lester Young's habit of nicknaming people "Lady." To Lester, Ella was "Lady Time," an apt title for an album that featured Ella singing with organ and drums only. Recorded on June 19 and 20, old friend (and Pearl Bailey's husband) Louie Bellson hit the skins, with organist Jackie Davis providing the rest of the accompaniment.

"Originally, the date started with bass player Joe Comfort, but Jackie played so well Granz thought the bass unnecessary," says Bellson. Jackie was very much in charge musically, with Louie just following Davis's lead. Ella rose to the creative occasion, being in fine voice and living up to her nickname. The first cut was a cover of a song both Fats Domino and Rick Nelson made popular, "I'm Walkin'." This five-and-a-half-minute rhythm tune was a straight swinger, with Ella using the lyrics, friends of the lyrics, new lyrics, and scat to propel her to the finish. This was also a rare occurrence where one of Ella's songs was not ended but faded off. Davis's manipulation of the organ was incredible, making it sound at various times like strings, bass, brass, piano, and, of course, organ. He was a true match to Ella's innate ability to use, manipulate, steal, and otherwise swing time. As Count Basie said, "He's a bitch."

The choice of songs for this album were very eclectic, going from the 1930s with "I Cried for You" to the 1940s with "And the Angels

Sing" to the 1950s with "That's My Desire" and finally to the 1960s with "that same old song," "Mack the Knife." This was the only studio version of that song, and the only time that Ella actually sang the correct lyrics all the way through. She wanted to bring something new to the song, to make it something a little different. She succeeded.

Lady Time was a totally satisfying album, whose originality and creativity were greatly appreciated by jazz lovers. Norman Granz again needs to be thanked for the musical environments in which he placed Ella, many of them invented by him.

Ella returned to New York one week later, this time playing Carnegie Hall as part of the still-titled Newport Jazz Festival on June 24. The closeness in bookings was due to the postponement of her last concert at Avery Fisher Hall. Tommy and the trio played for the first half of the concert, with Ella joining in the fun after the intermission. She was in such good voice that one would have thought they were listening to *Ella in Berlin*. Smiling and laughing all evening, Ella sang more than twenty songs, taking requests and filling them as quickly as they were shouted at her. She sang many of the same tunes, with the addition of a rousing "I Cried for You" and a version of "Angel Eyes" that garnered a standing ovation. At least five of her songs that night were done as spur-of-the-moment request fillers, including her two encores.

Tommy Flanagan's last gig with the trio was in late 1978 at the Salone de Provence in France. His health simply could not stand up to the rigorous demands of Ella's touring schedule, so he wisely chose a solo career that garnered him four Grammy nominations and the top vote in both *Down Beat* and *Jazz Times* polls. Norman Granz turned to Paul Smith for coverage until a full-time pianist was found. While Smith had not worked with Ella in concert since the early sixties, he had been instrumental in the Songbooks and several of her excellent albums. Paul wasn't thrilled with the idea of returning to the touring grind, but he had great regard for Ella and was happy to fill in.

Upon their first rehearsal together, Ella asked Paul if he noticed anything different in her voice. Paul, ever the diplomat, said no. Ella's retort was, "Just call me Molly McQuiver!" She was aware that her voice had changed in the almost thirty years since first working with Paul. Ella was too savvy to not be honest about her talent, and she wanted to let him know that she was aware of the changes.

A unique television appearance in November of 1978 paired Ella for the only time with that other diva of jazz, Sarah Vaughan. "Salute to Pearl Bailey" had the two ladies paired on some of Pearlie Mae's hits, with Pearl herself joining them for the finale of "St. Louis Blues." This union of singers has taken on almost mythic proportions among jazz fans, many of whom never saw the show but had heard of the broadcast.

The three albums released in 1978 were diverse, excellent, and original, but the two recorded in 1979 were legendary, although mysterious in their release. Ella's next was to have been an album called *Ella and Basie—The Perfect Match*. With songs orchestrated by Benny Carter (their first studio work together since *30 By Ella*, although the liner notes incorrectly called this their first collaboration since 1955), all eleven tunes were recorded on February 15, 1979, in one long session. This, it turns out somewhat confusingly, was not the album finally released with that name.

Ella and Basie appeared at Montreux again that summer, with their concert being recorded with digital mastering for the first time on Pablo. Also, the concert was excellent, a pure tour de force for Ella and the Basie band. Norman Granz decided to shelve the studio album temporarily and release the live one instead. He used the name, pictures, and most of the graphics already created for the studio set. The first pressings of the live album were released on a special red vinyl to signify that this digitally mastered album (on Sony equipment) was the beginning of a new era for Pablo.

The studio album was then released as her *next* one, with a new cover and title, *A Classy Pair*. Two of the songs originally recorded for this album were dropped, as they had been done live in Montreux.

Several months later, European imports of this album appeared in New York with the *original* title and graphics, including the two dropped songs but dropping two others to make room for them. Finally, the German arm of Pablo released a boxed set of CDs, and on this version of the album *all* of the songs appeared, although the commercial CD of the album does not contain the added songs. The boxed set, released independently of Granz, did not have covers for the CDs, with photographically shrunken versions of the back covers of the albums on the back of each CD. There was a well-written booklet included (written in both German and English), but the package was poorly done and it was less expensive to simply buy the CDs individually and get all the graphics and liner notes. Only die-hard fans would spend the extra money for two extra cuts on one out of ten CDs in the set.

The album that was finally released as A Classy Pair was a fine companion to the first full Ella/Basie connection for Verve. In fact, two of the songs ("Honeysuckle Rose" and "Ain't Misbehavin' ") were repeats, which said a lot for both Ella and the Count as the later versions were better. "Honeysuckle Rose" started as a solo for Basie in his inimitable style: not a note was wasted or overused. He set the tempo by the fourth bar, and Ella joined in at the second chorus with the rhythm section. At the tag of the second chorus, the band blasted in to trade time with Ella, who hit notes that would leave singers half her age panting and weak. Lady Time more than held her own as another instrument in the band, not only following along but acting as her own musical nuclear reactor to push the action along. Ella used a slightly altered version of this chart in her concerts from then on, always to roaring approval.

"Teach Me Tonight" got a second reading from Ella here. The pace is faster than the live version in 1975, but the arrangement remained relatively the same. Ella revisited "Just A-Sittin' and A-Rockin'," a favorite of hers that really gave her a chance to wail with Benny's solid arrangement. The same held true for "Don't Worry 'Bout Me," last heard from as a duet with Joe Pass in 1973 at Carnegie Hall. Where Ella gently approached the song with Joe so as not to bruise it, the attack here was head on. Ella munched through the song as though it were a favorite snack. Once again she was in top form vocally, as she seemingly stripped years off her voice. Playing all the songs from both Basie albums in shuffled fashion, it is difficult to distinguish the cuts from 1963 from those recorded in 1979, save for Ella's deeper vibrato and harder attack on her notes.

Taking on Frank Sinatra's "I'm Getting Sentimental Over You," the arrangement here was more Herb Alpert than Herb Ellis. Ella and the musicians again traded fours in the second chorus. "My Kind of Trouble Is You" featured Basie on the organ, as did "Dream a Little Dream" in 1963. "Sweet Lorraine" was another gender bender for Ella, gently done not unlike Nat Cole's version. The only out-of-place cut here was "Organ Grinder's Swing," not strange for its inclusion (both Ella and Basie were known to use liberal portions of this song in their jazz improvisations) but for the amount of time allotted to it.

The two deleted songs would have only put sweet icing on an already delicious cake. "Please Don't Talk About Me When I'm Gone" had been a standard for almost fifty years; it is amazing that Ella hadn't recorded it sooner. The third chorus, with its switch to a Charleston tempo, really blasted. Once again, Ella did tribute to a Billie Holiday tune with "Some Other Spring." It was the lushest, most full-bodied ballad she had done in years, and it was a shame that the studio version was not generally available.

Carnegie Hall was the scene for one of the most star-filled evenings with which Ella was associated in almost a decade. On April 14, 1979, Norman Granz produced a concert featuring a group which he called his "Pablo All-Stars," assuredly harking back to his halcyon days with the JATP tours. Featured on the bill were Ella, Joe Pass, Oscar Peterson, and bassist Niels Orsted-Pedersen (who was making his New York debut that night). Paul Smith rejoined Ella at this point, after a hiatus of more than fifteen years. (He agreed to fill in for six months, but returned two years later to accompany Ella until the end of the next decade.) The evening was awash with entrances and exits, as Ella sang with the trio; sang with Oscar; sang with Joe; sang with Joe, Oscar, and Niels; and allowed these talented musicians some time onstage by themselves. It was an extremely long concert, with Ella singing over twenty songs besides all of the instrumentals. Her repertoire that night consisted of material from her latest albums, as well as some spontaneous work with Oscar and Joe. This might have made for her next live album, were it not for her upcoming concert with Count Basie.

When the two performed at Montreux on July 12, 1979, the concert featured songs from various parts of Ella's catalogue. Strangely enough, none of the songs from their first collaboration (or "April in Paris," for that matter) were used here. Instead, the album opened with "Please Don't Talk About Me When I'm Gone," with the middle instrumental chorus deleted from the arrangement. To keep the pace hopping, they pounced on Marty Paich's arrangement of "Sweet Georgia Brown," not taking so much as a wrong breath along the way.

Dick Van Dyke and Barbara Feldon appeared in a farce called

Fitzwilly (1967); its jaunty theme song was called "Make Me Rainbows." Ella showed off her talent for taking this run-of-the-mill number and making something unique, stimulating, and engaging out of it. This song proved to be important in Ella's life a few years later.

"After You've Gone" first appeared on the *Rhythm Is My Business* album. Not bothering with the second set of lyrics, Ella rocked and rocketed the number. She gave a truly outstanding rendition of an already inventive orchestration.

The next two songs were performed with the trio, with one added guest musician. Generally, when Ella performed with a large group, four or five songs were done just with the trio in the middle of the concert. Keter Betts was the only member of the trio from recent years to appear at Montreux that summer. With Paul Smith still supplanting Tommy, Ella did fine. Tommy's talent was sorely missed by Ella, but he truly deserved the added recognition as a solo artist for he was rich in talent. Mickey Roker filled out the trio on drums. The trio was heard on two cuts from *Fine and Mellow*, " 'Round Midnight," and the title cut. Saxophonist Danny Turner doubled on flute for the break in " 'Round Midnight."

Time limitations forced Norman Granz to chop off the verse to "You've Changed," but otherwise this was the same arrangement from the *Whisper Not* album. Ella's "Honeysuckle Rose" appeared next, while the finale featured "St. Louis Blues." She had been doing this current arrangement for several years, giving the song the distinction of more different versions recorded by Ella than any other song. An encore featured Ella and Basie jamming through what was basically another version of "C Jam Blues," but here it is cutely titled "Basella." Interestingly enough, there were no liner notes for this album, and no graphics to indicate that this was a live album (after all, it was not called "Montreux '79"). Graphics or not, this was another one of those "must have" albums for any Ella collection, for it was simply great.

What about those cuts that were left off the album? Well, two of them appeared on *Digital III at Montreux*, an album of leftovers from live albums by Ella, Joe Pass, and Count Basie recorded at the festival using the Sony digital system. Like its predecessor, the first pressing was on red vinyl, and featured Ella and the trio. "I Don't Stand a Ghost of a Chance With You" also took its arrangement from *Fine and Mellow*, but the gem here was Ella's eight-plus-minute version of "Flying Home." The treatment was totally reworked from the Decca bop hit of the 1940s. It took the same musical themes but expounded and changed them. The reception for the song was great, and Ella did something she rarely did—an encore to the same song.

At the time, such an album was necessary, both to hold the extra songs and to publicize the digital remastering. It was a shame (no fault of Norman Granz, as Fantasy, Inc., bought these albums just as they were released on vinyl) that these songs were not simply inserted back into the concert where they belonged, along with the verse to "You've Changed." A CD could easily hold all that material, and it was anachronistic to bother to publicize digital mastering.

Around this time, Paul Smith solved a problem for Ella: Tommy Flanagan had been in charge of her music for quite a while, choosing her numbers for concerts and writing new arrangements on the road as she needed them. Unfortunately for Ella, Tommy was such a genius that he didn't need music—he just learned a piece and then played it from memory. Any new pianist didn't have a clue to Ella's "book," the lead arrangements for all the songs she did in her live concerts. Paul took great pains to write Ella such a book, using many of the Flanagan arrangements or embellishments and then adding more of his own as they toured. When Jimmy Rowles took over the following year, he was able to continue without very many noticeable seams, and added to the book himself. It took a gifted musician, secure man, and good friend to do what Paul did, and he was all of these. From 1956 until 1988, Paul was a huge support musically for Ella, second only to Tommy Flanagan for his effect on her music, and live concerts in particular. He was indispensable in helping her through her next vocal hurdles.

Chapter Thirty-two

1979–1980

*T*he 1970s, although starting out rocky with Ella's health and career problems, produced some of her most imaginative and creative work. She recorded sixteen albums in ten years, and suddenly there was a glut of Fitzgerald product on the market. MGM sold the Verve catalogue to Polygram which began to release it. Starting with *The Cole Porter Songbook*, each of the Songbooks was rereleased in stereo. The Christmas album, the Basie album (now subtitled *On the Sunny Side of the Street*); the Metronome 1956 collection; *Like Someone in Love*; *Hello, Love*; *Whisper Not*; and others were all given a new life, many on high-grade Japanese vinyl and some digitally remastered on vinyl. MCA rereleased her Decca catalogue on greatest hits albums, along with a shortened collection of her cuts with Gordon Jenkins, now called *Black Coffee*. Several compilations of Ella's early work appeared on the market, especially those which featured other singers in duets. She was at the third great plateau of her popularity and her powers, having outdistanced, outlasted, and outsung all of her contemporaries (except of course, Sinatra). She survived rock, disco, and new wave music trends, acknowledging the newer sounds without compromising her taste or style.

Ella won a Grammy for *The Perfect Match*, another in a series of awards she garnered during this period. To top off her year, she made her first appearance at New York's Radio City Music Hall on September 6, 1979. Appearing with the full Radio City Orchestra as well as her trio (still headed by Paul Smith), Ella brought an excitement that shone through her performance. Kicking off with "Give Me the Simple Life," her program included "Honeysuckle Rose," "Love Is Here to Stay," "My Ship," "Make Me Rainbows," and "After You've Gone" before cooling off to work with the trio.

Ella hadn't done "Miss Otis Regrets" lately; her voice cracked halfway through, and she was forced to belt the rest of the song, lest she crack again. Showman that she was, Ella wisely surprised the audience by doing "Mack the Knife" next, not only taking their minds off her temporary lack of perfection but throwing them a programming curve. Not expecting to hear the song until the encore (if they were lucky), the audience snapped, crackled, and popped as she sang it. Ella had no further vocal problems for the rest of the evening.

With the return of the orchestra, her next surprise was a rare nod to pop culture which delighted everyone. Ella Fitzgerald sang the theme song to the hit television show, "The Love Boat." An unrehearsed version of "The Sidewalks of New York" was her first encore after the usual huge standing ovation, followed by "Mr. Paganini." Ella came out for a third encore, unusual even for her. The audience did its normal shout festival of requests, and Ella quieted them long enough to say ". . . Now, now, that's the only reason we came back!" and went into a full version of "A-Tisket A-Tasket." Once again the audience was taken aback, knowing they were witnessing a rarity.

Flying to Chicago, Ella joined Count Basie and the guys, Joe Pass, Roy Eldridge, Zoot Sims, and her trio to tape an edition of "Soundstage" for PBS. She avoided the obvious, doing only one of the expected Ella-Basie songs, and chose instead to concentrate on tunes from the Songbooks.

She looked glamorous, changing outfits several times. Curiously, there was no audience in attendance, and therefore no applause. It was strange to see all that great talent do their unmatched thing, and finish a number to deafening silence. Ella was also heavier than she had been in years, perhaps weightier than ever. The added pounds affected her voice, as she had trouble getting it to do exactly what she wanted.

On November 27, 1979, Ella jetted to Washington, this time to attend a special White House reception thrown by President Carter for recipients of the Kennedy Center Honors. On December 2, Ella was greeted by a standing ovation as Peggy Lee outlined her career (up to that point, as Ella's career did not slow for several years) with witticisms and video clips. In a black suit with white satin blouse and stylish "wedge" wig, Ella sat in the president's box as Count Basie saluted her, then was joined by Joe Williams for "Alright, Okay, You Win." Peggy joined with Joe for a second chorus encore, then the Basie band vamped as Jon Hendricks joined the group with special lyrics for "One O'Clock Jump." The Honors show was broadcast on CBS on December 29, 1979, and the only thing missing was a live performance by The Lady herself.

Ella returned to touring with her trio as 1980 rolled around. Once again she turned to PBS, taping a "Previn and the Pittsburgh" episode with her old friend and musical collaborator, André Previn. Previn did a thorough interview with her, although it was obvious that much of it was edited to fit the hour time slot. Featured here were many songs that Ella rarely did live, if at all. Previn himself accompanied her on "Like Someone in Love." Paul and the trio backed Ella for several numbers. At Previn's request, Ella did one of her on-the-spot, impromptu, original songs, and it came off quite well. She was in excellent spirits but not in top voice, as she frequently sipped icewater saying ". . . They say Pittsburgh makes you dry!" More and more often she was inconsistent in live performances, sometimes being brilliant and other times really having to work hard to be the singer of old.

Early 1980 also saw yet another Fitzgerald win at the Grammy awards on February 27, 1980. Although not there in person to accept, she was honored for the belated release of *Fine and Mellow* as Best Vocal Performance–Female. Doing more television than she had in years, she also guested on an ABC-TV special starring Karen and Richard Carpenter called "Music, Music, Music" on April 26. The show opened with the entire cast (John Davidson was the other guest) and the Nelson Riddle Orchestra joining together for "Without a

Song." Besides doing a medley of torch songs, Ella was featured with a large orchestra and strings in "Ain't Misbehavin'," a concert arrangement that differed from the ones on the Basie albums. The song was done in one take, with only one false start for the orchestra who muffed the introduction after four bars. The wrap-arounds took many takes to tape (there was no live audience, applause was "sweetened" in later) in order to get the complicated camera work right.

Ella and Karen worked very well together, their voices blending beautifully. The medley started with Ella seated at a bar, with Karen walking in. One thing that the torch medley did offer was Ella's only chance to sing "This Masquerade," a song that suited her voice so perfectly that it is a shame she didn't run immediately into a studio and record it. Karen was obviously thrilled to be working with Ella, a sparkle in her eye and an unflagging smile showing her respect for the singer and her music.

After being referred to later as a genius by Richard Carpenter, Ella introduced Paul, Keter, and Bobby before doing her final solo for the evening: a shortened version of "How High the Moon," one of the rare times her performance of this song was captured for any sort of camera.

Mention must also be made of exceptional production values and the talents of the Carpenters. Karen's voice was its usual haunting bell, and Richard's virtuosity was highlighted by a number showcasing him on all manner of keyboards, from a grand piano to a toy piano. Bob Henry, producer and director, did a superb job with all concerned.

On May 21, 1980, Ella did a concert in New Brunswick, New Jersey, that ended in controversy. Appearing with her trio and the Garden State Symphonic Pops, she was in top voice. The controversy was that this was supposed to have been a fund-raiser for Local 204 of the American Federation of Musicians. Ella even cut her standard $25,000 fee by $10,000 in support of the musicians. Yet, the theater was only half full because the publicity on the concert contained erroneous dates and phone numbers, and last-minute sales were affected by inclement weather. Finally, officials stated that the show was *not* a fund-raiser, but if a profit *had* been made it would have gone to the union. Obviously, the entire affair had been mishandled, as Ella always sold out at this point in her career. While there were no profits, there was money enough for a champagne reception in Ella's honor in the mezzanine of the theater after the performance.

Awards and honors flooded in through 1980. On May 7, Ella was given the Will Rogers award by the Beverly Hills Chamber of Commerce and Civic Association at the annual Beverly Hills Ball. At a show hosted by television's Mike Douglas, Ella sang "Some Other Spring" and "After You've Gone." September 25 brought her an honorary Doctor of Music degree from Howard University. On October 10, 1980, Ella received the Lord & Taylor Rose award for "the person whose outstanding contribution in her field has enriched all of our lives." While she did not do a set that night at the party in her honor, she did do an unrehearsed ten-minute "scat challenge" with Jon Hendricks of Lambert, Hendricks, and Ross. The next day, an exhausted Ella received a Doctor of Human Letters from Talladega College of Alabama.

Ella then flew to Washington to appear at the Kennedy Center Honors to salute Count Basie. After being introduced by Walter Cronkite, she and the Basie band appeared from behind a curtain, and Ella swung into "Too Close for Comfort." Joe Williams then joined her, and the two of them dueted on a spirited "Honeysuckle Rose."

Ella's temper reared its head at one such charity function. "The only time I really lost my temper was one night in Pennsylvania," she would later say. "We were doing a benefit for the musicians' union— they were trying to bring the symphony back—and this fellow kept following me. If they [photographers] shoot close to where I had that hemorrhage, the moment that flashbulb hits, it's as if someone punched me in the eye. I said, 'Please, don't put the flash in my face!' He kept right on, and I started taking the camera from him and trying to hit him. I felt so bad afterward, because people like that don't mean any harm."

It was becoming clear that Ella's voice was going through a roller-coaster ride. Never yet even approaching poor delivery, she was, however, not often in good form. Some evenings she was in top voice, smoothly handling her performance with tremendous energy and vocal control. Other times, Ella had a dry throat, did not hit high notes well, and was unable to sustain a consistent level of energy. This pattern followed for the rest of her career, but Ella's concerts were never anything but successful, enjoyable experiences for her audience.

Ray, Jr., had long since left home to start a life for himself as a musician. Settling in Washington State, he was leading a small group in Seattle specializing in country music, having abandoned rock several years earlier. There was not a tremendous amount of time spent between mother and son. "They say he sings now—in the country style—but I haven't heard him," she was once quoted as having remarked. When she attended his wedding, she hadn't even met his fiancée prior to the ceremony. "I was waiting for this little colored girl to come down the aisle, and I looked and I saw this redhead! I think she's Scottish or Irish." Obviously, Ella wasn't even certain of her background. "A very sweet girl. They were supposed to come down last Christmas, but he had a job in Portland, so I said, as long as he's working and staying out of trouble, that's fine."

But was that fine? Money was no problem, and Ray could have been flown to see her whenever he chose. The unfortunate truth of the matter was that there wasn't a close bond among family members. The only consistent member to visit frequently was her niece. Ella lived her life to perform for adoring strangers but her own flesh and blood remained distant (unless they needed her for something).

Chapter Thirty-three

1980–1982

*N*orman Granz was always an extremely imaginative producer, surfacing with all the creative concepts for Ella's albums. One of his most creative was her next studio project, *Ella Abraca Jobim*. Returning to the Songbook series he had abandoned in 1964, this Jobim Songbook was creative not only in its concept but in its presentation. Norman wisely surrounded Ella with the jazz musicians she enjoyed working with (Clark Terry, Zoot Sims, Joe Pass), as well as with artists familiar with Brazilian music and the instruments necessary to give the album an authentic sound.

Recorded in Hollywood on September 17–19, 1980, and March 18–20, 1981, the album also featured percussionist Paulinho da Costa (who was also listed as associate producer), harmonica virtuoso Toots Thielemans, guitarist Oscar Castro-Neves, drummer Alex Acuna, bassist Abraham Laboriel, and rhythm guitarists Paul Jackson, Mitch Holder, and Roland Bautista. This was one of the few albums Ella recorded that lacked piano accompaniment. Erich Bulling arranged and conducted the two-record set with emphasis on guitars, harmonica, synthesizers, two horns, and Brazilian percussion instruments.

The album had a true feeling of Brazil. Many of the songs included had received earlier Ella treatments; she had been singing Jobim strains since the early 1960s. However, jacked up by all of the creative excitement, she plunged into this project facing the music anew. None of the cuts featured old vocal lines; Ella reworked every one of them to make them fresh and exciting. Nineteen songs appeared on the album, with only "So Danco Samba" and "Meditation" being conspicuously absent from the collection.

"The Boy From Ipanema" (again incorrectly given the wrong gender on the cover and label) was probably Ella's most often repeated Jobim number. She had been doing it as a solo song since the middle 1960s, but most recently had been featuring it as part of a bossa-nova medley. Here, Zoot Sims set the tempo and feeling with his tenor sax before Ella came in with the lyrics. Naturally, she did a scat here, careful to come up with a new vocal line rather than repeat her earlier performances. It is amazing that age did not seem to encroach on her ability to swing and to use time to her advantage. One could compare Ella to a Harlem Globetrotter: she did her vocal dribbles in meticulous time, and was able to turn on a dime, juggle, or dunk with equal ease. At this she was a champion, and no one, not Louis nor Billie nor Frank nor Carmen nor Sarah nor anyone else ever came even close to her.

"One Note Samba" was taken at the same tempo as her earlier versions; this time lyrics were featured before the de rigueur scatting. This song, if handled improperly, could have ended up being tedious, but there was never this fear when Ella was involved. Likewise, "Wave" appeared here with its lyrics intact before Zoot Sims played his sensitive solo.

This album showed the change in Ella's voice, which manifested itself in high notes that were more difficult to reach (her next albums would all be arranged in lower keys), vibrato problems (by the end of the decade, Ella would sing almost without vibrato to sidestep the problem), and a slight hoarseness that came and went. As she did before, Ella simply adapted and adopted. She kept her style but used her voice in different ways that suited her vocal equipment.

Another talent was Toots Thielemans, whose harmonica stylings floated throughout "Quiet Nights of Quiet Stars." Toots set the mood while the rhythm section created the easy swing. It had been twenty or so years since Ella first recorded "Desafinado" with Marty Paich; the treatment here was dissimilar. While the original used a pseudo-bossa rhythm, here the rhythm was traditional Brazil. The lyrics were also different, with more depth to them (although they were difficult to fit into the rhythm of the music). Lyrics like ". . . I put your picture in my trusty Roloflex / but all that I developed was a complex . . .") needed listening to more than once to appreciate fully the dark humor and use of internal rhythms.

Pablo originally released this Songbook as a two-record set holding over eighty minutes of music. Fantasy, Inc., released the collection as the last of Ella's albums digitally redone on CD, over ten years after it was recorded. CDs can hold much more music than vinyl records, but even a CD cannot hold eighty-plus minutes. Rather than release this collection as a two-CD set (as Verve had done with most of the other Songbooks), Fantasy chose to eliminate "Don't Ever Go Away" and "Song of the Jet" and release the music on a single CD. Except for those who bought the album originally, or live in cities that have stores carrying used records, these songs are now lost to the general buying public. In an era when so much was done to preserve both the music and integrity of older albums, more's the pity that a comparatively new album was allowed to be stripped so as not to include all of its original selections.

It is important that the work of artists such as Ella be preserved and made available to the public. Naturally, not every recording ever made by every artist can be offered, because there would be no market for them. However, when it comes to artists such as Ella, Frank Sinatra, Judy Garland, Nat Cole, Bing Crosby, the Beatles, Elvis Presley, Ethel Merman, Al Jolson, Barbra Streisand, and others, every effort should be made, because they were simply the very best at what they did, true originals.

Ella's recordings were constantly sought by directors for their films, more and more often as time went on. In the United Kingdom, a thirty-three-minute short by director Roger Christian called *The Dollar Bottom*, whose plot revolved around playground wheeler-dealing, used Ella's "Isn't It Romantic." Other upcoming films in this decade, such as *Torch Song Trilogy*, *Raging Bull*, and *When Harry Met Sally*, generously sprinkled Ella's voice throughout for much added atmosphere.

An unusual television appearance marked this time and place as Ella made her only foray onto a dramatic, episodic show. "The White Shadow" was a new hour-long drama on CBS centering around a white high-school basketball coach, played by Ken Howard, in a predominantly African-American neighborhood. In several episodes, the plot would spotlight on other characters to give Howard, who was in almost every scene of the shows, a little respite from the heavy demands of network television.

Writer Joshua Brand came up with an idea for a reunion show, a "whatever happened to . . . ?" episode spotlighting former students of Howard's. One alumnus, a cab driver played by Nathan Cook (who tragically died several years later from an allergy to medical treatment he was given), was to pick up a jazz singer at the airport and end up spending the day with her. Naturally, when anyone thought of jazz singers, they thought of Ella, so the part was written as an Ella prototype. At a production conference with Joshua, coordinating producer John Masius, and director Victor Lobl, the topic centered on just who should play this character, named Maxine Jeffries. They wanted someone who could sing, because the script called for a song. Names were bandied about, always with the question, "Who could play an Ella Fitzgerald character?" Finally, someone joked, "Well, let's hire Ella!" A call was made to Salle Productions (Ella's career was guided from there). Ella was *delighted* to appear on their program. "The White Shadow" was her nephew's favorite show.

A story conference was arranged in Ella's home, where her character was fleshed out. Several disguised incidents from Ella's own life were included: her character was in town to attend the funeral of her ex-husband, a jazz musician with whom she had always remained on friendly terms. Ray Brown must have swallowed hard at that one. The dialogue revealed "Maxine's" origins with Chick Webb, and her work with Benny Goodman, who broke the color barrier in jazz by hiring Lionel Hampton. Ella was concerned that she might be more of a burden than an asset. Director Victor Lobl had the script printed in extra-large letters so she could easily read it, then returned to her home to work with her on scenes so she would be comfortable during shooting.

Her scenes for episode 119, titled "A Day in the Life," were all done on location, commencing on February 12, 1981. Four actual sites were used: Burbank Airport, the Hollywood Freeway, Forest Lawn cemetery, and the Coconut Grove nightclub. Ella wore a gray suit and sunglasses. Her scenes at the airport were shot first, with care taken not to tire her or make her walk around too much. Between her poor eyesight, her weight, her diabetes, and arthritis, mobility was a major problem. A stand-in first went through all her scenes, so Ella could see exactly where she was required to move. After that, she rarely needed more than one take to be letter-perfect in her portrayal.

The next location was on the freeway, where the characters struggled with a flat tire. This was literally done on the freeway, as if the car had pulled over with a flat. There was no movement in this scene, just dialogue, so once the technicians were in place, the scene went quickly. Forest Lawn proved to be somewhat of a problem, as the grass was wet and soggy, making her walking difficult. Her heeled shoes were replaced by flats so she would not sink into the mud, and Nathan Cook held her arm to ensure steadiness. While the scene was not difficult in itself, it was unsettling for Ella as again she felt she was a burden. She never realized what a star she was.

The last (and best) scenes were shot at the long-closed Coconut Grove nightclub. It had been Hollywood's top spot for over forty years, but changing times and tastes had made it passé. It was used for private parties and charity functions and occasional film production work such as this. The shot of Ella and Nathan descending down the lengthy set of stairs took the longest to film, as Ella could not handle it in one take. The better moments revolve around Ella's singing, set in another room at the Grove that was being used as a closed boîte where Nathan's character liked to hang out. This cab-driver-cum-jazz-pianist character encouraged Ella to sing, and she did a superb job of lip-syncing to "Do Nothing 'Til You Hear From Me." Prerecorded with Paul Smith at the piano, the song sequence was shot with two cameras in several takes to get the best possible results. It was a salute to Ella's skill that viewers could not notice she wasn't singing live. Fans can check local video stores for this episode, as MTM released many of its shows for home video.

Ella hit the Grammys again (February 25, 1981), this time copping one as Best Jazz Vocal Performance–Female, for *A Perfect Match*. In a strange turn of events, she won the same award the following year (February 24, 1982) for *Digital III at Montreux*, which was, after all, an extension of the same performance.

Decca hit a financial sour note with Ella, one that brought her to Los Angeles Superior Court. Her attorney, Sam Krane, filed on her behalf a claim that MCA, the company that now owned Decca records and hence Ella's contract with them, had misrepresented her earnings and record sales. Sought in the suit was a rescinding of her contract, $49,727 in compensatory damages, and $1 million in punitive damages.

The lawsuit stemmed from two separate issues. First, MCA had licensed Ella's old recordings to a spate of subsidiary and unrelated labels for the purposes of reissues and collections throughout the world. Many of these labels "forgot" to report their sales to MCA, which was contractually bound to send Ella her percentage. Ella wanted her money. Second, Granz had stacks of Ella recordings he made during the JATP years that he wanted to release. If he could have broken her contract, he would have been free to issue these recordings.

This lawsuit, if won, would certainly have been in Ella's best interest, but it prevented the re-issue of her Decca recordings on CD until the suit was settled out of court in 1992. During this time, Ella continued her perpetual world tour. Paul Smith, tired of travel, found a regular gig in Long Beach, California, so Ella was forced to go elsewhere for a musical leader. She found one in Jimmy Rowles, who for years had worked with Billie Holiday and other jazz greats. Unfortunately, this was not the best musical marriage for Ella. As talented as Rowles was, he could not totally relinquish the spotlight to Ella. He often extemporized during concerts, and changed rhythms or chord structures without rehearsal. Ella always demanded of her musicians that both rhythm and music be kept as rehearsed, except in numbers where there was solo interplay between Ella and a particular musician, such as Joe Pass or Keter Betts. And at this point in her life, she needed that solid musical foundation to keep herself from going astray.

Ella's concert at Carnegie Hall on July 1, 1981, was a good example of what was wrong. In fine voice, she kicked off with her old arrangement of "All of Me," this time starting the song in tempo. It was obvious almost from the start that Rowles was disturbing her timing, that he played off the rhythm. Rowles was an accomplished pianist and arranger, and had this been a concert of his music, it would have been wonderful to watch and listen to his virtuosity.

However, Ella needed and deserved a different kind of support, and in number after number it was clear that she was missing the kind of work Paul Smith or Tommy Flanagan offered. Instead, Ella and Jimmy dueled for musical supremacy. Often, he wouldn't give her the notes she needed to stay in tune, and changed chords to suit his own vision. Keter and Bobby were forced to try and impose the sense of rhythm they knew she wanted, but the arrangements had a rushed sound.

It was a shame, for Ella was singing very, very well that night. Rowles did a revamp on "Take the 'A' Train." He began in waltz time, speeded the tempo up as if to follow a subway train that left the platform, traveled, and then slowed down at the next stop. Yet, even this number, when played by Paul Smith a year or two later, sounded much more cohesive and the musical intent much clearer. Ella's three high notes, blasted at the end to imitate a train's whistle, never failed to bring down the house.

Before "Baby Ain't I Good to You," someone from the balcony complained they couldn't hear (the acoustics were not up to par that evening, and eventually Carnegie Hall was closed and refurbished). When Ella asked, in all innocence, if the audience really couldn't hear, another voice in the balcony coming from a young black man shouted, "Just *work* those songs, Ella girl!" and everyone (including Ella) broke up with laughter.

During this same period, Ella appeared in Chicago, a concert that was broadcast over National Public Radio. Much of the first half of the concert was the same as a Pablo recital, with the exception of the opener, which was "Them There Eyes" (like "Goody-Goody," Ella almost never sang this song the same way twice). Ella loved "I'm Beginning to See the Light," working snatches of it into almost every concert. Rarely, however, did she sing the entire song with the trio (she often sang it in her duet turns with Joe Pass, but strangely they never recorded it). Here, Ella interrupted the song to do a recitative:

You know, when Duke Ellington wrote that song, he must have been thinking about all the lovers in the world. That's right! You know, when you'd go out with a fellah and you're dancing or something and he kisses you and you say, YEAH! I saw the light! Remember the days when everybody used to dance together?

Do you remember those days? Yeah, when you'd go home, the
back of your dress would be soakin' wet where the fellah's hand
was. All those beautiful ballrooms. The great Chick Webb,
Jimmy Dorsey, Jimmie Lunceford, Tommy Dorsey, oh those
were the days of the big bands! Yeah, you'd go in a ballroom
and you'd stand on a dime [segue to a few bars from "Ten Cents
a Dance" and "Moonlight Becomes You"]. Those were the days,
yeah. But you know, nowadays everybody they don't want to
dance together, all they want to do is push each other away.
They look up at the cat who plays and he says hey, Daddy, hit
me with those disco lights [trio does disco rhythm]. Enough of
that! But I dig it, you dig it, you dig it, you dig it? Yeah, those
were the days!

The White House beckoned and Ella gave a "command performance" on October 18, 1981. Ronald and Nancy Reagan were entertaining King Juan Carlos of Spain, and he requested to be entertained
by his favorite singer, Ella Fitzgerald.

Norman Granz reached back into the 1960s for Ella's next studio
album, her last one with a full orchestra. Featuring Nelson Riddle as
leader, arranger, and conductor, and recorded on February 4 and 5,
1982, *The Best Is Yet to Come* was a much anticipated album for Ella.

While the album *was* good, Riddle's arrangements were concept-
heavy, featuring four flutes, four French horns, and eight cellos. Noticeably missing were Riddle's trademark violins, harp, and xylophone
or vibes.

The deep, resonant sound of the instruments made for a very dark
album, as though the energy level of the entire collection was lacking.
Trying to accommodate the changes in Ella's voice, Riddle wrote the
arrangements in much lower keys than, for instance, Benny Green
had orchestrated the Basie album in 1979. These lower keys, which
were for the most part unfortunately necessary, added to the atmosphere. This album should have been called "Deep Purple," after one
of the songs in the collection.

Excepting all of this, the album did have some wonderful cuts, and
two of the songs *did* end up as part of Ella's live repertoire. For the
umpteenth time, Ella recorded "Don't Be That Way." While this was
a song worth singing, these repetitive recordings had a tendency to

be tiresome. "Autumn in New York" was last featured as a duet with Satchmo. The effect here was so somber that it lost the joy of the Big Apple in the fall, as if the song were about a lost love instead of a romantic season. Many old friends appear on the album, with Joe Pass, Jimmy Rowles, Shelly Mann, and Jim Hughart contributing their musicianship. The best work on this album, however, belonged to three songs that were as good as any of Ella's work with Riddle.

"God Bless the Child" perfectly fit Ella's voice and style. Borrowing nothing from Billie, she made the song totally her own. Time after time, Ella sang Lady Day's songs so successfully ("My Man," "Them There Eyes," "Good Morning Heartache," "Some Other Spring," "Fine and Mellow," "You've Changed," and others), yet never did she imitate Billie's interpretations, as great as they were. She was always secure enough to rely on her own good taste and style to make her own imprint.

"Deep Purple" had appeared briefly on *30 by Ella*. The arrangement here was imaginative, utilizing Riddle's concept to the fullest. The magic of Riddle's music was evident, for even when this song was done with a big band sans cellos or French horns, the orchestration held up. Ella explored the lower range of her voice, in a song truly calling for it. As with " 'Round Midnight," Ella did not fear or avoid the low notes. She plunged right in without a second's hesitation.

"The Best Is Yet to Come" was introduced by Tony Bennett in 1959, and always was a natural for Ella. The song was a finger-snapper, designed to be rhythmic without getting carried away with itself. Once again, the concept hurt the performance, for while it was a good cut, it could have been great had the arrangement not been so murky. The song should give the intention of a controlled explosion, promising a musical peak that it can't deliver. Ella was never given a chance to build that excitement, through no fault of her own. She was too much of a musician to sing against an arrangement.

Harvard Yard called as Ella was chosen the 1982 Hasty Pudding Club Woman of the Year. Given a parade through Harvard Square on February 17, 1982, Ella was taken to the theater, where she received her award and sang "I've Got a Crush on You," and then stayed to watch the annual all-male review, entitled that year "Sealed With a Quiche."

She returned to Carnegie Hall for her annual visit to the Jazz Festival held in New York every summer. Originally held in Newport (with adjuncts in New York) and called the Newport Jazz Festival, the yearly event's name changed with the corporate sponsor. Her two shows on June 2, 1982, with the Count Basie Orchestra, included live versions of recent recordings, old favorites, and a jam session. Her appearance came in the second half of the show.

"Too Close for Comfort" worked even better with brass, and Ella abandoned the words toward the end for a lively scat finish. "Teach Me Tonight" was a reprise from her last album with the Basie band, followed by "Deep Purple." Here the brass doubled for all those Riddle concepts, and what a difference it made. Ella got her chance to soar, for she was in marvelous voice for both shows. She even slightly altered the program. "Let's Do It" and "Old MacDonald" both benefited from the big band sound before she sang three songs with the trio. Paul Smith returned to conduct here, which ended the short-lived concert marriage with Jimmy Rowles. "God Bless the Child" found its place with the trio, where it remained for years as an integral part of the show, always a crowd pleaser. Rowles's arrangement of "Take the 'A' Train" endured after him, played better by Smith because he was more in sync with Ella. The encores were the de rigueur jam session with the sidemen from the band, followed by a quieter moment with the trio in a medley of "I'll See You in My Dreams" and "Dream" put together by Keter Betts.

With Paul back in the fold and her musical surroundings secure, Ella looked forward to smooth sailing. However, from this point on, it would always seem that just as soon as she overcame one problem, others sprung up in front of her.

Chapter Thirty-four

1983–1985

*F*or Ella 1983 was a year of transition: she lost some close friends, recorded three albums, and suffered the beginning of her worst health problems. In addition, she still took musical risks and broke new ground.

Continental Airlines was looking for a new gimmick to induce people to fly first class, and someone at the aeronautic brain trust decided to inaugurate live, big-name entertainment in the lounges of the 747 jets. Ella jumped at the chance to be the first performer to do an airplane concert. On January 12, 1983, she and the trio sang from Chicago to Denver, and then from Denver to Los Angeles. Dressed in casual attire, they performed for more than an hour to a select audience of passengers. The mini-concert included "The Continental." It was probably the smallest audience Ella had sung for in over forty years. A commemorative poster was commissioned by Continental, and a signed copy was displayed in the offices of Salle Productions.

In a legendary combination of talent and generations, Ella once again was a presenter at the Grammy awards, this time handing out the award for Best Jazz Instrumentalist–Solo. The Manhattan Transfer joined her onstage, and they were off and flying on "How High the Moon." Ella sang with them on the second chorus, and scatted her way through while the group swung through the lyrics. They would introduce this song in their concerts by noting that Ella made it famous, and that they had been fortunate enough to once sing it with her.

Joe Pass was appearing more frequently with Ella in concerts as an unbilled guest star, so it came as no surprise that the two recorded another studio album. *Speak Love* was recorded in Hollywood on March 21 and 22, with the sessions producing so many songs that several were withheld and released on an album three years later. Joe Pass had long been a fan of Kurt Weill's song "Speak Low" (introduced by Mary Martin in *Lute Song*), and it was his idea to adopt the title of the song for the title of the album. The song was given an easy, rhythmic approach.

Two months later, Ella flew to New York to record another duo album, this time reverting to her earlier voice and piano efforts with Ellis Larkins, Paul Smith, and Oscar Peterson. *Nice Work If You Can Get It* had all the right ingredients: André Previn on piano, Ella's vocals, the Gershwins providing the songs, and even Al Hirschfeld providing the cover.

Recorded on May 23, the album included the ten songs (three were in a medley) that had all been on the original Gershwin Songbook, and four of them were standard parts of Ella's live repertoire. Niels Orsted-Pedersen provided the occasional bass for this album, the third one of Ella's that was recorded digitally on the Sony system. Historically, this album was an enigma, because the concept had already been done so many times before, even by Ella. Ella and Ellis did this same kind of album with Gershwin tunes, and she of course had recorded the extensive *Gershwin Songbook* with Nelson Riddle, so it was odd these songs were chosen. There were still many melodies Ella had not gotten to, and certainly there were other songs worth a second look besides those of the Gershwin brothers. These are some of the reasons that *Nice Work If You Can Get It* is anticlimactic, having a déjà vu feeling. This collection just did not have the originality, inspiration, or vocal quality that an Ella Fitzgerald album deserved.

"But Not for Me" skipped the verse, went right to the chorus, and showed Ella with a troublesome vibrato. Previn did a middle chorus here in a minor that was very effective. "Let's Call the Whole Thing Off" began in waltz time before settling into its normal rhythm. While this was a cute gimmick, it gave up before having any real impact. "How Long Has This Been Going On?," although recorded by Ella so many times, was still done beautifully here. She really *knew* this song, and sang it differently every time. Her depth of understanding, not only of the lyrics but also of the music, the notes and chords and possible harmonies, shone through. This is the big winner on the album. "They Can't Take That Away From Me" was the biggest enigma on the set: it followed almost exactly the vocal line Ella used for more than twenty years on three live albums.

Four days after these recordings, Ella won the Peabody medal for Outstanding Contributions to Music in America at Johns Hopkins University in Baltimore.

Norman Granz planned a JATP reunion at this time, a thirty-year anniversary of the famous Tokyo concert. He took his troupe to the Yoyogi National Stadium in October of 1983, and such stalwarts as Oscar Peterson; Zoot Sims (in one of his last appearances as he was *very* ill); Eddie "Lockjaw" Davis; Harry "Sweets" Edison; Clark Terry; Al Grey; Joe Pass; Louis Bellson; Niels Orsted-Pedersen; J. J. Johnson; Martin Drew; and the trio of Paul Smith, Bobby Durham, and Keter Betts joined Ella in a concert that was much later released on a two-CD set called *Return to Happiness*.

Once again, Granz chose to break up Ella's set, reworking the order of the nine songs released and with limited applause. Her repertoire at this time included many songs that had never appeared on live albums, yet those released here hardly reflected that. "Flying Home" (done here in extended form with the All-Stars), " 'Round Midnight," the medley of "The Man I Love" and "Body and Soul," "Night and Day," and "They Can't Take That Away From Me" (the *fourth* live version with the same arrangement, besides the recently recorded studio version) had all been on live albums during the Pablo years. "Manteca" and "Willow Weep for Me" were taken from *Things Ain't What They Used to Be*, and both were excellent, especially "Willow Weep for Me." What might have been a highlight, "Blue Moon" seemed to have little energy behind it, which made it a pedestrian effort. Unfortunately, this was her last recorded live album released to date, and many of the wonderful songs she sang to live audiences throughout the 1980s and early '90s were never put to wax or disc. This entire concert was videotaped, but was never shown on American television.

On August 25, 1983, Ella appeared with Count Basie at Avery Fisher Hall in Lincoln Center. While the Count had noticeably slowed (he refrained from joining the band in several numbers) their turn was a crowd pleaser, warming up the 2,000 in attendance. Both Oscar Peterson and Joe Pass were guest artists, and Joe appeared after the interval. He seemed to be stalling for time, but finally the trio was introduced and Ella walked on.

From the moment she stepped onstage, it was obvious there was a problem. Ella was often tentative when appearing, partly because she always became nervous before a performance, and partly because the stage lights were blinding until her eyes adjusted. On this night, Ella seemed to wobble around the piano as she reached for her microphone, and did not greet the audience with any of her usual, friendly banter. The band started the opener ("Give Me the Simple Life"), and had to repeat the introduction, as Ella did not seem to recognize the song. While often forgetting lyrics, she had trouble with all of the words to this song.

Although the audience did not seem to notice that anything was awry, Ella fared no better on her second number, "Good Morning Heartache." She kept losing her balance, walking forward and back while staying close to the piano. She always performed at center stage, the piano to her right, the drums behind her and the bass slightly to her left. This concert was the last time this happened.

Ella seemed to be doing a cha-cha as she started her third number, "Make Me Rainbows." For those not familiar with Ella's rendition of this song, the band played alone after the first chorus, and Ella joined in after the bridge of the second chorus. As she sang ". . . make me sunsets . . ." and threw up her hand in the familiar gesture when she was cooking, both the rhythm and the movement threw her backwards, and she fell, with her head just missing the bandstand. While the audience breathed deeply as one, the band kept playing and, amazingly, Ella kept singing. She was unable to rise, so she just remained on the stage at a ninety-degree angle to the band, with the microphone in her hand as she continued singing. Several of the side-men attempted to pick her up, but her considerable girth made it awkward, so they just leaned her forward until she was standing. Just then, Ella sang the scarily ironic ". . . don't let me fall / 'til I'm all I can be . . ." and the audience went wild.

As she finished the song to a standing ovation, Ella quieted the audience as she attempted an explanation. Obviously shaken but apparently unhurt, she charmed her way out of what could have been a major embarrassment by saying, "Folks, I'm wearing brand new shoes tonight and you ladies know . . ." She never got further than that, because the audience applauded its approval, happily accepting this innocent explanation. Ella finished the concert with one hand hanging on to the piano, concentrating on her performance and the lyrics. Incredibly, she did a second show just seventy-five minutes after the end of the first one. Her second show proceeded well, although she took hold of the piano on her entrance. None of the reviews mentioned her fall; perhaps they all attended the second show, which had started at ten o'clock.

What happened? Obviously, the problem was more than just new shoes. Anyone familiar with Ella Fitzgerald could immediately rule out alcohol or drugs, as she somehow managed to avoid the pitfalls that befell many of her performing colleagues. While Ella enjoyed an occasional drink or a bottle of good champagne, she was not a drinker in the sense that she regularly imbibed. Drugs were out of the question, her strong religious beliefs sustaining her where others turned to mind-altering chemicals. The answer was a medical one: the years of touring and doing two shows a night, the years of carrying around extra weight, the stress of her numerous eye operations, all were finally taking their toll. She was sixty-six years old, with heart problems as well as troubling arthritis.

What the public would not know was that she also battled diabetes, and, in fact, one of her toes had been amputated. This was kept out of the press, both to save her possible embarrassment and so as not to interfere with possible future bookings. Her footing would never be sure again, and her wearing of high heels in public a foolhardy attempt at hiding her condition.

In a way, this fall was fortunate, because it forced Ella and her physicians to take action that probably saved her life and certainly extended her career for more years. Ella fell because she lost her balance due to a combination of dizziness, medication, and loss of footing caused by the surgery. Immediately, she was put on a stringent diet, and over the next two years safely and slowly lost close to one hundred pounds. It was these health problems that had most recently affected her voice. Ella's tours continued, her physicians wisely understanding that she was happiest (and therefore healthiest) when she sang for her public.

Ella's last few albums were held back from release to give the impression that she was recording albums every single year. The fact is, she did not record again in the studio until 1986, and then not again for another three years. In between, four albums were released annually so there would be a new Ella album from Pablo every year. Additionally, her Verve albums (now owned by Polydor) were widely available, and Decca (now owned by MCA) kept her hits in the stores. Her Capitol albums were still available in their abridged forms, with *30 by Ella* finally being rereleased. Even her Reprise albums had been reissued on subsidiary labels to owner Warner Brothers. There was no Ella dearth in record stores.

Also, technology was changing, and Polydor began to release its albums on the new format, the CD. By 1990, there were more than sixty different CDs available in the Ella Fitzgerald section in music stores. Also by 1990, Norman Granz was out of the recording business, and was for all intents and purposes retired. Fantasy, Inc., had bought Ella's albums as is, without any extra cuts or unreleased material. This was too bad, because there were almost always such cuts, and many labels (like Verve with Ella and Capitol with Sinatra) took advantage of the extra space available on the CD format to include previously unreleased material.

February of 1984 allowed Ella to bask again in the glow of the Grammy spotlight, when she won Best Jazz Vocal Performance–Female for *The Best Is Yet to Come*. She wasn't up to accepting her award in person.

Ella spent much of the year under doctors' care. She continued her weight reduction and the doctors tried to bring her diabetes under control. When she appeared at the Westbury Music Fair in Long Island, New York, in October, she seemed in fine spirits and in excellent voice. Obviously thinner but looking glamorous in a red sequined jacket and skirt with matching bow tie, she had to be helped down the aisle and onto the rotating stage of this theater-in-the-round by two ushers.

She did two shows that night, with Oscar Peterson as the opening act. Ella was a little taken aback because there was not a capacity crowd (". . . It's Saturday night, where is everybody?"). The place was about two-thirds full for both shows. Capacity crowd or not, Ella was loose and relaxed, and did a long set that featured many favorites such as "It's All Right With Me," "Sophisticated Lady," and "Old Mac-Donald." She continued holding onto the piano, as she did for the next several years until her doctors forced her to sit down while she sang.

Her schedule was rigorous, except that more and more often she was doing only one show a night. Previously, she often appeared in the second half of the set, following an opening group or musician. Now, she opened the show, doing ten or twelve songs before an intermission. After the break, the trio or Joe Pass or other musicians did two or three songs, and Ella returned (her gown always changed to look glamorous) to conclude the evening.

This was the case when Ella made her usual pilgrimage to Carnegie Hall on June 29, 1985. The audience was taken aback by her appearance. Wearing a slinky, beige gown with bugle beads, she not only had lost weight, but was practically svelte. Immediately holding on to the piano after entering to the usual riotous audience welcome, Ella reached into her mixed vocal bag that night, dipping more into the Decca years. The truly peak moment remembered from this concert was "Night in Tunisia." She dispensed with the words altogether and transformed it into scat. At the end, Ella and Keter Betts performed a musical duel as he tried to imitate her vocal gyrations on his bass. Unfortunately, this performance has not been recorded.

In August, Ella, Joe, and Oscar Peterson did a concert at Wolf Trap, the outdoor music center not far from Washington. Much of this performance was taped by PBS, and Ella's set included songs from the New York concert. The finale featured Ella, Joe, Oscar, and the trio bopping out "Four Brothers" as the credits unrolled. Her voice cracked trying to hit the notes. While in rehearsal for this concert, Ella felt ill, and complained to Paul Smith. He grabbed her arm (a familiar gesture between them) and was shocked by how cold it was.

Paul feared Ella's circulation was poor and advised her to see a doctor posthaste. She delayed until after the concert, when she was admitted to a local hospital for the treatment of fluid buildup in the lungs. She ceased performances for several months as a downward health spiral continued.

Chapter Thirty-five

1986–1990

*A*lthough many predicted that Ella's recording career was slowing down and perhaps over, she and Joe Pass went into the studio on February 25 and 28, 1986, for another album of duet performances. *Easy Living* was an unusual release, not only in its long list of fifteen entries, but also in the use of cuts recorded earlier but not released. After *Fitzgerald and Pass . . . Again* had included so many tunes, it was a surprise that *Speak Love* provided a relatively short program. Several more songs were recorded than released at that time, and these cuts (some discarded because they were rehearsal cuts) found their way onto this latest collection. There was an obvious difference in vocal quality between those songs recorded in 1983 and those in 1986. Additionally, many of the songs from 1986 sounded as if they too were rehearsal cuts, as they began and ended without much support from Joe, who usually framed those duets with his own brand of introductions and playoffs.

Part of the reason for this was the haste in which the album was recorded. Granz always pushed for quick recordings, trying to get a totally improvised approach to the jazz. Unfortunately, Ella was not feeling well, and was not thrilled with the choice of material Granz had selected this time. The selection posed major question marks to a chronicler of Ella's music. "Don't Be That Way" had been recorded as recently as 1982 for *The Best Is Yet to Come*, and Ella had cut it so often that no new interpretation could bring anything fresh to the song, especially since she and Joe had already done the number on their first album, *Take Love Easy*. "Don't Worry 'Bout Me" had a spectacular live version by Ella and Joe in 1973 at Carnegie Hall, and was redundant here.

The rest of the choices were more interesting, such as "My Ship." Both "I Want a Little Girl" and "I'm Making Believe" were seldom recorded. In the liner notes, Norman Granz referred to these songs as survivors, but it was Ella who was the survivor. She made these songs live again long after their time.

While a new recording by Ella was always welcome, one has to wonder at the lack of thought or imagination behind this one, especially at a time when she had been grappling with physical problems and hadn't recorded in three years. It isn't that the album is not enjoyable, although Ella was clearly not in good voice. At this point in her career, she deserved better. She did not record again for another three years, as she entered a bleak period of unhappiness.

Although Ella managed to continue her performing schedule, she was feeling ill frequently and continued to develop heart problems. On July 27, 1986, she was in a hotel room in Lewiston, New York, when she was rushed to Niagara Falls Medical Center. She had been performing at Artpark in Lewiston the night before, returning to her hotel after the show to rest. At approximately 11:00 A.M., the ambulance brought her to the center, where she was immediately placed in intensive care. Annie Chapman, spokesperson for the hospital, listed Ella as suffering from "heat exhaustion" and being in "fair" condition.

In reality, the doctors at first thought that Ella had suffered a heart attack; their diagnosis was changed to congestive heart failure and she was released three days later. She was flown directly to her home in Beverly Hills, where she withheld any decisions about her work schedule until her condition improved. It did not take long for her own doctors to diagnose that Ella was in critical condition and required radical treatment in order to keep her alive and healthy. She was admitted to Cedars-Sinai Hospital in Los Angeles on August 19, 1986, in preparation for the open-heart/bypass surgery performed on September 3. News was withheld from the press until it was certain that she would recover fully.

She was able to be moved out of ICU by the weekend, and returned to convalesce in the comfort of her home. Norman Granz wisely canceled Ella's engagements for the rest of the year. Once again at this point, many thought her career was over. It *was* certain that she could not possibly keep the kind of schedule she had been used to for the previous forty years; her doctors put their collective foot down about that. Ella, however, had other ideas about retirement. Singing had been her whole life; it meant everything to her. Ray, Jr., was in Seattle with his band, married, and had a daughter named Alice. Ella's favorite niece had married, and Norman Granz was living in Europe most of the year. The only thing that revitalized her spirit was getting up in front of an audience, and wisely but begrudgingly her doctors realized that to prevent Ella from singing could kill her just as fast as permitting her to perform. As one doctor said, "She could just as easily die on the toilet as she could on stage. She might as well sing and be happy." Reaching out to her fans was her therapy, and if she was going to leave this world, she wanted to do it with a microphone in her hand.

After an almost fifty-year wait, Ella and Van Alexander were given the Hall of Fame award at the annual Grammy presentation (February 24, 1987) for their "A-Tisket A-Tasket." Ella was not well enough to attend. For the most part, she spent the spring of 1987 recuperating and resting.

June was a month of honors. On the fourteenth, she was awarded the UCLA Medal for Musical Achievements, the school's highest honor to those whose achievements were of such important significance to merit recognition. As one of the recipients of the third annual National Medal of Arts (a medal intending to honor those who create the arts for the American people and those whose philanthropy make them available), Ella flew to Washington for a White House luncheon on the nineteenth. There was also a dinner given by Frank Hodsoll, the chairman of the National Endowment for the Arts, and a congressional reception hosted by Senator Edward Kennedy.

Ella did two "try-out" gigs in smaller towns to get her performing legs back before coming back to her hometown. Returning to Avery Fisher Hall on June 24, she again overwhelmed New York. Appearing with Paul Smith, Keter Betts, and Jeff Hamilton on drums, she was escorted onstage on the arms of two ushers who placed her on a high-rising stool as she began her first number. The audience wasn't certain what they would find, after reading of Ella's medical problems and heart surgery. Lean and beautiful, she wailed into a Charleston-tempoed "Old Black Magic," getting a second standing ovation before she could thank the audience. She began "I've Got the World on a String" by telling everyone how lucky she was, how singing was her therapy, and that next year she'd come back and dance! Except for a little breathiness on some of the up-tempo numbers, Ella swung solidly and there was no doubt that she and Mackie were back in town.

Norman Granz released *The Best of Ella Fitzgerald* in 1988, a collection of Ella on Pablo. The fourteen studio cuts found her with various musical accompaniments. While this was a most satisfying collection, especially for those who hadn't collected all of the original Pablo albums and for those cuts from albums (at that point) yet to be released on CD, it was hoped that future collections would contain unreleased material.

Ella was the recipient of the NAACP Image award for Lifetime Achievement in a show that was syndicated in early 1988. Saluted by Nancy Wilson and Al Jarreau, who did a modernized version of "A-Tisket A-Tasket," Ella was escorted to the podium, where she was visibly moved. As a thank-you, she fragily warbled "You Are the Sunshine of My Life," throwing in a scat chorus to the great approval of the audience. Several audience members were visibly crying. Again, columnists wrote that Ella would not, could not perform in concerts any longer. Surely, the evidence pointed in that direction, but it took lightning and thunder from above to finally stop her several years later. While these doubters were learning how to use the delete button on their PCs, Ella was back at work.

June 24, 1988, brought Ella back to Carnegie Hall as part of the JVC Jazz Festival. There was nothing new at this concert, with the exception of a rousing "Stompin' at the Savoy." Ella was in only fair voice, but clearly happy to be performing. One song would come out well, the next would be shaky, almost as if the chemicals in her body were on a roller coaster (and with all the medications she was taking, perhaps they were).

The only nerve-wracking part of the concert was Ella's tendency to inch her way forward toward the audience near the end of the show. This was done because she truly wanted to reach out to people. In recent concerts, a chair had been placed next to the piano should Ella feel the need to sit down, or find herself falling backwards. While she did not heed the advice of her doctors to sit while she sang, she certainly no longer took center stage to do her songs. Toward the end of her concert, she became adventurous, and moved away from the piano closer to her adoring fans, her "therapy." At one point, several members of the first-row audience stood up to catch Ella as it seemed she would take one step too many. She did not.

Ella made her annual appearance at the Hollywood Bowl on July 22 and once again garnered headlines. She continued her recent habit of, late in her set, slowly moving to the apron of whatever stage she was working on in order to better play to the crowd. That night in 1988 she took one step too many, and landed on the ledge in the first section of box seats at the Bowl. Luckily, the pond of water separating the stage from the seats had been replaced by box seats several years earlier. She injured a leg when she fell, and her trio and several of the audience members helped her back onstage as she quipped, "I'm okay, I'll just sing from down here!" As she returned to the stage, she wisecracked, "Now you can tell folks that Ella fell for *you*!" And she sang "Since I Fell for You."

Her doctors were in attendance that night (as they often were when she played in the Los Angeles area), and after ice was applied to her leg, she came out to join Joe Pass (sitting down this time) and finished the rest of the show, which contained many of the same numbers she had been doing for the previous few seasons. Much was made of this in the press, and again some wondered if it wasn't wise for Ella to retire from such appearances. They didn't need to wonder long, for Ella was yet to perform many memorable concerts (some in such good voice it was almost eerie) and win yet another Grammy award for her recording wizardry.

A regular venue now for Ella, she fared much better at Radio City Music Hall on February 11, 1989. Backed by pianist Keith Johnson (Paul couldn't make it), Keter, and drummer Frankie Capp, she did many of her usual songs, although now she was firmly ensconced on top of a stool. She sat on a stool from then on when she sang. As usual in her concerts at this time, the highlight was the appearance of Joe Pass at the second half, and their working together. Deliciously grooving, these two brought out the best in one another.

Although Ella no longer had a permanent contract with Pablo, Norman Granz decided it was time to get her back in recording harness and take advantage of her latest comeback. He produced *All That Jazz*, a success for Ella all around. The cover illustration was modern, based on a photograph by James W. Blackman. Phil Carroll's art direction was the first in many years to give one of Ella's albums a progressive, modern look without the use of out-of-focus pictures and outdated graphics. Recorded on March 15–16 and 20–22, 1989, the album was initially supervised by Norman (who stayed in the booth), with Ray Brown taking responsibility on the studio floor for what actually happened musically.

Two pianists were used, Kenny Barron and Mike Wofford, the latter taking up the piano slack, accompanying Ella in concerts after Paul Smith decided he no longer wanted to tour. Mike ended up carrying most of these chores for Ella from then on, although sometimes Paul pitched in. Born in San Antonio on February 25, 1938, Mike Wofford had been a highly respected name in jazz for over three decades, having worked with Sarah Vaughan, Benny Carter, Joe Pass, Zoot Sims, and others. He got his start with the Los Angeles jazz scene in the late fifties with the Lighthouse All-Stars. Familiar with his work and impressed by his rapport with Ella, Norman Granz tapped him to lead her trio henceforth.

Norman surrounded Ella with many of her old friends, such as Harry "Sweets" Edison, Benny Carter, Al Grey, Clark Terry, the aforementioned Ray Brown, and Bobby Durham returning to the fold after several years away from the trio. In musicianship, this album is reminiscent of *Fine and Mellow* back in 1974, with many of the same players. So much of Ella's studio work in the last decade had featured guitar, and while there was none this time, this amalgam of musicians provided a nice change of pace. Granz's liner notes took on a slightly morbid tone (". . . so many of her contemporaries have passed on . . ."), but they honestly stated for the first time in print that Ella's voice had changed.

While several of the songs had been recorded before, they hadn't been recorded to death, with only one song repeated from her much-sung repertoire, "Good Morning Heartache." The arrangement was much different from the one first recorded back in 1961 and repeated through the years. There was a long musical introduction (a brainstorm of Ray Brown's, as were many of the musical phrasings on this all-head-arrangement album) before Ella joined in with her vocal, and the spirit was less of pain than of melancholic acceptance.

The big winners on this set included "When Your Lover Has Gone," and "Baby, Don't You Quit Now" (written by former Ella accompanist Jimmy Rowles and the great Johnny Mercer), whose hauntingly bittersweet lyrics gave Miss Fitz a chance to show once again just how adept she was at handling this kind of material. The title cut, written by Benny Carter, was just plain fun and, to my knowledge, never recorded by anyone else. The over-seven-minute version of "The Nearness of You" was just glorious, the only true tour de force on the collection. This entire album carried the aural verisimilitude of being on Fifty-second Street in New York in its heyday. The only previously recorded tune that did not stand the test of time was "The Jersey Bounce." Although the standard was originally done by Ella in 1961 and featured in concerts since, its range and pace were not enhanced by a new recording at this point in her career.

When the Grammys were announced in February 1991, Ella once again was honored for Best Jazz Vocal–Female, for this (1989) album. Her private reaction to a friend: "They're just giving it to me 'cause I'm old and still around."

While her voice was still pleasing and comforting to listen to, much of the magic had vanished. Certainly the old style was there, but there wasn't enough voice to back it up. Surgeries, medications, stress, and age had stripped Ella of much of her breath control and vibrato, and her voice often just trailed off if she tried to press it too hard. She attempted to sing around her limitations, but was not happy with the final outcome of this studio effort. The sound that she had worked so hard to come by, the musical image it took all of her years at Decca to develop, was based on clarity, smoothness, and easy manipulation of a voice that could, on a good day, swing through almost four octaves. With that evenness of tone, that trademark smoothness, the voice that could move anywhere with equal facility all stripped away, she sadly lost much of her musical aura.

Strangely enough, there was still an almost hypnotic quality to her voice, especially in her ballad singing. In the late seventies and early eighties, it was her singing of the slow tempos that betrayed the deterioration of voice. Swing, snappy, or scat numbers still resounded and carried her through many of her performances. Now, her breath control could no longer handle the truly fast numbers, as old favorites like "Sweet Georgia Brown" and "Too Close for Comfort" had to be slowed down to give her room to breathe. The days of scatting her brains out as if on a sugar rush were over. Even when she *did* scat, the tempo was much slower. In the last few years of her concert career, it was the ballad that would most often offer a glimmer of Ella!, usually making the evening.

To celebrate her announced seventy-first birthday, the Society of Singers gave a black-tie gala to inaugurate a new trophy for Lifetime Achievement. She was honored on April 29, 1989, with the "Ella" (aptly named), and Bill Cosby emceed an evening that featured Dionne Warwick, the Pointer Sisters, Mel Tormé, the Manhattan Transfer, and Carol Burnett. Burnett had, on her variety show in the early seventies, parodied a singer in sequined gown and rolled down stockings with a big wig and thick glasses who sang "The Lady Is a Tramp." Benny Carter led the band.

In June Ella returned to Carnegie Hall for the fortieth annual year. Appearing on the twenty-sixth as part of the JVC Jazz Festival, she had a shaky start, sitting on a stool and forgetting both melody and lyrics to several of the songs in her set. Still nervous after all those years of staring into the lights at Carnegie Hall, she calmed down for the second half, and tossed off yet another brilliant twenty minutes with Joe Pass before finishing the evening with her trio (and Joe) behind her. More and more often now, Ella's concerts had an uneven feel, her second set usually stronger than her first. The appearance of Joe Pass almost always assured renewed vitality, and the two were booked together as often as possible. The highlight of this evening was Ella and Joe's massage of "Lady Be Good" as a lullaby, tenderly working through slow, brooding choruses.

Ella performed again at the Hollywood Bowl in a concert with the trio in early August of 1989. As she sat in a chair, she joked, "It's in my contract; after last time I have to sit down!" She sang several of the songs from her new album, but they were tentatively delivered, and Ella appeared irked. Old standbys such as "Shiny Stockings" and even "Mack the Knife" provided problems. "Mack" was almost sad, as she simply seemed to forget what she was doing. Over and over, she repeated, "Old Mackie, oh yeah, Old Mack," forgetting the signature lyrics she made up so many years before in Berlin. Several times the trio tried prompting her, but she seemed unable to catch on. Finally, Mike Wofford gave her the obvious musical cue to end the song, and she made as hasty an exit as someone who was barely able to walk could.

The low spots in Ella's life rarely lasted long because there was so much activity. Even with her performing schedule pared down from the whirlwind it had once been, there was always something on the horizon, something to balance the scales. Edith Kiggen produced a show, *Hearts for Ella*, on February 12, 1990, at Lincoln Center, a Valentine's Day tribute the proceeds of which were to benefit the American Heart Association. This concert was a shot in the arm for Ella, for not only was it another honor, not only did it come at a point in her life where her always-insecure self-image needed a boost, but the collection of her peers and loved ones who appeared was tremendous. Ella walked down the aisle at Avery Fisher Hall to a standing ovation that went on and on as she took her seat.

New York City mayor David Dinkins presented her with a crystal apple, and recalled her show business debut in 1934 ("when you were fifteen, and I was seven"). Lena Horne and Itzhak Perlman traded hosting chores, with Lena reading a page of verse by Oscar Peterson accompanied by Ray Brown on bass. Perlman then brought on Benny Carter, saying his musicians needed no introduction (which brought a laugh as the first man out, a stagehand, received applause from the eager audience). What a lineup of virtuoso talent: Ray Brown, Hank Jones, Herb Ellis, Louie Bellson, Stan Getz, Phil Woods, Dave Sanborn, Jimmy Heath, Nick Brignola, Al Grey, Urbie Green, Slide Hampton, Jack Jeffers, Red Rodney, Jon Faddis, Clark Terry, and Joe Wilder played together while Benny led them. They all took a slice at "How High the Moon," each improvising full choruses. "Ornithology" and a new piece called "First Lady" closed the Carter set.

The Manhattan Transfer, always in awe of Ella, sang a movement from Duke Ellington's "A Portrait of Ella Fitzgerald" from the *Ellington Songbook*. George Shearing riffed "Lulu's (Ella's) Back in Town," and he accompanied Joe Williams on "Blues in My Heart."

Perlman reappeared to duet with Bobby McFerrin on "Blue Skies," and Dizzy Gillespie inflated his expansive cheeks for "I Waited for You," taking a turn at the vocal as well. The first half finished with Honi Coles and the Copacetics, dancing along with a new light, Savion Glover.

Forty minutes later, the second half began with Cab Calloway (in his de rigueur white tie and tails) leading the band for "A-Tisket A-Tasket." Paying respects as well as love for his and Ella's twenty years together, pianist Tommy Flanagan did "Mr. Paganini," including all of her riffs that he had heard countless numbers of times while accompanying her. James Moody came out for "Stompin' at the Savoy," choosing sidemen from the musicians present the way a child would pick favorite pieces of candy from a box of expensive chocolates: Flanagan, Rodney, Hampton, Getz, and others. Joe Williams joined them to sing one of Ella's original compositions, "You Showed Me the Way." Quincy Jones, so much a part of Ella's recording and television history, came out to reminisce and conduct a Benny Carter arrangement of his own "Stockholm Sweetnin'."

Lady Lena returned to the stage to speak of wanting to sing like Ella when she was getting her musical feet wet, then Melissa Manchester and the Manhattan Transfer's Janis Siegel and Cheryl Bentyne came out to tackle "Crazy People" and "It's You" much in the style of the Boswell Sisters (Perlman tried his hand at jazz violin for this one). Oscar Peterson broke it up with "Who Can I Turn To?" then took on Perlman with "Summertime" and "Stormy Weather," which really needed Joe Pass (who couldn't make it that night and was sorely missed despite the all-star lineup). Moody took a turn at reminiscing, then read a verse called "Hearts for Ella" that appeared in the program and gave the evening its name.

Taking Ella's original Decca recording of "Lady Be Good," Benny Carter capped the evening by breaking down Ella's scatting and orchestrating it for the band. In between the famous scat phrases, these jazz giants took turns on improvised solos, leaving pop music at the door and making this a solid jazz evening, a night that must have pleased Norman Granz no end.

The only act that could follow would be Ella herself, led to the stage by Joe Williams. The band played Carter's arrangement of "Honeysuckle Rose" while the audience stood, cheered, whistled, stomped, and generally made a loving fool of itself. At the second chorus, just to make certain that no one misconstrued her not performing that night as a lack of ability, Ella scatted through the remainder of the number, hitting high notes that must have hurt the ears of every dog on the Upper West Side of Manhattan.

More speeches, plaques, and affectionate screaming occurred, until finally Ella turned to Joe Williams and asked, "Is this it?" A question like that to a jazz musician is like a gauntlet thrown down to one of King Arthur's knights. "It is unless you're going to sing something," countered Joe. With Oscar at the piano Ella blew the assemblage away with the one, the only, the original "Oh, Lady Be Good." It's not that Ella minded the tribute to her song, but she wasn't through with it yet. The New York Chapter of the Heart Association (with the help of American Express who sponsored the evening) established the Ella Fitzgerald Research Fellowship with the money raised at the benefit. And Ella, whom the newspapers wrote about as being frail, left New York for London, San Francisco, New Haven, and traveled back for Radio City.

Before leaving Manhattan, however, Ella journeyed to Radio City Music Hall to appear on the Grammy awards as a presenter with Natalie Cole for Album of the Year. Natalie had recently scored a personal success with her album of songs her father had made famous, *Unforgettable*. The following year, the award she was helping to present would be hers, but this year Natalie had to settle for singing with Ella Fitzgerald for 50 million people, reprising Father Nat's (and Ella's) old chestnut "Straighten Up and Fly Right" to a standing ovation.

Traveling to Europe in late May, Ella was given France's top award for excellence in the arts. Named Commander of Arts and Letters, she received the award (a bronze medal with a green and white ribbon) from Culture Minister Jack Lorung on May 30. That night Ella gave a concert in Paris.

The First Lady of Song again became the First Doctor of Song as Ella received an honorary Doctor of Music degree from Princeton University on June 13, 1990. Feeling well and enjoying the honor from an Ivy League school that would have made it difficult for African Americans to matriculate back when Ella was of college age, she had big plans looming in the immediate future. Unfortunately, the best laid plans . . .

Chapter Thirty-six

1990–End of Career

$\mathcal{E}$lla was looking forward to an extensive European tour in the summer of 1990, the highlight of which was to headline at a "Gala for Ella" aboard an ocean liner sponsored by the North Sea Jazz Festival in The Netherlands. On July 9, Ella collapsed in her Holland hotel room and was rushed to Bronovo Hospital in The Hague, where her friend and physician Dr. Clifford Booker informed the press she was suffering from exhaustion. While it was rumored in the papers that she had suffered another heart attack, it was untrue. Her diabetes was getting worse.

She did have to cancel her show at the Gala, as well as the rest of her European tour, and was flown home to Beverly Hills after a hospital rest.

Benny Carter had been a huge part of the Valentine's Day tribute to Ella in New York. Benny and the band joined Ella in Hollywood for a Bowl appearance in August, repeating "Lady Be Good" and several other songs before Ella appeared. She made her entrance, and it was apparent from the outset that she was in total control. Looking beautiful in a specially made gown for sitting in, Ella set the pace with "Sweet Georgia Brown," immediately following it with "Too Close for Comfort." She was in top form, not just for this period of her life but for any period. In song after song, "Satin Doll," "All That Jazz," "As Time Goes By," "Honeysuckle Rose," "Teach Me Tonight," "It's All Right With Me," and others, Ella conquered the audience. Her voice was strong and clear, her range impressive and her mood jubilant. The show was a total triumph, and she hadn't even started the second half. After the intermission, Ella did a set with the trio, concentrating on old standards that had been requested. "The Lady Is a Tramp," "Agua de Beber," a Cole Porter medley, "Night and Day" . . . all were gems. Closing with a spectacular version of "Mack the Knife," Ella was joined by Benny and several of his sidemen for a jam session, indicating for the first time in the evening the slightest hint of fatigue. It was amazing in its scope, impressive that someone who had been so ill, whose recent efforts had been sketchy at best, could perform with such facility and sheer excellence. This was the last of the truly great concerts, for she would never again be able to repeat a show with such energy, vocal consistency, and breath control.

One of Ella's favorite performers had been Sammy Davis, Jr., and although not doing well herself she was distressed upon learning of his final illness. She quickly agreed to appear with Quincy Jones and his orchestra in a salute to this little giant, taped by CBS in the late fall and broadcast in January of 1991. Ella capped the evening of top celebrities by being led onto the stage by Arsenio Hall and Eddie Murphy to sing "Too Close for Comfort." Wearing a slinky black sequined gown (made for standing, not sitting) and looking beautiful, she was clearly the star of the evening (not counting Sammy, of course).

Making a brief return to the recording studio, Ella was reunited with longtime friend Billy May that January. A Japanese film company had come to May, to arrange Maurice Jarre's "The Setting Sun," a song that would be played over the closing credits of the film with the same name. Originally, Sinatra was approached and May wrote the orchestration in his key. However, after hearing the song, Sinatra turned it down. The next person approached was Ella. Billy reorchestrated the number to suit her range and style, and this version was good enough to get Ella's okay. It took two sessions to get it right; she didn't have enough voice to record one song on the first session. Unfortunately, audiences in the West will probably never hear the song, as neither Billy May, Lee Hirschberg (the engineer for the two sessions), nor Ella were given a copy of it. As soon as she was finished singing, the folks from Japan took their tape and made a hasty departure for the airport.

During this period, Frank Sinatra was celebrating his seventy-fifth birthday, and it was Miss Fitz's pleasure to give him the second annual Ella award, presented by the Society of Singers. The society had named this prestigious award after The Lady, presenting it to her as the first recipient the previous year. For Sinatra, Ella hosted the evening, opening with "There Will Never Be Another You." She had to encore it before introducing the rest of the talent that night, which included Peggy Lee, Vic Damone, Diahann Carroll, Steve Lawrence, Eydie Gorme, Jack Jones, Tony Danza, and others. At the finale, Ella and Sinatra dueted on "The Lady Is a Tramp" (harking back to their television version from 1967), and they encored with it three times before the star-studded audience let them go. Many of the highlights from the evening were taped by CBS for inclusion in a special saluting Sinatra's career, and it's a shame the entire evening wasn't taped just as it happened. Ella and Frank together were dynamite.

Her health was riding its usual roller coaster; time spent feeling better and hopeful about resuming her career full-time was followed by periods of illness and unpublicized hospital stays. As one associate contends, perhaps Ella was in a state of denial. "She really believed she would go back on the road in a week, two weeks, two months," recalls a colleague. "Nothing mattered but the next concert. Health was only important in that it improved enough to keep performing. Nothing else was important, not friends, not family, not social life, nothing. She was obsessed with continuing her work. It's all she thought she had."

Ella made two false starts on albums during this period. Going into the studio with her trio, Harry Edison and a couple of the sidemen from her last album, the group recorded a couple of standards. Unfortunately, Ella was not satisfied with the results, nor was she the following day when she began recording *Ella and Joe*, the next leg of her work with Pass. A few cuts were recorded, including "What a Difference a Day Makes," but again Ella was not pleased. There was not enough material from either session to make a CD release. Perhaps Norman Granz, or his successors, will eventually release what product there was.

Ella double-timed New York in two performances in the spring and early summer of 1991. Her first was at Radio City Music Hall, appearing on April 15 with Louie Bellson's band and her trio. The highlight of the evening was a Cole Porter medley, and Ella's swinging "It's All Right With Me" with the band. She was presented with the Cole Porter Society's "You're the Top" award from Margaret Cole Richards (the composer's cousin), a crystal sculpture engraved, "In recognition of outstanding achievements for sustaining the Cole Porter legend, and for winning new audiences to appreciate his genius."

After another engagement at Carnegie Hall with her trio (June 27), California concerts filled out Ella's performing year, bringing her back to the Hollywood Bowl in August (with her trio and Joe Pass) and on to an appearance with the San Francisco Symphony in early November. The former featured many of the usual songs, along with Pass duets. The latter was more absorbing, as she sang many numbers not included in her recent concerts. "S'Wonderful," the *My Fair Lady* medley, "Deep Purple," "Love Is Here to Stay," and others got some fresh air, with Ella in fair voice but having a great deal of trouble with the lyrics.

Part of the problem stemmed from her last-minute decision to fill several requests from fans, changing the lineup and inserting songs she had no time to rehearse and with which the orchestra had been unable to familiarize themselves. Another problem was the stool she was supposed to sit on. She tried to mount it but it wobbled, and she was forced to stand during the entire concert when she simply wasn't up to it. It is hard to believe that the San Francisco Symphony Hall did not have another stool in the building which could have been brought to her after the first or second number. Additionally, while her voice was comparatively strong, she kept apologizing for her sniffles, a legend who was still nervous about being good enough. Ella never really accepted the fact that she was *so* popular, or that she was unconditionally loved from the moment she walked on stage.

It is a curiosity that as controlling as the folks at Salle Productions were (Granz was in Europe, himself ironically the victim of cataracts, heart problems, and diabetes), it sometimes seemed that Ella appeared with little thought to the presentation. Often she wore little makeup or no lipstick. Her once chic wigs were now confined to what seemed to be the cheap, department-store variety, and they looked as if they hadn't been washed or set in months. In San Francisco, she was brought out with the tag from her blouse sticking up behind her neck for all to see. The gowns she wore no longer looked glamorous; indeed they looked as if they had been quickly made with inferior materials. This is in contrast to her stage persona during the previous thirty years, where her wigs and gowns were expensive and dazzling. Certainly, a special stool could have been custom made for her, one that would be both comfortable and sturdy for her appearances. Certainly, a wireless mike could have kept her from tripping over unnecessary wires, and a body mike could have saved her arthritis-ridden hands from aching by holding a microphone for almost two hours. Certainly, no one thought of these things.

Her longtime traveling companion and road manager, Pete Covella, had passed away, and loyal Val Valentin was pressed into service. He accompanied her, saw to her needs, and worked in the Salle offices in Beverly Hills between gigs. The man who once was responsible for engineering the albums of Ella Fitzgerald, Frank Sinatra, Connie Francis, and Sammy Davis, Jr., who was one of the original voting members of the National Academy of Recording Arts and Sciences (NARAS) that gives out the Grammys, was now making travel arrangements, taking her to doctor appointments, and generally holding her hand. His devotion to both Fitzgerald and Granz was almost beyond the call and there was practically nothing he wouldn't do for them. Unfortunately, Ella needed a stronger, more experienced hand.

The early winter of 1992 returned Ella to television for yet another salute, this time to Muhammad Ali. Ella had originally planned to sing "Too Close for Comfort" with Quincy Jones's big band, much as she had on the previous salute to the late Sammy Davis, Jr. At the last minute, Ella decided she wasn't up to the full orchestra rehearsals required (for the musicians, that is, as Ella could sing this one in her sleep) and instead substituted her trio led by Mike Wofford. Ella looked well but sounded very shaky.

Deciding to forgo her regular forays to the summertime jazz festival in New York for the great expanse of Radio City Music Hall, Ella made her now annual appearance there on May 2, 1992. The first half of the evening featured her with a small orchestra doing many of the same songs she had done at the Hollywood Bowl with Benny Carter's organization. The more interesting (and shorter) second half had guest artist trumpeter Clark Terry soloing until Ella joined him for "Willow Weep for Me." Terry sat in with the trio for the rest of the evening, which found Ella (as was usually the case) more relaxed and experimental with her vocals.

Returning home to Beverly Hills, Ella prepared for a special evening at the Beverly Hilton as the University of Southern California held their Friends of Music Night, dubbed "Ella." Looking chic in a flowered print gown with a gold ball hanging from a long gold chain around her neck, Ella was joined by some old friends from the halcyon days: drummer Louie Bellson, pianist Gerald Wiggins, saxophonists Buddy Collette and Marshall Royal, trumpeter Snooky Young, and, although not of the same generation, Dave Stone on bass. The USC Jazz Combo performed "A-Tisket A-Tasket," while the man who cowrote the song with Ella, Van Alexander, came out to croon "When Ella Sings," an original Steve Allen composition. Joe Williams appeared, singing a sentimental "The Very Thought of You" directly to Ella, and then rocked the room with "I'd Rather Drink Muddy Water" as he involved the audience in the song. Finally, after several minutes of video clips from the 1960s, master of ceremonies Chuck Niles (from jazz radio station KLON in Long Beach, California) introduced Ella. While not doing a full set, she did an engaging jam session that included the bop tune that started it all, "Lady Be Good."

Ella made her twelfth incursion on the Hollywood Bowl on July 15. Appearing with her trio and Benny Carter's big band at a festival sponsored by ARCO, she looked elegant and confident, although she was wearing surgical stockings and specially made shoes that made it easier for her to walk as yet another toe had been lost to diabetes. High heels were now out of the question. Once again there was a slow start until she warmed up, and the highlight of the evening was a tender version of the rarely done "What Will I Tell My Heart." Supported by the trio and Benny's plaintive saxophone, Ella was hoarse throughout the night. The presentation was unusual, in that Benny simply walked out from the wings after she had begun singing, started playing until the song was over, and then walked off again without even looking at the audience. When Ella did not remember the words to the bridge, she imitated Benny's sax as they traded moans back and forth until the reprise of the chorus. This song was one last proof of another facet of Ella's artistry: she did not rely on the same old numbers. There was always something new in an Ella Fitzgerald concert, even at this stage of the game.

She had taken to meeting with Mike Wofford a few days before each concert to decide on material. While her extensive repertoire was always a hallmark of her concerts, these days she limited her choices to those she felt comfortable with and might want to do for fans' requests. Mike generally brought a list of songs to Ella, which she then accepted or changed at her level of comfort. Many songs, such as "Agua de Beber" or "The Lady Is a Tramp," appeared at every concert now, as well as "Mack the Knife." Rarely would Ella spontaneously do songs shouted out by the audience, and some of her old numbers were now simply out of her vocal range. Yet, she was musically wise and knew how to pace her shows to please the audience and always perform at the absolute top level of her powers, whatever they might be on a given day.

In the fall of 1992, all of her scheduled performances were canceled until April 1993 because of the fragility of her health. The latest surgery on her foot had not been healing, and infections kept the wound open. Multiple visits to doctors to reopen and clean her foot left her weak and in pain. Walking had become almost impossible, and privately Ella was confined to a wheelchair. She continued to fight deteriorating health but wanted to continue her performing schedule when she could. She had taken a notion to record an album in Spanish, an idea that she was sure would delight fans in the Spanish-speaking countries around the world, as well as the growing number of American residents who counted it as their native tongue. The number of concerts she did each year had dwindled to a handful, and now resumption was uncertain.

When not performing, she led a very quiet life, going to regular doctor appointments and sneaking a few of her favorite hot dogs. Much time was spent in front of the television, especially when the Dodgers or the Lakers were on the tube. The years of world travel, parties, and restaurants had left Ella with a real need to be in her luxurious home, resting and waiting for the next concert date. Ella the woman was not a social animal; she seldom left the house, did not chat on the phone to friends, and spent little time with family. She lived to perform, her energies being stored up for the next time she could walk out on that stage and share her vocal gifts with her admirers, who still packed every seat when she appeared. She was carefully taken care of by a protective staff, both at her home and in her production office, who saw to it that her needs were met and that absolutely no one bothered her for any reason. While some might feel that this degree of protection and inactivity would be sad for someone of Ella's accomplishments (and advanced years), it was necessary if she chose to continue to perform and maintain the health level needed to face the footlights. And Ella needed to face the footlights!

"Every tour I ever made with her convinced me that singing is her whole life," once recalled guitarist Barney Kessel. "I remember once in Genoa, Italy, we sat down to eat and the restaurant was empty except for Lester Young and his wife and Ella and me. So while we waited to give our breakfast order I pulled out my guitar and she and Lester started making up fabulous things on the blues. Another time, when we were touring Switzerland, instead of gossiping with the rest of the troupe on the bus, she and I would get together and take some song like 'Blue Lou' and sing it every way in the world. She'd do it like Mahalia Jackson and like Sarah and finally make up new lyrics for it. She would try to exhaust every possibility, as if she were trying to develop improvisation to a new point by ad-libbing lyrically, too, the way Calypso singers do."

"Ella even does that on shows," recalled another musician who toured with her for years. "If there's a heckler, she'll interpolate a swinging warning to him in the middle of a number, or the mike'll go wrong and she'll tell the engineer about it in words and music. But she's terribly sensitive socially. Whenever she hears a crowd mumbling she feels they are discussing her—and always unfavorably. I think she lays so much stress on being accepted in music because this is the one area of life into which she feels she can fit successfully. Her marriage failed; she doesn't have an awful lot of the normal activities most women have, such as home life, so she wraps herself up entirely in music. She wants desperately to be accepted."

Ella had always understood the need for acceptance, especially with children. A crusader for the health and education of the younger generations, she had for quite some time personally funded all of the expenses for the Ella Fitzgerald Day Care Center in the Watts neighborhood of Los Angeles. For years she was a frequent visitor and in-person booster, until her health declined to a point where these visits became impossible. "I'd usually be there when they had the Christmas celebrations," she once recalled. "I'd sing for them. They give little shows for the kids." Another time, Ella recounted, "I was singing 'Old MacDonald,' and at the end of the song, the little ones stood up and applauded just like grown folks!" The children continued to stay in touch with her, sending her handmade gifts and cards covered with good wishes. She made one more visit to the center in April 1993, close in time to her supposed seventy-fifth birthday. Wheelchair bound and frail, she delighted in seeing what her money was providing, especially after the devastating riots in Los Angeles the year before.

On April 10, 1993, the Dream Street Foundation, a not-for-profit organization that provided camping experiences for children with life-threatening diseases, put on a tribute to Ella with a special award presented to her by Quincy Jones. D. Mitchell DePew, who coordinated the program, was thrilled that she was able to make it. Only two weeks before, she had been bed-ridden in the hospital, so ill that some thought she would not ever come out.

Ella became supportive because her podiatrist, Dr. Mark Weiss, was involved with Dream Street, and his wife, Marilyn, was on the board of directors. The invitation was sent in a CD case, opening like a normal CD. The guests, who paid $200 each to attend, dined on porterhouse steak, chocolate-dipped strawberries, and ice cream. A silent auction for a car, vacations, and fur coats raised over $100,000. Ella arrived in a wheelchair, her seat for the entire evening, not rising to perform or even receive the award. Quincy brought it to her at her table, and Joe Williams came out on the floor and sang right to her. She joined him in a few seconds of scat, but obviously had been very ill. Smiling but not attentive, she appeared to be only a shell of her former self. For all intents and purposes, this is how she celebrated what the public perceived as her birthday. "This was such a perfect tribute," recalls DePew, "it was magic, having worked so hard for it and having it work out so well with Ella showing up."

For Ella's public seventy-fifth birthday celebration, a great deal of time and expense was expended by two of her former record companies. Decca began to finally release (after the settling of Ella's lawsuit with them) all of her best recordings, the reissues carefully produced by Orrin Keepnews. *The 75th Birthday Collection* was produced by Orrin with Milt Gabler, her producer of so many years before. Many of her Decca hits were featured, along with extensive liner notes. This author was honored to contribute liner notes to some of the other Decca Fitzgerald CD projects.

Michael Lang at Verve (a newly revitalized company that has once again begun recording upcoming artists in the jazz world as well as making the Verve catalogue available on CD) had, with the aid of Phil Schaap, combed the vaults looking for any and all Ella recordings. They unearthed much gold, some of which was reissued in a compilation set called *Ella Fitzgerald—First Lady of Song* that gave an overview to Ella's career on Verve. This collection was beautifully done, released in a special CD case that harked back to the look of the old 78 rpm albums, with the notes (mine) in front and the three CDs carried in sleeves at the back.

For several years, die-hard fan, struggling actor, and Ella impersonator Andy Powell had taken flowers to Miss Fitz at her home on her birthday. Once he was allowed in the first time (on a fluke, she happened to be there and was feeling well), he returned annually to pay his respects. On her seventy-fifth birthday, he did not fail:

"I was really surprised they let me in, considering what I had heard about her health," remembered Powell. "They led me upstairs to her bedroom, where she was sitting up in a chair with a couple of blankets over her legs. She looked very ill, without any energy or spark in her eye. A nurse took the flowers and she said, 'Oh, thank you, darlin.' I gave her my best wishes and made a hasty exit, for it was obvious she was in no condition to visit. I really felt sad when I left."

When the Hollywood Bowl mailed out its subscription brochure for the summer of 1993, many were surprised to see Ella booked for an entire weekend. Called "An Ella Fitzgerald Weekend at the Bowl," she was to appear with the Bowl Symphony Orchestra for the nights of July 9 and 10. By the time most people had received their brochure, the dates were canceled and Ella replaced by another act. The Bowl had to redo its brochure and mail it out a second time. Ella simply wasn't up to performing. The concert days were over. The studio days were over. The career was over.

Ella never healed from the operations to remove her toes. Because of severe diabetes, gangrene set in. Doctors hoped to treat her, but in the fall of 1993 first one and then the other of her legs were amputated. With her condition already frail, her health was in the worst condition it had ever been. While those close to her knew the truth, the press was strangely quiet about her health. Finally, Mary Jane Outwater, Norman Granz's right hand person, leaked the information to the public in early April of 1994. Even the newspaper reports couldn't agree on the facts. The Daily News' Wire Services reported:

> Fitzgerald's Legs Amputated
> Both of Ella Fitzgerald's legs have been amputated, according to Wednesday's New York Daily News.
>
> The paper, which couldn't confirm its report, said the jazz great was recuperating in Europe. Its sources said the singer, who has long suffered with diabetes, developed gangrene and required surgery.
>
> Fitzgerald will be 76 on April 25.

However, the Associated Press had a different statement:

> Complications from diabetes forced the amputation of jazz singer Ella Fitzgerald's legs, a spokeswoman said, but she is home and doing well.
>
> The surgeries were performed last year, said spokeswoman Mary Jane Outwater, but were only recently disclosed.
>
> "It's been done a long time ago, and of course she's fine and she's at home," said Outwater. Asked why there was no announcement at the time, she said, "I really can't tell you. All I can tell you is that it was done."
>
> Fitzgerald wasn't available for comment.

Even at this point, the facts of her private life are shrouded in misinformation. Surely, it would do her career no good. Ella would never be able to sing again. Why the subterfuge? More of the same illogical paranoia that accompanied almost every release of information about her since her career began.

In May, Ella suffered a loss with the death of Joe Pass from stomach cancer. This author knew Pass had been ill, but I had been asked by Joe not to write about it. I first met him the day after his first treatment for cancer. Joe had invited me to his Chatsworth, California, condo to talk. He greeted me in the parking lot, and I almost didn't recognize him. Thin and pale, he looked as if he had aged ten years since I had last seen him perform the year before. He was a quiet but gracious host, but in short order he was wincing in pain. The following is an excerpt from our conversation that day:

GMF: What's the matter? Are you ill?

Joe: No, it's just. [Starts to cry] I don't know why I'm telling you this. I'm having problems [tapping his stomach]. They don't know what to do for it. They started something yesterday. It's making me sick.

GMF: Do you want me to leave?

Joe: No, please stay. I don't know when I'll feel better.

GMF: Have they diagnosed it?

Joe: Yes. The big one. Please don't tell anyone. I have to work. [Starts to cry again] This will be so hard for my daughter.

GMF: Is there anything I can do for you?

Joe: There's nothing anyone can do. It's funny. Tommy [Flanagan] has been sick, too [he'd recently had heart surgery at that time]. Ella's going to outlive all of us.

Ella didn't outlive all of them, but she certainly survived a lot of them: Louis and Sarah and Billie and Basie and Duke and Pass and Prez and Bird and Dizzy and Chick and Strayhorn and Pearl and Riddle and Getz and Goodman and Dinah . . . almost from the day of her birth, Ella has been a survivor.

Ella Fitzgerald's legacy is so large, her presence will be felt for decades to come. Every singer with a measure of discernment has and will continue to steal liberally from her. She has set the tone for good music for almost sixty years, and has set standards in taste, quality, musicality, and musicianship that will never be surpassed. She got the title the First Lady of Song the old-fashioned way: she gave her life for it.

WHEN ELLA SINGS
Music and Lyrics By Steve Allen

VERSE:
Ever since the night
She claimed the right
   to sing the blues,
The fact that we love Ella
Can hardly be considered news.
Nobody ever could sing better
And she'll prove it tonight, if we let her.

CHORUS:
When Ella sings
Then Ella swings.
She makes your heart remember lots of wonderful things.
When Ella wails
Ella prevails.
She makes us all rejoice
Because that voice
   has wings,
And all the while
You've got to smile
   When Ella sings.
When she sings Kern
   The others learn
That though it's fate
They'll simply have to wait
   their turn,
Cause East or West
It's just the best,
   When Ella sings.

And all the upper-class gentry,
They stand in line when she appears.

They know
That it's so
Ella-mentary;
Always lovely music to our ears.

What magic sounds
When she's around,
And now she's here
It's all so clear
Why she's renowned.
Beggars or kings
The mem-ry clings,
    when Ella sings.

Appendices

Appendix One
Ella's Top Tens

Ella's Top Ten Albums

The following are my nominations for the ten best LP or CD albums Ella made. They are in descending order of excellence.

1. *Ella and Basie!*, Verve 1963
2. *Fitzgerald and Pass . . . Again*, Pablo 1976
3. *The Complete Ella in Berlin* (Mack the Knife), Verve 1960
4. *Ella Fitzgerald Sings the George and Ira Gershwin Songbook*, Verve 1959
5. *Fine and Mellow*, Pablo 1974
6. *A Perfect Match*, Pablo 1979
7. *Montreux '77: Ella Fitzgerald With the Tommy Flanagan Trio*, Pablo 1977
8. *Ella at Duke's Place*, Verve 1965
9. *Ella in Rome: The Birthday Concert*, Verve 1958
   Ella Sings the Cole Porter Songbook, Verve 1956 (tie)
10. *Ella Swings Gently With Nelson*, Verve 1962

Ella's Top Ten Songs

Simply, the ten best songs she ever recorded in the studio. No particular order.

1. April in Paris (The Metronome All-Stars 1956, Verve)
2. Street of Dreams (*Ella Swings Gently With Nelson*, Verve 1962)
3. Oh, Lady Be Good (Decca, 1947)
4. Miss Otis Regrets (*The Cole Porter Songbook*, Verve 1956)
5. Sweet Georgia Brown (*Whisper Not*, Verve 1966)
6. Black Coffee (Decca, 1948)
7. Love Is Here to Stay (*Ella Sings The George and Ira Gershwin Songbook*, Verve 1959)
8. A-Tisket A-Tasket (Decca, 1938)
9. Lullaby of Birdland (Decca, 1952)
10. 'Tis Autumn (*Fitzgerald and Pass . . . Again*, Pablo 1976)

Ella's Ten Best Live Cuts

The best of her live albums, in no particular order.

1. I Loves You Porgy (*Ella in Rome: The Birthday Concert*, Verve 1958)
2. Too Close for Comfort (*Montreux '77: Ella Fitzgerald With the Tommy Flanagan Trio*, Pablo)
3. Mr. Paganini (*Ella in Hollywood*, Verve 1961)
4. Mack the Knife (*Ella in Berlin*, Verve 1960)
5. Something to Live For (*The Stockholm Concert—1966*, Pablo)
6. Sweet Georgia Brown (*A Perfect Match*, Pablo 1979)
7. The Boy From Ipanema (*Ella at Montreux*, Pablo 1975)
8. How High the Moon (*Ella in Berlin*, Verve 1960)
9. 'Round Midnight (*A Perfect Match*, Pablo 1979)
10. Body and Soul (*Ella and Billie at Newport*, Verve 1957)

Appendix Two

100 Songs Ella
Never Recorded

The following are 100 excellent songs that for one reason or another Ella never recorded. Some of them are lesser known songs from the worlds of pop and Broadway; others are little recorded standards or jazz songs from the big band era. This should end all discussions that there are no good songs left to record.

1. Love Look in My Window
2. Time Heals Everything
3. The Coffee Song
4. The Last Dance
5. Please Be Kind
6. Pennies From Heaven
7. I Have Dreamed
8. This Is All I Ask
9. Oh, You Crazy Moon
10. Whispering

11. Drinking Again
12. What Are You Doing the Rest of Your Life?
13. Didn't We
14. Send in the Clowns
15. A Taste of Honey
16. A Sleepin' Bee
17. But Beautiful
18. Firefly
19. For Once in My Life
20. I Got Lost in His Arms
21. They Say It's Wonderful
22. Small World
23. If I Love Again
24. It Had to Be You
25. To You
26. Smile
27. Lazy Afternoon
28. Last Night When We Were Young
29. What a Little Moonlight Can Do
30. Don't Explain
31. Miss Brown to You
32. Make Someone Happy
33. As Long as He Needs Me
34. More
35. I Wish You Love
36. Zing! Went the Strings of My Heart
37. Memories of You
38. Chances Are
39. The Twelfth of Never
40. Four Brothers
41. Friendly Star
42. Rum and Coca-Cola
43. I'll Walk Alone
44. Straighten Up and Fly Right
45. Old Cape Cod
46. Never, Never Land
47. I'll Be Around
48. In the Wee Small Hours of the Morning
49. You're Getting to Be a Habit With Me
50. We'll Be Together Again
51. Guess I'll Hang My Tears Out to Dry
52. I Thought About You

53. Am I Losing My Mind?
54. This Masquerade
55. An Earful of Music
56. The Lonesome Road
57. I Cover the Waterfront
58. I'm a Fool to Want You
59. Autumn Leaves
60. A Cottage for Sale
61. I'll Never Smile Again
62. Nevertheless
63. Fools Rush In
64. Should I?
65. When the World Was Young
66. I'll Remember April
67. There Will Never Be Another You
68. I'll Be Seeing You
69. Love and Marriage
70. Be Careful, It's My Heart
71. I Never Knew (Till I Met You)
72. Alone Too Long
73. Meditation
74. Maybe This Time
75. All That Jazz (by Kander & Ebb)
76. The World We Knew
77. I Remember Johnny Hodges
78. Never Will I Marry
79. Feelings
80. Sugar
81. *The Wiz* Medley
82. Blow Gabriel Blow
83. Eadie Was a Lady
84. Here's to the Ladies Who Lunch
85. How Do You Keep the Music Playing?
86. Love in a Home
87. If He Walked Into My Life
88. What a Wonderful World
89. That's Him
90. It's a Quiet Thing
91. I Confessed to the Breeze
92. Java Jive
93. Memory
94. Please

Appendix Three

Complete Listing of
Media Appearances

The following is a listing of Ella's appearances in films and on television, as well as some of her radio work. All of her films are covered, but it is impossible to be totally accurate with her radio and television appearances as they are too numerous, and often network records have been lost to the sands of time. This listing is in chronological order.

Camel Caravan—November 10, 1936 (Radio)
The Lucidin Program—Three times a week, 1936–1937 (Radio)
The Goodtime Society—Weekly, 1936–1937 (Radio)
Live From the Savoy Ballroom—December 1936, three remotes (Radio)
Live From Lavigi's—April and May 1939 (Radio)
George Jessel's Celebrities—August 23, 1939 (Radio)
Live From Roseland—1940 (Radio)
Ride 'Em Cowboy (Film)
Saturday Night Swing Show—April 5, 1947 (Radio)
The Dave Garroway Show—May 1947 (Radio)

The Kraft Music Hall—1948 (Radio)
Jubilee—May 25, 1948 (Armed Forces Radio)
Jubilee—June 1, 1948 (Armed Forces Radio)
The Toast of the Town—July 18, 1948
Eddie Condon's Floorshow—April 23, 1949
Bing Crosby Chesterfield Show—November 9, 1949 (Radio)
Bing Crosby Chesterfield Show—November 23, 1949 (Radio)
Bing Crosby Chesterfield Show—May 3, 1950 (Radio)
Summer Nights' Dreams—July 23, 1950
Bing Crosby Chesterfield Show—November 29, 1950 (Radio)
Kriesler Bandstand—1951
A Salute to Bing Crosby—January 9, 1951 (Radio)
Bing Crosby Chesterfield Show—November 28, 1951 (Radio)
New York Cardiac Telethon—March 14, 1952
Damon Runyon Memorial Fund Telethon—June 7–8, 1952
Saturday Night Dance Party—June 28, 1952
NBC's "All-Star Review"—August 16, 1952
Bing Crosby General Electric Show—December 18, 1952 (Radio)
Bing Crosby General Electric Show—January 1, 1953 (Radio)
Bing Crosby General Electric Show—December 13, 1953 (Radio)
Bing Crosby General Electric Show—December 27, 1953 (Radio)
Bing Crosby General Electric Show—February 14, 1954 (Radio)
Pete Kelly's Blues—1955 (Film)
Finian's Rainbow (aborted animated film version, 1955)
Colgate Variety Hour—July 24, 1955
Tennessee Ernie Ford Show—December 9, 1955
Ford Star Jubilee ("I Hear America Singing")—December 17, 1955
The Tonight Show—April 2, 1956
The Ford Show—August 31, 1956
Frankie Laine Time—September 8, 1956
The Ford Show—December 27, 1956
The Ed Sullivan Show—March 24, 1957
The Nat "King" Cole Show—September 10, 1957
The Nat "King" Cole Show—November 11, 1957
St. Louis Blues—1958 (Film)
Swing Into Spring—April 8, 1958
The Frank Sinatra Show—May 9, 1958
The Dinah Shore Chevy Show—October 12, 1958
Milton Berle Starring in the Kraft Music Hall—December 3, 1958
The Garry Moore Show—January 13, 1959
The Bell Telephone Hour—February 10, 1959
The Dinah Shore Chevy Show—March 8, 1959

The Eddie Fisher Show—March 17, 1959
Swing Into Spring—April 10, 1959
The Garry Moore Show—October 13, 1959
The Pat Boone–Chevy Showroom—October 29, 1959
The Bell Telephone Hour—November 20, 1959
The Sunday Showcase—November 29, 1959
Person to Person—December 1959
An Afternoon With Frank Sinatra—December 13, 1959
Let No Man Write My Epitaph—1960 (Film)
The Dinah Shore Chevy Show—January 10, 1960
The Garry Moore Show—March 29, 1960
The Academy Awards Telecast—April 4, 1960
The Dinah Shore Chevy Show—December 11, 1960
The Kennedy Inauguration—January 20, 1961
An Evening With Ella Fitzgerald—Granada TV, April 12, 1961
The Jo Stafford Show—July 1961
What's My Line—January 21, 1962
The Lively Ones—August 2, 1962
The Lively Ones—September 6, 1962
The Dinah Shore Show—April 17, 1963
The Ed Sullivan Show—May 5, 1963
The Tonight Show Starring Johnny Carson—May 13, 1963
The Steve Allen Show—July 3, 1963
The Garry Moore Show—1964
The Ed Sullivan Show—February 2, 1964
An Evening With Ella and Roy—July 1964 Japanese TV
Today Salutes Duke Ellington—November 5, 1964
The Ed Sullivan Show—November 29, 1964
The Ed Sullivan Show—March 7, 1965
The Bell Telephone Hour—September 26, 1965
The Andy Williams Show—November 15, 1965
The Dean Martin Show—December 16, 1965
The Dean Martin Show—April 10, 1966
The Kraft Music Hall—April 25, 1966
The Andy Williams Show—September 11, 1966
The Tonight Show Starring Johnny Carson—October 25, 1966
The Danny Kaye Show—November 16, 1966
The Andy Williams Show—January 1, 1967
The Hollywood Palace—February 18, 1967
The Dean Martin Show—March 16, 1967
The Best on Record—May 24, 1967
The Tonight Show—October 26, 1967

Frank Sinatra, A Man and His Music Plus Ella Plus Jobim—November 13, 1967

The Carol Burnett Show—December 25, 1967

The Ed Sullivan Show—April 28, 1968

Pat Boone in Hollywood—Fall, 1968

The Joey Bishop Show—October 24, 1968

Ella and the Duke—Syndicated TV Special—1968

The Tonight Show Starring Johnny Carson—December 5, 1968

The Hollywood Palace—January 11, 1969

The Ed Sullivan Show—January 12, 1969

The Sandler and Young Show—June 4, 1969

Personality—June 10, 1969

The Carol Burnett Show— November 10, 1969

The Ed Sullivan Show—November 23, 1969

The Glen Campbell Goodtime Hour—March 1, 1970

The Tonight Show Starring Johnny Carson—April 2, 1970

The Andy Williams Show—October 17, 1970

The Flip Wilson Show—November 26, 1970

This Is Tom Jones—December 25, 1970

Timex All Star Swing Festival—July 1972

The Tonight Show Starring Johnny Carson—January 11, 1973

Arthur Fiedler and the Boston Pops—July 1973

Harlem Homecoming—February 10, 1974 (WNBC-TV local show)

Live at Ronnie Scott's—BBC-TV, April 1974

CBS News Special Report: A Salute to Duke—May 24, 1974

The Mike Douglas Show—July 8, 1975

The Mike Douglas Show—February 19, 1976

Dinah!—April 7, 1976

The Tonight Show Starring Johnny Carson—April 28, 1976

Dinah!—October 5, 1977

The Mike Douglas Show—November 11, 1977

Salute to Pearl Bailey—November 1978

Soundstage—1979

The Kennedy Center Honors—December 29, 1979

The Grammy Awards—February 27, 1980

The Carpenters Special: Music, Music, Music—April 26, 1980

Previn and the Pittsburgh—1980

The Kennedy Center Honors—December 1980

The Captain and Tennille Special—1981

The Grammy Awards—February 25, 1981

The White Shadow—March 16, 1981

The Grammy Awards—February 24, 1982

PM Magazine—1983
The Grammy Awards—February 28, 1983
Live at Wolftrap—August 1985
Ebony—1986
NAACP Image Awards—1988
All-Star Salute to Sammy Davis, Jr.—January 1991
The Best of Ed Sullivan—1991
All-Star Salute to Muhammad Ali—Winter 1992
The Tonight Show Starring Johnny Carson—May 1992 (Last Johnny Carson
  show, clip from 1973)
The Best of the Grammys—December 1993
Jazz in the Night—December 31, 1993 (National Public Radio Broadcast of
  1981 Edinburgh concert)

Appendix Four
Complete Discography

The following is a complete listing of the recordings of Ella Fitzgerald in chronological order. Every original recording is listed, as well as the major compilations and reissues. While every effort has been made to be thorough, there may be bootlegs or duplicate issues of the same album not listed.

The name of the song is followed by the record number and date of original recording.

The following recordings were all made for Decca on 78 rpm unless otherwise indicated; all Decca vinyl 33 rpm and CD compilations follow afterward.

I'll Chase the Blues Away 02602 6/12/35 (Brunswick) [w/Chick Webb Orch.]
Love and Kisses 494 6/12/35 [w/Chick Webb Orch.]
Rhythm and Romance 558 10/12/35 [w/Chick Webb Orch.]
I'll Chase the Blues Away 640 10/12/35 [w/Chick Webb Orch.]
My Melancholy Baby 7729 3/17/36 (Brunswick) [w/Teddy Wilson Orch.]
All My Life 7640 3/17/36 (Brunswick) [w/Teddy Wilson Orch.]
Crying My Heart Out for You 785 4/7/36 [w/Chick Webb Orch.]

Under the Spell of the Blues 831 4/7/36 [w/Chick Webb Orch.]
When I Get Low I Get High 1123 4/7/36 [w/Chick Webb Orch.]
Sing Me a Swing Song (and Let Me Dance) 830 6/2/36 [w/Chick Webb Orch.]
A Little Bit Later On 831 6/2/36 [w/Chick Webb Orch.]
Love, You're Just a Laugh 1114 6/2/36 [w/Chick Webb Orch.]
Devoting My Time to You 995 6/2/36 [w/Chick Webb Orch.]
(If You Can't Sing It) You'll Have to Swing It 1032 10/29/36 [w/Chick Webb Orch.]
Swingin' on the Reservation 1065 10/29/36 [w/Chick Webb Orch.]
I Got the Spring Fever Blues 1087 10/29/36 [w/Chick Webb Orch.]
Vote for Mr. Rhythm 1032 10/29/36 [w/Chick Webb Orch.]
Goodnight My Love 25461 11/5/36 (Victor) [w/Benny Goodman Orch.]
Oh, Yes, Take Another Guess 25461 11/5/36 (Victor) [w/Benny Goodman Orch.]
Didja Mean It? 25469 11/5/36 (Victor) [w/Benny Goodman Orch.]
My Last Affair 1061 11/18/36 [Ella Fitzgerald and Her Savoy Eight]
Organ Grinder's Swing 1062 11/18/36 [Ella Fitzgerald and Her Savoy Eight]
Shine 1062 11/19/36 [Ella Fitzgerald and Her Savoy Eight]
Darktown Strutters' Ball 1061 11/19/36 [Ella Fitzgerald and Her Savoy Eight]
Oh, Yes, Take Another Guess 1121 1/14/37 [w/Chick Webb Orch.]
Love Marches On 1115 1/14/37 [w/Chick Webb Orch.]
Big Boy Blue 1148 1/14/37 [Ella Fitzgerald and Her Savoy Eight]
There's a Frost on the Moon 1114 1/15/37 [w/Chick Webb Orch.]
Dedicated to You 1148 2/3/37 [Ella Fitzgerald and Her Savoy Eight]
Wake Up and Live 1173 3/24/37 [w/Chick Webb Orch.]
You Showed Me the Way 1220 3/24/37 [w/Chick Webb Orch.]
Cryin' Mood 1273 3/24/37 [w/Chick Webb Orch.]
Love Is the Thing, So They Say 1356 3/24/37 [w/Chick Webb Orch.]
All or Nothing at All 1339 5/24/37 [Ella Fitzgerald and Her Savoy Eight]
If You Should Ever Leave 1302 5/24/37 [Ella Fitzgerald and Her Savoy Eight]
Everyone's Wrong But Me 1302 5/24/37 [Ella Fitzgerald and Her Savoy Eight]
Deep in the Heart of the South 1339 5/24/37 [Ella Fitzgerald and Her Savoy Eight]
Just a Simple Melody 1521 10/27/37 [w/Chick Webb Orch.]
I Got a Guy 1681 10/27/37 [w/Chick Webb Orch.]
Holiday in Harlem 1521 10/27/37 [w/Chick Webb Orch.]
Rock It for Me 1586 11/1/37 [w/Chick Webb and His Little Chicks]
I Want to Be Happy 15039 12/17/37 [w/Chick Webb Orch.]

The Dipsy Doodle 1587 12/17/37 [w/Chick Webb Orch.]
If Dreams Come True 1716 12/17/37 [w/Chick Webb Orch.]
Hallelujah! 15039 12/17/37 [w/Chick Webb Orch.]
Bei Mir Bist Du Schoen 1596 12/21/37 [Ella Fitzgerald and Her Savoy
    Eight]
It's My Turn Now 1596 12/21/37 [Ella Fitzgerald and Her Savoy Eight]
It's Wonderful 1669 1/25/38 [Ella Fitzgerald and Her Savoy Eight]
I Was Doing All Right 1669 1/25/38 [Ella Fitzgerald and Her Savoy Eight]
A-Tisket A-Tasket 1840 5/2/38 [w/Chick Webb Orch.]
Heart of Mine 2721 5/2/38 [w/Chick Webb Orch.]
I'm Just a Jitterbug 1899 5/2/38 [w/Chick Webb Orch.]
This Time It's Real 1806 5/3/38 [Ella Fitzgerald and Her Savoy Eight]
(Oh, Oh) What Do You Know About Love? 1967 5/3/38 [Ella Fitzgerald and
    Her Savoy Eight]
You Can't Be Mine (and Someone Else's Too) 1806 5/3/38 [Ella Fitzgerald
    and Her Savoy Eight]
We Can't Go on This Way 1846 5/3/38 [Ella Fitzgerald and Her Savoy Eight]
Saving Myself for You 1846 5/3/38 [Ella Fitzgerald and Her Savoy Eight]
If You Only Knew 1967 5/3/38 [Ella Fitzgerald and Her Savoy Eight]
Pack Up Your Sins and Go to the Devil 1894 6/9/38 [w/Chick Webb Orch.]
MacPherson Is Rehearsin' (to Swing) 2080 6/9/38 [w/Chick Webb Orch.]
Everybody Step 1894 6/9/38 [w/Chick Webb Orch.]
Ella 2148 6/9/38 [w/Chick Webb Orch.]
Wacky Dust 2021 8/17/38 [w/Chick Webb Orch.]
Gotta Pebble in My Shoe 2231 8/17/38 [w/Chick Webb Orch.]
I Can't Stop Loving You 2310 8/17/38 [w/Chick Webb Orch.]
Strictly From Dixie 2202 8/18/38 [Ella Fitzgerald and Her Savoy Eight]
Woe Is Me 2202 8/18/38 [Ella Fitzgerald and Her Savoy Eight]
I Let a Tear Fall in the River 2080 8/18/38 [Ella Fitzgerald and Her Savoy
    Eight]
FDR Jones 2105 10/6/38 [w/Chick Webb Orch.]
I Love Each Move You Make 2105 10/6/38 [w/Chick Webb Orch.]
It's Foxy 2309 10/6/38 [w/Chick Webb Orch.]
I Found My Yellow Basket 2148 10/6/38 [w/Chick Webb Orch.]
Undecided 2323 2/17/39 [w/Chick Webb Orch.]
'Tain't What You Do (It's the Way That Cha Do It) 2310 2/17/39 [w/Chick
    Webb Orch.]
One Side of Me 2556 2/17/39 [w/Chick Webb Orch.]
My Heart Belongs to Daddy 2309 2/17/39 [w/Chick Webb Orch.]
Once Is Enough for Me 2451 3/2/39 [Ella Fitzgerald and Her Savoy Eight]
I Had to Live and Learn 2581 3/2/39 [Ella Fitzgerald and Her Savoy Eight]
Sugar Pie 2665 3/2/39 [w/Chick Webb Orch.]

It's Slumbertime Along the Swanee 2389 3/2/39 [w/Chick Webb Orch.]
I'm Up a Tree 2468 3/2/39 [w/Chick Webb Orch.]
Chew-Chew-Chew (Your Bubble Gum) 2389 3/2/39 [w/Chick Webb Orch.]

Ella Sings, Chick Swings Olympic Records 7119 Recorded at the Savoy Ballroom, Spring 1939
  Oh, Johnny, I Want the Waiter With the Water, 'Tain't What You Do, I'm Confessin' That I Love You

Don't Worry 'Bout Me 2451 4/21/39 [Ella Fitzgerald and Her Savoy Eight]
If Anything Happened to You 2481 4/21/39 [Ella Fitzgerald and Her Savoy Eight]
If That's What You're Thinking 2581 4/21/39 [Ella Fitzgerald and Her Savoy Eight]
If You Ever Change Your Mind 2481 4/21/39 [Ella Fitzgerald and Her Savoy Eight]
Have Mercy 2468 4/21/39 [w/Chick Webb Orch.]
Little White Lies 2556 4/21/39 [w/Chick Webb Orch.]
Coochi-Coochi-Coo 2803 4/21/39 [w/Chick Webb Orch.]
That Was My Heart 2665 4/21/39 [w/Chick Webb Orch.]

Collector's Classics, TAX CD 3706-2 recorded May 4, 1939
  Live performance, including New Moon and Old Serenade, I Never Knew Heaven Could Speak, If I Didn't Care, Chew-Chew-Chew

Betcha Nickel 2904 6/29/39 [Ella Fitzgerald and Her Famous Orchestra]
Stairway to the Stars 2598 6/29/39 [Ella Fitzgerald and Her Famous Orchestra]
I Want the Waiter (With the Water) 2628 6/29/39 [Ella Fitzgerald and Her Famous Orchestra]
That's All, Brother 2628 6/29/39 [Ella Fitzgerald and Her Famous Orchestra]
Out of Nowhere 2598 6/29/39 [Ella Fitzgerald and Her Famous Orchestra]
My Last Goodbye 2721 8/18/39 [Ella Fitzgerald and Her Famous Orchestra]
Billy (I Always Dream of Billy) 2769 8/18/39 [Ella Fitzgerald and Her Famous Orchestra]
Please Tell Me the Truth 2769 8/18/39 [Ella Fitzgerald and Her Famous Orchestra]
I'm Not Complainin' 3005 8/18/39 [Ella Fitzgerald and Her Famous Orchestra]
You're Gonna Lose Your Gal 2816 10/12/39 [Ella Fitzgerald and Her Famous Orchestra]

After I Say I'm Sorry 2826 10/12/39 [Ella Fitzgerald and Her Famous Or-
chestra]
Baby, What Else Can I Do? 2926 10/12/39 [Ella Fitzgerald and Her Famous
Orchestra]
My Wubba Dolly 2816 10/12/39 [Ella Fitzgerald and Her Famous Orches-
tra]
Moon Ray 2904 10/12/39 [Ella Fitzgerald and Her Famous Orchestra]

The following songs were issued on an album called *Collector's Classics*.
They are live radio remotes. There are no Decca release numbers for
them. There are also several unissued cuts, which are listed as such:

1/22/40 Traffic Jam, A Lover Is Blue (unissued), Dodging the Dean,
'Tain't What You Do, I'm Confessin', What's the Matter With Me (unissued), I Want the Waiter (With the Water)

1/25/40 This Changing World (unissued), Oh, Johnny, Thank Your Stars
(unissued)

Is There Somebody Else? 2988 1/26/40 [Ella Fitzgerald and Her Famous
Orchestra]
Sugar Blues 3078 1/26/40 [Ella Fitzgerald and Her Famous Orchestra]
The Starlit Hour 2988 1/26/40 [Ella Fitzgerald and Her Famous Orchestra]
What's the Matter With Me? 3005 1/26/40 [Ella Fitzgerald and Her Famous
Orchestra]
Baby, Won't You Please Come Home? 3186 2/15/40 [Ella Fitzgerald and
Her Famous Orchestra]
If It Weren't for You 23126 2/15/40
Sing Song Swing 3126 2/15/40
Imagination 3078 2/15/40
Busy As a Bee X-1937 2/15/40

Two broadcasts were released on Sunbeam Records 205:
2/26/40 Sugar Blues, It's a Blue World, Is There Somebody Else?, One
Moment Please
3/4/40 Chew-Chew-Chew, Sing Song Swing, Starlit Hour

One broadcast was released on Jazz Trip Records 5:
3/40 Oh, Johnny, I Want the Waiter (With the Water), I'm Confessin'

Deedle-De-Dum 3324 5/9/40 [Ella Fitzgerald and Her Famous Orchestra]
Gulf Coast Blues 3324 5/9/40 [Ella Fitzgerald and Her Famous Orchestra]

Shake Down the Stars 3159 5/9/40 [Ella Fitzgerald and Her Famous Orchestra]

I Fell in Love With a Dream 3199 5/9/40 [Ella Fitzgerald and Her Famous Orchestra]

Five O'Clock Whistle 3420 9/25/40 [Ella Fitzgerald and Her Famous Orchestra]

So Long 3420 9/25/40 [Ella Fitzgerald and Her Famous Orchestra]

Louisville, K-Y 3441 9/25/40 [Ella Fitzgerald and Her Famous Orchestra]

Cabin in the Sky 3490 11/8/40 [Ella Fitzgerald and Her Famous Orchestra]

Taking a Chance on Love 3490 11/8/40 [Ella Fitzgerald and Her Famous Orchestra]

I'm the Lonesomest Gal in Town 25123 11/8/40 [Ella Fitzgerald and Her Famous Orchestra]

The One I Love (Belongs to Somebody Else) 3608 1/8/41 [Ella Fitzgerald and Her Famous Orchestra]

Three Little Words 3608 1/8/41 [Ella Fitzgerald and Her Famous Orchestra]

Hello Ma! I Done It Again 3612 1/8/41 [Ella Fitzgerald and Her Famous Orchestra]

Wishful Thinking 3612 1/8/41 [Ella Fitzgerald and Her Famous Orchestra]

I'm the Lonesomest Gal in Town 3666 1/8/41 [Ella Fitzgerald and Her Famous Orchestra]

The Muffin Man 3666 1/8/41 [Ella Fitzgerald and Her Famous Orchestra]

Keep Cool, Fool 3754 3/31/41 [Ella Fitzgerald and Her Famous Orchestra]

No Nothing 3754 3/31/41 [Ella Fitzgerald and Her Famous Orchestra]

My Man (Mon Homme) 4291 3/31/41 [Ella Fitzgerald and Her Famous Orchestra]

I Got It Bad (and That Ain't Good) 3968 7/31/41 [Ella Fitzgerald and Her Famous Orchestra]

Melinda the Mouse 3968 7/31/41 [Ella Fitzgerald and Her Famous Orchestra]

I Can't Believe That You're in Love With Me 25124 7/31/41 [Ella Fitzgerald and Her Famous Orchestra]

When My Sugar Walks Down the Street 18587 7/31/41 [Ella Fitzgerald and Her Famous Orchestra]

Can't Help Loving Dat Man 25126 7/31/41 [Ella Fitzgerald and Her Famous Orchestra]

I Must Have That Man 25126 7/31/41 [Ella Fitzgerald and Her Famous Orchestra]

Jim 4007 10/6/41 [Ella Fitzgerald and Her Famous Orchestra]

This Love of Mine 4007 10/6/41 [Ella Fitzgerald and Her Famous Orchestra]

Somebody Nobody Loves 4082 10/28/41 [Ella Fitzgerald and Her Famous Orchestra]

You Don't Know What Love Is 4082 10/28/41 [Ella Fitzgerald and Her
    Famous Orchestra]
I'm Thrilled 4073 11/5/41
Make Love to Me 4073 11/5/41
Who Are You? 4291 11/5/41
I'm Getting Mighty Lonesome for You 4315 3/11/42
When I Come Back Crying (Will You Be Laughing at Me?) 4315
    3/11/42
All I Need Is You 18347 3/11/42
Mama Come Home 18347 3/11/42
My Heart and I Decided 18530 7/31/42
(I Put a) Four Leaf Clover in Your Pocket 18472 7/31/42
He's My Guy 18472 7/31/42
Cow Cow Boogie 18587 11/3/43
Once Too Often 18605 3/21/44
Time Alone Will Tell 18505 3/21/44
I'm Making Believe 23356 8/30/44
Into Each Life Some Rain Must Fall 23356 8/30/44
And Her Tears Flowed Like Wine 18633 11/6/44
I'm Confessin' That I Love You 18633 11/6/44
I'm Beginning to See the Light 23399 11/6/44
That's the Way It Is 23399 11/6/44
It's Only a Paper Moon 23425 3/27/45
Cry You Out of My Heart 3/27/45 (unissued)
Cry You Out of My Heart 23425 3/28/45
A Kiss Goodnight 18713 8/29/45
Benny's Coming Home on Saturday 18713 8/29/45
Flying Home 23956 10/4/45
Stone Cold Dead in De Market 23546 10/8/45
Peetootie Pie 23546 10/8/45
That's Rich V-DISC 603 10/12/45
I'll Always Be in Love With You V-DISC 569 10/12/45
I'll See You in My Dreams V-DISC 730 10/12/45
The Frim Fram Sauce 23496 1/18/46
You Won't Be Satisfied 23496 1/18/46
I'm Just a Lucky So-and-So 18814 2/21/46
I Didn't Mean a Word 18814 2/21/46
(I Love You) For Sentimental Reasons 23670 8/29/46
It's a Pity to Say Goodnight 23670 8/29/46
That's Rich V-DISC 569 10/12/46

I'll Always Be in Love With You 10/12/46
Guilty 23844 1/24/47
Sentimental Journey 23844 1/24/47
Budella V-DISC 775 1/24/47
A Sunday Kind of Love 23866 3/19/47
That's My Desire 23866 3/19/47
Oh, Lady Be Good 23956 3/19/47
You're Breakin' in a New Heart 7/11/47 (unissued)
Don't You Think I Oughta Know? 24157 7/22/47
You're Breakin' in a New Heart 24157 7/22/47

It Happened One Night: Dizzy Gillespie, Ella Fitzgerald, Charlie Parker in Concert: Natural Organic 7000 Recorded September 29, 1947
Almost Like Being in Love, Stairway to the Stars, Lover Man, Flying Home, Lady Be Good, How High the Moon

I Want to Learn About Love 24581 12/18/47
That Old Feeling 28049 12/18/47
My Baby Likes to BeBop 24232 12/20/47
NOTE: My Baby Likes to BeBop has been wrongfully given the date of 4/27/49 in all previous discographies due to misinformation in Decca files. The date on the original acetate is the one above, and is the correct date. Also note that the name of the song is BeBop, not Rebop, as has been listed in some discographies.

No Sense 24538 12/20/47
How High the Moon 24387 12/20/47
My Baby Likes to Rebop 24332 12/20/47
I've Got a Feeling I'm Falling 24232 12/23/47
You Turned the Tables on Me 24387 12/23/47
Robbins' Nest 24538 12/23/47
I Cried and Cried and Cried 12/23/47 (unreleased)
Tea Leaves 24446 4/29/48
My Happiness 24446 4/30/48
It's Too Soon to Know 24497 8/20/48
I Can't Go on Without You 24497 8/20/48
To Make a Mistake Is Human 24529 11/10/48
In My Dreams 24529 11/10/48
NOTE: The following LPs, released in the 1980s with limited distribution, carried radio broadcasts of Ella and Ray Brown's combo from the Royal Roost Club in late 1948 and early 1949. A CD issue follows, that carried all of the songs broadcast and recorded by Ella.

Hooray for Ella Fitzgerald Session Records 105 Recorded 1948
Old Mother Hubbard, Mr. Paganini, There's a Small Hotel, How High the Moon, Robbins' Nest, As You Desire Me, Thou Swell, Flying Home, Someone Like You, Again, In a Mellow Tone, Lemon Drop, I Hadn't Anyone 'Till You

Ray Brown • Ella Fitzgerald Alto Records AL 706 Recorded 1948
Lady Be Good, I Never Knew, Love That Boy, It's Too Soon to Know, Mr. Paganini, Royal Roost Bop Boogie, Tiny's Blues, Bop Goes the Weasel, Heat Wave, Old Mother Hubbard, Flying Home

Ella Fitzgerald—Starlit Hour Hollywood CD HCD-406 Recorded 1948
Flying Home, Lemon Drop, Mr. Paganini, How High the Moon, Old Mother Hubbard, There's a Small Hotel, Robbins' Nest, As You Desire Me, Thou Swell, The Starlit Hour, Sing Song Swing

Ella Fitzgerald—The Royal Roost Sessions With the Ray Brown Trio and Quartet Cool Blue C&B CD112 Released 8/93
Recorded November 27, 1948:
Ool-Ya-Koo, Love That Boy, Mr. Paganini, It's Too Soon to Know, I Never Knew, How High the Moon
Recorded December 4, 1948:
Heat Wave, Old Mother Hubbard, Bop Goes the Weasel, Ool-Ya-Koo, Flying Home
Recorded April 15, 1949:
Old Mother Hubbard, Mr. Paganini, There's a Small Hotel, How High the Moon
Recorded April 20, 1949:
Robbins' Nest, As You Desire Me, Thou Swell, Flying Home
Recorded April 30, 1949:
Someone Like You, Again, In a Mellowtone, Lemon Drop

I Couldn't Stay Away 24562 1/14/49
Old Mother Hubbard 24581 1/14/49
Someone Like You 24562 1/14/49

JATP at Carnegie Hall Clef Records Recorded February 11, 1949 Unissued
Robbins' Nest, I Got a Guy, Old Mother Hubbard, Flying Home, Lover Man, Royal Roost Bop Boogie

Don't Cry, Cry Baby 24644 2/28/49
Baby, It's Cold Outside 24644 2/28/49
Happy Talk 24639 4/28/49
I'm Gonna Wash That Man Right Out of My Hair 24639 4/28/49
Black Coffee 24646 4/28/49
Lover's Gold 24646 4/28/49

A CD was issued by Parrot containing all of the music from the Bing Crosby
radio shows of the late forties and early fifties featuring Ella Fitzgerald.
While the dates span several years, I include it now as the first date follows
the chronological order.

Ella Fitzgerald & Bing Crosby—*"My Happiness"* Parrot PARCD 002 Re-
leased 2/93
Recorded Nov. 9, 1949:
  Way Back Home, a Dreamer's Holiday, My Happiness
Recorded May 3, 1950:
  Stay With the Happy People, I Hadn't Anyone 'Til You
Recorded November 29, 1950:
  Basin Street Blues, Can Anyone Explain?, Silver Bells, Marshmallow
  World, Memphis Blues
Recorded November 28, 1951:
  Undecided
Recorded December 18, 1952:
  Medley: Trying/My Favorite Song/Between the Devil and the Deep Blue
  Sea, Rudolph the Red-Nosed Reindeer
Recorded January 1, 1953:
  Chicago Style, Medley: I Hadn't Anyone 'Till You/If You Should Ever
  Leave/I Can't Give You Anything But Love
Recorded December 13, 1953:
  White Christmas, Moanin' Low
Recorded December 27, 1953:
  Someone to Watch Over Me, Istanbul, Looking for a Boy
Recorded February 14, 1954:
  That's A-Plenty, Taking a Chance on Love

Crying 34708 7/20/49
A New Shade of Blue 34708 7/20/49

JATP at Carnegie Hall Clef Records Recorded September 18, 1949 Unissued

First set: Robbins' Nest, A New Shade of Blue, Just a Lucky So-and-So, Somebody Loves Me, Basin Street Blues, Old Mother Hubbard, Flying Home

Second set: Black Coffee, Lady Be Good, A-Tisket A-Tasket, How High the Moon, Perdido

JATP at Carnegie Hall Verve CD Collection *The Complete Charlie Parker on Verve* Late Show September 18, 1949
Flying Home, How High the Moon, Perdido

JATP: The Ella Fitzgerald Set Verve Records 815 147 1
Recorded September 18, 1949 at Carnegie Hall:
Robbins' Nest, Black Coffee, Just a Lucky So-and-So, Somebody Loves Me, Basin Street Blues, Flying Home

Recorded September 19, 1953, at Carnegie Hall:
My Bill, Why Don't You Do Right?

Recorded September 17, 1954, at Carnegie Hall:
A Foggy Day, The Man That Got Away, Hernando's Hideaway, Later

In the Evening 24780 9/20/49
Talk Fast, My Heart, Talk Fast 24780 9/20/49
I'm Waitin' for the Junkman 24868 9/20/49
Basin Street Blues 24868 9/20/49
I Hadn't Anyone 'Til You 24900 9/21/49
Dream a Little Longer 24900 9/21/49
Foolish Tears 24773 9/21/49
A Man Wrote a Song 24773 9/21/49
Fairy Tales 24813 11/7/49
I Gotta Have My Baby Back 24813 11/7/49

Ella Fitzgerald's Souvenir Album DL-5084 Released 1/23/50
Cabin in the Sky, Can't Help Lovin' That Man, I Can't Believe That You're in Love With Me, I Got It Bad and That Ain't Good, The One I Love Belongs to Somebody Else

Studio session in conjunction with JATP unreleased film, 1950 (all cuts unissued):
Don't Cry Joe, Laura, You Go to My Head, I'll Remember April, Run, Joe, Run, The Boy Next Door, My Old Flame, Night and Day, The Way You Look Tonight, The Hucklebuck

Baby Won't You Say You Love Me 24917 2/2/50
Doncha Go 'Way Mad 24917 2/2/50
Solid as a Rock 24958 3/6/50
I've Got the World on a String 27120 3/6/50
Sugarfoot Rag 24958 3/6/50
Peas and Rice 27120 3/6/50
Mississippi 27061 5/9/50
I Don't Want the World 27061 5/9/50
Ain't Nobody's Business 27200 5/9/50
I'll Never Be Free 27200 5/9/50
Can Anyone Explain? 27209 8/15/50
Dream a Little Dream of Me 27209 8/15/50
Looking for a Boy 27369 9/11/50
My One and Only 27368 9/11/50
How Long Has This Been Going On? 27370 9/11/50
I've Got a Crush on You 27370 9/11/50
But Not for Me 27369 9/12/50
Soon 27371 9/12/50
Someone to Watch Over Me 27368 9/12/50
Maybe 27371 9/12/50

Ella Sings Gershwin DL-5300
    Contains all of eight Gershwin songs recorded on September 11–12, 1950

Santa Claus Got Stuck in My Chimney 27255 9/26/50
Molasses, Molasses 27255 9/26/50
Little Small Town Girl 27419 12/20/50
I Still Feel the Same About You 27419 12/20/50
Lonesome Gal 27453 1/12/51
The Bean Bag Song 27453 1/12/51
Chesapeake and Ohio 27602 3/27/51
Little Man in a Flying Saucer 27578 3/27/51
Because of Rain 27602 3/27/51
The Hot Canary 27578 3/27/51
Even As You and I 27634 5/24/51
If You Really Love Me 27634 5/24/51
Love You Madly 27693 5/24/51
Mixed Emotions 27680 6/26/51
Smooth Sailing 27693 6/26/51
Come On A-My House 27680 6/26/51
It's My Own Darn Fault DL8695 7/18/51

I Don't Want to Take the Chance 27948 7/18/51
There Was Never a Baby 27724 7/18/51
Give a Little, Get a Little 27724 7/18/51
Oops! 27901 11/23/51
Necessary Evil 27901 11/23/51
Baby Doll 27900 12/26/51
What Does It Take 28034 12/26/51
Lady Bug 27900 12/26/51
Lazy Day 28034 12/26/51
Airmail Special 28126 1/4/52
Rough Riding 27948 1/4/52
A Guy Is a Guy 28049 2/25/52
Nowhere Guy 28707 2/25/52
Gee But I'm Glad to Know You 28131 2/25/52
Goody-Goody 28126 2/25/52
Ding-Dong Boogie 28321 6/26/52
(If You Can't Sing It) You'll Have to Swing It (Mr. Paganini) Part I 287754
    6/26/52
(If You Can't Sing It) You'll Have to Swing It (Mr. Paganini) Part II 287754
    6/26/52
Angel Eyes 28707 6/26/52
Early Autumn 29810 6/26/52
Preview 28321 6/26/52

Top Tunes by Top Artists DL-5421 Released 7/21/52
    A Guy Is a Guy

Trying 28375 8/11/52
The Greatest Thing There Is 28930 8/11/52
Walkin' by the River 28433 8/11/52
My Bonnie Lies Over the Ocean 28375 8/12/52
Ella's Contribution to the Blues 29810 8/12/52
My Favorite Song 28433 8/12/52
Basin Street Blues 10/15/52 (unissued)
Who Walks in When I Walk Out 28552 11/23/52
Would You Like to Take a Walk 28552 11/23/52
I Can't Lie to Myself 28589 11/30/52
Don't Wake Me Up 28589 11/30/52

Top Tunes DL-5443 Released 1/5/53
    Trying

Careless 28671 2/13/53
Blue Lou 28671 2/13/53
I Wonder What Kind of Man 28930 2/13/53

Jazz at the Philharmonic Europe Jazz EJ 1050 Recorded live in Paris, March
 3, 1953
 Lester Leaps In

Ella Fitzgerald Sings, Vol. I ED-2014 Released 5/4/53
 For Sentimental Reasons, Guilty, It's Only a Paper Moon, Stairway to the
 Stars

Ella Fitzgerald With Louis Armstrong ED-2027 Released 5/25/53
 Dream a Little Dream of Me, The Frim Fram Sauce, Would You Like to
 Take a Walk, You Won't Be Satisfied

Smooth Sailing ED-2028 Released 6/1/53
 Flying Home, How High the Moon, Lady Be Good, Smooth Sailing

When the Hands of the Clock 28762 6/11/53
Crying in the Chapel 28762 6/11/53

Ella Fitzgerald Sings, Vol. II ED-2040 Released 6/15/53
 I'm Beginning to See the Light, I'm Making Believe, Into Each Life Some
 Rain Must Fall

Ella Fitzgerald Sings, Vol. III ED-2049 Released 7/6/53
 Cabin in the Sky, My Happiness, My Last Affair, That's My Desire

Unreleased JATP Concert Recorded September 11, 1953
 S'posin', Bill, Lover Come Back to Me, The Birth of the Blues, Angel
 Eyes, Love You Madly, Babalu, Why Don't You Do Right?, One O'Clock
 Jump

JATP in Tokyo Pablo CD PACD-2620-104-2
 Recorded November 4, 7 or 8, 1953
 On the Sunny Side of the Street, Body and Soul, Why Don't You Do
 Right, Lady Be Good, I Got It Bad and That Ain't Good, How High the
 Moon, My Funny Valentine, Smooth Sailing, Frim Fram Sauce, Perdido,
 Sweethearts on Parade/Dixie (After-hours session, unissued)

An Empty Ballroom 29259 12/23/53
If You Don't, I Know Who Will 29259 12/23/53
Melancholy Me 29008 12/23/53
Somebody Bad Stole De Wedding Bell 29008 12/23/53
Moanin' Low 29475 12/31/53
Taking a Chance on Love 29475 12/31/53

Curtain Call, Vol. 6 DL-7026 Released 2/8/54
  A-Tisket A-Tasket, Undecided

I Wished on the Moon 29137 3/24/54
Baby 29137 3/24/54
I Need 29137 3/24/54
Who's Afraid? 29137 3/24/54
I'm Glad There Is You ED-2148 3/24/54
What Else Could I Do? ED-2150 3/24/54
What Is There to Say? ED-2148 3/24/54
Makin' Whoopee ED-2149 3/24/54
Until the Real Thing Comes Along ED-2149 3/24/54
People Will Say We're in Love ED-2148 3/24/54
Please Be Kind ED-2148 3/30/54
Imagination ED-2149 3/30/54
My Heart Belongs to Daddy ED-2150 3/30/54
You Leave Me Breathless ED-2150 3/30/54
Nice Work If You Can Get It ED-2150 3/30/54
Stardust ED-2149 3/30/54
Lullaby of Birdland 29198 6/4/54
Later 29198 6/4/54

Ella and Ellis DL-8068 Released 8/9/54
  Includes all of the songs from the 3/29–30/54 recording dates

Ella Sings Gershwin DL-4451 Released 8/12/54
  Includes all of the songs from the 9/11–12/50 recording dates plus Oh,
  Lady Be Good, Nice Work If You Can Get It, Ellington's I'm Just a Lucky
  So-and-So, and McHugh-Adamson's I Didn't Mean a Word I Said (last
  two with Billy Kyle and His Trio)

Unreleased JATP Session Recorded September 18, 1954
  That Old Black Magic, Hey There

US All-Stars in Berlin CD Jazz Band EBCD 2113-2 Recorded February 1955
Papa Loves Mambo, Perdido

You'll Never Know DL-8155 4/1/55
Thanks for the Memory DL-8155 4/1/55
It Might As Well Be Spring DL-8155 4/1/55
I Can't Get Started DL-8155 4/1/55
Old Devil Moon 29580 4/27/55
Lover Come Back to Me 29580 4/27/55
Between the Devil and the Deep Blue Sea DL-8155 4/27/55
That Old Black Magic DL-8155 4/27/55
Hard Hearted Hannah 29689 5/3/55
Pete Kelly's Blues 29689 5/3/55
Ella Hums the Blues DL-8149 5/3/55
Soldier Boy 29648 8/1/55
A Satisfied Mind DL-8695 8/1/55

One Night Stand With Stan Kenton and Music '55 Joyce 1130
How High the Moon, Someone to Watch Over Me, Skylark, Stardust

My One and Only Love 29746 8/5/55
Impatient Years 29665 8/5/55
But Not Like Mine 29665 8/5/55
(Love Is) The Tender Trap 29746 8/5/55

There have been numerous LP reissues of material from the Decca vault since Ella left the label in 1955. Listed below are those by Decca (or their parent company MCA). There have also been dozens of compilation albums using material from the Decca years that have been released by other companies, many of them in Europe and Japan. They are too numerous and redundant to list here.

Ella: Songs in a Mellow Mood DL-8068 Released 1955
I'm Glad There Is You, What Is There to Say?, People Will Say We're in Love, Please Be Kind, Until the Real Thing Comes Along, Makin' Whoopee, Imagination, Stardust, My Heart Belongs to Daddy, You Leave Me Breathless, Baby What Else Can I Do?, Nice Work If You Can Get It

Songs from Pete Kelly's Blues DL-8166 Released 7/25/55
Hard Hearted Hannah, Pete Kelly's Blues, Ella Hums the Blues

Sweet and Hot DL-8155 Released 11/7/55
Thanks for the Memory, It Might as Well Be Spring, You'll Never Know, I Can't Get Started, Moanin' Low, Taking a Chance on Love, That Old Black Magic, Lover Come Back to Me, Between the Devil and the Deep Blue Sea, You'll Have to Swing It

Lullabies of Birdland DL-8149 Released 1/6/56
Lullaby of Birdland, Rough Ridin', Angel Eyes, Smooth Sailing, Lady Be Good, Later, Ella Hums the Blues, How High the Moon, Basin Street Blues, Air Mail Special, Flying Home

Ella Sings Gershwin DL-8378 Released 11/12/56 (reissue of DL-4451)
Contains all of the songs from the 9/11–12/50 recording dates

Ella and Her Fellas DL-8477 Released 6/15/57
You Won't Be Satisfied, That's the Way It Is, Stone Cold Dead in De Market, I Gotta Have My Baby Back, Sentimental Journey, The Frim Fram Sauce, It's Only a Paper Moon, Dream a Little Dream of Me, Baby It's Cold Outside, A-Tisket A-Tasket, Would You Like to Take a Walk, Don'cha Go 'Way Mad

The First Lady of Song DL-8695 Released 1957
My One and Only Love, The Impatient Years, But Not Like Me, I've Got the World on a String, An Empty Ballroom, You Turned the Tables on Me, Ella's Contribution to the Blues, That's My Desire, A Satisfied Mind, Careless, Give a Little–Get a Little, Blue Lou

Miss Ella Fitzgerald and Mr. Gordon Jenkins Invite You to Listen and Relax
DL-8698 Released 4/28/58
I Wished on the Moon, Baby, I Hadn't Anyone Till You, A Man Wrote a Song, Who's Afraid, Happy Talk, Black Coffee, Lover's Gold, I'm Gonna Wash That Man Right Out of My Hair, Dream a Little Longer, I Need, Foolish Tears

The Best of Ella Fitzgerald DL-8759 Released 8/11/58
A-Tisket A-Tasket, Undecided, Stairway to the Stars, Into Each Life Some Rain Must Fall, It's Only a Paper Moon, Flying Home, (I Love You) For Sentimental Reasons, Lady Be Good, How High the Moon, It's Too Soon

to Know, Basin Street Blues, I Hadn't Anyone Till You, I've Got the World
on a String, Mixed Emotions, Smooth Sailing, (If You Want to Sing It)
You'll Have to Swing It, Walkin' by the River, An Empty Ballroom, I
Wished on the Moon, That Old Black Magic, Lover Come Back to Me,
My One and Only Love, (Love Is) The Tender Trap

For Sentimental Reasons DL-8832 Released 2/7/59
(I Love You) For Sentimental Reasons, Baby Doll, Because of Rain, I'm
Confessin', Don't You Think I Oughta Know, Guilty, Mixed Emotions, A
Sunday Kind of Love, That Old Feeling, There Was Never a Baby Like
Mine, Walkin' by the River

Billie, Ella, Lena, Sarah Harmony HL-7125 Released 1959
Compilation with two Ella Fitzgerald cuts: My Melancholy Baby and All
My Life

Ella's Golden Favorites DL-4129 Released 3/13/61
Goody-Goody, Stairway to the Stars, Angel Eyes, Old Devil Moon, Taking
a Chance on Love, Cow-Cow Boogie, Lover Come Back to Me, A Sunday
Kind of Love, A-Tisket A-Tasket, My Happiness, Stone Cold Dead in De
Market, I Got It Bad and That Ain't Good

Early Ella: Great Ballads by Ella Fitzgerald DL-4447 Released 1962
Mixed Emotions, It's Too Soon to Know, Baby Doll, Walkin' by the River,
Melancholy Me, Someone Like You, I Hadn't Anyone Till You, So Long,
Gee But I'm Glad to Know You Love Me, Even As You and I, Crying

Stairway to the Stars DL-4446 Released 1/20/64
Stairway to the Stars, I Was Doing All Right, All or Nothing at All, You
Can't Be Mine, My Last Affair, Organ Grinder's Swing, Five O'Clock
Whistle, You Don't Know What Love Is, Undecided, Everyone's Wrong
But Me, Don't Worry 'Bout Me, If You Should Ever Leave

Smooth Sailing DL-4487 Released 10/16/67
Smooth Sailing, Basin Street Blues, Preview, Lady Be Good, Rough Rid-
ing, How High the Moon, Lullaby of Birdland, Flying Home, Angel Eyes,
Air Mail Special, Ella Hums the Blues, Later

Ella Fitzgerald: Memories CB-20024 Released 1973
Thanks for the Memory, You'll Never Know, Moanin' Low, Old Devil

Moon, Between the Devil and the Deep Blue Sea, Please Be Kind, Makin' Whoopee, Stardust, You Leave Me Breathless, Baby What Else Can I Do

The Best of Ella Fitzgerald, Vol. 2 MCA2-4016 Released 9/24/73
It Might as Well Be Spring, I Can't Get Started, Blue Lou, Lullaby of Birdland, Stone Cold Dead in De Market, Goody-Goody, You Turned the Tables on Me, That's My Desire, Guilty, That Old Feeling, A Kiss Goodnight, A Sunday Kind of Love, Sentimental Journey, There Was Never a Baby Like My Baby, Careless, Cow-Cow Boogie, Taking a Chance on Love, You Don't Know What Love Is, Baby Doll

Ella Fitzgerald: The Early Years Part I GRD-2-618 2-CD Set Released 10/92
I'll Chase the Blues Away, Love and Kisses, Rhythm and Romance, Under the Spell of the Blues, When I Get High I Get Low, Sing Me a Swing Song, A Little Bit Later On, Love You're Just a Laugh, You'll Have to Swing It, Vote for Mr. Rhythm, My Last Affair, Organ Grinder's Swing, Shine, Darktown Strutters' Ball, Oh, Yes, Take Another Guess, You Showed Me the Way, Cryin' Mood, If You Should Ever Leave, Everyone's Wrong But Me, Just a Simple Melody, I Got a Guy, Rock It for Me, I Want to Be Happy, The Dipsy Doodle, If Dreams Come True, Hallelujah!, Bei Mir Bist Du Schoen, It's My Turn Now, It's Wonderful, I Was Doing All Right, A-Tisket A-Tasket, Heart of Mine, I'm Just a Jitterbug, You Can't Be Mine, If You Only Knew, Pack Up Your Sins and Go to the Devil, MacPherson Is Rehearsin', Everybody Step, Wacky Dust, Strictly From Dixie, FDR Jones, It's Foxy, I Found My Yellow Basket

Ella Fitzgerald—The 75th Birthday Collection GRD-2-619 2-CD Set Released 3/93
A-Tisket A-Tasket, Undecided, Don't Worry 'Bout Me, Stairway to the Stars, Five O'Clock Whistle, Cow-Cow Boogie, Into Each Life Some Rain Must Fall, It's Only a Paper Moon, Flying Home, Stone Cold Dead in De Market, You Won't Be Satisfied, I'm Just a Lucky So-and-So, I Didn't Mean a Word I Said, Lady Be Good, How High the Moon, My Happiness, Black Coffee, In the Evening When the Sun Goes Down, Basin Street Blues, I've Got the World on a String, Ain't Nobody's Business But My Own, Dream a Little Dream of Me, Smooth Sailing, Air Mail Special, Rough Ridin', Goody-Goody, Angel Eyes, Mr. Paganini, Preview, Blue Lou, I Wished on the Moon, Until the Real Thing Comes Along, Lullaby of Birdland, That Old Black Magic, Old Devil Moon, Lover Come Back to Me, Between the Devil and the Deep Blue Sea, Hard Hearted Hannah, My One and Only Love

Ella Fitzgerald: The Early Years Part II GRD-2-623 2-CD Set Released 10/93

Undecided, 'Tain't What You Do, My Heart Belongs to Daddy, Chew-Chew-Chew (Your Bubble Gum), Don't Worry 'Bout Me, If You Ever Change Your Mind, Little White Lies, Coochi-Coochi-Coo, Betcha Nickel, Stairway to the Stars, I Want the Waiter (With the Water), Out of Nowhere, My Last Goodbye, Billy (I Always Dream of Billy), You're Gonna Lose Your Gal, After I Say I'm Sorry, Moon Ray, Sugar Blues, The Starlit Hour, What's the Matter With Me, Baby Won't You Please Come Home, If It Weren't for You, Imagination, Deedle-De Dum, Shake Down the Stars, Gulf Coast Blues, Five O'Clock Whistle, Louisville, K-Y, Taking a Chance on Love, Cabin in the Sky, I'm the Lonesomest Gal in Town, Three Little Words, The One I Love Belongs to Somebody Else, The Muffin Man, Keep Cool Fool, No Nothing, My Man, I Can't Believe That You're in Love With Me, I Must Have That Man, When My Sugar Walks Down the Street, I Got It Bad (and That Ain't Good), Can't Help Lovin' That Man

Pure Ella GRD-636 Released 2/94

This CD features all of the Decca Ella Fitzgerald–Ellis Larkins recordings.

Ella Fitzgerald: The War Years GRD 2-CD Set Released 9/94

Jim, This Love of Mine, Somebody Nobody Loves, You Don't Know What Love Is, Make Love to Me, Mama Come Home, My Heart and I Decided, He's My Guy, Cow-Cow Boogie, Once Too Often, Time Alone Will Tell, I'm Making Believe, Into Each Life Some Rain Must Fall, and Her Tears Flowed Like Wine, I'm Confessin', I'm Beginning to See the Light, That's the Way It Is, It's Only a Paper Moon*, Cry You Out of My Heart, A Kiss Goodnight, Flying Home*, Stone Cold Dead in De Market, Peetootie Pie, The Frim Fram Sauce, You Won't Be Satisfied, I'm Just a Lucky So-and-So, I Didn't Mean a Word, (I Love You) For Sentimental Reasons, It's a Pity to Say Goodnight, Guilty, Sentimental Journey, A Sunday Kind of Love, That's My Desire, Oh, Lady Be Good, Don't You Think I Oughta Know?, You're Breaking in a New Heart, I Want to Learn About Love, That Old Feeling, My Baby Likes to BeBop, No Sense, How High the Moon*, How High the Moon†

---

*Previously unissued alternate take.
†Second previously unissued take.

The following recordings were released on the Verve label unless otherwise indicated:

Jazz At the Philharmonic: The Ella Fitzgerald Set 815-147 1 Recorded September 18, 1949:
Robbins' Nest, Black Coffee, Just a Lucky So-and-So, Somebody Loves Me, Basin Street Blues, Flying Home

Recorded September 19, 1953:
My Bill, Why Don't You Do Right?

Recorded September 17, 1954:
A Foggy Day, The Man That Got Away, Hernando's Hideaway, Later

Ella Fitzgerald and the Dave Brubeck Quartet at the Shrine Auditorium Recorded January 21, 1956, all titles unissued:
And the Angels Sing, Joe Williams' Blues, Air Mail Special, S'Wonderful, Cry Me a River, Lullaby of Birdland, Medley: Fools Rush In/Glad to Be Unhappy

Singles Session Recorded January 25, 1956
Stay There (MGV 10012), The Sun Forgot to Shine This Morning (MGV 10021), It's Only a Man, Too Young for the Blues (MGV 2036)

Ella at Zardi's Recorded February 2, 1956, all titles unissued:
It All Depends on You, Tenderly, Why Don't You Do Right?, In a Mellow Tone, Joe Williams' Blues, A Fine Romance, How High the Moon, Gone With the Wind, Bernie's Tune, S'Wonderful, Glad to Be Unhappy, Lullaby of Birdland, (Love Is) The Tender Trap, And the Angels Sing, I Can't Give You Anything But Love, Little Boy, A-Tisket A-Tasket, My Heart Belongs to Daddy, Air Mail Special, I've Got a Crush on You

Singles Session 10128 Recorded February 8, 1956
Beale Street Blues

The Cole Porter Songbook, Vol. I V-4001,CD 821 989-2
Recorded February 7, 1956: Miss Otis Regrets, Too Darn Hot, Do I Love You?, Just One of Those Things, Everytime We Say Goodbye, Get Out of Town, I Am In Love, From This Moment On
Recorded February 8, 1957: All Through the Night, Anything Goes, In the

Still of the Night, Always True to You in My Fashion, Let's Do It, Begin the Beguine.
Recorded February 9, 1956: I Get a Kick Out of You, All of You

The Cole Porter Songbook, Vol. II V-4002, CD 821 990-2
Recorded February 7, 1956: I Love Paris, Ridin' High, Easy to Love, It's All Right With Me, Why Can't You Behave
Recorded February 8, 1956: You Do Something to Me, Love For Sale, It's Delovely, Ace in the Hole, So In Love, I Concentrate on You
Recorded February 9, 1956: What Is This Thing Called Love, You're the Top, I've Got You Under My Skin, Don't Fence Me In.
Recorded March 27, 1956: Night and Day, You're the Top (unissued), Love For Sale (unissued), I Concentrate on You (unissued).
NOTE: The unisssued cuts were released in 1993 on *The Complete Ella Fitzgerald Songbooks.*

Singles Session 10012 Recorded March 27, 1956
Beautiful Friendship, I Had to Find Out for Myself (unissued)

Metronome All-Stars 1956 UMV 2510 Recorded June 26–27, 1956
April in Paris, Everyday I Have the Blues, Party Blues, Salty Lips (unissued)

One O'Clock Jump MGV-8288 Recorded June 26–27, 1956
Too Close for Comfort

Jazz at the Hollywood Bowl MGV 8231-2 Recorded August 15, 1956
This Can't Be Love (unreleased), Beautiful Friendship (unreleased), I Could Have Danced All Night (unreleased), Lady Be Good (unreleased), Love for Sale, Just One of Those Things, Angel Eyes (unreleased and lost), Little Girl Blue, Too Close for Comfort, I Can't Give You Anything But Love, Air Mail Special, You Won't Be Satisfied, Undecided, When the Saints Go Marching In

Ella and Louis 825 373-2 Recorded August 16, 1956
Can't We Be Friends, Isn't This a Lovely Day?, Moonlight in Vermont, They Can't Take That Away From Me, Under a Blanket of Blue, Tenderly, A Foggy Day, Stars Fell on Alabama, Cheek to Cheek, The Nearness of You, April in Paris

Singles Session 10021 Recorded August 21, 1956
The Silent Treatment

The Rodgers and Hart Songbook, Vol. I MGV 4022 and CD 821 579-2

Recorded August 21, 1956: This Can't Be Love, The Lady Is a Tramp, I've Got Five Dollars

Recorded August 28, 1956: Johnny One Note, I Wish I Were In Love Again

Recorded August 29, 1956: Manhattan, To Keep My Love Alive, With a Song in My Heart

Recorded August 30, 1956: Have You Met Miss Jones?, A Ship Without a Sail, Spring Is Here, It Never Entered My Mind, Little Girl Blue

Recorded August 31, 1956: You Took Advantage of Me, Where or When, Dancing on the Ceiling, The Blue Room

The Rodgers and Hart Songbook, Vol. II MGV 4023 and CD 821 580-2

Recorded August 21, 1956: Lover, Lover (unreleased mono version)

Recorded August 28, 1956: Give It Back to the Indians, Ten Cents a Dance, Mountain Greenery

Recorded August 29, 1956: There's a Small Hotel, I Didn't Know What Time It Was, Bewitched, Wait Till You See Her, Thou Swell, Everything I've Got

Recorded August 30, 1956: I Could Write a Book, My Funny Valentine, My Romance, Here in My Arms, My Heart Stood Still

Recorded August 31, 1956: Isn't It Romantic?

NOTE: Mono version of Lover released on *The Complete Ella Fitzgerald Songbooks.*

Singles Session: Recorded September 4, 1956

Everything I've Got Belongs to You

The Duke Ellington Songbook CD 837 035-2

Recorded September 4, 1956: Cottontail, Do Nothing Till You Hear from Me, Just A-Sitting and A-Rocking, Solitude, Satin Doll, Rocks In My Bed, Sophisticated Lady, Just Squeeze Me, It Don't Mean A Thing If It Ain't Got That Swing, Azure, I Let a Song Go Out of My Heart, In a Sentimental Mood, Don't Get Around Much Anymore, Prelude to a Kiss

Recorded June 24, 1957: Day Dreams, Take the "A" Train, I Got It Bad and That Ain't Good

Recorded June 25, 1957: Drop Me Off in Harlem, I Ain't Got Nothin' But the Blues, Lost in Meditation, Everything But You

Recorded June 26, 1957: Rockin' in Rhythm, Clementine, I Didn't Know About You, I'm Beginning To See the Light, I'm Just a Lucky So-and-So

Recorded June 27, 1957: Caravan, Perdido, All Too Soon, Be-Bop, Chelsea Bridge, Rehearsal (unissued), Chelsea Bridge (unissued), The E & D Blues

Recorded August 1957: Portrait of Ella Fitzgerald
Recorded October 17, 1957: Mood Indigo, In a Mellow Tone, Love You
Medley, Lush Life, Squatty Roo
NOTE: Alternate cut of Chelsea Bridge and Rehearsal cut were issued on
The Complete Ella Fitzgerald Songbook.

Single Session: V-10031 Recorded January 14, 1957
Hear My Heart, Hotta Chocolotta

Jazz At The Philharmonic 1957: Americans in Sweden TAX CD 3703-2 Re-
corded April 29, 1957
You Got Me Singing the Blues, Angel Eyes, Lullaby of Birdland, Tenderly,
Do Nothing Till You Hear From Me, April in Paris, I Can't Give You
Anything But Love, Love for Sale, It Don't Mean a Thing (If It Ain't Got
That Swing)

Ella and Billie at Newport MGV 8232 Recorded July 4, 1957
This Can't Be Love, I Got It Bad (And That Ain't Good), Body and Soul,
April in Paris, I've Got a Crush on You, Air Mail Special, I Can't Give You
Anything But Love

Unissued Session Recorded July 23, 1957
Ill Wind, These Foolish Things, Comes Love
NOTE: These cuts, vocals without Louis Armstrong, originally appeared
on the LP version of *Ella and Louis Again,* but were deleted from the
CD issue.

Ella and Louis Again CD 825 374-2
Recorded July 23, 1957: They All Laughed, Autumn in New York, Stompin'
at the Savoy, Gee Baby Ain't I Good to You, Let's Call the Whole Thing
Off, Love Is Here to Stay, Learnin' the Blues
Recorded August 13, 1957: Don't Be That Way, I Won't Dance, I've Got
My Love to Keep Me Warm, I'm Putting All My Eggs in One Basket, A
Fine Romance

Singles Session Recorded July 24, 1957
A-Tisket A-Tasket, How Long Has This Been Going On?, Angel Eyes,
Don'cha Go 'Way Mad (unissued)
NOTE: Angel Eyes and Don'cha Go 'Way Mad were issued on *Ella Fitz-
gerald—The First Lady of Song* in 1993

Porgy and Bess V6-4011-2 CD 827 475-2
Recorded August 18, 1957:
  Overture, Summertime, My Man's Gone Now, I Got Plenty of Nothing, Bess You Is My Woman Now, It Ain't Necessarily So, A Woman Is a Sometime Thing, They Pass By (unissued)
Recorded August 28, 1957:
  I Wants to Stay Here, The Buzzard Song, What You Want Wid' Bess?, Oh Doctor Jesus, Medley: Here Come De Honey Man/Crab Man/Oh Dey's So Fresh and Fine, There's a Boat Dat's Leaving Soon for New York, Bess Oh Where's My Bess?, Oh Lawd I'm on My Way

Ella at the Opera House MGV 8264 CD 831 269-2
Recorded September 29, 1957:
  It's Alright With Me, Don'cha Go 'Way Mad, Bewitched, These Foolish Things, Ill Wind, Goody-Goody, Moonlight in Vermont, Them There Eyes, Stompin' at the Savoy
Recorded October 7, 1957:
  It's All Right With Me, Don'cha Go 'Way Mad, Bewitched, These Foolish Things, Ill Wind, Goody-Goody, Moonlight in Vermont, Stompin' at the Savoy, Lady Be Good

Like Someone in Love CD 314 511 524-2
Recorded October 15, 1957:
  There's a Lull in My Life, More Than You Know, What Will I Tell My Heart, I Never Had a Chance, Close Your Eyes, We'll Be Together Again, Then I'll Be Tired of You, Midnight Sun, I Thought About You, You're Blasé
Recorded October 28, 1957:
  I'll Never Be the Same, Night Wind, Hurry Home, How Long Has This Been Going On?, Lost in a Fog, Everything Happens to Me, What's New?, So Rare

The Irving Berlin Songbook, Vol. I MGV-4019-2 CD 829 534-2
Recorded March 13, 1958
  All By Myself
Recorded March 14, 1958
  You Can Have Him, I Used to Be Color Blind
Recorded March 17, 1958
  You're Laughing At Me, Russian Lullaby, Get Thee Behind Me Satan, How About Me, How Deep Is the Ocean
Recorded March 18, 1958

Let's Face the Music and Dance, Puttin' on the Ritz, Cheek to Cheek, Lazy, Remember
Recorded March 18, 1958
Let Yourself Go, Alexander's Ragtime Band, Top Hat, White Tie and Tails, Swinging Shepherd Blues (unissued), Teach Me How to Cry (unissued)
NOTE: Swingin' Shepherd Blues was issued on *Ella Fitzgerald—First Lady of Song* in 1993.

The Irving Berlin Songbook, Vol. II MGV-4019-2 CD 829 535-2
Recorded March 13, 1958
Isn't This a Lovely Day, Slumming on Park Avenue, I'm Putting All My Eggs in One Basket, Always
Recorded March 14, 1958
How's Chances, No Strings
Recorded March 17, 1958
Suppertime, You Keep Coming Back Like a Song, Reaching for the Moon, Now It Can Be Told, Change Partners
Recorded March 18, 1958
Blue Skies, Heat Wave, The Song Is Ended, It's a Lovely Day Today, I've Got My Love To Keep Me Warm

Swing Into Spring Sandy Hook CD 2057 Recorded April 9, 1958
Riding High, I Got a Right to Sing the Blues, Hard Hearted Hannah, St. Louis Blues, Gotta Be This or That

Ella in Rome CD 835 454-2 Recorded April 25, 1958
St. Louis Blues, These Foolish Things, Just Squeeze Me, Angel Eyes, That Old Black Magic, Just One of Those Things, I Loves You Porgy, It's Alright With Me, I Can't Give You Anything But Love, When You're Smiling, A Foggy Day, Midnight Sun, The Lady Is a Tramp, Sophisticated Lady, Caravan, Stompin' at the Savoy
NOTE: This CD is a compilation of the afternoon and evening concerts, where the same program was repeated and the best of both shows was used. There are unissued tracks of these same songs that were not chosen.

Unissued Session: July 1, 1958
Your Red Wagon, Traveling Light
NOTE: Your Red Wagon was issued on *The Essential American Singers* in 1993.

Ella at Mr. Kelly's Recorded August 10–12, 1958 (unreleased)
Your Red Wagon, Nice Work If You Can Get It, I'm Glad There Is You,
How Long Has This Been Going On?, Across the Alley From the Alamo,
Perdido, The Lady Is a Tramp, Witchcraft, Bewitched, Summertime, In
the Wee Small Hours of the Morning, St. Louis Blues, Lover, On the
Sunny Side of the Street, Willow Weep for Me, My Heart Belongs to
Daddy, The Lady Is a Tramp, Too Close for Comfort, Love Me or Leave
Me, Porgy and Bess Medley, How High the Moon, Exactly Like You,
Come Rain or Come Shine, Stardust, S'Wonderful, Royal Roost Bop Boo-
gie, You Don't Know What Love Is, In the Wee Small Hours of the
Morning, My Funny Valentine

Ella Swings Lightly CD 314 517 535-2
Recorded November 22, 1958:
You Hit the Spot, What's Your Story Morning Glory?, Just You Just Me,
As Long as I Live, Teardrops From My Eyes, My Kinda Love, Blues in
the Night, If I Were a Bell, You're an Old Smoothie
Recorded November 23, 1958:
Little White Lies, Gotta Be This or That, Moonlight on the Ganges, Little
Jazz, You Brought a New Kind of Love to Me, Knock Me a Kiss, 720 in
the Books, Oh What a Night for Love (long version), Little Jazz (alternate
take), Dreams Are Made for Children, Oh What a Night for Love (single
version)

Ella Fitzgerald Sings Sweet Songs for Swingers V6-4032
Recorded November 24, 1958:
Sweet and Lovely, Let's Fall in Love, Makin' Whoopee, I Remember You,
Moonlight Serenade, Can't We Be Friends, Out of This World, My Old
Flame, East of the Sun, Lullaby of Broadway
Recorded July 11, 1959:
Gone With the Wind, That Old Feeling

The George and Ira Gershwin Songbook CD 825 024-2
Recorded January 5, 1959:
Beginner's Luck, How Long Has This Been Going On?, The Man I Love,
A Foggy Day, Soon, Bidin' My Time, He Loves and She Loves, Love Is
Here to Stay, Isn't It a Pity?, They Can't Take That Away From Me,
Fascinating Rhythm, I Got Rhythm
Recorded January 7, 1959:
Clap Yo' Hands, Slap That Bass, You've Got What Gets Me, Somebody
Loves Me, Cheerful Little Earful

NOTE: Somebody Loves Me and Cheerful Little Earful originally recorded for *Gershwin Songbook*, but used in compilation LP *Get Happy* because Ira did not write the lyrics. Both songs included in *The Ella Fitzgerald Songbook*.

Recorded January 8, 1959:
But Not for Me, Lady Be Good, I've Got a Crush on You, Embraceable You, Lady Be Good (alternate take)
NOTE: Alternate take for Lady Be Good is included in *The Ella Fitzgerald Songbook*.

Recorded March 18, 1959:
Of Thee I Sing, I Was Doing All Right, I Can't Be Bothered Now, Funny Face, Lorelei
Recorded March 26, 1959:
My One and Only, Let's Call the Whole Thing Off, Nice Work If You Can Get It, Someone to Watch Over Me, Looking for a Boy, They All Laughed, Love Walked In, Let's Kiss and Make Up, But Not for Me
NOTE: Alternate take for But Not for Me was used in single release, included in *The Ella Fitzgerald Songbook*.

Recorded July 15, 1959:
That Certain Feeling, Boy Wanted, "The Half of It Dearie" Blues, Shall We Dance?, Boy! What Love Has Done to Me
Recorded July 16, 1959:
Sam and Delilah, S'Wonderful, By Strauss, Who Cares?, My Cousin in Milwaukee, Strike Up the Band, Treat Me Rough
Recorded July 17, 1959:
Things Are Looking Up, Just Another Rhumba, For You for Me for Evermore, Stiff Upper Lip, Oh So Nice
Recorded July 18, 1959:
The Real American Folk Song, Somebody From Somewhere, Aren't You Kind of Glad We Did, Love Is Sweeping the Country
Recorded August 20, 1959:
Ambulatory Suite, The Preludes (orchestral pieces included in the original boxed set but not in the CD version; reissued on *The Ella Fitzgerald Song Book*)

Unissued Session Recorded March 25, 1959
Pennies From Heaven, It's a Good Day, Detour Ahead

The Best of the Jazz Singers Denon CD DC-8517 Recorded August 1959
   Lover Come Back to Me, Angel Eyes, I'm Beginning to See the Light,
   My Heart Belongs to Daddy, Just One of Those Things, I Can't Give You
   Anything But Love, Sophisticated Lady, Air Mail Special

Get Happy V6-4036
Recorded July 24, 1957:
   You Turned the Tables on Me, Gypsy in My Soul, Goody Goody, St. Louis
   Blues
Recorded March 13, 1958:
   Blue Skies
Recorded July 11, 1959:
   Moonlight Becomes You, You Make Me Feel So Young
Recorded January 5, 1959:
   Somebody Loves Me, Cheerful Little Earful
Recorded September 3, 1959:
   Like Young, Cool Breeze, Beat Me Daddy Eight to the Bar

Ella in Berlin (Mack the Knife) MGV-4041 CD 825 670-2
Recorded February 13, 1960
   Gone With the Wind, Misty, The Lady Is a Tramp, The Man I Love,
   Summertime, Too Darn Hot, Lorelei, Mack the Knife, How High the
   Moon

The Complete Ella in Berlin Recorded February 13, 1960; released 8/93
   All of the songs above, plus Love Is Here to Stay, That Old Black Magic,
   Love for Sale, Just One of Those Things, that were taken from the ten-
   inch version of the concert and a tape transcription of the concert intended
   for radio broadcast.

The Intimate Ella CD 839 838-2
Recorded April 14, 1960:
   Black Coffee, Angel Eyes, I Cried for You, I Hadn't Anyone Till You, My
   Melancholy Baby, Misty
Recorded April 19, 1960:
   I Can't Give You Anything But Love, Then You've Never Been Blue,
   September Song, One for My Baby, Who's Sorry Now?, I'm Getting Sen-
   timental Over You, Reach for Tomorrow

Hello Love MOIR Records Album 124 Released 1960
Recorded July 24, 1957:
   Tenderly, Stairway to the Stars, Moonlight in Vermont

Recorded October 28, 1957:
Everything Happens to Me, Lost in a Fog, So Rare
Recorded March 25, 1959:
You Go to My Head, Willow Weep for Me, I'm Thru With You, I've
Grown Accustomed to His Face (unissued), Spring Will Be a Little Late
This Year

Have Yourself a Jazzy Little Christmas CD 840 501-2
Recorded September 3, 1959
The Secret of Christmas, The Christmas Song (unissued), White Christ-
mas (alternate version from session July 15, 1960), Have Yourself a Merry
Little Christmas (July 15, 1960)

Ella Wishes You a Swinging Christmas CD 827 150-2
Recorded July 15, 1960:
Jingle Bells, Santa Claus Is Coming to Town, Rudolph the Red-Nosed
Reindeer, Frosty the Snowman, We Three Kings of Orient Are and O
Little Town of Bethlehem (issued only in Europe)
Recorded July 16, 1960:
Have Yourself a Merry Little Christmas, What Are You Doing New Year's
Eve?, Let It Snow!, Winter Wonderland
Recorded August 5, 1960:
Sleigh Ride, The Christmas Song, Good Morning Blues, White
Christmas

The Harold Arlen Songbook Vol. I V6-4057 CD 817 527-2
Recorded August 1, 1960:
Hooray for Love, I've Got the World on a String, Let's Take a Walk
Around the Block, Accentuate the Positive
Recorded August 2, 1960:
Sing My Heart, Sing My Heart (unreleased), Let's Take a Walk Around
the Block (unreleased)
Recorded January 14, 1961:
Blues in the Night, Stormy Weather, That Old Black Magic
Recorded January 15, 1961:
My Shining Hour, This Time the Dream's on Me, Ill Wind
Recorded January 16, 1961:
Let's Fall in Love, Between the Devil and the Deep Blue Sea
NOTE: The two unissued cuts were alternate takes that were released on *The
Complete Ella Fitzgerald Songbooks.*

The Harold Arlen Songbook Vol. II V6-4058 CD 817 528-2
Recorded August 1, 1960:
  When the Sun Comes Out, As Long As I Live, It's Only a Paper Moon,
  The Man That Got Away
Recorded August 2, 1960:
  Get Happy, Ding Dong! The Witch Is Dead
Recorded January 14, 1961:
  One For My Baby, I've Got a Right to Sing the Blues, Heart and Soul
  (unissued)
Recorded January 15, 1961:
  It Was Written in the Stars, Over the Rainbow
Recorded January 16, 1961:
  Come Rain or Come Shine, Happiness Is a Thing Called Joe, Out of This
  World
  NOTE: Heart and Soul was not issued with the *Arlen Songbook*, but later
  appeared on the CD compilation *Ella Fitzgerald—First Lady of Song*.

Unissued Session: Recorded January 23, 1961
  Slow Boat to China, You're Driving Me Crazy, Spring Can Really Hang
  You Up the Most, This Year's Kisses, 'Round Midnight, The One I Love
  Belongs to Somebody Else, I Got a Guy, This Could Be the Start of
  Something Big, Stella by Starlight
  NOTE: The One I Love Belongs to Somebody Else, I Got a Guy, and This
  Could Be the Start of Something Big released on CD version of *Clap
  Hands, Here Comes Charlie!*

Ella Returns to Berlin CD 837 758-2 Recorded February 11, 1961
  Give Me the Simple Life, Take the "A" Train, Slow Boat to China, Med-
  ley: Why Was I Born/ Can't Help Loving That Man/ People Will Say We're
  in Love, You're Driving Me Crazy, Rock It for Me, Witchcraft, Anything
  Goes, Cheek to Cheek, Misty, Caravan, Mr. Paganini, Mack the Knife,
  'Round Midnight, Joe Williams' Blues, This Can't Be Love

Ella Sings Cole Porter V-4049
  Reissue of *Cole Porter Songbook, Vol. I*

Ella Sings More Cole Porter V-4050
  Reissue of *Cole Porter Songbook, Vol. II*

Unissued Session Recorded April 5, 1961, at Northwestern University
  St. Louis Blues, Mr. Paganini

Ella in Hollywood V6-4052, UMV 2636

This Could Be the Start of Something Big, I've Got the World on a String, You're Driving Me Crazy, Just in Time, It Might As Well Be Spring, Take the "A" Train, Stairway to the Stars, Mr. Paganini, Satin Doll, Blue Moon, Baby Won't You Please Come Home, Air Mail Special, A-Tisket A-Tasket (issued only on *Compact Jazz*)

NOTE: The above is the actual running order of the album. There was so much recorded that was unused that I have broken them down by date. What follows is what still survives in the Verve vaults; even more was recorded at the time.

Recorded May 11, 1961:

Mr. Paganini (unissued)

Recorded May 12, 1961:

Mr. Paganini, Lover Come Back to Me (unissued), You Brought a New Kind of Love to Me (unissued), Across the Alley From the Alamo (unissued), I'm Glad There Is You (unissued), 'Round Midnight (unissued), Take the "A" Train (unissued), A-Tisket A-Tasket

Recorded May 13, 1961 (all unissued):

I Found a New Baby, On the Sunny Side of the Street, Am I Blue?, I've Got a Crush on You, It's Alright With Me, Caravan, Blue Moon, Lullaby of Birdland, A-Tisket A-Tasket, Imagination, Mack the Knife, Joe Williams' Blues, Give Me the Simple Life, Mr. Paganini, 'Round Midnight, Just Squeeze Me, This Could Be the Start of Something Big, S'Wonderful, In the Wee Small Hours of the Morning, How High the Moon

Recorded May 14, 1961:

Just in Time, Rock It for Me (unissued), S'Wonderful (unissued), St. Louis Blues (unissued), I've Got the World on a String, It's Alright With Me (unissued), Mr. Paganini (unissued).

Recorded May 16, 1961:

I Found a New Baby (unissued), Deep Purple (unissued), You're Driving Me Crazy, Blue Moon, This Could Be the Start of Something Big, Baby Won't You Please Come Home, Slow Boat to China (unissued), Take the "A" Train (unissued), Li'l Darlin' (unissued), Caravan (unissued), in the Wee Small Hours of the Morning (unissued), Mack the Knife (unissued), Joe Wiliams' Blues (unissued)

NOTES: Ella introduced Gig Young from the audience that night. Slow Boat, Caravan, and Joe Williams' Blues were originally planned to be on the album and were pulled at the last minute.

Recorded May 17, 1961:
   Mr. Paganini (unissued), Satin Doll, S'Wonderful (unissued), Air Mail
   Special
Recorded May 18, 1961 (all unissued):
   The Lady's in Love With Me, Love Is Here to Stay, Come Rain or Come
   Shine, Anything Goes, This Could Be the Start of Something Big, Candy,
   Little Girl Blue, You're Driving Me Crazy, Mack the Knife, Blue Moon,
   Joe Williams' Blues, S'Wonderful, Give Me the Simple Life, Slow Boat to
   China, Am I Blue?, Lullaby of Birdland, But Not for Me, Take the "A"
   Train, In the Wee Small Hours of the Morning, Witchcraft, A-Tisket A-
   Tasket, Mack the Knife, I've Got a Crush on You, Joe Williams' Blues
   NOTE: Ella introduced both Carl Reiner and Mack David (lyricist of
   Candy) from the audience.

Recorded May 19, 1961 (all unissued except for It Might As Well Be Spring):
   This Could Be the Start of Something Big, Witchcraft, Gone With the
   Wind, It Might as Well Be Spring, Happiness Is a Thing Called Joe, It's
   Delovely, The Lady Is a Tramp, That Old Black Magic, Lullaby of Bird-
   land, Just Squeeze Me, Mr. Paganini, Stompin' at the Savoy, S'Wonderful,
   Nice Work If You Can Get It, I Can't Get Started, Give Me the Simple
   Life, Caravan, Little Girl Blue, One for My Baby, This Could Be the Start
   of Something Big, Lorelei, Across the Alley From the Alamo, A-Tisket A-
   Tasket
Recorded May 20, 1961 (all unissued):
   Lover Come Back to Me, Too Close for Comfort, Little White Lies, On
   the Sunny Side of the Street, Accentuate the Positive, Little Girl Blue,
   Anything Goes, Take the "A" Train, Mr. Paganini, This Could Be the Start
   of Something Big, I Found a New Baby, Slow Boat to China, Medley: Am
   I Blue?/Blue and Sentimental/Baby Won't You Please Come Home, My
   Heart Belongs to Daddy, Perdido, Witchcraft, In the Wee Small Hours
   of the Morning
Recorded May 21, 1961:
   Love for Sale (unissued), Stairway to the Stars, Mr. Paganini (unissued),
   Take the "A" Train, Mack the Knife (unissued), Exactly Like You (unis-
   sued)

Clap Hands, Here Comes Charlie! V6-4053 CD 835 646-2
Recorded January 23, 1961:
   The One I Love Belongs to Somebody Else, I Got a Guy, This Could Be
   the Start of Something Big
Recorded June 23, 1961:
   My Reverie, Stella by Starlight, 'Round Midnight, Born to Be Blue

Recorded June 24, 1961:
  Night in Tunisia, You're My Thrill, Jersey Bounce, Signing Off, Cry Me a River, This Year's Kisses, Good Morning Heartache, Clap Hands, Here Comes Charlie!, Spring Can Really Hang You Up the Most, Music Goes 'Round and 'Round

Unreleased Session Recorded August 25, 1961, in Copenhagen
  Mr. Paganini, Ich Fuhle Mich Crazy
  NOTE: This was released as a single in Germany only, sung in German.

Jazz Round Midnight CD 843 621-2 Compilation
  The Man I Love, Reaching for the Moon, Blue Moon, Moonlight Becomes You, Love Is Here to Stay, With a Song in My Heart, How Deep Is the Ocean?, September Song, Good Morning Heartache, 'Round Midnight, I Got It Bad (And That Ain't Good), One for My Baby, Cry Me a River, Do Nothing Till You Hear From Me

All Star Festival UNM-1 Recorded November 15, 1961
  All of Me
  NOTE: All of Me was recorded at the same time as the following Nelson Riddle albums, and was included in the CD release of *Ella Swings Brightly With Nelson*. It was used on this special release by the United Nations at the time of its recording.

Ella Swings Brightly With Nelson V6-4054 CD 519 347-2
Recorded November 13, 14, and 15, 1961:
  When Your Lover Has Gone, Love Me or Leave Me, I Hear Music, What Am I Here For?, I Only Have Eyes for You, The Gentleman Is a Dope, Mean to Me, Alone Together, Pick Yourself Up
Recorded December 27, 1961:
  Don't Be That Way, I'm Gonna Go Fishing, I Won't Dance
Recorded April 10, 1962
  Call Me Darling

Ella Swings Gently With Nelson V6-4055 CD 519 348-2
Recorded November 13, 14, and 15, 1961:
  Darn That Dream, Georgia on My Mind, I Can't Get Started
Recorded December 27, 1961:
  It's a Pity to Say Goodnight
Recorded April 9 and 10, 1962:
  Sweet and Slow, Street of Dreams, Imagination, The Very Thought of

You, It's a Blue World, He's Funny That Way, I Wished on the Moon, My One and Only Love, Body and Soul, Call Me Darling (only issued in the United Kingdom, but released on both Riddle albums on CD)

Rhythm Is My Business V6-4056 Recorded January 30–31, 1962:
Rough Ridin', Broadway, You Can Depend on Me, Runnin' Wild, Show Me the Way to Go Out of This World 'Cause That's Where Everything Is, I'll Always Be in Love With You, Hallelujah I Love Him So, I Can't Face the Music, No Moon at All, Laughin' on the Outside, After You've Gone, If I Could Be With You (unissued), Taking a Chance on Love (unissued)

Unissued Sessions from the Crescendo Night Club
Recorded June 29, 1962:
Misty, Hallelujah I Love Him So, Joe Williams' Blues, Bill Bailey, Mack the Knife, All of Me, It Might As Well Be Spring, The Lady Is a Tramp, Little Girl Blue, On the Sunny Side of the Street, My Heart Belongs to Daddy, Hard Hearted Hannah, Broadway, He's My Kind of Boy, It Had to Be You, All of Me, Bewitched, Exactly Like You, I've Got a Crush on You, How Long Has This Been Going On?, C'est Magnifique, On the Sunny Side of the Street, Bill Bailey
Recorded June 30, 1962:
He's My Kind of Boy, Teach Me Tonight, Exactly Like You, C'est Magnifique, On the Sunny Side of the Street, When Your Lover Has Gone, Teach Me Tonight, Taking a Chance on Love, Good Morning Heartache, Clap Hands, Here Comes Charlie, C'est Magnifique, It Had to Be You, Exactly Like You, Hallelujah I Love Him So, Exactly Like You, Perdido, Angel Eyes, Old Man Mose, Bill Bailey, Bill Bailey (encore), All of Me, He's My Kind of Boy, My Heart Belongs to Daddy, Too Close for Comfort, Teach Me Tonight, Too Darn Hot (stopped by Ella, then she extemporizes into), Ella's Twist, It's Too Darn Hot, Bewitched
NOTE: Old Man Moses and Bill Bailey (released as Verve single 10288) were also recorded at this time and released as a single, but they are not the versions listed above.

Singles Session Recorded October 1, 1962:
Desafinado, Stardust Bossa Nova, A Felicidad

Ella Sings Broadway V6-4059
Recorded October 1, 1962:
Steam Heat

Recorded October 2, 1962:
   I Could Have Danced All Night, Whatever Lola Wants, Guys and Dolls, Hernando's Hideaway
Recorded October 3, 1962:
   Somebody Somewhere, No Other Love, Dites-Moi, Warm All Over
Recorded October 4, 1962:
   Almost Like Being in Love, If I Were a Bell, Show Me

The Jerome Kern Songbook V6-4060 CD825 669-2
Recorded January 5, 1963:
   A Fine Romance, I'll Be Hard to Handle, I'm Old Fashioned
Recorded January 6, 1963:
   The Way You Look Tonight, Yesterdays, Can't Help Loving That Man, Why Was I Born?
Recorded January 7, 1963:
   Let's Begin, All the Things You Are, You Couldn't Be Cuter, She Didn't Say Yes, Remind Me

Ella and Basie! V6-4061 CD 821 576-2
Recorded July 15 or 16, 1963:
   Honeysuckle Rose, 'Deed I Do, Into Each Life Some Rain Must Fall, Them There Eyes, Dream a Little Dream of Me, Tea for Two, Satin Doll, I'm Beginning to See the Light, Shiny Stockings, Ain't Misbehavin', On the Sunny Side of the Street
Recorded July 16, 1963:
   My Last Affair, Robbins' Nest (unissued)

These Are the Blues V6-4062 CD 829 536-2
Recorded October 28, 1963:
   Jailhouse Blues, See See Rider, Trouble in Mind, How Long How Long Blues, Cherry Red, Hear Me Talking to Ya
Recorded October 29, 1963:
   In the Evening When the Sun Goes Down, You Don't Know My Mind, Down Hearted Blues, St. Louis Blues, Jam Session (unissued)

Verve's Choice: The Best of Ella Fitzgerald V6-4063
   Mack the Knife, Beautiful Friendship, (You'll Have to Swing It) Mr. Paganini, Lorelei, Goody-Goody, Desafinado, Bill Bailey, Won't You Please Come Home, Shiny Stockings, A-Tisket A-Tasket, How High the Moon

Unissued Session Recorded live February 3, 1964:
 You'd Be So Nice to Come Home To, I'm Beginning to See the Light,
 This Is My Last Affair, Dream a Little Dream of Me, Goody-Goody, I
 Love Being Here With You, Ten Cents a Dance, Deep Purple, Witchcraft,
 Them There Eyes, Shiny Stockings, The Lady Is a Tramp, Bill Bailey,
 Perdido, Mack the Knife

Hello Dolly! V6-4064
Recorded March 3, 1964:
 How High the Moon, Volare, The Thrill Is Gone, Memories of You, Pete
 Kelly's Blues, There I've Said It Again (unissued)
Recorded March 4, 1964:
 Lullaby of the Leaves, Miss Otis Regrets, My Man, I'll See You in My
 Dreams (unissued), There Are Such Things (unissued)
Recorded April 7, 1964:
 Hello Dolly!, People, Can't Buy Me Love, The Sweetest Sounds

Unissued Session Recorded May 27, 1964, from a live television show
 I'm Beginning to See the Light, Satin Doll

Ella at Juan-les-Pins V6 4065 CD POCJ-1925
Recorded July 28, 1964:
 Hello, Dolly!*, Day-In Day-Out, Just a-Sittin' and a-Rockin', I Love Being
 Here With You*, People, Someone to Watch Over Me, Can't Buy Me
 Love, Them There Eyes, The Lady Is a Tramp, Summertime, Cutie Pants,
 I'm Putting All My Eggs in One Basket*, St. Louis Blues, Perdido, Mack
 the Knife*, Honeysuckle Rose
Recorded July 29, 1964:
 Hello Dolly*, Day-In Day-Out*, Just a-Sittin' and a-Rockin'*, I Love Be-
 ing Here With You*, People*, Someone to Watch Over Me*, Can't Buy
 Me Love*, Them There Eyes*, The Lady Is a Tramp*, Summertime*,
 Cutie Pants*, I'm Putting All My Eggs in One Basket*, St. Louis Blues*,
 Goody-Goody, The Boy From Ipanema, They Can't Take That Away
 From Me, You'd Be So Nice to Come Home To, Shiny Stockings, Some-
 where in the Night, I've Got You Under My Skin, The Cricket Song, How
 High the Moon
 NOTE: An asterisk (*) means cut was unissued.

Ella in Nippon Unreleased album recorded various dates in July 1964.
 This was meant to be a deluxe album, including non-Ella cuts by the Roy
 Eldridge Quartet, recorded in the studio, in concert, and from television,
 with both a full orchestra and the quartet.

NOTE: While very little had been known about these recordings until recently, other sources list the date as late 1963. However, after seeing the television special some of the material is taken from, it is my considered opinion that this tour of Japan happened after her concert in Juan-les-Pins.

Produced for Issue:
  Cheek to Cheek, Deep Purple, Too Close for Comfort, I Love Being Here With You, Fly Me to the Moon, S'Wonderful, I've Got You Under My Skin, Hallelujah I Love Him So, Misty, Whatever Lola Wants, Bill Bailey, Ella's Blues
Material Not Planned for Issue:
  Cheek to Cheek, Can't Help Lovin' Dat Man, Shiny Stockings, Bill Bailey, Take the "A" Train, A-Tisket A-Tasket, Hallelujah I Love Him So, Ella's Blues, Mack the Knife, Ain't Misbehavin', My Last Affair, Perdido

Unreleased Session Recorded October 19, 1964
  I've Grown Accustomed to His Face, All the Live Long Day, I'm a Poached Egg, Traveling Light
  NOTE: These songs were released in Europe but not in the United States.

The Johnny Mercer Songbook V6-4067 CD 823 247-2
Recorded October 19–21, 1964:
  Too Marvelous for Words, Early Autumn, Day-In Day-Out, Laura, This Time the Dream's on Me, Skylark, Single-O, Something's Gotta Give, Traveling Light, Midnight Sun, Dream, I Remember You, When a Woman Loves a Man

Unreleased Session Recorded October 22, 1964
  I've Got Your Number, Thanks for the Memory, Old MacDonald, I Said No, When Sunny Gets Blue, Spring Can Really Hang You Up the Most, Melancholy Serenade

Unissued Session Recorded October 23, 1964
  Ringo Beat, I'm Falling in Love
  NOTE: These songs were released in Europe but not in the United States.

Unreleased Session Recorded March 7, 1965, on the "Ed Sullivan Show"
  It Don't Mean a Thing (If It Ain't Got That Swing), Do Nothin' Till You Hear From Me, Scatted Medley of Ellington songs

Ella in Hamburg V-4069 Recorded March 26, 1965
  Walk Right In, That Old Black Magic, Body and Soul, Here's That Rainy
  Day, And the Angels Sing, A Hard Day's Night, Ellington Medley, The
  Boy From Ipanema, Don't Rain on My Parade, Angel Eyes, Smooth Sail-
  ing, Old MacDonald, Duke's Place, The Shadow of Your Smile
  NOTE: Both Duke's Place and Shadow of Your Smile were recorded with
  the Duke Ellington Orchestra before the rest of the concert and were
  released as a single in Europe as #10408.

Unreleased Session Recorded June 25, 1965
  Time After Time, Whisper Not, You've Changed, Lover Man

Unreleased Session Recorded June 26, 1965
  Wives and Lovers, Matchmaker Matchmaker, Sweet Georgia Brown,
  Don't Rain on My Parade

Unreleased Session Recorded July 6, 1965
  She's Just a Quiet Girl, We Three
  NOTE: These songs were released in Europe but not in the United States.

Ella at Duke's Place V6-4070 Recorded October 1965
  Something to Live For, A Flower Is a Lovesome Thing, Passion Flower,
  I Like the Sunrise, Azure, Imagine My Frustration, Duke's Place, Brown-
  skin Gal in the Calico Gown, What Am I Here For?, Cottontail

Unreleased Session Recorded April 5, 1966
  The Shadow of Your Smile, You're Gonna Hear From Me
  NOTE: These songs were released briefly in Europe as a single.

Whisper Not V6-4071 Recorded July 20, 1966
  Sweet Georgia Brown, Whisper Not, I Said No, Thanks for the Memory,
  Spring Can Really Hang You Up the Most, Old MacDonald, Time After
  Time, You've Changed, I've Got Your Number, Lover Man, Wives and
  Lovers, Matchmaker Matchmaker

Ella and Duke at the Côte d'Azur V6-4072-2 Recorded July 27–29, 1966:
  Jazz Samba, Going Out of My Head, Misty, Lullaby of Birdland, How
  Long Has This Been Going On?, The More I See You
Recorded July 27, 1966 (unissued):
  Let's Do It, Satin Doll, Cottontail

Recorded July 28, 1966 (unissued):
Thou Swell, Satin Doll, Something to Live For, Let's Do It
Recorded July 29, 1966:
Thou Swell*, Satin Doll*, Wives and Lovers*, Something to Live For*, Let's Do It*, Sweet Georgia Brown*, Mack the Knife*, Cottontail*, Going Out of My Head*, Jazz Samba*, Lullaby of Birdland*, The Moment of Truth*, Just Squeeze Me, It Don't Mean a Thing (If It Ain't Got That Swing), Mack the Knife
NOTE: An asterisk (*) means these cuts were unissued.

The Best of Ella Fitzgerald V6-8720
People, Sweet and Slow, Broadway, The Thrill Is Gone, I Won't Dance, Show Me, See See Rider, Honeysuckle Rose, When Your Lover Has Gone, Gone With the Wind, Don't Be That Way

The History of Ella Fitzgerald 2-V6S-8817
Mack the Knife, Pete Kelly's Blues, Volare, Angel Eyes, Old MacDonald, Hello Dolly, People, Can't Buy Me Love, The Sweetest Sounds, Miss Otis Regrets, Walk Right In, Wives and Lovers, Here's That Rainy Day, And the Angels Sing, A Hard Day's Night, The Boy From Ipanema, Don't Rain on My Parade, Time After Time, I Said No, Matchmaker Matchmaker

The World of Ella Fitzgerald MGM-567
Reissue of "Clap Hands, Here Comes Charlie!"

MGM Golden Archives Series—Ella Fitzgerald Compilation
I Won't Dance, You're Blase, Midnight Sun, Honeysuckle Rose, Downhearted Blues, Don't Be That Way, Can't We Be Friends, I'm Gonna Go Fishin', When Your Lover Has Gone, Cottontail

Compact Jazz—Ella Fitzgerald CD 831 367-2 Compilation
Mack the Knife, Desafinado, Mr. Paganini, I Can't Get Started, A Night in Tunisia, A-Tisket A-Tasket, Shiny Stockings, Smooth Sailing, Goody-Goody, Rough Ridin', The Boy From Ipanema, Sweet Georgia Brown, Duke's Place, Misty, Somebody Loves Me, How High the Moon

Compact Jazz—Ella Fitzgerald Live CD 833 294-2 Compilation
Lady Be Good, Summertime, Honeysuckle Rose, Body and Soul, Squeeze Me, These Foolish Things, Stompin' At the Savoy, Baby Won't You Please Come Home, You'd Be So Nice to Come Home To, The More I See You,

I've Got a Crush on You, I Can't Give You Anything But Love, The Man I Love, Take the "A" Train

For the Love of Ella Fitzgerald CD 841 765-2 Compilation
A-Tisket A-Tasket, Lady Be Good, Stompin' at the Savoy, How High the Moon, Mr. Paganini, Sweet Georgia Brown, Mack the Knife, Caravan, A Night in Tunisia, Rockin' in Rhythm, Honeysuckle Rose, I Got Rhythm, A Fine Romance, On the Sunny Side of the Street, Party Blues, Cottontail, Misty, Sophisticated Lady, Midnight Sun, Solitude, How Long How Long Blues, I Loves You Porgy, Summertime, Mood Indigo, Laura, Stormy Weather, Autumn in New York, These Foolish Things, I Can't Get Started, See See Rider, I Love Paris, Blues in the Night

The Essential Ella Fitzgerald: The Great Songs CD 314 517 170-2 Compilation
Lady Be Good, There's a Lull in My Life, Little Jazz, Drop Me Off in Harlem, Angel Eyes, Ding! Dong! the Witch Is Dead, A-Tisket A-Tasket, Summertime, Into Each Life Some Rain Must Fall, Spring Can Really Hang You Up the Most, Pick Yourself Up, Cool Breeze, Imagine My Frustration, Mack the Knife, Dream

The Stockholm Concert—1966 Pablo CD 2308-242-2
Recorded August 1966
Imagine My Frustration, Duke's Place, Satin Doll, Something to Live For, Wives and Lovers, So Danco Samba, Let's Do It, Lover Man, Cottontail

Singles Session Salle Records Recorded at the Greek Theater, Los Angeles, September 1966:
The Moment of Truth, These Boots Are Made for Walking, Stardust (unreleased), I'm Just a Lucky So-and-So (unreleased)

La Nuova Musica, Volume 2 Stradivarius CD STR 10009
Recorded April 30, 1967
How High the Moon, Lover Man, So Danco Samba, St. Louis Blues, Mack the Knife, Cottontail

The Best of Ella Live Verve V6-8748
It has been reported that this was a live concert recorded in 1967, including songs already recorded by Ella in the past. This was a live hits compilation and was not new material.

The Greatest Jazz Concert in the World Pablo CD 2625-704-2
Recorded July 1967
> Don't Be That Way, You've Changed, Let's Do It, On the Sunny Side of the Street, It's Only a Paper Moon, Day Dream, If I Could Be With You, Between the Devil and the Deep Blue Sea, Cottontail

Ella Fitzgerald—The First Lady of Song Verve CD 314-5117-898-2
Released 4/93
> Perdido, Lullaby of Birdland, Too Young for the Blues, Too Darn Hot, Miss Otis Regrets, April in Paris, Undecided, Can't We Be Friends?, Bewitched, Just a-Sittin' and a-Rockin', I'm Just a Lucky So-and-So, Air Mail Special, A-Tisket A-Tasket, Baby Don't You Go 'Way Mad [sic], Angel Eyes, I Won't Dance, Summertime, Lady be Good, More Than You Know, Lush Life, Blue Skies, Swingin' Shepherd Blues, These Foolish Things, Travelin' Light, You're An Old Smoothie, Makin' Whoopee, How Long Has This Been Going On?, Detour Ahead, Mack the Knife, How High the Moon?, Black Coffee, Let It Snow, Get Happy, Heart and Soul, Mr. Paganini, A Night in Tunisia, I Can't Get Started, Don't Be That Way, After You've Gone, Hernando's Hideaway, A Fine Romance, 'Deed I Do, Hear Me Talkin' to Ya, Can't Buy Me Love, Day-In Day-Out, Something's Gotta Give, Here's That Rainy Day, Something to Live For, You've Changed, Jazz Samba, It Don't Mean a Thing (If It Ain't Got That Swing)

The Ella Fitzgerald Songbook Boxed Set Released 12/93 CD Compilation
> All of the songs from all of the Verve Songbooks, plus extra songs previously unreleased.

The Ella Fitzgerald CD Songbook Sampler Released 9/93 CD Compilation
> Sixteen songs taken from her Verve Songbooks

The Ella Fiztgerald CD Songbook Sampler, The Ballads. Released 9/94 CD Compilation
> Sixteen more songs taken from her Verve Songbooks

The following recordings were released by Capitol records unless otherwise indicated:

Brighten the Corner ST-2685 CD CDP 7 95151 2 Recorded February 1967
> Abide With Me, Just a Closer Walk With Thee, The Old Rugged Cross, Brighten the Corner Where You Are, I Need Thee Every Hour, In the Garden, God Be With You Till We Meet Again, God Will Take Care of You, The Church in the Wildwood, Throw Out the Lifeline, I Shall Not

Be Moved, Let the Lower Lights Be Burning, What a Friend We Have
in Jesus, Rock of Ages

Ella Fitzgerald's Christmas ST-CDP 7 94452 2
Recorded July 19 and 21, 1967
   O Holy Night, It Came Upon a Midnight Clear, Hark! the Herald Angels
   Sing, Away in a Manger, Joy to the World, The First Noel, Silent Night,
   O Come All Ye Faithful, Sleep My Little Jesus, Angels We Have Heard
   on High, O Little Town of Bethlehem, We Three Kings, God Rest Ye
   Merry Gentlemen

F. S.—The Television Years Retrospect Album 508
   Bootleg recordings of Frank Sinatra televisions shows, including those
   with Ella on May 9, 1958, December 13, 1959, and November 13, 1967.

Misty Blue ST-2888 CDP 7 95152 2
Recorded December 20, 1967:
   I Taught Him Everything He Knows, Turn the World Around, Don't
   Touch Me, Walking in the Sunshine
Recorded December 21, 1967:
   Misty Blue, It's Only Love, The Chokin' Kind, Born to Lose
Recorded December 22, 1967:
   Evil on Your Mind, Don't Let That Doorknob Hit You, This Gun Don't
   Care

The Big Bands' Greatest Vocalists Joyce Album 6045 Recorded May 1968
   Pick Yourself Up, Misty Blue, It's Up to Me and You, The Sweetest Sound,
   Volare, I Taught Him Everything, You Couldn't Be Cuter, All the Things
   You Are, Turn the World Around, Duke's Place, Evil on Your Mind, Born
   to Lose

Singles Session Capitol 02212 Released 6/10/68
   It's Up to Me and You, Brighten the Corner

Singles Session Capitol 02267 Recorded July 1968 (Recorded at the same
   time as the following album)
   Hawaiian War Chant, It's Only Love

30 By Ella ST-2960 CDP 7 48333 2 Recorded July 1968
   Medley #1: My Mother's Eyes, Try a Little Tenderness, I Got It Bad
   (and That Ain't Good), Everything I Have Is Yours, I Never Knew (I

Could Love Anybody), Goodnight, My Love
Medley #2: Four or Five Times, Maybe, Taking a Chance on Love, El-
mer's Tune, At Sundown, It's a Wonderful World
Medley #3: on Green Dolphin Street, How Am I to Know, Just Friends,
I Cried for You, Seems Like Old Times, You Stepped Out of a Dream
Medley #4: If I Give My Heart to You, Once in Awhile, Ebb Tide, The
Lamp Is Low, Where Are You, Thinking of You
Medley #5: Candy, All I Do Is Dream of You, Spring Is Here, 720 in the
Books, It Happened in Monterey, What Can I Say After I Say I'm Sorry
Medley #6: No Regrets, I've Got a Feeling You're Fooling, Don't Blame
Me, Deep Purple, Rain, You're a Sweetheart

Unissued Session Verve Studios Recorded October 21, 1968
A Place for Lovers, Lonely Is

The Sunshine of Your Love (also called *Watch What Happens* and *Love You
Madly*) MPS CD-POCJ-2166, Album 821 290-1 Recorded May, 1969
Hey Jude, Sunshine of Your Love, This Girl's in Love With You, Watch
What Happens, Alright Okay You Win, Give Me the Simple Life, Useless
Landscape, Old Devil Moon, Don'cha Go 'Way Mad, A House Is Not a
Home, Trouble Is a Man, Love You Madly

Jazz Ladies LRC Ltd. CDC-9076 Recorded live in Paris, 1969
I Won't Dance, That Old Black Magic, Medley: It Happened in Monterey/
No Regrets/It's a Wonderful World, Cabaret, Love You Madly, A Man
and a Woman, Alright Okay You Win, People, I Concentrate on You, Mr.
Paganini

The following recordings were released by Reprise records. Please note that
while the albums were recorded and released two years apart, the CD release (Reprise 9 26023-2) features both albums:

Ella RS-6354 Recorded May 26, 28, 29, and 30, 1969
Get Ready, The Hunter Gets Captured by the Game, Yellow Man, I'll
Never Fall in Love Again, Got to Get You Into My Life, I Wonder Why,
Ooo Baby Baby, Savoy Truffle, Open Your Window, Knock on Wood

Unreleased Session Recorded December 1969
Try a Little Bit, Timer, The Flim Flam Man, Lucky, Once It Was Alright
Now

Things Ain't What They Used to Be RS-6432 Recorded March 1971
Sunny, Mas Que Nada, A Man and a Woman, Days of Wine and Roses,
Black Coffee, Tuxedo Junction, I Heard It Through the Grapevine, Don't
Dream of Anybody But Me, Things Ain't What They Used to Be, Willow
Weep for Me, Manteca, Just When We're Falling in Love, In the Mood
(unreleased)

The Lady Is A Tramp CD JAZZ DOOR 1268 Live in Belgrade Released
August, 1994
Recorded February 21, 1961:
Too Close for Comfort, A Foggy Day, Medley: Get Out of Town/Easy to
Love, You're Driving Me Crazy, Cheek to Cheek, Caravan, Lady Be Good,
'Round Midnight, The Lady Is a Tramp, Mr. Paganini
Recorded May 18, 1971:
Lullaby of Birdland, Medley: Mood Indigo/Do Nothing Till You Hear
From Me/It Don't Mean A Thing If It Ain't Got that Swing, The Days of
Wine and Roses, Something, Summertime, Mack the Knife, Put a Little
Love in Your Heart, How High the Moon

The following recordings were released on Pablo records unless otherwise
indicated:

Ella a Nice OJCCD-442-2 Recorded July 21, 1971
Night and Day; Medley: Get Out of Town/Easy to Love/You Do Some-
thing to Me; Medley: Body and Soul/The Man I Love/I Loves You Porgy;
Medley: the Boy From Ipanema/Fly Me to the Moon/O Nosso Amor/
Cielito Lindo/Madalena/ Agua de Beber; Summertime; They Can't Take
That Away From Me; Medley: Mood Indigo/Do Nothing Till You Hear
From Me/It Don't Mean a Thing (If It Ain't Got That Swing); Something;
St. Louis Blues; Close to You; Put a Little Love in Your Heart

Ella Loves Cole Atlantic Records Recorded February 13, 1972
I've Got You Under My Skin, I Concentrate on You, My Heart Belongs
to Daddy, Love for Sale, So Near and Yet So Far, Down in the Depths,
Just One of Those Things, I Get a Kick Out of You, All of You, Anything
Goes, At Long Last Love, C'est Magnifique, Without Love

Jazz at the Santa Monica Civic '72 PACD-2625-701-2 Recorded June 2, 1972
L.O.V.E., Begin the Beguine, Indian Summer, You've Got a Friend,
What's Going On?, Night and Day, Spring Can Really Hang You Up the
Most, Little White Lies, Madalena, Shiny Stockings, Medley: Too Darn

Hot/It's Alright With Me, Street Beater, I Can't Stop Loving You, C Jam Blues

Newport Jazz Festival—Live at Carnegie Hall Columbia Records
Recorded July 5, 1973
    This recording was originally released as a two album set; the CD version released in the United States is on two separate CDs on the CBS label.
    Volume 1:
    I've Gotta Be Me, Down in the Depths (unissued), Good Morning Heartache, Miss Otis Regrets, What's Goin' On? (unissued), Medley: Don't Worry 'Bout Me/These Foolish Things, Any Old Blues, A-Tisket A-Tasket, Indian Summer, Smooth Sailing, You Turned the Tables on Me, Nice Work If You Can Get It, I've Got a Crush on You
    Volume 2:
    Medley: Taking a Chance on Love/I'm in the Mood for Love; Lemon Drop; Some of These Days; People

Take Love Easy CD PACD-2310-702-2 Recorded August 28, 1973
    Take Love Easy, Once I Loved, Don't Be That Way, You're Blasé, Lush Life, A Foggy Day, Gee Baby Ain't I Good to You?, You Go to My Head, I Want to Talk About You

Fine and Mellow CD PACD-2310-829-2 Recorded January 8, 1974
    Fine and Mellow, I'm Just a Lucky So-and-So, A Ghost of a Chance With You, Rockin' in Rhythm, I'm in the Mood for Love, 'Round Midnight, I Can't Give You Anything But Love, The Man I Love, Polka Dots and Moonbeams

Ella in London CD PACD-2310-829-2 Recorded April 11, 1974
    Sweet Georgia Brown, They Can't Take That Away From Me, Everytime We Say Goodbye, The Man I Love, It Don't Mean a Thing (If It Ain't Got That Swing), You've Got a Friend, Lemon Drop, The Very Thought of You, Happy Blues

Ella and Oscar CD PACD-2310-759-2 Recorded May 19, 1975
    Mean to Me, How Long Has This Been Going On?, When Your Lover Has Gone, More Than You Know, There's a Lull in My Life, Midnight Sun, I Hear Music, Street of Dreams, April in Paris

Singles Session Recorded May, 1975
    Roxy, I Am My Own Best Friend

Ella at Montreux CD PACD-2310-751-2 Recorded July 17, 1975
Caravan, Satin Doll, Teach Me Tonight, Wave, It's All Right With Me,
Let's Do It, How High the Moon, The Boy From Ipanema Medley, 'Tain't
Nobody's Business If I Do

The Montreux Collection Pablo Album 2625-707 Recorded July 17, 1975
The Man I Love

Fitzgerald & Pass . . . Again CD PACD-2310-772-2 Recorded January 29–
30 and February 8, 1976
I Ain't Got Nothin' But the Blues, 'Tis Autumn, My Old Flame, That Old
Feeling, Rain, I Didn't Know About You, You Took Advantage of Me,
I've Got the World on a String, All Too Soon, The One I Love (Belongs
to Somebody Else), Solitude, Nature Boy, Tennessee Waltz, One Note
Samba

Montreux '77: Ella Fitzgerald With the Tommy Flanagan Trio CD OJCCD-
376-2 Recorded July 14, 1977
Too Close for Comfort, I Ain't Got Nothin' But the Blues, My Man, Come
Rain or Come Shine, Day by Day, Ordinary Fool, One Note Samba, I Let
a Song Go Out of My Heart, Billie's Bounce, You Are the Sunshine of
My Life

Dream Dancing CD PACD-2310-814-2 Recorded February 13, 1972, and
June 9, 1978
Features all of the songs from *Ella Loves Cole* plus Dream Dancing and
After You.

Lady Time CD PACD-2310-825-2 Recorded June 19-20, 1978
I'm Walkin', All or Nothing at All, I Never Had a Chance, I Cried for
You, What Will I Tell My Heart, Since I Fell for You, And the Angels
Sing, I'm Confessin' (That I Love You), Mack the Knife, That's My Desire,
I'm in the Mood for Love

A Classy Pair (Also known in Europe as *Ella and the Count*) CD PACD-
2312-132-2 Recorded February 15, 1979
Organ Grinder's Swing, Just a-Sittin' and a-Rockin', My Kind of Trouble
Is You, Ain't Misbehavin', Some Other Spring•, Teach Me Tonight, I'm
Gettin' Sentimental Over You, Don't Worry 'Bout Me, Honeysuckle Rose,
Sweet Lorraine, Please Don't Talk About Me When I'm Gone•

NOTE: An asterisk (*) means these cuts were released only on boxed-set and European versions.

A Perfect Match CD PACD-2312-110-2 Recorded July 12, 1979
Please Don't Talk About Me When I'm Gone, Sweet Georgia Brown, Some Other Spring, Make Me Rainbows, After You've Gone, 'Round Midnight, Fine and Mellow, You've Changed, Honeysuckle Rose, St. Louis Blues, Basella

Digital III at Montreux CD PACD-2308-223-2 Recorded July 12, 1979
I Don't Stand a Ghost of a Chance With You, Flying Home
NOTE: Reports that Ella sang on the other cuts on this album are incorrect. Ella only sang on the two cuts listed above.

Ella Abraca Jobim: Ella Fitzgerald Sings the Antonio Carlos Jobim Songbook
PACD-2630- 201-2 Recorded September 17–19, 1980, and
March 18–20, 1981
Dreamer, This Love That I've Found, The Boy From Ipanema, Somewhere in the Hills, Photograph, Wave, Triste, Quiet Nights of Quiet Stars, Water to Drink, Bonita, Desafinado, He's a Carioca, Dindi, How Insensitive, One Note Samba, A Felicidade, Useless Landscape, Don't Ever Go Away and Song of the Jet (not released on the CD version)

The Best Is Yet to Come CD PACD-2312-138-2
Recorded February 4–5, 1982
Don't Be That Way, God Bless the Child, I Wonder Where Our Love Has Gone, You're Driving Me Crazy, Any Old Time, Good-Bye, Autumn in New York, The Best Is Yet to Come, Deep Purple, Somewhere in the Night

Speak Love CD PACD-2310-888-2 Recorded March 21–22, 1983
Speak Low, Comes Love, There's No You, I May Be Wrong (But I Think You're Wonderful), At Last, The Thrill Is Gone (Medley), Gone With the Wind, Blue and Sentimental, Girl Talk, Georgia on My Mind

Nice Work If You Can Get It: Ella Fitzgerald and André Previn Do Gershwin
CD PACD-2312-140-2 Recorded May 23, 1983
A Foggy Day, Nice Work If You Can Get It, But Not for Me, Let's Call the Whole Thing Off, How Long Has This Been Going On?, Who Cares?, Medley: I've Got a Crush on You/Someone to Watch Over Me/Embraceable You, They Can't Take That Away From Me

Return to Happiness: Jazz At The Philharmonic PACD-2620-117-2 Disc 2
Recorded October 1983
Manteca, Willow Weep for Me, All of Me, Blue Moon, Night and Day,
They Can't Take That Away From Me, Medley: The Man I Love/Body
and Soul, 'Round Midnight, Flying Home

Easy Living CD PACD-2310-921-2
Recorded March 21–22, 1983:
   On Green Dolphin Street, Why Don't You Do Right, Slow Boat to China,
   Love for Sale, By Myself
Recorded February 25–28, 1986:
   My Ship, Don't Be That Way, My Man, Don't Worry 'Bout Me, The Days
   of Wine and Roses, Easy Living, I Don't Stand a Ghost of a Chance With
   You, Moonlight in Vermont, I Want a Little Girl, I'm Making Believe

The Best of Ella Fitzgerald CD PACD-2405-421-2 Compilation Released
February 1988
   Dreamer, You're Blasé, Fine and Mellow, Honeysuckle Rose, I Wonder
   Where Our Love Has Gone, Street of Dreams, I'm Walkin', This Love
   That I've Found, I'm Getting Sentimental Over You, Any Old Time, How
   Long Has This Been Going On?, Since I Fell for You, Don't Be That Way,
   You Go to My Head

All That Jazz CD PACD-2310-938-2 Recorded March 15–16 and
20–22, 1989
   Dream a Little Dream of Me, My Last Affair, Baby Don't You Quit Now,
   Oh Look At Me Now, The Jersey Bounce, When Your Lover Has Gone,
   That Old Devil Called Love, All That Jazz, Just When We're Falling in
   Love, Good Morning Heartache, Little Jazz, The Nearness of You

Quest Warner Brothers 926020-2 Quincy Jones Album Recorded in 1989
   Ella appears as cameo guest artist on the following tracks:
   Wee B. Dooinit, Birdland, Jazz Corner of the World

Japanese Movie Soundtrack: The Setting Sun Recorded at Warner Brothers
   Studios January 1991
   Ella sings the title track

Unreleased Sessions Salle Productions Recorded Spring, 1991
   Several tracks recorded, with Joe Pass and Ella, and with small group
   similar to that on *All That Jazz*. These were recorded in back-to-back,

one-day sessions. There are *not* enough tracks to release a full-length CD. They were not released because Ella was unhappy with her vocal quality. She wanted to redo some of the numbers and record some more, but became too ill to continue. The only title known is a duet with Joe Pass of What a Difference a Day Makes. Album with Joe was to be called *Ella and Joe*.

I'll Take Manhattan (Single remix and rerelease) Verve 867 516-2 Released 1991
A single rerelease of Manhattan and the Lady Is a Tramp, with Manhattan shortened and remixed for the television show "I'll Take Manhattan" on Norwegian Verve.

Stars of the Apollo Columbia Legacy C2K-53407 Released 1993
28-song compilation of Apollo stars' original recordings. Ella sings *All My Life* (with Teddy Wilson Orchestra) 3/17/36.

921
Fit

Fidelman, Geoffrey
Mark.

First lady of song.

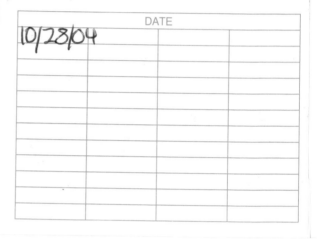

DATE			
10/28/04			